LATIN WORDS
of Common English

BY

EDWIN LEE JOHNSON, A.M., Ph.D.

ASSOCIATE PROFESSOR OF LATIN AND GREEK
VANDERBILT UNIVERSITY

D. C. HEATH AND COMPANY

BOSTON	NEW YORK	CHICAGO
ATLANTA	SAN FRANCISCO	DALLAS
	LONDON	

PREFACE

In the Classical Investigation of a few years ago the most widely approved ultimate objective of secondary Latin study was found to be the "increased ability to understand exactly and use accurately English words of Latin origin." Since that time the new textbooks, especially those for the first-year courses, have emphasized this feature of the study. The value of this emphasis is manifest in the elementary class: English words take on new meaning, and interest is aroused in the persistent life of an ancient language sometimes reported to be dead. But as the student proceeds with his courses in Latin or his reading in English, it is no longer enough for him to recognize English words of Latin origin; he has a right to know something further of the how and why of forms and meanings. Why do we have 'expose' but 'exponent,' 'invention' but 'pension'? How is 'royal' related to 'regal'? What of the b of 'humble' from *humilis*, or the *sh* of 'finish' from *finio?* What connection of meaning between 'Jove' and 'jovial,' between 'hearse' and 'rehearse,' between Latin *posse* and English 'posse'? When and how came the Latin words into English? Hundreds of questions like these the student may ask, and he deserves to be answered. It is to satisfy such a need that this volume has been prepared. Its purpose is to supplement what the elementary textbooks may have given and point the way to further study. It continues the story of Latin words at home and abroad, in church and market place, in court and camp; words formed and transformed, used and abused, from the time of the Caesars till the present day; words, finally, revealing a kinship with those of our own speech from a very remote period of the past.

iii

The long story is to be told briefly: "a big book is a big evil." The account here given must not be technical; it cannot be exhaustive. It is important rather that the presentation of the subject be understandable for the student, serviceable to the teacher, and convenient for any who may have occasion to consult the book. Brevity and simplicity will mean a wider usefulness.

The "common English" of the title is the English of our ordinary reading, whether in the newspaper and the magazine or in our standard literature. Scientific terms are excluded, but the line between the scientific and the common is not always easy to draw. 'Mandamus,' 'coefficient,' 'dementia,' belong to certain special fields of study, yet the layman may meet them in his casual reading. Linguistic principles are given only as they may be illustrated in derived or cognate English words. Thus, while the book may find its primary place in the Latin class, it is an English study as well, and in fact only a slight acquaintance with Latin is prerequisite to its use.

While this work was in preparation I sent copies of a prospectus to a large number of teachers, with a request for criticisms. For the encouragement offered and the helpful suggestions made in replies from these teachers I am sincerely thankful. Particularly I am indebted to Professor Roland G. Kent of the University of Pennsylvania, who has aided me in dealing with several perplexing questions. I am under obligation also to Professor R. B. Steele of Vanderbilt University and to Professor W. L. Carr of Teachers College, Columbia University, for their critical reading of the manuscript, and to Professor Walter H. Storer of Vanderbilt University for valuable assistance on the chapter dealing with French-English forms.

August, 1931.   E. L. J.

CONTENTS

PAGE

PREFACE iii

ABBREVIATIONS AND TYPOGRAPHICAL KEY viii

PART I — THE HISTORY OF LATIN WORDS IN ENGLISH

CHAPTER

I. ROME AND THE ANGLO-SAXONS 3

II. THE INFLUENCE OF CHRISTIANITY 11

III. THE NORMAN CONQUEST 18

    French and English Doublets, 24. French in State, 26; in War, 26; in Law, 27; in Art, 29; in Religion, 30. Norman and Parisian Doublets, 32.

IV. THE REVIVAL OF LEARNING 35

    English and Latin Doublets, 36. French and Latin Doublets, 42. Popular and Literary French Doublets, 45. Latin Words through Italian, 50; Spanish, 57; Portuguese, 60.

PART II — THE FORMS AND MEANINGS OF LATIN WORDS IN ENGLISH

I. LATIN WORDS MADE ENGLISH 63

    Nouns, 63. Adjectives, 77. Adverbs and Prepositions, 81. Inflectional Forms, 82.

II. LATIN WORDS AND PHRASES BORROWED IN ENGLISH . . 88

    Latin Words, 88. Abbreviations, 98. Proverbs and

CHAPTER   PAGE

Quotations, 101. Mottoes of States, 107; of Colleges,
107. Latin Titles in Literature, Art, and Music, 109.

III. WORD FORMATION IN LATIN   114

I. The Formation of Nouns: Nouns Made from
Other Nouns, 114; from Adjectives, 118; from Verbs,
124. II. The Formation of Adjectives: Adjectives
Made from Nouns, 136; from Verbs, 151. III. The
Formation of Verbs: Verbs Made from Nouns and
Adjectives, 163; from Other Verbs, 165. IV. Com-
pounds, 170: Dependent, 171; Descriptive, 173;
Possessive, 174; Prepositional, 175; Prefixes, 176.
V. Combinations of Sounds, 183. VI. Vowel Grada-
tion, 191.

IV. FRENCH-ENGLISH FORMS OF LATIN DERIVATIVES . .   193

I. Treatment of Vowels in Final Syllables, 195.
II. Treatment of Vowels in Other Unaccented Syllables,
196. III. Treatment of Vowels in Accented Syllables,
197. IV. Vowels Influenced by y (consonantal i), 198.
V. Treatment of Consonants: Consonants Dropped,
200; Added, 201; Changed (assimilated, palatalized),
201; Other Consonant Changes, 204. VI. Forms of Derived Verbs in English, 205. French Words Adopted
into English, 212.

V. CHANGES OF FORM AND MEANING   215

VI. COINED WORDS AND HYBRIDS   248

I. Coined Words, 248. II. Hybrids, 256: Latin
Prefix + Non-Latin Base, 256; Non-Latin Prefix
+ Latin Base, 257; Latin Base + Non-Latin Suffix,
258; Non-Latin Base + Latin Suffix, 259; Compounds
of Latin and Non-Latin Elements, 260.

CHAPTER PAGE
VII. DERIVATIVE NAMES 263

      Personal, 263. Geographical, 267. Months, 271.
Signs of the Zodiac, 273. Commercial, 273. Numeral
Signs, 274.

PART III — COGNATE WORDS

I. COGNATE WORDS 279

CONCLUSION 289

BIBLIOGRAPHY. 291

GENERAL INDEX. 295

INDEX OF WORDS 301

ABBREVIATIONS

abl., ablative

acc., accusative

adj., adjective

AF, Anglo-French, the French current in England after the Norman Conquest

AS, Anglo-Saxon (Old English), to approximately A.D. 1100

Cl. Lat., Classical Latin, approximately 100 B.C. to A.D. 100

dim., *dimin.*, diminutive

Eng., English

fem., feminine

Fr., French

Germ., German

Grk., Greek

inf., infinitive

Ital., Italian

Lat., Latin

lit., literally

Low Lat., Low or Vulgar Latin, Latin of the common crowd (vulgus); see 158, 159

masc., masculine

Med. Lat., Mediæval Latin, approximately A.D. 476–1500

Mid. Eng., Middle English, approximately A.D. 1100–1500

Mod., Modern

N., note

NED, A New English Dictionary; see Bibliography

nom., nominative

OF, Old French, approximately A.D. 600–1200

OHG, Old High German, to approximately A.D. 1100

Old Lat., or *O. Lat.*, Old Latin, before 100 B.C.

Old Sax., Old Saxon, the language of the Saxons while still in Germany

Old Sp., Old Spanish, to the twelfth century

pers., person

pf., perfect

pl., plural

Port., Portuguese

pple., participle

pres., present

sing., singular

Sp., Spanish

voc., vocative

Cross-references are made by section numbers unless page is indicated (p.).

TYPOGRAPHICAL KEY

Latin words in boldfaced type:	**videre**
Meanings in italics:	*see*
Words cited from other languages than Latin (except in lists) in single quotation marks:	Fr. 'voir'
Derived words in small capitals:	VISION
Cognate words in boldfaced italics:	***wit***

Part I

THE HISTORY OF LATIN WORDS
IN ENGLISH

CHAPTER I

ROME AND THE ANGLO-SAXONS

1. At the time of Rome's first contact with Britain, the inhabitants of the island were of the Celtic race, a people related in life and language to the Greeks, the Romans, and the Germans, as members of the great Indo-European family (220). In the spring of 58 B.C. Julius Caesar as governor of Gaul had begun his campaigns among those other Celtic tribes north of the Alps, and in two and a half years the Roman legions carried their conquests as far as the western coast. From here Caesar resolved to pass over into Britain, if to do nothing more than to visit the island, observe its people, and learn something of its geography, for it was then, for the most part, an unknown country to the people of the continent. Late in August 55 B.C. he landed with two legions near the present site of Dover, defeated the Britons in battle, and in less than a month returned to his camp on the Gallic coast.[1]

The next year he crossed the Channel again and advanced as far as the Thames, but, as Tacitus tells us, although he frightened the inhabitants by his success in arms and gained possession of the coast, he may be said to have directed attention to the country rather than to have conquered it.[2] Not until 43 A.D., during the reign of Claudius, was the conquest of the island undertaken again. At this time the Romans founded a colony, the beginning of an occupation that by the end of the first century had firmly established the power of the Empire in this new territory. Under this

---

[1] Caesar, *Gallic War*, IV, 20–36.
[2] Tacitus, *Agricola*, 13; Caesar, *Gallic War*, V, 8–23.

power rose walled towns in the midst of cultivated and
productive fields, a great system of military roads was introduced, forts and works of defence were constructed, tyran-
nical governors were put in charge, and the native Celts
reduced to practical slavery. For three centuries this oppressive rule continued; then with the year 410 the legions were
called away, for Rome, the conqueror of the barbarians, was
herself threatened by the barbarian invaders from the north.

Thus was begun an intercourse between a great empire of
antiquity and what was to become a great empire of modern
times, an intercourse which in time should influence the
language of that later people more profoundly than it influenced their political and military life. It was, however, a
meager beginning as far as language was concerned. These
Celts adopted but few words from their enemies. During
the long period of Roman occupation, while Latin probably
became common enough in the cities and among the educated
classes, the great mass of the native population, in marked
contrast to what had happened in Gaul and Spain, held
tenaciously to their own speech. And upon the withdrawal
of the Romans the Celtic language resumed its place with
few traces of Latin remaining.

2. Before we inquire what these traces were, there are
other characters to be presented in our story. The Roman
conquest had never extended beyond the Forth, and the
departure of the legions opened the way for the Picts and
the Scots of the north to have their turn at their neighbors
in the south, weakened as they were by the centuries of
Rome's oppression, and plundered by pirate bands along
their coast. These Britons in their desperate situation,
according to Bede's account,[1] invited the German tribes
along the North Sea, those indeed who had furnished the
pirates, to come to their aid. In the year 449 a band of
Jutes under the leadership of Hengist and Horsa, responding

---

[1] *Ecclesiastical History*, I, 11–12.

to the call, not only drove back the Picts and the Scots but also found territory for themselves. They were followed in 477 by their kinsmen the Saxons, and later (547) by the Angles, who eventually gave their name to the country (Angle-land). If modern historical research, no longer venerating the Venerable Bede, discredits much of the story and finds that Hengist and Horsa were but mythical characters or symbolic names, the fact remains that there settled in Britain, beginning in the fifth century or earlier, many immigrants belonging to the Low German branch of the Teutonic people, and the language which they spoke and which came to be called the Anglo-Saxon was in reality a German dialect.

3. Long before these people left their continental home, they had felt the influence of Roman civilization, and Roman soldiers pressing northward in the German wars had left their imprint on the German language. Especially words of Latin origin found as a common possession of other German groups, as well as of the invaders of Britain, may reasonably be assigned to a period prior to their separation. However, scholars are not agreed as to just what Latin words Jutes, Angles, and Saxons had adopted before their migration, and any list of such words may need revision as we consult this or that new authority. The significant fact is that our continental ancestors met and talked with Roman troops and traders and found some of their words worth borrowing, and German tribes invading Roman provinces brought back Latin terms which became widely adopted. Furthermore, whatever words may be ruled out of this group must be ruled into another received a little later when these Germans met the Latin influence again in Britain, and the result is much the same both for our Anglo-Saxon forebears and for us.

4. Whether blazing the way before the army or following in its rear, the Roman trader was as nearly omnipresent as

Roman power. He was known as **mango,** or establishing a shop and an inn, he became **caupo.** Suspiciously like **mango** is the Anglo-Saxon word 'mangere,' later altered into MONGER, still preserved in compounds like fish-MONGER and scandal-MONGER. **Caupo** apparently passed into the German 'kaufen,' the Anglo-Saxon 'ceapian,' *buy,* the noun 'ceap,' *price* or *market* (as in 'Cheapside'), and our adjective CHEAP, as indicating the good bargain we have made or missed. And apparently we have kept from CHAP-man, *trading-man,* the colloquial CHAP. The **caupones** must have known their patrons, for their chief article of merchandise seems to have been **vinum.** The Germans took it name and all, called it 'win,' and passed it on to us as WINE. Even the cup from which they drank it was Latin (though originally Greek), 'calic,' from **calix, calicis,** which was afterward lost but borrowed again both in the French form CHALICE and in the Greek form CALYX. BUTTER and CHEESE were probably in the merchant's stock, the one a Greek word, 'butyrum' (βούτυρον), AS 'butere,' the other Lat. **caseus,** AS 'cese.' A receptacle was **cista** (Grk.); the German repeats it as 'cist,' later to be pronounced CHEST, although Middle English kept also 'chiste,' and indeed some even yet, uncontaminated by learning, would call it 'chist.' **Catillus,** *a little bowl* (cf. **catinulus**), diminutive of **catinus,** *a bowl,* became AS 'cetel' or 'cytel' and later, perhaps from Scandinavian influence (20), KETTLE, sometimes called 'kittle'; **culter,** *knife,* was received as 'culter'; then COLTER and COULTER. Grain was ground at a MILL (*i.e.,* 'miln'), the Lat. **molina,** adopted as 'mylen' or 'myln'; or it was pounded in a MORTAR, AS 'mortere,' from **mortarium,** a word received again centuries later through the OF 'mortier.' Some of this food needs to be cooked and our primitive kinsman learns the process and takes the noun **coquus** (later **cocus**) as 'coc,' COOK, while the place of cooking, **coquina,** becomes 'cycene' or 'cicen,' and we know it as KITCHEN.

5. Of fruits and vegetables the Lat. **pirum** (through a late fem. **pira**) is represented in Anglo-Saxon by 'pera' or 'peru,' our PEAR; **prunum** (Grk.) became 'plume,' PLUM.[1] **Cerasum** became 'ciris' or 'cirs,' CHERRIES, as **pisum** (**pisa**) became 'pise,' PEAS, but CHERRY and PEA were of later development (CHERRY, 202). For serving food there was the 'disc,' *i.e.*, DISH, the Lat. (Grk.) **discus.** Articles sold by weight introduced the Lat. **pondus** or **pondo** (lit. *by weight*), to become 'pund,' later POUND (172). The Grk.-Lat. **sericum,** from 'Seres' as a name for the Chinese, came to be 'seolc,' SILK;[1] so there arose a need for lineal measurement and **uncia** was adopted as 'ynce,' INCH. **Uncia** meant *a twelfth part* (of a foot), practically our inch, the Roman foot (**pes**) being 11.65 inches of our measure.

6. Wares were paid for with a coin which the native called 'mynet,' furnishing us MINT as a place for making coins. But the Latin was **moneta,** so used because the Roman mint was in the temple of Juno Moneta, the latter name being that of an ancient goddess in classical times identified with Juno. This same **moneta** at a later time became MONEY (OF 'moneie'). The road built for the passage of the army was **via strata,** *paved way* (**sternere, stratus,** *strew*), and the participle was kept as 'straet,' STREET (cf. Germ. 'Strasse'). And on this road a measure of distance, 'mil,' a MILE, was adopted from the Lat. **milia,** in the sense of **mille passus,** *a thousand* (double) *steps,* or *paces* (plural **milia passuum**). SATURDay, the only name of a day of the week drawn from Latin, may possibly be listed with this group. It is a half translation of **Saturni dies,** *the day of* (the planet) *Saturn,* and in Anglo-Saxon was 'Saeternes-daeg.'

7. The words thus far cited are nouns, but a few adjectives may also belong to this period. CRISP from Latin **crispus,**

[1] PLUM and SILK must have come indirectly from Latin or Greek, evidently through some language that changed the *r* to *l*.

curling, has been assigned here, and some regard Low Lat. **excurtus** (Lat. **curtus**) as responsible for AS 'sceort,' with its threefold survival in SHORT, SHIRT, and SKIRT (20).

We are not surprised that these Latin forms were somewhat altered upon their adoption, for they came by word of mouth; the speaker's Latin was far from perfect and his hearers were quite like the rest of us in misunderstanding strange words.

It is noticeable that practically all these words are simple terms for concrete and commonplace things. Language always reflects life. Our German ancestor at this time dealt not in abstractions, nor did he care for philosophy. His concern was what he should eat, what he should drink, and, in some degree, wherewithal he should be clothed. And had he desired the abstract and the philosophic, he could hardly have obtained them from the Roman soldier or the Roman trader.

8. Something like this then — possibly less than this — was the Latin vocabulary which the Low German tribes, later known as Anglo-Saxons, carried with them when they came into Britain forty years and more after the Romans had left the island. The Latin words they were to find there were the very few which had been kept over by the Celts. The Romans soon after their arrival had constructed here also a military road from the present Richborough near Dover to their permanent camp on the River Dee (**Deva**). This **via strata,** the name perhaps lingering here just as among the Germans, was the beginning of the road-building in Britain which has left to the present day its evidence of how well these Romans wrought. **Strata** was kept with variant spelling in a number of names of places, as STRATford, *Street-ford;* STREATham, *Street-home;* STRATton, *Street-town.* The camp was **castra,** which became AS 'ceaster' and survived also in the names of towns (eventually meaning *town*), -CASTER in the north, -CESTER in the midland country, and -CHESTER in the south. So we have the following:

CHESTER, AS 'Ceaster,' the *camp*.

COLNCHESTER, AS 'Colnceaster,' the *camp on the River Colne*.

DONCASTER, AS 'Doneceaster,' the *camp on the River Don*.

EXETER, shortened from 'Ex-an-ceaster,' the *camp on the Exe*, or *stream*.

GLOUCESTER, AS 'Gleaw-ceaster' or 'Gleawan-ceaster,' **Glevum** being the Roman name of the place, and variously explained as *bright*, *fair*, or connected with **glaeba**, *soil*, GLEBE.

LEICESTER, possibly for **Legionis-castra**, *camp of the legion*.

MANCHESTER, AS 'Mameceaster,' 'Mamechestre,' etc., a combination of the British name of the place (probably 'Mamucio') with **castra.**

PORCHESTER, for 'Port-ceaster,' Lat. **portus,** the *harbor camp*.

ROCHESTER, AS 'Hrofes-ceaster,' *Hrof's camp*.

WINCHESTER, AS 'Wintan-ceaster,' 'wintan' meaning the *plain* or *open country*, the *camp of the plain*.

WORCESTER, AS 'Wigera-ceastre,' 'Wygracestre,' 'Wirecestre,' and many other forms, the first element being a local British name.

9. About the camp the Romans constructed a wall and a ditch, **vallum** and **fossa. Vallum** remained in the Celtic speech to be passed on to the newcomers as 'wal,' then WALL; **fossa** was kept in certain names, combining with native words, as Fossway, Fossbrooke, and Fossbridge. **Portus,** *harbor*, became PORT, and likewise entered into proper names, like FreePORT and PORTsmouth.[1] **Vicus,** *a village*, seems to survive in AS 'wic,' which remains in WARWICK and GreenWICH.[2] **Colonia,** COLONY, *a settlement of soldiers*, may explain '-coln' of LINCOLN, as also COLNE. **Lacus,** AS 'lacu,' later LAKE, and **mont-em,** AS 'munt,' MOUNT, also probably belong to this period. Even if a word or two of the group

[1] We may not in all cases be certain whether PORT in local names represents **portus,** *a harbor*, or **porta,** *a gate*, since it early came to mean a market town and the distinction of 'harbor town' might not be kept.

[2] On the continent also OHG '-wich' was a *dwelling-place* or *town*, Dutch 'wijk,' *a district*. Compounds made with this as a native word and those with -WICH (-WICK) from **vicus** cannot always be distinguished.

given as continental should be included here, as some would treat 'mil,' MILE, and 'win,' WINE, we still have less than a dozen Latin words kept over in Britain after nearly four hundred years of Roman control.   So little did these sturdy Celts admire or imitate their conquerors.

CHAPTER II

THE INFLUENCE OF CHRISTIANITY

10. The next occasion for contact between Rome and the Anglo-Saxons was the coming of the Christian missionaries. The story is a familiar one: how Gregory of Rome, passing by the slave market of the Forum one day, saw the blue-eyed, yellow-haired youths there for sale, and inquired who they were; on being told that they were Angles, he replied, "Not Angles, but angels" (**Non Angli, sed angeli**), and vowed he would one day bring Christianity to this people. Years afterward Gregory was made pope and the coveted opportunity came. In 597 he sent out Augustine with forty monks on this mission.[1] They were received by Ethelbert, king of Kent, and settling at Canterbury, they were permitted to build a cathedral and a monastery. Thus was a center established from which should radiate not only the doctrines of a new faith, but also the language in which the ritual of that faith was said. Indeed these religious teachers used Latin to a large extent in their conversation as well as in their church services. Of the multitude of Latin words received under church influence during the next few centuries, the following are examples, some of them also illustrations of the altered spelling of words heard and not seen:

[1] Christianity had indeed made its way to Britain before the end of the second century, unopposed by the Romans as long as their power was respected. But in 303 Diocletian, interpreting loyalty to Christ as disloyalty to Rome, began a persecution of the Christians throughout the Empire which postponed the Christianizing of the island till the time of Gregory. The influence of Irish missionaries must not be forgotten as aiding the work of Augustine (16).

11

Latin	Anglo-Saxon	Modern English
altare, *altar*	altar [1]	ALTAR
candela (from **candere,** *shine*)	candel	CANDLE
credo, *I believe*	creda	CREED (58)
fons, fontis, *fountain*	fant	FONT (FOUNT, 172)
missa, (**mittere,** *send,* 202, MASS)	maesse	MASS (but the mass-book is still MISSAL)
nona (**hora**), *ninth hour*	non-tid	NOON(tide)
nunna, or **nonna** (Low Lat.)	nunne	NUN
palla, *cloak*	paell	PALL
scrinium, *box, case, writing-desk*	scrin	SHRINE
templum, (*temple,* CONTEMPLATE, 202)	templ or tempel	TEMPLE
versus, *a turning* (**vertere,** *turn*)	fers	VERSE (202)

Since the Christian church was in its early history largely a Greek institution, a goodly number of words introduced at this time from Latin were in fact Greek, *e.g.*, 'alms,' 'bishop,' 'canon,' 'deacon,' 'devil,' 'martyr,' 'minster,' 'monk,' 'priest,' and 'psalm.'

11. Not always was the Latin adoption due to the lack of an equivalent Anglo-Saxon term: the borrowed word sometimes took its place alongside a native word or even supplanted it. The convert sometimes preferred an Anglo-Saxon equivalent, as when for PATRIARCH (Lat.-Grk. **patriarcha**), *ruling father,* he used for a time 'heah-faeder,' *high father,* or 'eald-faeder,' *old father;* for 'baptize' (Grk.), literally *dip,* he had 'dyppan,' or 'ful-wian,' *fully consecrate;* for 'evangelist' (Grk.), *the bringer of good tidings,* he had 'godspeller' ('gospeler'); and instead of 'discipul,' his modification of the Lat. **discipulus,** *a learner,*[2] he could use

---

[1] The Old French forms 'alter' and 'auter' were later borrowed; hence Mid. Eng. 'auter.'

[2] He would naturally associate **discipulus** with **discere,** *learn,* but see 121 (end).

'leornere,' *learner*, or 'leornung-mann,' *learning man*.   He might even compound Latin or Greek words with his own: as 'preosthad,' *priesthood* and 'Christendom,' *Christendom*, *Christianity* ('-had,' denoting state or condition, '-dom,' position or jurisdiction).

12. The missionaries brought many words not peculiarly church terms.   We find, for example, such as the following surviving in Modern English:

Latin	*Anglo-Saxon*	*Modern English*
buxus, *box*	box (a bush)	BOX
cappa (Low Lat.), *hood, cape*	caeppe	CAP (Mid. Eng. CAPE, then COPE)
culina, *kitchen*	cylen	KILN
cupa, *cask*, (Late) **cuppa,** *drinking vessel*	cuppe	CUP (cf. CUPOLA, 48)
feniculum, *little hay*, diminutive of **fenum,** *hay*	fenol	FENNEL
linum, *flax*	lin	LINen (210)
matta (Late), *mat*	meatta	MAT
palma, *palm tree* [1]	palm	PALM
palus, *stake*	pal	POLE (later PALE, PALing)
papaver, *poppy*	popig	POPPY
pilum, *pier*	pil	PILE
pinna,[2] *point, pinnacle*	pinn	PIN
pinus, *pine tree*	pin (treow)	PINE (tree)
pix, picis, *pitch*	pic	PITCH
planta, *sprout, shoot*	plante	PLANT
pulvinus, *cushion*	pyle (Mid. Eng. pilwe)	PILLOW
puteus, *well*	pyt or pytt	PIT

[1] The later meaning of **palma,** *i.e.*, *palm tree*, was adopted into English first.   The earlier meaning was *palm of the hand*, which came to us through the French.   The tree was so called because of its hand-shaped leaves.

[2] Early confused with **penna,** and thus coming to mean *feather*, but related to **spina,** *thorn*, rather than to **penna** ('pet[s]na ').

Latin	Anglo-Saxon	Modern English
secula, sicilis, *sickle* (**secare,** *cut*)	sicel, sicol	SICKLE
soccus, *a kind of slipper*	socc	SOCK
solea, *sandal*	sole	SOLE (cf. **solum,** *ground,* SOIL)
tegula (**tegere,** *cover,* 121)	tigel, tigol	TILE

13. Here again the borrowed words are mostly nouns, but there were a few verbs, as 'scrifan,' SHRIVE, from **scribere,** for **scribere** came over with the technical meaning, *draw up a law;* hence *impose a legal obligation,* and thus *prescribe a penance.*[1] 'Offrian' from the Latin **offerre** meant *make a sacrifice,* the ordinary OFFER being of later introduction (135). There are also DIGHT, AS 'dihtan,' *compose, prepare, equip,* from Latin **dictare;** 'spendan,' SPEND, from **expendere** (or **dispendere**), *weigh out;* and 'stoppian,' STOP, from Low Lat. **stupare,** made from **stupa** (**stuppa**), *tow,* used to stop a leak.

14. During the four hundred years intervening between the coming of the missionaries and the Norman Conquest a total variously estimated from three hundred to five hundred words had been adopted from Latin. Many of these were seldom used and failed to survive in common English, yet so large a number constitutes no inconsiderable element in the development of the language, especially in view of the fact that the majority of the English-speaking people found their own vocabulary sufficient for their needs. In the brief list given above we observe again the preference for concrete terms, although the stage of abstract thinking had now been reached. As Professor Jespersen has said, "The Anglo-Saxon principle of adopting only such words as were easily assimilated with the native vocabulary, for the most part names of concrete things, and of turning to the greatest

---

[1] Skeat, *Dict.,* s.v. shrove-tide.

possible account native words and roots, especially for abstract notions — that principle may be taken as a symptom of a healthful condition of a language and a nation." [1]

15. When the Low German tribes came into Britain they had already a system of writing which we know as "runic." The Teutonic word 'rūn' suggested something of the mystery attaching in the earliest times to written characters, and the mass of the people looked upon runes as carrying some magic influence.[2] It may have been partly on this account that the Christian missionaries sought to substitute the Latin alphabet. At any rate the introduction of Latin characters for Anglo-Saxon writing belongs to this period. But the resemblance of a number of the runic signs to Latin, that is to say Greek, characters is too close to be explained as a coincidence and somewhere these north-European people had met such characters before. Indeed evidence points to the North Etruscan alphabet as a connecting link. We may note the following correspondences:

Runic [3]	Latin
ᛒ	B
ᚦ	D (Ð below)
ᚡ	F
ᚺ	H
ᛁ	I
ᚲ	K or C (ancient form ᚲ)
ᛚ	L (Greek Λ)
ᛘ	M
ᚱ	R
ᛋ	S (ᛋ)
ᛏ	T

[1] *Growth and Structure of the Eng. Lang.*, 47.

[2] Gothic 'runa,' *whisper* or *secret*. Chaucer, *Friar's Tale*, 1550, has 'rouned in his eere,' *i.e.*, *whispered in his ear*.

[3] The runic alphabet is called 'futhork' from the values of its first six characters, *f, u, th, o, r,* and *k*.

With this much in common, the adoption of the Roman alphabet by the Anglo-Saxons must not have been difficult. The alphabet then adopted, however, was not quite the same as the English of the present time. Two runic characters were kept: þ, called 'thorn,' equivalent to *th* (as in 'thin'), and p, called 'wen,' with the value of *w* and superseded by double *u* after the Norman Conquest. A modified form of *d*, Ð, ð, called 'edh,' was also used for the sonant *th* (as in 'then'), but not always carefully distinguished from þ. It was not until about the end of the fifteenth century that both of these were discarded for the Roman *th*. Even then þ was kept in the words 'the' and 'that,' 'þe' and 'þat.' Later, when it was confused in form with *y*, 'the' was often written 'ye,' as may still be seen in advertisements and announcements affecting the antique.

In English *j* was not distinguished from *i* until the seventeenth century; and the complete separation of *u* and *v* was effected about the same time.[1] *K* was of rare occurrence, as in Latin, its place being supplied by *c*. *Qu* was regularly represented in Old English by *cw;* after the Conquest, the usage varied, and not until about the end of the thirteenth century was *cw* discontinued and *qu* finally established. *Z* was a late introduction, as foreign to Anglo-Saxon as it had been to Latin.

16. We must not overlook the fact that Christianity had already made its way into Ireland (A.D. 440) and had become so well established that Irish missionaries coöperated with Augustine in the effort to Christianize their Anglo-Saxon neighbors. Irish books were written in an Irish form of Roman characters (omitting *x* and *y*), and thus the new alphabet, as well as the new religion, came into England from two directions at the same time. In fact, with more

---

[1] In this work *j* and *v* are used for consonantal *i* and *u* of Latin words in order the better to link derivatives in English with their Latin sources.

Irish than Roman Christians engaged in the actual work of teaching, the written characters first used on the island must have come from that source and shown what Earle called "a distinct Hibernian physiognomy." [1] It should be added that a few of the words listed above as introduced by Christian missionaries seem to have come by way of Ireland rather than directly from Rome.

[1] *Philology of the English Tongue*, § 92.

CHAPTER III

THE NORMAN CONQUEST

17. The military conquest of Gaul, like that of Britain, was but the beginning of a larger Roman conquest in life and language. During the reign of Augustus the Gallic territory was becoming Romanized not only in its provincial administration and its courts, but also in its public celebrations, its commerce, and its literature. If as early as 69 B.C., as Cicero relates, Gaul was crowded with traders, filled with Romans, and no one of the Gauls transacted any business without the presence of a Roman citizen,[1] how much more constant and intricate must have been the intercourse after the country had been fully opened by Caesar's legions. Magistrates of the courts were Romans, cases were pleaded and edicts were issued in Latin, and a knowledge of the language became practically indispensable to those involved in business affairs or aspiring to official position. Under Claudius schools were opened in Gaul and an interest in Roman literature was fostered. The lower classes of course cared for none of these things, yet they too were learning their Latin, with traders and soldiers for their daily instructors. Thus as the years went on, alongside the Latin of the schools there was a Latin, mispronounced, misunderstood, and mixed with Celtic, which spread over the country and became the **sermo rusticus** or **sermo militaris** of the fourth century. Religion again played its part, for the spread of Christianity through this section contributed very largely to the use of Latin among the people.

[1] *Oratio pro Fonteio*, 1.

18. The language situation was further complicated by the coming of the Germans into Gaul. Opposed at first by the Romans, they were later allowed to settle in the northern part, Goths and Burgundians having already established themselves in the south. About the time that their kinsmen the Jutes were passing over to Britain, a division of these Germans, called Franks, invaded Gaul, secured control of all the northern part, and when Clovis, leader of the tribes and "king of the Franks," had been converted to Christianity (A.D. 496), the entire country was thrown open to the invaders, a country destined in the centuries following to accept their name and be known as France. But what of the language? The Romans had imposed their language on the conquered Gauls, the Gallo-Romans now imposed theirs on the conquering Franks, not, however, without the introduction of many Germanic words in turn. This linguistic product continued to be modified and corrupted till by the end of the seventh century as **lingua Romanica** it had wandered rather far from its parent Latin. Yet the kinship was still recognizable. To speak in this language was **loqui romanice,** the adverb giving us the term ROMANCE (202), and the Romance languages still furnish abundant testimony to their Latin origin.

19. Near the end of the ninth century the Norsemen (North-men) sailing down the coast began their inroads on French (Frankish) territory. A band of these Scandinavian rovers, under the leadership of Hrolf or Rollo, sailed up the Seine, fought successfully with the French, and in 912, when peace had been made, Charles the Simple granted them territory as a fief of the French crown. This territory lying along the channel coast and the river valley, from its new settlers as Normans, came to be known as Normandy. As the Franks had adopted the language of the Gallo-Romans, with added German words, so the Normans adopted the language of the Franco-Gallo-Romans, with many additions from Scandinavian sources, and the result was a Norman French dialect for this northwestern section.

20. A history of the English language would take account of another movement of Scandinavian tribes, particularly the Danes, who began their plundering of the English coast near the end of the eighth century and during the ninth and tenth overran the country with such success that the Dane Canute in 1016 became ruler of England. This fact requires mention here only by reason of the possibility that there were a few Latin words among those furnished to the language by the Danish invaders. KETTLE for the earlier 'cetel' (4) seems to belong here; as also SKIRT (cf. SHIRT and SHORT, 7), Low Lat. **excurtus**; and KINDLE, Lat. **candela**, (10; Old Norse 'kyndill,' *a torch*).

21. But we are far more concerned with the Northmen who settled across the Channel. The English people were not long in coming in touch with Normandy. In the year 1000 King Ethelred II, known as the Unready,[1] in the midst of his troubles with the Danes, invaded Normandy as sheltering and supporting the Danish fleet, and after a disastrous defeat, made a treaty with the Duke Richard and married his sister Emma. Edward the Confessor,[2] son of Ethelred and Emma, came to the English throne in 1042, having been educated in the Norman court under his uncles, the Dukes of Normandy. He naturally assigned positions in church and state to Normans, and adopted French as the language of his court. The Latin contact with English was beginning again.

When Edward died in 1066, Harold was chosen king. Some two years before, as Earl of Wessex, he had visited Normandy and taken an oath with his cousin William, Duke of Normandy, to assist him in obtaining the English crown. Or, according to a doubtful but more interesting story, he

---

[1] 'Rede' meant *counsel;* the king's lack of judgment earned him this title.

[2] So called from his reputation for sanctity.

was shipwrecked on the Norman coast, fell thus into the hands of William, and was forced to swear such an oath on a whole chest of sacred relics. The relics proved unavailing, for when upon the death of Edward, William asserted his claim to the English throne, he was opposed by Harold's armies. In the Battle of Hastings the English were defeated, Harold was killed, and the Duke of Normandy became King of England.

22. With the new king came a great company of dignitaries and officials speaking French. Had these Normans and their French retained the aggressive strength that once belonged to the Romans and their Latin, or had the new language been thrust upon a people less sturdy and less loyal than the English, French might have prevailed to the practical displacement of English. As it was, changes in the latter were not enforced by the conquerors, nor were they by any means immediate. With hostile feeling between the ruling class and the common people, the two languages continued for two centuries side by side with little influence of the one upon the other. At length the line of separation between English and Norman came to be less clearly drawn, and with the loss of Normandy to the English under King John (1204), the Normans in England began to be identified with the native people. French, from being the language of the conqueror, came to be the language of culture and fashion. Normans learned to speak English, and English French, till the scale finally turned in favor of English, but English with perhaps the greatest infusion of foreign words ever received into one language from another. And the significant thing for our present study is that the vast majority of these French words were merely modified Latin words.

English, however, did not cease to be a Teutonic language, even though the influx of French words continued through the fourteenth century. No legislative measure had ever required the use of French, but an act of Parliament in 1363 did require that English be the language of the law courts, in the very period, in fact, when French was being so freely introduced. It is significant that even in the sixteenth century Sir John Cheke, Professor of Greek at Cambridge, attempted to turn the New Testament into pure English, with such changes as *hunderder* for *centurion*, *crossed* for *crucified*, and *moond* for *lunatyke*.[1] It is also significant that his attempt failed.

23. Many French words of course displaced native words; *e.g.*,

French-English	Latin	Native English
AGRICULTURE	**agricultura**	earth-tilth
beSIEGE (cf. SIEGE, 29)	**-sedere**, *sit*	besittan, *sit by*
beTRAY	**-tradere**, *give over*	bewray
CONFESSOR	**confessor**	shrift-father (SCRIFAN, 13)
DESPAIR (verb, then noun)	**desperare**	unhope
IGNORANCE	**ignorantia**	unwisdom, or uncunningness
MEDIATOR	**mediator** (Late)	middler
NOBLE	**nobilis**	aethel, cf. Ethel
PENANCE (43)	**poenitentia**	daed-bot (*deed-bettering*) [2]
PRECIOUS (176)	**pretiosus**	dearworth
REDEEMer	**redimere**, *buy back*	again-buyer
REPENT	**re-paenitere**	afterthink
SAVIOUR	**Salvator**	Haelend, *Healer*, or *making whole*
SOLSTICE (140)	**solstitium**	sunstead

24. A religious treatise published in 1340 was called 'Ayenbite of Inwyt,' *i.e.*, 'Again-bite of In-wit,' for which

[1] McKnight, *English Words and Their Background*, p. 115.

[2] 'Bot' was *compensation;* hence 'daed-bot' was *amends for a* (wrong) *deed*, a sign of repentance.

in words of French-Latin origin we should say *Remorse of Conscience*. On the other hand the Saxon word at times could hold its own against the French: while OF 'veneison,' Lat. **venationem,**[1] was taken as VENISON, 'cerf,' Lat. **cervum,** never supplanted the native word 'stag'; PRINCE and DUKE came through the French from Lat. **principem** and **ducem,** yet the Fr. 'roi' and 'reine,' Lat. **regem** and **reginam,** never dethroned the good Saxon 'king' and 'queen.'

25. In many instances the two words, French and English, survived side by side yet with some difference of usage, sometimes reflecting the social conditions of the time. No better illustration of this perhaps can be given than the words which Scott put into the mouth of Wamba in his conversation with Gurth in the story of Ivanhoe. When the swineherd has called upon the jester to help him round up the scattered herd, the jester declines the invitation, advising him to leave the herd to their destiny, "which," he adds, "whether they meet with bands of travelling soldiers, or of outlaws, or of wandering pilgrims, can be little else than to be converted into Normans before morning, to thy no small ease and comfort."

"The swine turned Normans to my comfort!" quoth Gurth; "expound that to me, Wamba, for my brain is too dull and my mind too vexed to read riddles."

"Why, how call you those grunting brutes running about on their four legs?" demanded Wamba.

"Swine, fool — swine," said the herd; "every fool knows that."

"And swine is good Saxon," said the Jester; "but how call you the sow when she is flayed, and drawn, and quartered, and hung up by the heels like a traitor?"

"Pork," answered the swineherd.

"I am very glad every fool knows that, too," said Wamba, "and pork, I think, is good Norman French; and so when

---

[1] For the accusative in this and succeeding paragraphs, see 160.

the brute lives and is in charge of a Saxon slave, she goes by her Saxon name; but becomes a Norman and is called pork when she is carried to the castle-hall to feast among the nobles. What dost thou think of this, friend Gurth, ha?"

"It is but too true doctrine, friend Wamba, however it got into thy fool's pate."

"Nay, I can tell you more," said Wamba in the same tone; "there is old Alderman Ox continues to hold his Saxon epithet while he is under the charge of serfs and bondsmen such as thou, but becomes Beef, a fiery French Gallant, when he arrives before the worshipful jaws that are destined to consume him. Mynheer Calf, too, becomes Monsieur de Veau in the like manner; he is Saxon when he requires tendance, and takes a Norman name when he becomes a matter of enjoyment."

26. Wamba's examples along with other similar doublets may be thus arranged for comparison:

Anglo-Saxon	Old French	Latin	Modern English
swin	porc	**porcum**	swine, PORK
oxa	boef	**bovem**	OX, BEEF
cealf	veel (later, veau)	**vitellum**	calf, VEAL
beginnan	commencier (later, commencer)	**com + initiare**	begin, COMMENCE
blomo (OS)	flor, flour (later, fleur)	**florem**	bloom, FLOWER, FLOUR [1]
deop	profond, profund	**profundum**	deep, PROFOUND (172)
deor	veneison	**venationem**	deer, VENISON
folc	peuple (167)	**populum**	folk, PEOPLE
haelan	cure (noun)	**curam** (*care*)	heal, CURE

[1] Originally *flower of wheat;* the two spellings were formerly interchangeable.

Anglo-Saxon	Old French	Latin	Modern English
spaec for spraec	langue (also language, 177)	**linguam**	speech, LANGUAGE (u from Fr. 'langue')
stream	riviere	**riparia** (Low Lat. fem., cf. 101, from **ripa**, *bank*)	stream, RIVER
wif	espouse (180)	**sponsam** (**spondere**, *promise*, *betroth*)	wife, SPOUSE
wrecca (*an outcast*)	miserable	**miserabilem**	wretched, MISERABLE

27. The pairs of words common in legal and religious phraseology are often to be traced to this tendency to adopt the new and not part with the old. Such are the following:

AID and abet: OF 'aider,' Lat. **adjutare**, *help*, later shortened to 'aiutare' and 'aitare'; 'abet' also through the French, but of Scandinavian origin.

acknowledge and CONFESS: Lat. **confiteri, confessus**, *confess*.

ACT and deed: Lat. **actum**, *deed*, from **agere**, *do*.

ASSEMBLE and meet together: Fr. 'assembler,' from Low Lat. **assimulare**, not the same as the classical **assimulare** (also spelled **assimilare**), *make like*, but made from **ad**, *to*, and **simul**, *at the same time, bring together* (*at the same time*).

head and CHIEF: OF 'chef' or 'chief' from Lat. **caput** (178).

PARDON and forgive: the OF 'pardoner' was Low Lat. **perdonare**, *grant, remit, condone*, and this **perdonare** may itself have been modeled after the German 'vergeben,' our word *forgive*. Thus the words may be doublets.

PRAY and beseech: OF 'preier,' 'prier,' Lat. **precari** (173b).

SAFE and sound: Fr. 'sauf,' Lat. **salvum**, *safe* (179).

USE and wont: OF 'us,' Lat. **usum** (uti, *use*).

will and TESTAMENT: Fr. 'testament,' Lat. **testamentum**, *a will* (90).

The supremacy of the Norman French in state, war, law, art, and religion is indicated in words like the following, surviving in these fields: [1]

28. State:

AUTHORITY: OF 'autoritet,' Lat. **auctoritatem**, from **auctor** (80).

CHANCELLOR: OF 'chancellier,' Low Lat. **cancellarium** (CANCEL, 35).

COUNCIL: Fr. 'concile,' OF 'cuncile,' Lat. **concilium**; whether from **con-calare**, an old word for *call together*, or from **con** + **celare**, *get under (one) roof together*, authorities are divided. In any case it is not to be confused with COUNSEL, Lat. **consilium**, of like origin with **consulere**, CONSULT (cf. **consul**, 52).

COUNTRY: OF 'contree,' from Lat. **contra**, *over against* (202).

COURT: OF 'cort,' Lat. **cortem** (**cohortem**), *an enclosed place for a tribunal* (see COHORT, 202).

CROWN: contracted from OF 'coronne,' Lat. **coronam**, *a garland.*

ESQUIRE: OF 'escuyer' (180), from Low Lat. **scutarius, scutum**, *a shield;* hence *a shield-bearer.*

GOVERN: OF 'governer,' Lat. **gubernare** (from Greek), literally *steer* a ship.

MINISTER: OF 'ministre,' Lat. **ministrum** (**minister**), *a servant* (54).

POWER: OF 'poer' (the *w* merely carrying over from one vowel to the other) from **potere**, which was substituted in Low Latin for **posse**, *be able.*

REALM: OF 'realme,' as if from a Low Lat. '**regalimen,**' (cf. **regimen**, 89).

REIGN: OF 'regne,' Lat. **regnum.**

SOVEREIGN: OF 'soverain,' Low Lat. **superanus**, from **super**, *above*, the *g* being inserted through association with REIGN.

STATE: OF 'estat' (180), Lat. **statum**, from **stare**, *stand; a standing*, so an *established order* (cf. **status**, 52).

29. War:

ARMOR (ARMOUR): OF 'armure,' Lat. **armaturam** (87).

ARMS: OF 'armes,' Lat. **arma**, *arms.*

[1] The alteration of forms is presented in Chapter IV of Part II.

ARMY: English representation of OF 'armee,' fem. pple. of 'armer,' Lat. **armata**, from **armare** (cf. ARMADA, 50).

ASSAULT: OF 'assalt,' Lat. **ad** + **saltus**, *a leap, a leaping at* or *on.* From the verb **salire** and the same prefix came OF 'assailer,' Eng. ASSAIL, of like meaning.

BATTLE: OF 'bataille'; Low Lat. **batalia** was used for the classical **pugna.**

CAPTAIN, CHIEFTAIN: OF 'capitain,' 'chevetaine,' Low Lat. **capitanus**, from **caput,** *head* (36).

COLONEL: through the Fr. 'colonel,' from the Ital. 'colonnello,' and Lat. **columna;** *commander of a little column* (48).

ENEMY: OF 'enemi,' Lat. **inimicus**, **in** + **amicus**, *not-friend.* Directly from (Late) Latin, however, is the adjective INIMICAL (39).

LIEUTENANT: Fr. 'lieu tenant,' Lat. **locum tenentem** (59, 190), *place-holding, one who holds* temporarily another's *place.*

NAVY: OF 'navie,' Lat. **navia**, *a boat* (cf. **navis**, *ship*).

OFFICER: OF 'officier,' from Low Lat. **officiarius**, Lat. **officium**, *service* (OFFICE, 202).

PEACE: OF 'pais,' Fr. 'paix,' Lat. **pacem.**

PRISON: OF 'prison,' representing Lat. **prensionem**, *a seizing,* action noun (85) of **prendere, prensus,** *i.e.,* **prehendere,** *seize.* Cf. SURPRISE (French), from Med. Lat. **superprendere,** *take unawares.*

SERGEANT: OF 'sergant' or 'sergent,' made through Low Latin from **servientem**, *serving.* Cf. SERVANT, which is also a French pple. (202).

SIEGE: OF 'siege,' *a seat,* connected through Low Latin with **sedere**, *sit; a sitting* about a place. Cf. **ob-sidium,** *a sitting over against,* and hence *a siege.*

SOLDIER: OF 'soldier,' Low Lat. **soldarium**, *one receiving pay* for fighting (see 202).

TOWER: OF 'tur,' later 'tour,' Lat. **turrim**, *a (military) tower.*

30. Law:

ACCUSE: Fr. 'accuser,' Lat. **accusare**, from **ad causam;** hence *call to account.*

ATTORNEY: OF 'atorne,' a pple. of 'atorner,' *appoint,* Lat. **ad** + **tornare,** TURN (in a lathe); *turned to, i.e., appointed to* a case.

CRIME: Fr. 'crime,' Lat. **crimen,** from the same root as **cernere,** *decide;* so *a judicial decision, a charge;* then a CRIME.

DEFENDANT: pres. pple. of Fr. 'defendre,' from Lat. **defendere,** *strike down, ward off* (cf. FENCE, 202). A DEFENDANT then was one who wards off an assailant.

JUDGE: OF 'juge,' Lat. **judicem (judex), jus + dic,** the root of **dicere,** *say,* **dicare,** *make known; one who declares the right or law.*

JURY: OF 'juree,' fem. pple. of 'jurer' from Lat. **jurare,** *swear, take an oath;* hence *a group of sworn men.*

JUSTICE: the Old French rendering of the Lat. **justitia,** from **justus,** JUST, **jus,** *right* (76, 111).

PENALTY: The Lat. **poenalis** (98), from **poena** (Grk. poinē, ποινή) and so meaning *pertaining to punishment,* appears in OF and Eng. PENAL, from which was made OF 'penalite', Med. Lat. **poenalitatem;** and this became Eng. PENALTY.

PLAINTIFF: the Fr. 'plaintif,' from Lat. **plangere, planctus,** with the suffix **-ivus** (120). The verb is properly *to beat,* but since one beats his breast in grief, it means also *lament.* The term then applies to one who has been grieved or wronged, or thinks he has.

PLEAD: The Lat. **placitum,** from **placere,** meant *the thing that is pleasing,* therefore *a decision,* then (through Low Latin) *a court* where decisions are given, and finally the *presenting of a case* in court. From **placitum** came the Old French noun 'plaid,' the verb 'plaider,' and from these the Eng. PLEAD.

PROPERTY: The OF 'proprete,' like our PROPRIETY (73) came from Lat. **proprietatem,** the abstract noun from **proprius,** Eng. PROPER, *i.e., one's own.*

SESSION: through the French from Lat. **sessionem,** *a sitting,* **sedere, sessus,** *sit* (85).

SUIT: like SUITE, Fr. 'suite,' Low Lat. **sequita,** Med. Lat. **secta,** from **sequi,** *a following;* so *a legal process.*

SUMMON, through OF 'somoner,' goes back to the Lat. **summonere (sub-monere),** *remind privately.* Cf. the use of "warn" in the sense of *serve legal notice.*

TENURE: French of the Low Lat. **tenuram,** *a holding,* from **tenere,** *hold.*

31. Art:

BEAUTY: From the Lat. **bellus,** *fair, handsome* (cf. EMBELLISH), Low Latin made a noun in -tat- (72). **Bellitatem** appeared in Old French as 'beltet' and 'biaute' (Fr. 'beauté'), spelled into English as BEAUTY. Cf. BEAU, 158 N.

CHISEL: OF 'chisel' and 'cisel,' from Low Lat. **sciselum, scindere,** *cut apart, split;* or not improbably, like Ital. 'cesello,' going back to **caedere,** *cut.*

CLOISTER: OF 'cloistre,' Lat. **claustrum** (93), *an enclosure,* from **claudere, clausus,** *shut* (cf. INCLUDE, EXCLUDE).

COLOR: This is the Latin nom. form, having come to us, however, through **colorem,** OF 'colur,' or 'colour' (52 N). The same root gives **cel-are,** CONCEAL, COLOR being a *covering* for a surface.

DESIGN: The noun is made from the verb, which, coming from OF 'designer,' is Lat. **designare** (**signum,** *a mark,* SIGN), *mark down, i.e., mark fully.*

FIGURE: Fr. 'figure,' Lat. **figuram,** shows the root **fig** which gives also **fingere, fictus,** *form.* FIGURE, therefore, is the thing *formed* (cf. FIGMENT and FICTION).

IMAGE: Fr. 'image,' Lat. **imago, imaginem** (see **farrago,** 52). Cf. **imitari,** IMITATE.

MORTAR: OF 'mortier,' Lat. **mortarium,** originally the *vessel in which things were pounded;* also the *substance pounded.* Cf. MORTAR, 4.

PAINT: OF 'paint' or 'peint,' pf. pple. of the verb from Lat. **pingere** (root **pig**). It is therefore of the same origin with PIGMENT, PICTURE, and DEPICT. And PAINTED is doubly a passive participle.

PILLAR, through the OF 'piler,' and Low Lat. **pilare,** goes back to Lat. **pila,** *a stone pier,* a PILE, with adjective suffix **-aris** (99).

PLUMB, with its older spelling PLOMB, is the Fr. 'plomb,' Lat. **plumbum,** which means *lead;* so a *mass of lead* hung on a line for securing the vertical. PLUMB down therefore is *straight* down, and the word passes over colloquially to mean *absolutely* or *entirely,* PLUMB different from its first meaning.

PORTRAIT: OF 'pourtrai(c)t,' Med. Lat. **protractus,** *image,* **protrahere,** *draw,* PORTRAY; Cl. Lat. **protrahere** *draw forth.*

32. Religion:

MIRACLE: Fr. 'miracle,' Lat. **miraculum,** *what excites wonder* (91), made from **mirari,** *wonder at* (cf. **mirus,** *wonderful,* **nimirum,** *doubtless, i.e., no-wonder,* and the English derivative ADMIRE).

PRAY: OF 'preier' comes from Lat. **precari,** *pray;* **prex, precis,** *prayer.*

PREACH: OF 'precher was made from Lat. **prae-dicare,** *proclaim;* direct Latin derivative, PREDICATE.

PURGATORY: **purgare,** *cleanse,* **purgator,** *a cleanser,* **purgatorius,** *cleansing;* OF 'purgatoire'; hence *a place of cleansing* (71) preparatory to heaven.

RELIGION: The French is also 'religion,' from **religionem.** The origin of the Latin word is a matter of dispute. "A binding back" of man to God (root of **ligare,** cf. LIGAMENT, LIGATURE) is perhaps better religion than etymology. Cicero, for all that the ancients are commonly wrong on derivation, seems to be more nearly right when he says that those who *examined again* and *went over carefully* (**relegerent**) all things pertaining to the worship of the gods, were called **religiosi.**[1] So **religens** came to mean *revering the gods.* Cf. **diligens,** *careful,* DILIGENT, and **neg-ligens** (**nec +** **legens**[2]), *not careful,* NEGLIGENT, 75.

SACRIFICE: The same word in French, coming from Lat. **sacrificium,** *a making* SACRED, *a thing made* SACRED, **sacer + facere.**

SAINT is merely the French form of the Lat. **sanctum,** pf. pple. of **sancire,** which has the same root **sac-** as the first element of SACRIFICE above.

SAVIOUR: OF 'saveor,' 'salveor,' from the Lat. **salvatorem,** agent noun from **salvare,** itself made from the adjective **salvus,** SAFE; a SAVIOUR is *one who makes safe.*

SERMON: the same as the French, from Lat. **sermonem,** *talk, discourse.* Strangely enough it is related to the Eng. 'swear' (AS 'swerian'), both the SERMON and the swearing involving positive declarations. So also 'an-swer.'

SERVICE: OF 'servise,' or 'service,' Lat. **servitium,** literally, *the work of a slave* (**servus**). Cf. MINISTRY, 71.

---

[1] *De Natura Deorum*, 2, 28, 72.

[2] Unless *g* is a particle (Grk. 'ge,' γε) as in **negotium,** 128 NEGOTIATE.

TRINITY: the English form of OF 'trinite,' representing **trinitatem,** *a triad, i.e.,* the three persons of the Godhead. The abstract noun (72) was made from the adjective **trini,** *threefold.*

VIRGIN: OF 'virgine,' Lat. **virginem (virgo),** *a maiden.*

33. The physicians of the day also used French, as is suggested by such words as the following:

CORDIAL: Fr. 'cordial,' an adjective from **cor, cordis,** *heart;* hence meaning *pertaining to the heart;* so *stimulating, reviving,* and thus applied to a preparation that stimulates. Cf. 41, HEARTY.

HUMOR: OF 'humor,' Lat. **humorem,** *liquid* or *moisture.* From the time of the Greek physician Galen it was supposed that four humors or kinds of moisture in the body — blood, phlegm, choler (yellow bile), and black bile — were responsible not only for ailments, but also for different temperaments, as sanguine, phlegmatic, choleric, and melancholy. Then the word was applied especially to that turn of mind which appreciates the ludicrous, and we get so far from the meaning of moisture that a reference even to "dry humor" is not humorous.

PATIENT, the same as in Old French, is the pres. pple. **patientem (patiens)** of **pati,** *suffer;* hence *the sufferer.*

PESTILENCE, Fr. 'pestilence,' is the Lat. **pestilentia,** made from **pestilens, pestilentis,** *infected* or *unhealthy.* **Pestilens** is in participial form, as if a verb had been made from the adjective **pestilis,** *pestilential, i.e., connected with a plague,* or PEST, **pestis.**

Along with such words came also medical terms from Greek through Latin, passed on to English by the French, as 'physic,' *relating to nature;* 'practitioner,' *one who practices* (a flagrant specimen of hybrid, 211); 'diet,' one's *living* or *mode of living,* then *an allowance of food;* 'surgeon,' for 'chirurgien,' made by adding *-en* (**-anus**) to 'cirurgie,' from Low Lat.-Grk. **chirurgia,** lit. *handwork;* with such perversity did our forefathers spell.

34. If all our French words had been adopted into English in a single brief period or from the same French dialect, doubtless we should find little variation in the treatment of their sounds; there would have been uniformity in their representation of the original vowels and consonants. As a matter of fact such words represent two general periods and at least two sections of France. Words entering English as a direct result of the Conquest came from the dialects used in Normandy or Picardy, the northern part of the country. These words, as we have observed, were accepted slowly and belonged in general to the century 1250–1350. There followed perhaps a half century of ebb in the tide of new words, after which, whether by associations of war or by a growing interest in continental literature, England established new contacts with France and began once more to receive French words, this time from the Parisian dialect of the central section. From the end of the fourteenth century to the present time our borrowing has been from this dialect. Already in Chaucer's time two dialects were distinguished. In his Prologue (ll. 124–126) it is said of the Prioresse,

> And Frensh she spak ful faire and fetisly,
> After the scole of Stratford-atte-Bowe,
> For Frensh of Paris was to hir unknowe.[1]

35. In a small number of words we have survivals in English of these dialectal differences in French, particularly the variation between the hard *c* of Picard and the *ch* of Parisian French, representing the Latin *c* before *a*. The following doublets will illustrate:

CALDRON, CHALDRON. Both are made through Old French from Lat. **caldaria** (with French suffix '-on'), *a pot for boiling*, **caldus** meaning *hot*, a shortened form of **calidus**. CALDRON has retained practically its original meaning, while CHALDRON became a receptacle for measuring, and now a little used English measure for coal and coke only.

---

[1] 'Fetisly,' *properly;* 'scole,' *school;* 'unknowe,' *unknown;* Stratford-at-Bow was near London.

CANCEL, CHANCEL. The Old French had both 'canceler' (verb) [1] and 'chancel' from Lat. **cancelli,** *crossbars, lattice work,* such as formerly enclosed a part of a church or a seat of judgment; hence our word CHANCEL. As cross lines used to mark out what has been written, we have it in the form CANCEL.

CAPITAL, CHAPTER. The Latin **capitellum** is a diminutive of **capitulum** and **capitulum** is a diminutive of **caput,** but the derivatives have lost the meaning of a *small little head.* By way of Picardy **capitellum,** denoting *the head* of a column, became 'capitel,' later CAPITAL on analogy of CAPITAL from the Lat. adjective **capitalis** (see CATTLE below). By the other route **capitulum** became OF 'chapitle,' then 'chapitre' (Mod. Fr. and Mid. Eng.), and was finally shortened for us into CHAPTER, as *a heading* or *division* of a treatise.

CATCH, CHASE. The Old French forms were 'cachier' and 'chacier,' from the Low Lat. **caciare,** coming apparently (through an intermediate **'captiare')** from **captare,** *seize, lay hold of,* a frequentative of **capere,** *take.*

CATTLE, CHATTEL. The Old French made both 'catel' and 'chatel' from Low Lat. **capitale** or **captale** meaning *property,* in which sense we have later CAPITAL denoting wealth (a thing important enough to stand "at the head," **caput**). But early property was largely **vivum capitale,** *live stock,* the meaning we have kept in CATTLE, while CHATTELS (pl.) is used for *goods* or *property* in a more general sense.

36. Some other words apparently like these in the use of *c* and *ch* are to be differently explained:

CARD, CHART. The French forms are 'carte' and 'charte'; the former, however, was a fourteenth century adaptation of Ital. 'carta,' used first for *a playing card,* and then extended to other meanings belonging already to 'charte.' The word, while taken from Lat. **charta,** *a sheet of paper* (papyrus), was originally Greek (χάρτης). CARD seems to be a mere corruption of Fr. 'carte.'

[1] The use of 'canceler' as a scholarly term may also allow these words a place in 43.

CAMPAIGN, CHAMPAGNE. From Lat. **campania** (**campus,** *field*), *the level country* around Rome, the French made the name of another level country, 'Champagne.' This the English adopted to apply to the light wine coming from that province. 'Campagne' seems to have been taken from the Ital. 'campagna.' [1] It became in English CAMPAIGN denoting first military operations in the open field; later also the more or less warlike operations of a political contest.

CAPTAIN, CHIEFTAIN. The latter represents a twelfth century French spelling 'chevetain,' from Low Lat. **capitanus** or **capitaneus,** *a head* or *leader* of soldiers (**caput,** *head*). 'Capitain,' our CAPTAIN, was a fourteenth century adaptation of the same word, possibly influenced by Ital. capitano.'

CAVALRY, CHIVALRY. The former came through Italian, and then French, the latter from Old French (see CAVALRY, 48).

[1] So NED s.v. CAMPAIGN, but Brachet, Gram. Hist. de la Langue Fr., p. 48, gives *campagne* and *champagne* as examples of dialectal differences, and mentions *campagne* as one of a few instances of the preservation of the *c*-form in Modern French.

CHAPTER IV

THE REVIVAL OF LEARNING

37. In the fourteenth century there began in Italy a movement which is commonly known in its broader phases as the Renaissance, in its intellectual aspect as the Revival of Learning. Its earliest exponent and greatest leader was Petrarch, Italian poet and classical scholar, who died in 1374. Continuing some two centuries after Petrarch's time and extending to other parts of Europe, the movement was marked by a breaking away from mediæval traditions, by searching investigations into things long unquestioningly accepted, by relentless criticism of established systems of philosophy and science. It found its standards of life in the classic literature of Greece and Rome, and naturally gained impetus when the capture of Constantinople by the Turks in 1453 sent Christian scholars and ecclesiastics far and wide over western Europe, carrying with them their ancient manuscripts.

38. During the latter years of the fifteenth century the Revival reached England, in the time of Henry VII, and later found in Henry VIII an influential patron. Here, then, was another and significant meeting of English with Latin. Latin had long been the language of scholarship and theology, but here was a new interest created in classical study. The religious and philosophic discussion inspired by the Protestant Reformation, as a part of the general movement, discussion so commonly carried on in Latin, did its part to open the way for the coming of new Latin words into English. These words, moreover, introduced by scholars from published works into written documents or printed books, came more strictly in their Latin forms than the earlier words conveyed by speech only and modified, if not mutilated, by their speakers. In fact, so faithful did both French and English become to the original Latin that we may at times be uncertain whether their borrowings are independent or, if not, which has adopted the borrowed word from the other.

39. The enrichment of our vocabulary is again manifest when we observe how large a number of doublets [1] we have from the adoption of a new Latin word alongside the native English word.

It must not be supposed that definitely from the end of the fifteenth century the tendency to adopt words from literary Latin began to show itself. It is convenient to let our study of such derivatives center in the Revival of Learning, but the thirteenth and fourteenth centuries also furnished literary words. And in the following lists of doublets we are not so much concerned with the exact date of admission as with the fact that classical study was increasing the number of English synonyms. [2]

Examples, English and Latin, are the following:

anger, IRE: Lat. **ira**, *anger.*

behead, DECAPITATE: Low Lat. **decapitare, decapitatus,** *take off* (**de-**) *the head* (**caput, capitis**).

bodily, CORPORAL: **corporalis,** from **corpus,** *body* (98).

choose, SELECT: **seligere, selectus, se-,** *apart* (145) + **legere,** *choose.*

cleave, DIVIDE: **di-videre,** *separate;* probably the same root as in **vidua,** and Eng. 'widow.'

cloak, PALLIATE: **palliatus,** from **pallium,** *a cloak* (107).

---

[1] The term *doublets* is used in these paragraphs in two senses: it designates (a) two words of like meaning and often of like formation but coming from different sources, as here (§ 39) and §§ 25, 26, and 41; and (b) two forms from a common original, as in §§ 35, 36, 42, 43, 44.

[2] It must be remembered that doublets, like other synonyms, have not exactly the same meaning and use. While similar in meaning they are rarely, if ever, interchangeable.

earthly, TERRESTRIAL: To **terrestri(s)** from **terra**, *earth*, has been added another adjective suffix -AL (98, 204).

fat, CORPULENT: **corpulentus**, from **corpus**, *body* (106).

fiery, IGNEOUS: **igneus** from **ignis**, *fire* (110).

fire, CONFLAGRATION: **Conflagratio**, *a burning*, is the action noun (85) from **conflagrare**, *be wholly consumed by fire*, or (later) *consume*.

forerunner, PRECURSOR: **praecursor**, *forerunner;* **cursor**, agent noun from **currere**, *run* (80).

foresee, PROVIDE: **pro-videre**, *see beforehand;* also 'foresight' and PROVISION.

foretell, PREDICT: **prae-dicere, -dictus**, *say beforehand* (133).

friendly, AMICABLE: **amicabilis**, *friendly* (42).

gainsay, CONTRADICT: **contra-dicere, -dictus**, *speak against* (133).

handbook, MANUAL: formerly MANUEL, which is the French spelling, now returned to the Latin form **manual-is**; from **manus**, *hand* (98). Lat. **manuale** was *a bookcase* or *book-cover*, and in Late Latin *a handbook*.

height, ALTITUDE: **altitudo**, quality noun of **altus**, *high* (78).

hide, CONCEAL: **con-celare**, *conceal*.

learned, ERUDITE: **erudire, eruditus**, *polish, instruct* (see ERUDITION, 85).

lie, PREVARICATE: **praevaricari, praevaricatus**, *walk crookedly* (202).

loving, AMATORY: From the familiar verb **amare** was made the agent noun **amator** (80) and from this the adjective **amatorius** (102). **Amator** comes to us only in the French form AMATEUR (194).

name, APPELLATION: **appellare**, *call by name;* **appellatio**, action noun (85).

oversee, SUPERVISE: **super-videre, -visus**, an exact equivalent; also 'oversight,' SUPERVISION.

scare, TERRIFY: from **terrificare**, *frighten*, on the analogy of French words in '-fier' from Lat. -ficare (187). The Latin verb is from **terrificus**, TERRIFIC, itself a compound of **terror** and **facere**, *make fright*.

shield, PROTECT: **pro-tegere, -tectus**, *cover before, furnish a shelter in front of*.

small, DIMINUTIVE: The Latin adjective was **deminutivus** (120) from **deminuere,** *lessen* (**minus,** *less*). There seems to have been a confusion of spelling with **diminuere** (**dis-**), *break into small pieces.* Furthermore it should be noted that the English DIMINISH is not made from either of these verbs, but after MINISH had been made through the French from a Low Latin word going back to **minutia** (52), the compound was made with the prefix **di-** (**dis-**).

sparkle, SCINTILLATE: **Scintillare, scintillatus,** *sparkle,* was made from the noun **scintilla,** *spark* (52). The noun SCINTILLATION was first taken over from the French; then the verb came directly from the Latin.

starry, STELLAR: **stellaris,** adjective from the noun **stella,** *star* (99).

straightway, IMMEDIATELY: **Mediare, mediatus,** from **medius,** *middle,* meant *divide in the middle* or *be in the middle,* giving our MEDIATE (124). Thus with the negative **in-,** IMMEDIATE, *not through a middle way;* hence *direct.*

sunny, SOLAR: **solaris,** adjective from **sol,** *sun* (99).

teacher, INSTRUCTOR: agent noun (80) of **in-struere,** *build* (*into*), *set in order, provide for, provide with information.*

thin, EMACIATED. The Latin verb is **emaciare, emaciatus,** *make lean,* **e-,** *out, i.e., out and out, very,* and the base of **macies,** *leanness.*

truth, VERACITY: like Fr. 'veracité,' Med. Lat. **veracitatem** (**veracitas**); **verax,** *truthful,* VERACIOUS.

unfriendly, INIMICAL. The adjective **inimicalis** belongs to Late Latin but is regular in its formation from **inimicus** as a noun (98).

unload, EXONERATE: **exonerare, exoneratus,** from **ex-** with **onus, oneris,** *burden;* hence, *disburden,* lit. *take the burden out* or *off.*

unreadable, ILLEGIBLE: The adjective was made from the negative prefix **in-** with LEGIBLE, from **legibilis** (116), **legere,** *read;* 'illegibilis' does not occur in Latin. For 'unreadable,' see 118.

uproot, ERADICATE: **eradicare, eradicatus,** lit. *root out,* **radicare** from **radix, radicis,** *root,* which we have also in RADICAL and RADISH (Fr. 'radis').

wholesome, SALUBRIOUS: SALUBRIOUS is made as if from 'salubriosus' (94) but the Latin word is **salubris** from **salus, salutis,** *safety, health.*

40. Sometimes our native noun has no corresponding adjective, and we have drawn on the Latin to supply the lack, or the native and derived adjectives have quite different meanings or uses:

ear, AURAL: as if 'auralis,' from **auris**, *ear* (98); AURAL, however, is a coined word.

eye, OCULAR: **ocularis**, *pertaining to the eye*, **oculus** (99).

foot, PEDAL: **pedalis**, *pertaining to the foot*, **pes, pedis** (98).

hand, MANUAL: through French from **manualis**, *pertaining to the hand*, **manus** ('handbook,' 39). Our own adjective 'handy' is either *skilled in using the hand*, or *suited to be used by the hand*.

head, CAPITAL: through the French from **capitalis, caput, capitis**, *head* (98); *at the head* of its kind, *excellent;* or *relative to the life (head)*, as 'CAPITAL punishment.' Note the different meaning of the native 'heady.'

lip, LABIAL: Late Lat. **labialis**, *of* or *made by the lips;* **labia (labium)**, *lip;* as 'LABIAL sound' (98).

mind, MENTAL: Late Lat. **mentalis**, *pertaining to the mind*, **mens, mentis** (98).

moon, LUNAR: **lunaris** from **luna**, *moon* (99).

mouth, ORAL: ORAL, coined in -AL (-alis, 98), from **os, oris**, *mouth*.

son, FILIAL: **filialis** not classical, but a later formation on the analogy of adjectives in -al (-alis, 98), from **filius**, *son* (**filia**, *daughter*).

tail, CAUDAL: a coined word like AURAL; **cauda**, *tail* (205).

throat, GUTTURAL: coined, as in French, from **guttur**, *throat*. 'Throaty' is close in meaning to GUTTURAL, *hoarse-sounding*.

wound, VULNERABLE: the Late Lat. **vulnerabilis** from the verb **vulnerare** (116), *wound;* **vulnus, vulneris**, *a wound*.

Again, these nouns themselves may be used as adjectives but still in a different sense, usually in an ordinary or direct meaning, the derivative adjective tending to learned use, as: 'ear' muffs, AURAL surgery; 'hand' saw, MANUAL labor; 'tail' end, CAUDAL extremity; 'throat' trouble, GUTTURAL consonant.

41. Practically of the same group as the English-Latin doublets are those of which the Latin word has come through the literary French and therefore preserves its Latin form. Such are the following:

almighty, OMNIPOTENT: **omni-potens, -potentis,** participial form from **posse,** *all-able, all-powerful.*

bitterness, ACERBITY: **acerbitas, acerbitat-em,** from **acerbus,** *bitter* (72).

bloody, SANGUINE: **sanguineus,** *bloody,* or *bloodthirsty.* This literal meaning, however, has passed over to SANGUINARY (**sanguinarius,** 101) and SANGUINE denotes a full blood supply; hence *ardent, hopeful* (cf. HUMOR, 33).

boyish, PUERILE: **puerilis** from **puer,** *boy* (100).

bravery, VALOR: action noun of **valere,** *be strong* (81).

building, EDIFICE: **aedificium, aedes + facere** (140).

burdensome, ONEROUS: **onerosus** from **onus, oneris,** *burden* (94). Cf. unload, EXONERATE (39).

buy, PURCHASE: PUR- is a French variation of Latin **pro,** *for;* CHASE goes back through Low Latin to **captare,** *seize, lay hold of* (35); the OF 'purchaser' meant *pursue eagerly.* PURCHASE was formerly used in English of the gain of a pirate, later gain by labor, and especially gain by payment.

deadly, MORTAL: **mortalis** from **mors, mortis,** *death* (98). To the Latin meaning *subject to death* we have added that of *causing death* or *resulting in death.*

dwelling, RESIDENCE: RESIDENCE is made on analogy of nouns in -ENCE, Lat. -entia from pres. pples. (75), **residens** being the pres. pple. of **residere,** RESIDE, *remain behind, tarry, abide;* a RESIDENCE is a place where one may stay and sit down (**sedere,** *sit*).

fear, TERROR: **terror,** action noun of **terrere,** *frighten* (81).

fearful, TIMID: **timidus,** *fearing,* verbal adjective from **timere,** *fear* (112).

feather, PLUME: **pluma,** *a feather.*

feeling, SENTIMENT: OF 'sentement,' Med. Lat. **sentimentum** from **sentire,** *feel* (90).

freedom, LIBERTY: OF 'liberte,' Lat. **libertat-em,** *freedom,* **liber,** *free.*

heal, CURE: The verb CURE is from the noun, Lat. **cura,** *care, attention* (26). Giving attention to a malady implies its cure. Note that 'heal' goes back to AS 'hāl,' *whole, hale.*

hearten, ENCOURAGE: OF 'encourager,' 'en-' being the prefix **in-,** and the noun 'courage,' derived from the Lat. **cor,** *heart,* with the suffix -AGE, Lat. -**aticum** (177).

hearty, CORDIAL: **cordialis** from **cor, cordis,** *heart* (98). Cf. 33.

heavenly, CELESTIAL: OF 'celestiel,' as if from '**celestialis.**' But the Latin adjective from **caelum,** *heaven,* is **caelestis,** -AL being here again added by analogy (204).

kingdom, REIGN: Fr. 'regne,' Lat. **regnum,** *the government* or *power of a king,* **rex.**

kingly, ROYAL: OF 'roial' ('roi,' *king*), Lat. **regalis,** from **rex, regis,** *king.* Cf. OF 'realme,' from an assumed Low Lat. '**regalimen,**' Eng. REALM.

limb, MEMBER: Fr. 'membre,' Lat. **membrum,** *member.*

lonely, SOLITARY: Fr. 'solitaire,' Lat. **solitarius,** *alone* (101, for **solitat-arius**), **solitas** (-**tatis**), *loneliness.*

manly, VIRILE: Fr. 'viril,' Lat. **virilis,** from **vir,** *man* (100).

manslaughter, HOMICIDE: Fr. 'homicide,' Lat. **homicidium,** homi- for **homini-** (**homo**), *man* and -**cid-** from **caedere,** *cut down* or *slay* (140).

old, VENERABLE: VENERABLE means primarily *worthy of reverence,* **venerabilis** from **venerari,** *revere* (116). Its application to the aged is secondary and even there it always carries its first meaning.

soften, MOLLIFY: OF 'mollifier,' Lat. **mollificare** (187); **mollis,** *soft, mild.*

sorrow, GRIEF: OF 'gref' or 'grief,' Lat. **gravis,** *heavy* (178). Cf. Matthew 26 : 37, "sorrowful and very heavy."

speech, ORATION: action noun of **orare,** *speak* (85).

speed, VELOCITY: **Velocitas** is the abstract noun from **velox,** *swift* (72).

steadfast, FIRM: **firmus,** *steadfast.*

storm, TEMPEST: OF 'tempeste,' representing Low Lat. **tempesta.** The Classical Latin word was **tempestas,** which first, like the related word **tempus,** meant *time* or *season;* from this it became *weather;* then *bad weather.*

tidings, REPORT: We had first the verb through the French from **re-portare,** *carry back;* then the noun.

wish, DESIRE: OF 'desirer,' modified form of **desiderare,** *long for.*

withstand, RESIST: Lat. **resistere** was *stand back, stand still, withstand.*

womanly, FEMININE: OF 'feminin,' Lat. **femininus,** from the noun **femina** (104).

work, LABOR: OF 'labour,' Lat. **labor** (54).

worldly, MUNDANE: changed from the Fr. 'mondain' to follow the Latin spelling, **mundanus** (103), from **mundus,** *world.*

yearly, ANNUAL: Fr. 'annuel,' the English spelling following the Lat. **annual-is,** a Late Latin adjective from **annus,** *year.* Cf. ANNALS, 98.

young, JUVENILE: Fr. 'juvenil,' Lat. **juvenilis,** from **juvenis,** youth (100).

42. We find another series of doublets representing French and Latin, since in many cases a word was introduced directly which had already been adopted in a modified form from the earlier French:

ABRIDGE, ABBREVIATE: both from **abbreviare, abbreviatus,** *shorten,* from **ad** and **brevis,** *short.*

AGGRIEVE, AGGRAVATE: **aggravare, aggravatus,** *add to the weight of,* from **ad** and **gravis,** *heavy.*

AMIABLE, AMICABLE: The OF 'aimiable,' *friendly,* was the Lat. **amicabilis** (**amicare,** 116), which came into English directly as AMICABLE. But 'aimiable' was confused with 'aimable,' Lat. **amabilis** (**amare**) and AMIABLE means *lovable.*

CAITIFF, CAPTIVE: **captivus,** one *taken,* adjective and then noun from **capere,** *take* (120).

CHANT, CANT: Lat. **cantare,** frequentative (130) of **canere,** *sing;* CANT, *sing hypocritically, talk deceitfully.* Both also are used as nouns. Cf. ENCHANT and INCANTATION, *sing on* or *over, pronouncing a mystical formula.*

CHARNEL, CARNAL: two representations of **carnalis,** from **caro, carnis,** *flesh, pertaining to flesh;* but CHARNEL means *containing dead bodies,* as a 'CHARNEL vault.'

COUNT, COMPUTE: **computare,** *think together, sum up, reckon* (137, N).

COY, QUIET: **quietus,** pf. pple. of **quiescere** (or originally of **quiere**), *be at rest* (202). Old French made it 'coit,' then 'coi,' our COY.

DEFEAT, DEFECT: DEFEAT, first verb, then substantive, *an un-*

making, its prefix going back to the Lat. **dis-, -FEAT** the Lat. **-factum, -fectum; DEFECT** directly from the Lat. **deficere, defectus,** *fail* (cf. FEAT and FACT).

ESTEEM, ESTIMATE: **aestimare, aestimatus,** *value,* made evidently from an adjective form from **aes,** *bronze, money.* Besides 'estimer' giving ESTEEM, Old French had 'esmer' (**aestimare**) and 'aesmer' (**adaestimare**) from which came Mid. Eng. 'eimen,' 'aimen,' and finally AIM.

FEAT, FACT: both representing **factum,** pf. pple. of **facere,** *do,* the latter *a thing done,* the former, *a thing remarkably done.*

GARNER, GRANARY: **granarium** (or pl. **-ia**), *a place for grain,* **granum** (71).

MAYOR, MAJOR: comparative of **magnus;** *greater, superior* (53).

NOURISHMENT, NUTRIMENT: **nutrimentum,** *food* (90); **nutrire,** NOURISH (186).

POIGNANT, PUNGENT: **pungens, pungentis,** pres. pple. of **pungere,** *pierce, prick.* Cf. POINT from **punctum;** see PUNCH (202).

POOR, PAUPER: **Pauper,** adopted into English as a noun, was altered in Old French to 'povre' and 'poure,' becoming Eng. POOR; so the noun **paupertatem** through Old French became Eng. POVERTY.

PURSUE, PROSECUTE: Old French changed **pro-** to 'por-' or 'pur-' (AF 'pur-') and Low Lat. **sequere** (for **sequi**) to 'suir'. **Prosequi** thus became 'poursuir' and Eng. PURSUE; from **prosecutus** comes directly our PROSECUTE (133).

PURVEY, PROVIDE: **pro-videre,** *see beforehand;* **pro-** changed to AF 'pur-' and **videre** (OF 'veoir') to AF 'veier,' 'purveier' becoming PURVEY.

RAY, RADIUS: Lat. **radius,** *a rod, a spoke of a wheel,* a RAY from a center of light; OF 'raye.' Cf. RADIUM, and RADIO.

REASON, RATIO: Lat. **ratio** in meaning is one of those accommodating words which can be all things to all men; from **reri, ratus,** *think,* it may apply to *the thinking faculty,* and through OF 'raisun' becomes REASON (170); from *a reckoning* it is transformed to *a relation* in RATIO. See REASON, RATION, 43.

RESPITE, RESPECT: Lat. **respectus,** *a looking back* (**re + specere**), *regard* or *consideration.* The OF 'respit' meant *a delay of time* granted to a debtor, *i.e.,* the *regard* or *respect* shown his case.

RESTRAIN, RESTRICT: RESTRAIN (Mid. Eng. 'restreinen') represents OF 'restreindre,' Lat. **restringere,** *bind back, hold in check;* from the pf. pple. of this verb, **restrictus,** we have made RESTRICT, with somewhat similar meaning (133).

RULE, REGULATE: Lat. **regulare, regulatus,** *direct,* was made from the noun **regula,** *a straight stick;* root of **regere,** *rule.* Old French has the same noun 'riule' and 'reule,' from which by an easy step comes RULE, first the noun and then the verb.

SEVER, SEPARATE: **separare, separatus; se-,** *apart,* **parare,** *arrange* (202 COMPARE). Of this verb Old French made 'sevrer,' passed on to English as SEVER.

SIR, SENIOR: comparative of **senex,** *old, old man.* The earlier English form, like the French, was SIRE, a weakened form of the OF 'senre.'

SPICE, SPECIES: **Species,** adopted into English (52), meant *appearance* (**specere,** *look*); then *kind.* SPICE, OF 'espice,' was first used in the sense of SPECIES; then particularly SPECIES of aromatic herbs.

STRAIT, STRICT: **strictus,** pf. pple. of **stringere,** *draw tight* (cf. the pres. pple. derivative STRINGENT). STRAIT comes from the Old French spelling 'estreit,' and means *narrow.* 'Straight' is an English word on the same root.

SURE, SECURE: The preposition **se,** *without* (145), uniting with **cura** made the adjective **securus,** *without care* (202); through OF 'segur' it became 'seur' and 'sur,' Mod. Fr. 'sûr,' Eng. SURE (173b).

TRAIT, TRACT: **tractus,** *a drawing out, a stretch,* **trahere,** *draw;* so an *extent of country* (**extendere,** *stretch out*). TRAIT was earlier spelled in both French and English 'traict.' The meaning is *a drawing, stroke, touch;* then *a distinguishing feature.*

TREASON, TRADITION: Lat. **traditio** from **tradere,** *deliver, i.e.,* **trans + dare,** *give over.* So a story *handed down* is TRADITION, while the *handing over* of the state to its enemies was OF 'traison,' and became Eng. TREASON.

Compounds of **currere,** *run,* come directly from Latin, the noun **cursus,** *a running,* through French; so we have CONCUR, *run together,* RECUR, *run back,* but CONCOURSE and RECOURSE.

43. The scholarly study of Latin on the part of the French brought into their language anew words which had already been received in the altered form of the popular speech. Both French words, the earlier and the later, or the popular and the literary, received into English, gave us still another series of doublets of Latin origin:

BENISON, BENEDICTION: Lat. **benedictionem,** *well-saying,* from **bene + dicere,** *say,* was changed in Old French to 'beneison.'

CHANCE, CADENCE: CADENCE came into French from Low Lat. **cadentia,** *a falling* (**cadere,** *fall*), *falling* of the voice. The same word became OF 'chaance,' or 'cheance,' and applied to what *falls to* or *befalls* one. [1]

CONCEIT, CONCEPTION: Lat. **conceptio** from **concipere, conceptus,** literally, *take together;* to take hold is to grasp, to grasp is to get an idea. The OF 'conceipt,' then CONCEIT, refers to a fanciful idea, also to a fanciful idea about oneself.

DAINTY, DIGNITY: **Dignitat-em,** *worthiness, rank,* became OF 'deintie,' taking on the meaning of *a delicacy;* so first in Eng. 'deinte,' and 'dainte'; later DAINTY as noun, *value, delicacy;* then as adjective *elegant.* Likewise we took DIGNITY from OF 'dignite.'

DEPOT, DEPOSIT: both representing Lat. **depositum,** *placed down, stored;* DEPOT, the later form of OF 'depost.' (It was the verb DEPOSIT that came first from the French.)

ESTATE, STATE: From **statum** (nom. **status**), Old French made 'estat' (180). Derived from **stare, status,** *stand,* the Latin word meant *a standing, position, condition, public condition, government,* etc. The simpler form of the word in English, though still from the French, follows more closely the Latin (cf. **status,** 52).

FASHION, FACTION: Lat. **factionem** was spelled 'faceon' or 'fachon' in Old French, easily becoming Eng. FASHION; **factio** was *a doing, a taking sides,* a FACTION; but the French word meant also *form* or *shape, i.e.,* FASHION (cf. 176).

FEALTY, FIDELITY. The latter form comes regularly through the

---

[1] Cf. **casus,** from the same root, used of a throw of the dice, Juvenal, 1, 90.

French from Lat. **fidelitatem** (72), *faithfulness;* OF 'fealte' gave us FEALTY.

FORGE, FABRIC: FABRIC is our spelling of the Fr. 'fabrique,' Lat. **fabrica,** *a workshop,* changing in meaning from the shop to the product; Old French, however, kept the Latin meaning more nearly, with a development of spelling something like this: **fabricam, fabr(i)ca, fabrca,** 'faurca,' 'faurga,' 'forga,' FORGE.

FRAIL, FRAGILE: The later French form represents Lat. **fragilis,** *breakable* (**frangere,** *break,* 114); the older form lost the *g* (173b), and 'fraile' became Eng. FRAIL.

GENTLE, GENTILE: both English words through OF 'gentil,' from Lat. **gentilis** (100); **gens, gentis,** *clan* or *tribe;* a man of one's own tribe is considered GENTLE; he may be a GENTLEman and therefore GENTEEL, so spelled to preserve the sound of the Fr. 'gentile'; but if he belongs to another tribe, the outside people, he is a GENTILE.

HOTEL, HOSPITAL: The old form HOSTEL (cf. HOSTELRY) was the Old French spelling of the Low Lat. **hospitale. Hospitalis,** from **hospes, hospitis** (98), meant *relating to guests,* and **hospitalia** were *apartments for guests.* Later came the meaning of *apartments for sick guests.* When the French had changed the old form 'hostel' to 'hôtel,' the English borrowed also this form.

LEAL, LOYAL, LEGAL: From **lex, legis,** was made **legalis** (98), and from this the OF 'leial' (Eng. LEAL, *faithful*); from this adjective later, following the noun 'loi' (for **legem,** 167), came LOYAL. The literary French word 'legal' merely preserves the Latin form. English was interested enough in the subject to borrow all three.

MANURE, MANOEUVRE: The Low Latin noun was made from the Lat. **manu + operari,** *work with the hand.* **Manuopera** became Fr. 'manoeuvre' and meant *manipulation, handling of troops,* and so *strategic movement.* The verb MANURE in English formerly meant *cultivate* or *till* (by manual labor); then *make productive,* and so *fertilize.*

OBEISANCE, OBEDIENCE: OBEISANCE was formerly used in the sense of OBEDIENCE; then came to be an act of respect. The Lat. **obedire** or **oboedire** has the same root as **audire,** *to listen to.* Cf. Eng. "listen to" for *give heed to* or OBEY.

ORISON, ORATION: Lat. **orare, oratus,** was *to speak, argue,* or *plead a case* (from one's mouth, **os, oris**). If the pleading was with a deity, **orare** became *pray.* So **orationem** was either *speech* or *prayer.* With the latter meaning is ORISON (OF); in the former sense it became Fr. and then Eng., ORATION.

PARCEL, PARTICLE: **Particula** from **pars, partis,** was a (double) diminutive (**-cu-la,** 68), *a (very) little part.* The French form 'particule' was shortened into Eng. PARTICLE. The Fr. 'parcelle,' from Low Latin appearing in Ital. 'particella,' became Eng. PARCEL, especially in the sense of *a very small package.*

PENANCE, PENITENCE: **Paenitere,** occurring very often as impersonal **paenitet,** meant *repent.* Its pres. pple. was **paenitens,** whence **paenitentia** (75), OF and Eng. PENANCE. But Old French gave us also the learned forms PENITENT, and PENITENCE.

PITY, PIETY: Lat. **pietatem** meant *dutiful conduct toward parents or gods;* in Late Latin it came to mean *compassion,* which easily accompanied such conduct; OF 'pite' ('pitet'); later 'pieté.'

POISON, POTION: Lat. **potionem** (**potio**) was formed from the verb **potare, potus,** *drink.* The popular French form was 'poison' (170), which from meaning merely *a drink,* came to mean *a harmful or deadly drink;* a POTION is less dangerous.

RANSOM, REDEMPTION: Lat. **redemptio, redimere** (**red + emere**), **redemptus,** *buy back.* **Redemptionem** (154) became OF 'raenson,' which appeared in English as RANSOM. Both words have kept more or less literally the meaning of *a buying back.*

RAVIN, RAPINE: RAVIN is also written RAVINE and RAVEN, and is the same word as RAVINE meaning *a gorge* (made by a stream that carries things away by violence); all meanings go back to the Lat. **rapina,** *a snatching away,* **rapere,** *snatch;* in the earlier French it meant *violence* and even in English once meant *a flood, a violent stream of water.*

REASON, RATION: REASON from **rationem** (**ratio**) has been given above (42). From the meaning *reckoning,* RATION becomes *a calculated allowance,* especially for soldiers.

ROYAL, REGAL: Old French took over the Lat. **regalis,** adjective from **rex, regis,** *king* (98), as 'real'; then 'royal' (167); REGAL is the literary form. REAL in this sense is now obsolete in English. Cf. LEAL, LOYAL, LEGAL. REAL meaning *true* or *actual* is a different word, the Low Lat. **realis** from Lat. **res,** *thing, fact.*

SAMPLE, EXAMPLE: Of the Lat. **exemplum,** Old French made 'essample' and 'assample'); then revising the word after Latin, had 'example' and 'exemple.' This variety naturally had its effect in English, and we have ENSAMPLE for an earlier 'asample,' and SAMPLE for an earlier 'essample'); also the Latinized French form EXAMPLE, and along with these EXEMPLARY and EXEMPLIFY. **Exemplum** was made from **eximere, ex-emere,** *take out, select* a specimen (**ex-em-lum,** 154).

SPIRIT, SPRITE: The Lat. **spiritus** from the root of **spirare,** *breathe, blow,* meant *a breath.* Like the breath is the invisible part of man; the soul is therefore **spiritus.** Old French altered **spiritus** into 'esprit' (180), which later French has kept. By borrowing both words English has both SPIRIT and SPRITE (not to mention ESPRIT in 'ESPRIT de corps'). A mere misspelling of SPRITE accounts for our adjective SPRIGHTLY.

44. A small group of doublet forms show admission first from the older French, and then from Modern French; for example:

CHIEF, CHEF: Both occurred in Old French; 'chef' is also Modern French and a late borrowing; Lat. **caput;** CHEF, the *head* of the cooks.

CORPSE, CORPS: The latter is our borrowing from the Modern French. From the Lat. **corpus,** *a body,* the one form of the word has been restricted to a dead body, the other to a group of soldiers or officials.

FEAST, FÊTE: The OF 'feste,' from which we get FEAST, was the Lat. **festa,** pl. of **festum,** *festival* or *holiday* (see FESTAL, 205). Modern French altered it to 'fête.'

HOSTEL, HOTEL: The older French form belongs also to older English. See HOTEL, HOSPITAL, 43.

MEDLEY, MÊLÉE: The Mid. Eng. 'medlee' is the same as the fem. pple. of OF 'medler,' *mix,* made from Low Lat. **misculare,** from Lat. **miscere;** but the French word had the forms 'medlee' and 'meslee'; hence MÊLÉE, which also is a *mixture.*

45. Some words upon coming into English have assumed different forms with a corresponding difference of meaning, and are more properly called variants than doublets:

CANCER, CANKER: The Lat. **cancer, cancri,** was first *a crab;* then a spreading crawling *tumor,* eating into the flesh. As the sore may be a corroding ulcer, the word may apply to corroding in the case of other things; CANKER becomes also a verb in this sense.

COURTESY, CURTSY: The OF 'corteisie' from the adjective 'courteis' or 'courtois' meant *politeness,* such as belongs to the royal court (28).[1] The shortened form CURTSY has been restricted to one particular form of politeness.

MASTER, MISTER: For the loss of *g* as the Lat. **magistrum (magister)** became OF 'maistre,' see 173b. The form MASTER seems to be a combination of the Old French word and AS 'maegester.' **Mag-is-ter** is a double comparative of the word meaning *great* (**magnus,** compar. adv. **magis**). The MASTER is *more greater,* and in a like formation, the MINISTER is *more smaller* (54); MISTER, a pronunciation of MASTER in proclitic use with a name, written Mr. From about the end of the seventeenth century, MASTER and MISTER became separate words.

MODE, MOOD: The Fr. MODE is from Lat. **modum (modus),** *measure* or *manner;* the variant MOOD is used, especially in grammar, of a verb form to denote manner of action. The confusion of this word with the native English 'mood' meaning *disposition* may have affected somewhat the signification of both words.

PERSON, PARSON: The Lat. **persona** was *a mask.* The mask indicated the rôle, the character which the actor played, and since "all the world's a stage, and all the men and women merely players," PERSON designates an actor in the drama of life. The important and honored PERSON of the church community of former days was the PARSON, a spelling corresponding to an old pronunciation (cf. 'clerk' and 'Clark'). His place of acting more-

---

[1] Milton, *Comus,* 322 ff.: . . . courtesy,
    Which oft is sooner found in lowly sheds
    With smoky rafters than in tapestry halls
    And courts of princes, where it first was named. . : :

over was the PULPIT, Lat. **pulpitum** (or pl. **pulpita**), *a stage* for actors (201).

46. In the lists given above the following examples of triplets in meaning may already have been observed:

> blessing, BENISON, BENEDICTION
> faithfulness, FEALTY, FIDELITY
> foresee, PURVEY, PROVIDE
> friendly, AMIABLE, AMICABLE
> kingly, ROYAL, REGAL
> kingdom, REIGN, REALM
> lawful, LOYAL, LEGAL (and LEAL)
> speech, ORISON, ORATION

Also:

> HOSTEL, HOTEL, HOSPITAL
> REASON, RATION, RATIO
> STATE, ESTATE, STATUS (52)

47. Among the words of Latin origin conveyed to us through the French not a few had their development in Italian, from which language they were borrowed by the French. Certain of the changes which Latin underwent as it passed into Italian will need to be observed. We note that with the disappearance of final **m** of the accusative (158), **-am, -em, -um,** became respectively *-a, -e, -o;* **b** between vowels commonly became *v*, while **t** in like position either remained or changed to *d;* **ct, pt,** and **vt,** by assimilation, became *tt; l* after an initial consonant appears as *i;* **-ntia(m)** as *-nza;* while groups of three consonants were likely to lose the middle one.

48. Some of the words reaching us by the Italian-French route are these:

ALARM: This French word was in Italian 'all'arme,' *to arms, i.e.,* 'alle arme,' Lat. **ad illa arma.**

ALERT: Fr. 'alerte' was the Ital. 'all'erta' for 'a la erta,' Lat. **ad** illam **erectam,** *on the height,* 'erta' (for 'ercta,' **erectam,** *raised up*) being the steep place or height on which one stands to watch; hence *on the look-out.* Note the tautology of our phrase "on the alert," as some people have "the la grippe."

ALTO: Lat. **altum,** *high;* this part in music was once sung by the highest male voice, though now by the lowest female voice. (Cf. CONTRALTO, 49).

ARCADE: the French spelling of Ital. 'arcata,' fem. pple. form (cf. Lat. **arcuata),** *arched,* Lat. **arcus,** *a bow.*

BULLETIN: Lat. **bulla** was *a seal* (cf. BULL, 202). An Italian diminutive of this is 'bulletta,' *a passport* or *a lottery ticket;* a second diminutive is 'bulletino,' *a ticket.* And from this comes BULLETIN as *a public announcement.* From **bulla** as *a knob,* the French have given us their diminutive 'boulet' as BULLET, *a little ball.*

CABBAGE: Ital. 'capuccio,' from Lat. **caput,** means *a little head,* (Fr. 'caboche'). Our word therefore is from **caput** and "cabbage head" is tautological.

CARNIVAL: The Italians call the last three days before Lent 'carnovale' or 'carnevale,' the Med. Lat. **carnelevamen,** *removal of meat* (**carnem levare,** 89). This occurred also as 'carne-levale' and was shortened to 'carnevale.' The second part was then sometimes supposed to be **vale,** *farewell,* and the word was erroneously explained as *farewell meat!*

CAVALRY: The Low Lat. **caballus (-um),** *horse,* changed to 'cavallo' in Italian. The rider of the horse was 'cavaliere,' Eng. CAVALIER, *i.e., knight.* Knighthood was 'cavalleria,' and this word reached us by way of the French as CAVALRY. But the OF 'chevalrie' became Eng. CHIVALRY. CAVALRY and CHIVALRY are therefore doublets (36).

CITADEL: Ital. 'cittadella,' *a small town,* diminutive of 'cittade,' *i.e.,* 'cittate,' whence 'città,' from Lat. **civitatem (civitas).** The *little state* has thus in English become only *a fortress.*

COLONEL: The Italian word means *a little column,* diminutive of 'colonna,' Lat. **columna;** hence *the officer in command of a little column* (at the head of a regiment). Its older spelling 'coronel,' as it is also in Spanish (*r* for *l* by dissimilation, 155), accounts for the present pronunciation.

COLONNADE: French form from Ital. 'colonnata' (*columned*), *a range of columns*, Lat. **columna.**

CONCERT: the noun from the verb CONCERT (cf. a 'CONCERTed plan'). This verb (Ital. 'concertare') apparently represents Lat. **concertare,** *contend with*, which is far from indicating harmony. It is probably a mistake for 'consert,' **conserere, consertus,** *join* or *fit together*.

CORRIDOR: literally *a runner*. Ital. 'correre' is the Lat. **currere,** and '-dore' represents the Lat. **-tor-em,** the suffix of agent nouns (80). The Italian word, however, was confused with one in '-orio,' Lat. **-orium,** and came to mean *a place for running*. Cf. Lat. **cursor, cursorius** (102).

COSTUME: a doublet of CUSTOM, both being from the Lat. **consuetudinem (consuetudo).** Coming by way of the OF 'coustume,' this becomes CUSTOM, by way of Italian COSTUME, as a CUSTOMARY dress. Cf. HABIT for both *customary act* and *dress*, 88.

CUPOLA: Low Lat. **cupa** was a *cask* or *vat*, later a CUP. Ital. 'cupola' is a diminutive, like **cupula** in Latin. A CUPOLA therefore is a *little cup* (inverted).

DUEL: the Old French form of Ital. 'duello,' Med. Lat. **duellum,** *a combat between two persons* (**duo**); not the O. Lat. **duellum (bellum)** in which the connection with **duo,** if any, was simply in the conflict between two hostile parties.

FAÇADE: The Ital. 'facciata' represented in this word means *the front of a building*, lit. *faced*, from 'faccia,' which is the Lat. **faciem (facies),** FACE.

FRACAS: The Ital. 'fracassare' means *break to pieces*, *i.e.*, 'fra-' (originally Lat. **infra;** cf. Eng. 'break up, down,' etc.) + 'cassare,' which is Lat. **quassare,** *shatter* (kept in Eng. QUASH). The débris left over therefore marks the genuineness of the FRACAS.

GAMBOL: An old spelling was 'gambold' or 'gambaud,' perhaps erroneously for 'gambade,' since the Italian is 'gambata,' 'gamba,' *a leg*, and Lat. **gamba,** *a hoof;* GAMBOL is then the *movement of a leg or hoof*.

LAVENDER: The *r* does not belong to this word, the French being 'lavande,' and the Italian 'lavanda,' from Lat. **lavare,** *wash* (cf. LAVA, 49). The plant was used in washing or laid in with washed clothes on account of its fragrance. The name of the plant is also applied to the color of its flowers. See LAUNDRY, 202.

MODEL: The Lat. **modulus,** diminutive of **modus,** was *a little measure.* Similarly from 'modo' (or as if from a double diminutive **'modellus'**) the Italian made 'modello,' from which comes MODEL. The little measure thus became a pattern and a pattern should be a standard.

POMADE: Ital. 'pomata,' with participial suffix from 'pomo,' *apple,* Lat. **pomum,** as if *appled* (cf. 107). This unguent for the hair seems to have been made originally from apple juice.

SALAD: Lat. **sal,** *salt,* Ital. 'sale'; the Italian verb is 'salare.' Of its pf. pple. 'salato,' the fem. 'salata' as a noun became Fr. 'salade' and thence Eng. SALAD. SALAD then is literally *salted.*

SERENADE: The Lat. **serenus,** *bright, calm,* SERENE (originally *hot, dry*), appears in the Ital. 'serenare,' *make clear.* The fem. pple. 'serenata' became Fr., then Eng. SERENADE, the gentle music suitable to a *clear, calm* evening. Since Ital. 'serenata' is *an evening song,* there may have been some confusion with **serus,** *late,* **sera** (*i.e.,* **sera hora**), *a late hour, evening.*

TERRACE: The French form of the Ital. 'terracia,' from **terra,** *earth,* the suffix '-acia' being the Lat. **-acea** (110).

49. But the English were by no means entirely dependent upon their French neighbors for their supply of Italian words. They became widely enough acquainted with the countries of the continent and their literature to do some borrowing directly.

Examples are the following:

ATTITUDE: the same word as APTITUDE, Ital. 'attitudine,' representing Lat. **aptitudinem,** from **aptus** (78), *suited,* Eng. APT.

BELLADONNA: Lat. **bella domina,** *beautiful lady,* is Ital. 'bella donna.' The name was applied to the deadly nightshade because the plant was used by the ladies to dilate the pupils of their eyes and make them more beautiful.

CAPER: a shortening of an old form CAPREOLL, made from Ital. 'capriolare,' *leap about like a goat,* 'capriolo' being a diminutive of 'caprio' ('capro'), Lat. **caprum** (**capreolum**), *goat.* The English has thus happened to return to the Latin nominative **caper.** CAPRICE, a French form (Ital. 'capriccio'), apparently gets its meaning from the sudden and uncertain movements of the goat.

CARICATURE: Ital. 'caricatura,' from 'caricare,' *load,* Low Lat. **carricare,** *load a wagon,* Lat. **carrus,** CAR, *wagon,* a word originally borrowed from the Gauls. The CARICATURE, accordingly, represents an excess (a *carload*) of drawing.

CONTRALTO: 'contra alto,' *i.e.,* Lat. **contra,** *against,* **altum,** *high.* The voice pitched over against the high or tenor voice is CONTRALTO.

DILETTANTE (pl.-I): participle of 'dilettare,' *delight,* (reflexive) *take pleasure in,* Lat. **delectare;** one who finds pleasure in the fine arts but not a professional. Cf. AMATEUR, 194.

DITTO: This is the Italian spelling of the Lat. **dictum,** pf. pple. of **dicere,** *say; the thing that has been said* (cf. **dictum,** 52). But DITTY is OF 'dite' (dité), *a composition,* or *poem,* from **dictatum** (130).

DUET: Ital. 'duetto,' made with a diminutive suffix from 'due,' *i.e.,* the Lat. **duo,** *two.*

EXTRAVAGANZA: Ital. 'estravaganza' or 'stravaganza.' The English reverts to the Latin spelling of the first part; like EXTRAVAGANCE, made from **extra,** *beyond,* with **vagans, vagantis,** pres. pple. of **vagari** (as if a noun in **-ntia,** 75), *wander.* This form of musical or dramatic composition wanders far beyond the normal.

FALSETTO: diminutive of 'falso,' Lat. **falsum,** FALSE; applied to a voice FALSE in that it goes above its natural range.

FINALE: This word, applied to the conclusion of a symphony or drama, is Lat. **finalem, finis,** *end* (98).

GENERALISSIMO: GENERAL, Lat. **generalis,** as an adjective, means pertaining to the **genus,** or *race* (98). The Ital. '-issimo' is Lat. **-issimum,** superlative ending. The GENERAL, then, has command of the troops of the tribe at large; the GENERALISSIMO is a "*superlative general.*"

GRANITE: Ital. 'granito,' pf. pple. form, *having a granular surface,* 'grano,' *grain* of corn, also of sand, being the Lat. **granum.**

GUSTO: the Italian form of the Lat. **gustum (gustus),** *a tasting, taste;* hence *a relish.* GUST was also in use in early English. Cf. DISGUST, "*bad taste.*"

INCOGNITO: Lat. **incognitum, in-,** *not,* + **cognitum,** pf. pple. of **cognoscere,** *know; un-known.*

INFERNO: Lat. **infernum,** belonging to the lower regions (**inferna;** cf. **inferior,** 54); *hell.*

INFLUENZA: the same word as INFLUENCE, Low Lat. **influentia,** *a flowing in,* from **in** + **fluere,** *flow* (75). There is a reference (as also formerly in the word INFLUENCE) to the effect once supposed to be produced on men by the heavenly bodies, this epidemic catarrhal affection being formerly attributed to that cause.

INFURIATE: From Ital. 'infuriare' the pf. pple. 'infuriato' came into English as INFURIATE, adjective; then verb. The Italian verb was made from Lat. **in furia,** *in a* FURY.

INTAGLIO: From the Lat. **talea,** *a stick* or *twig, a cutting,* Low Latin made the verb **taleare,** *cut* (cf. TAILOR, 202); so Ital. 'in-tagliare' is *to cut in, carve,* or *engrave,* and INTAGLIO is a gem *cut in* or hollowed out.

ISOLATE: Ital. 'isolato,' Lat. **insulatum,** *made into an island.* ISOLATE thus is the same in origin as INSULATE.

LAVA: This Italian word, first applied to a torrent of rain overflowing the streets, is literally *the flow, the wash,* from the Lat. **lavare,** *wash,* Eng. LAVE. In Naples it denoted the stream (of molten matter) issuing from Vesuvius.

LEVANT: The Ital. 'levante' shows the pres. pple. stem of the Lat. **levare,** *raise,* (**se levare,** *rise*), and, like ORIENT from **oriri,** *rise,* designates the rising place of the sun, and so the east shores of the Mediterranean. Cf. PONENT, from **ponere,** *place, put down;* as LEVANT is east, PONENT is west, like OCCIDENT from **occidere,** *fall, set.* Milton, *Paradise Lost,* 10, 704, has "The Levant and Ponent winds."

MADONNA: 'madonna,' Italian for **mea domina,** *my lady,* the same as MADAME and MADAM.

MALARIA: This is 'mal' aria,' *i.e.,* 'mala aria,' *bad air;* 'aria,' *atmosphere,* also *air* of a song, from Lat. **aer** (Grk.).

MINIATURE: The Latin word **minium,** meaning *red lead,* is said to have been borrowed along with the paint from Spain. From this the Italians made the verb 'miniare,' *paint in miniature,* since this kind of painting was done in red lead. The pf. pple. of 'miniare' is 'miniato,' and from this 'miniatura' became Eng. MINIATURE. There is then no connection with MINIMIZE or DIMINISH.

MOTTO: the Italian form of Low Lat. **muttum** meaning *a grunt* (**mutire**, *mutter*). But MOTTO became *a word, a saying*, and in this sense was received into English.

OPERA: the Latin for *service* or *work* passed on to us through the Italian with the meaning of *a musical drama*.

ORATORIO: Beginning with the Lat. **os, oris,** *mouth*, we have **orare,** *to one who speaks* (102); **oratorium,** an ORATORY, *place for prayer* (71); Ital., then Eng. ORATORIO, *a sacred musical composition.* Cf. (**ars**) **oratoria,** *art of speaking,* ORATORY.

PIANO: The Latin adjective **planum (planus),** PLAIN (PLANE), *level,* became in Ital. 'piano,' with also the meaning *gentle, soft.* To this was added also 'forte,' Lat. **fortem (fortis),** *strong, loud,* and the name PIANOFORTE was applied to the instrument invented in 1717 which produced sounds either soft or loud.

PORTICO: PORTICO is Italian as PORCH ('porche') is French of the Lat. **porticum (porticus),** *a colonnade* or *piazza.* Cf. **porta,** *gate.*

PRIMA DONNA: Lat. **prima domina,** *first lady.*

PROFILE: literally, *foreline,* 'pro-' as in Latin, *before,* and 'filo' the Lat. **filum,** *a thread.* **Filum** from *thread* came to mean *line.* *Foreline* is *outline;* hence *side view.*

QUARTET: 'Quartetto' in Italian is diminutive of 'quarto,' Lat. **quartum (quartus),** *fourth* (cf. QUART, QUARTER, etc.).

QUOTA: The Lat. adjective **quotus,** *how much, how many*, was made from the indeclinable **quot,** *how many;* **quota (pars),** *how great (a part)*, came into Italian, and thence into English as QUOTA, *a share.* From the same word we have QUOTE (through the French), since Low Lat. **quotare** was *to tell how many, tell the number* by chapters and verses, and QUOTE from giving a reference became *to repeat* the words.

SCAMPER: The Ital. 'scampare,' *escape,* or *get out of danger,* was made from Lat. **ex + campus,** *i.e., get out of the field* of battle. The earlier English form SCAMP survives as a noun, *a fugitive,* and therefore *a vagabond* or *rascal,* while the verb refers now to the agility rather than to the cowardice of the SCAMP. Cf.

DECAMP, Fr. 'decamper' (Lat. **dis-**), *get away from the field.*

SOLO: Italian for Lat. **solum,** *alone,* SOLE.

SOPRANO: The Ital. 'soprano' is the Low Lat. **superanus, super,** *above,* suffix **-anus,** and is therefore of the same origin as SOVEREIGN (28).

STANZA: From **stare,** *stand,* pres. pple. **stans, stantis,** came Low Lat. **stantia** (75), *a stopping-place, a room,* Ital. 'stanza.' STANZA thus indicates a place to stand or stop.

STILETTO: diminutive of 'stilo,' *a knife* (also, as in English, STYLE), Lat. **stilum (stilus),** a STYLUS, erroneous spelling of **stilus** (58).

STUDIO: the Italian spelling of Lat. **studium,** *application, zeal,* STUDY; from Late Latin the word denotes *a place of study.* Cf. STUDENT, 123.

TARANTULA: The name ('tarantola') was made in the Middle Ages from 'Taranto,' the Italian form of **Tarentum,** the city in southern Italy, where this kind of spider was found.

TERRA COTTA: the Lat. **terra cocta,** *cooked earth* **(coquere).**

TRIO: The Italian word was made on the analogy of 'duo' = DUET; Lat. **tres, tria,** *three.*

UMBRELLA: an Italian diminutive of 'ombra' (spelled also 'ombrella' and 'ombrello'), Lat. **umbra,** *shade.*

VIRTUOSO: the Italian form of **virtuosum** (94) from **virtus,** *manliness* **(vir,** *a man*). **Virtus,** then, was *courage* in war; it was *excellence* in character or skill. Excellence in artistic skill makes the VIRTUOSO; Ital. pl. 'virtuosi.'

VISTA: the fem. pple. of Ital. 'vedere,' Lat. **videre, visus,** and so meaning *sight;* then *view,* or *prospect.*

VOLCANO: the Italian form of Lat. **volcanum** or **vulcanum (-us),** VULCAN, *the god of fire.* From designating Aetna, the chief fire mountain, also the one where in ancient mythology Vulcan had his forge, VOLCANO became the name of any mountain from which fire issues.

50. Spanish also has furnished a considerable number of our Latin derivatives, either directly or through the French. Here, as in Italian (47), we may note the loss of final **-m** (cf. 160), with **-u(m)** becoming *-o.* Between vowels, **c** and **t** became respectively *g* and *d* unless *e* or *i* followed. In some

places *t* represents Lat. **ct**; and in some words *-nza* occurs
for **-ntia(m)**. The fem. pf. pple. in *-ada* (Lat. **-ata-m**),
through French, appears in English in *-ade*, widely extended
to non-Latin words as lemon*ade*, orange*ade*, even Welch*ade*.
The following are examples of Latin words coming to us
through the Spanish:

ALLIGATOR: The Lat. **ille**, *that*, became the article 'el' in Spanish,
and **lacertum** (nom. **lacertus**), *a lizard*, became 'lagarto.' ALLI-
GATOR is but a corruption of 'el lagarto,' *the lizard*. LIZARD also
is a respelling of Fr. 'lezard' from **lacertus**.

AMBUSCADE: through the Fr. 'embuscade' from Sp. 'emboscada,'
'emboscar,' Low Lat. **imboscare, -atus**; **in** + **boscus**, *a wood*,
BUSH (through Germanic). AMBUSCADE then is a *hiding in the
wood* or *in the bushes;* so also AMBUSH.

ARMADA: the feminine of 'armado,' the pf. pple. of 'armar,' Lat.
armare, armata; hence *armed, equipped* (fleet).

ARMADILLO: a diminutive of the pple. 'armado' (see ARMADA);
it thus means the *little armored animal*.

BONANZA: *fair weather at sea, prosperity*, as if for **'bonantia,'** *good-
ness* (**bonus**).

CARGO: The Mediæval Latin word was **carricum**, *a load*, made
from **carrus** which has been noted above as a Celtic word (CARI-
CATURE, 49).

CLOVE: taken from the Sp. 'clavo,' *a nail* or *a clove*, Lat. **clavum**
(**clavus**), *a nail*, from the resemblance of shape. It would doubtless have come to us as 'clave' but for the influence of a native
English word 'clove' (*bulb*) which caused the change of *a* to *o*.

COMRADE: The Sp. 'camarada,' *company* or *partner*, was derived
from 'camara,' *a room*, Lat. **camera** (52), Eng. CHAMBER. The
COMRADE therefore occupies a room with one, as a COMPANION
eats bread with one (COMPANIONship, 210).

CORK: This is our spelling of the Sp. 'corcho,' probably from Lat.
corticem (**cortex**), *bark*.

DESPERADO: The Old Spanish form representing Lat. **desperatum**,
pf. pple. of **de-sperare**, *be out of hope* (**spes**), *be desperate* (cf.
DESPAIR 23, DESPERATION, 85).

DOMINO: As meaning *a hood, a masquerade dress*, or *a garment* of the canons of a cathedral, the DOMINO was named from the church official by whom it was worn (cf. DOMINIE, 58), Lat. **dominum**. The game of DOMINOES was probably so called from the color of the pieces, black like the garments of this name.

FLOTILLA: a diminutive of the Sp. 'flota,' *fleet*, a fem. form going back to Lat. **fluctus**, *a wave*. The meaning of the Spanish word, Skeat remarks, must have been influenced by the Dutch 'vloot,' a *fleet*, to which are related Eng. 'fleet' and 'float.'

MATADOR: Lat. **mactare**, *sacrifice* or *kill*, became Sp. 'matar.' MATADOR, corresponding to Lat. **mactator,** means primarily *a slayer*.

MOSQUITO: diminutive of Sp. 'mosca,' *fly*, Lat. **musca;** *a little fly*.

NEGRO: Spanish for Lat. **nigrum (niger),** *black*.

PARADE: From Lat. **parare**, *prepare*, came Sp. 'parar' in the sense of *stop* or *halt*. So 'parada' was first *a halting*, and then *a parade*. Taken over by the French as 'parade' it was *a halting* on horseback for stately display and added something of the meaning of *adorn* from the Fr. 'parer' of the same origin.

PECCADILLO: 'pecadillo,' diminutive of Sp. 'pecado,' *sin*. The Latin is **peccatum**, neut. pple. of **peccare**, *sin*. The English returns to the Latin spelling with two *c's*.

RENEGADE: Sp. 'renegado,' pf. pple. of 'renegar,' from Lat. **re + negare, negatus,** *deny again*. Specifically, *one who has denied* the faith. Earlier in English the Latin word had been borrowed and corrupted into 'runagate,' lit. *run-a-way*. Cf. also RENEGE, *refuse* to follow suit in cards, and its colloquial form RENIG.

SASSAFRAS: the French spelling of the Sp. 'sasafras,' seemingly derived from Lat. **saxifraga,** which (through French) furnishes the name for another plant SAXIFRAGE. **Saxifraga (herba)** means *stone-breaking* plant, **saxum frangere** (root **frag**), and according to Pliny [1] this plant was so called from its supposed virtue of breaking up stone in the bladder. Stone in the bladder however was **calculus** (52), and more probably the name refers to the fact that the plant often grew in clefts of rocks.

SOMERSAULT: The older form was SOBERSAULT, a modification of the Fr. 'soubresaut' (179; cf. OF 'sombresaut'); these represent the Sp. 'sobresalto,' Lat. **supra-saltum (saltus),** *over-leap*. What

[1] *Natural History*, 22, 30, 3.

mispronunciation can do to disguise a word is further illustrated in our colloquial SUMMERSET.

TORNADO: a word apparently coined in Spanish form from 'tornar,' *turn, return*, Lat. **tornare**, TURN in a lathe. Cf. our 'twister.' There seems to have been a confusion of this verb with 'tronar,' *thunder*, 'tronada,' *thunderstorm*.

51. We have only a few Latin words coming to us by way of the Portuguese.[1] Some common ones are these:

ALBINO: literally *whitish*, from 'albo' (cf. 104), Lat. **album (-us)**, *white*.

FETICH, FETISH: The French furnished us the word, having made their 'fetiche' from the Port. 'feitico,' *artificial*, and as a noun *sorcery*, Lat. **facticium**, *made by art, not naturally produced* (**facere**, *make*); hence the same originally as FACTITIOUS (176).

JUNK: 'Junco' is the Portuguese word from Lat. **juncum (juncus)**, *a rush*, and was applied to pieces of rope made of rushes.

MARMALADE: The Portuguese word was 'marmelada' ('-ada,' Lat. **-ata**) from 'marmelo,' *a quince*. 'Marmelo' was formed, with dissimilation of consonants (155), from Lat. **melimelum**, a borrowed Greek word meaning *honey apple* (μελίμηλον), originally a sweet apple produced by grafting the apple on a quince tree. "Orange marmalade" is something of a contradiction.

MOLASSES: an English spelling of Port. 'melaço,' from Late Lat. **mellaceum**, *must, i.e., honeylike*, **mel**, *honey*, with the suffix **-aceus** (110).

PARASOL: This is the Portuguese compound from 'parar,' *ward off* (lit. *prepare for, prepare against*), and 'sol,' *sun*, Lat. **parare** and **solem**. The word comes through the French and might equally well have been the Ital. 'parasole.'

[1] Changes from the Latin forms, it will be observed, are much the same as those in Spanish (50).

PART II

THE FORMS AND MEANINGS OF
LATIN WORDS IN ENGLISH

CHAPTER I

LATIN WORDS MADE ENGLISH

52. Many words have been fully adopted into English in exactly or practically the same form as they had in Latin, and we find ourselves speaking not only the modified Latin discussed in the preceding chapters, but also the very forms of scores and scores of words which Cicero and Vergil used. Even those unfriendly to classical study daily employ the language which they affect to dislike. The words of the following lists, incomplete as they are, one could ill afford to lose from his vocabulary. First we may observe certain nouns transferred to English:

abdomen: a word of uncertain origin; the Latin meaning unchanged in English.

aborigines: a plural made from the phrase **ab origine** (143), *from the beginning,* applied first to the prehistoric people of Italy.

actor [1]: *a doer, a performer,* agent noun (80) of **agere,** *do.*

acumen: action noun from **acuere,** *sharpen* (89); cf. **acer,** *sharp.*

administrator [1] (fem. **-trix**): agent noun (80), of **administrare,** *to be servant to* (**minister**), *assist, manage.*

afflatus: afflare (**ad-flare**), *blow upon;* hence *a blowing* or *breathing upon* (one), *inspiration.*

agitator [1]: **agitare,** *put in motion, drive;* **agitator,** the agent noun (80), is *one who sets things moving.*

---

[1] Many nouns with suffixes **-tor** (agent, 80) and **-or** (action, 81) appear in English in exactly the form of their Latin nom. sing. Not all of these, however, are "Latin words made English." A large number of them have undergone changes in coming through French, or through Low Latin and Old French, then in English have been restored to their Latin nom. spelling. ORATOR came to us from **oratorem,** through the OF 'orateur,' the AF 'oratour,' eventually Latinized again for us into ORATOR; it is therefore not an adopted Latin word in the same

album: neuter of **albus,** *white,* a *"white book";* in political life at Rome, a *white tablet* for edicts or registrations.

albumen: literally *whiteness,* **albus,** *white;* the noun occurs but once in classical Latin, in **albumen ovi,** *white of an egg.*

alumna (pl. **-ae**): *foster-daughter,* fem. of **alumnus,** q.v.

alumnus (pl. **-i**): *nursling, foster-son,* from **alere,** *nourish;* hence the *son* of an institution, which is the *fostering mother,* **alma mater** (59); **-mnus** (cf. Grk. '-menos') a participle suffix.

amanuensis: a word used first by Suetonius,[1] and made from the phrase **servus a manu,** *a servant "from the hand,"* applied to a scribe writing from dictation; with the omission of **servus, a-manu** added the adj. suffix, **-ensis** (109), and **a-manu-ensis** became *a clerk* or *secretary.*

animal: *a breathing thing,* from **anima,** *breath* (cf. ANIMATE, **animus,** etc.; also **animalculum,** 68).

animus: *soul, courage, feeling.* The corresponding Greek word means *wind.* Cf. **anima,** *breath,* and **spiritus,** *a blowing,* SPIRIT (43).

antenna (pl. **-ae**): *sail-yard,* possibly connected with the root of **tendere,** *stretch.* The "yards" of an insect are his feelers; the resemblance between the sail-yard and an aërial wire is also evident.

antrum (pl. **-a**): a Latinized form of a Greek word (ἄντρον) meaning *a cave;* hence *a cavity* (cf. **sinus** below).

apex: *top, summit.*

apparatus: literally, *preparation,* **ad,** *to, for,* and **parare,** *make ready;* then *equipment* or *instrument.*

appendix: **ad,** *to,* and **pendere,** *hang;* something that *hangs upon* or is *joined to* either a book or the intestines.

aquarium: **aqua,** *water* (71); *a place for water.*

arbiter: *one who goes to* something in order to observe it; hence an

---

sense as is **sponsor,** taken over bodily and directly from the Latin. For convenience and accuracy, therefore, agent and action nouns received from the French (either popular or literary) are reserved for examples under 80, 81, while only those of direct adoption are included in the present list. Even with this general division we cannot always be certain to which group a word belongs (38).

[1] *Life of Nero,* 44; *Life of Titus,* 3.

umpire or *judge;* **ar-,** an Old Latin form for **ad,** and **-biter** from an old verb **betere,** *go.*

arbor: This word for *tree* we use in the phrase 'Arbor Day'; an ARBOR for vines is Mid. Eng. 'erber,' OF 'herbier,' Lat. **herbarium** (see below).

arcana: *things shut up,* neut. pl. of **arcanus,** from **arcere,** *enclose;* hence *secrets* or *mysteries.*

area: *a vacant space of level ground, a threshing-floor;* so any *plane surface.*

arena: *sand; a sand-covered place* for athletic contests, as the space in the amphitheatre for gladiatorial combats.

assessor: *one who sits by,* agent noun (80) of **assidere (ad-sedere),** *sit beside, a judge's assistant;* later he has the duty of fixing taxes.

auditorium: from **auditor** (80), *hearer,* was made the adjective **auditorius,** *relating to a hearer,* or *to hearing* (102); so the neuter, *a place for hearing* (71).

augur: The Roman **augur** practiced divination by observing the birds. This word accordingly has been explained as derived from **avis,** *bird,* with **gerere,** *do, manage, have to do with.* We are told that the early Romans said **auger**[1]; if so, the *e* of the second syllable was evidently assimilated to the *u* of the first. The origin of the word, however, is uncertain. Cf. AUSPICES, INAUGURATE, 202.

aura: *air, breeze, breath of air;* now a supposed psychic influence emanating from the human body.

aurora: *the dawn,* personified also as the goddess of the morning. **Aurora borealis,** *the northern aurora, i.e., the northern lights;* **borealis** from **Boreas** (Grk.), *the north wind.*

axis (pl. **axes**): *axle.*

bacillus: Lat. **bacillus** or **bacillum,** a diminutive meaning *a little staff;* so called from its shape. Possibly **imbecillus,** or **imbacillus,** *weak,* was made from this, meaning literally *without a staff;* so *unsupported,* Eng. IMBECILE.

basis: While coming to us from Latin and retaining its Latin

---

[1] The Latin grammarian Priscian (Lat. Gram. II, 27, 17 Keil): **Antiqui auger et augeratus pro augur et auguratus dicebant:** *The ancients used to say auger and augeratus for augur and auguratus.*

plural, **basēs,** this is really the Greek word for *pedestal* and the same as our borrowed French form BASE.

boa: a word of doubtful origin. We often add **constrictor,** a coined agent noun of **constringere,** *bind together, squeeze.*

cadaver: the *fallen body* of a man; hence *a corpse;* **cadere,** *fall,* also *fall dead, die.*

caesura: *a cutting* (of a verse of poetry), from **caedere,** *cut* (87).

calculus: *a pebble,* diminutive of **calx, calcis,** *a stone,* from which we get also CHALK; the pebble was used in counting (see 68).

camera: *a box* or *room* (cf. CHAMBER, 174). As a name for the common photographic apparatus the word is an abbreviation for **camera obscura,** *dark room.* (Grk. καμάρα.)

campus: *a field,* now the *field* for school buildings; in the form CAMP, coming to us through the French, it was applied especially to the field occupied by an army, but now also to the field of a very peaceful sojourn out-of-doors.

cancer: *a crab, a crablike tumor* (45). The Tropic of Cancer refers to the sign of the Crab in the zodiac (217).

candelabrum: Lat. **candela,** from **candere,** *glow,* gives the Eng. CANDLE; **candelabrum** (92) was *a candlestick.*

captor: *a taker,* agent noun of **capere,** *take* (80).

censor: The verb **censere** meant *estimate* or *assess.* Censor (80) was one who had charge of valuation of citizens' property. Later he supervised their moral conduct, and in this sense we have adopted the word.

census: censere, *estimate* (88); *a reckoning, a rating* and *a registering* of Roman citizens and their property.

cerebrum: *brain;* **cerebellum** is a diminutive of this, *a little brain* (69).

circus: *a circle, a ring; a circular theatre, e.g.,* the **Circus Maximus,** said to have been built by Tarquinius Priscus; so *a circular place* for exhibitions, and the modern **circus.**

cirrus: *a curled lock of hair.* The fleecy cloud of this name presents a surface resembling ringlets.

clangor: action noun (81) of **clangere,** CLANG.

coadjutor: *a helper,* agent noun (80) of **coadjuvare,** *help.*

codex: the *trunk* of a tree; then *wooden planks* or *tablets* fastened together and smeared with wax to serve as a book; used now of a book or manuscript, or of a digest of laws. Through the French it becomes CODE.

cognomen: Nomen, *name*, in compounds was confused with the root gno-, *know*, and thus arose **co-gnomen, a-gnomen, i-gno-minia; noscere ... cognoscere** was felt to require **nomen ... cognomen.** A comparison of cognates of Greek and other languages does not justify a gno- for **nomen.** Co-, *with;* a name along with another name is a **cognomen.**

compendium: from **com-pendere** (82), *weigh together, a weighing together* became *a short cut, a saving,* and *an abridgment.*

competitor: agent noun from **com-petere** (80), *seek along with* some one.

consensus: action noun from **con-sentire** (88), *feel together; feeling together* is *agreement.*

consul: one of the two highest magistrates of the Roman state; evidently from **consulere,** *consult,* or of like origin with it. Cf. COUNSEL (28, COUNCIL). The **consul** must have been a COUNSELOR.[1]

copula: *a tie,* or *band.* The noun was made with diminutive suffix (**co-ap-ula**) from **co-apere,** *fasten together.*

cornea: fem. of **corneus,** *horny;* **cornu,** *horn* (222); the *horny* coat of the eyeball.

cornucopia: strictly **cornu copiae,** *horn of plenty.* According to an old legend it was the horn of Amalthea, the goat which furnished milk for the infant Zeus (Jupiter). From this horn, afterward placed among the stars, flowed ambrosia and nectar.

corolla: *a little crown,* diminutive of **corona** (**coron-la,** 69); the *little crown* of a flower.

corona: a CROWN (Grk. 'corōnē,' κορώνη); *e.g.,* the CROWN surrounding the sun in a total eclipse.

creator: *a maker,* agent noun of **creare** (80), *make, create.*

creditor: agent noun of **credere** (80), *believe, trust* (see 58, CREED).

---

[1] Varro, *De Lingua Latina* 5, 80: **Nominatus qui consuleret populum et senatum,** *So named because he consulted the people and the senate.* Various etymologies have been offered for **consul, consulere, consilium:** from **sal-,** *go, leap,* hence *come with* one into conference; from **sed-, sod-,** with *l* for *d* (cf. **dacruma, lacrima**), hence *sit with;* or from **cons-** as ablaut form of **cens-** in **censere,** *estimate, judge.*

crux: a CROSS, as an instrument of torture. We use it of a difficult point of cardinal importance. Cf. CRUCIAL.

curator: *caretaker*, agent noun of **curare**, *care for* (80).

curriculum: *a race course* (**currere**, *run*); a program of studies became an educational race course. Of like meaning is CAREER; from **carrus** (49, CARICATURE). Late Latin had **carraria** (**via**), the *wagon road;* hence Fr. 'carrière,' *race course*, Eng. CAREER.

data: *things given*, or *granted to be true;* **datum** is the pf. pple. of **dare**, *give*. It was used by the Romans in stating the time and place of writing; hence DATE. Cf. our phrase in proclamations and official documents, "*Given* under my hand," etc.

decemvir: a singular of **decemviri**, *the ten-men board*, especially the board appointed in 410 B.C. to revise and codify the Roman laws. For the form cf. TRIUMVIRATE, 70.

delirium: **Lira** was *a ridge* between two furrows; then *a furrow*. **Delirare** was *to go out of the furrow* (**de lira**, 143); hence *to be deranged* ("*get off the track*"), and from this was made the noun. To describe the **delirium** resulting from the use of alcohol, we add **tremens**, *trembling* (**tremere**, *tremble*), **delirium tremens.**

dementia: *mindlessness;* **de-**, *away*, **mens, mentis**, *mind; being out of one's mind*.

demonstrator: *one who shows*, agent noun of **demonstrare** (80), *show*.

detritus: a *wearing away;* action noun of **deterere**, *wear away* (88). We apply it to loosened fragments of rock.

dictator: *one who makes a declaration* or *prescribes;* agent noun of **dictare** (80), frequentative of **dicere**, *say; he who "has the say."*

dictum: *a thing said*, pf. pple. of **dicere**, *say;* especially *a thing said* with real or fancied authority behind it.

Dives: *rich*. From its use in the Vulgate version of the parable of the Rich Man and Lazarus, it has come to be applied to that character as a proper name.

divisor: *a divider*, agent noun (80) of **dividere**, *divide*.

doctor: *a teacher*, agent noun of **docere**, *teach* (80); most frequently for **medicinae doctor**, *teacher of medicine*.

educator: *a bringer up* (of children), *a tutor;* agent noun of **educare**, *rear*, EDUCATE (80).

ego: *I*, the conscious individual. Cf. EGOTISM, EGOTIST with

Greek suffixes and an inserted *t* (probably from some *t*-stem with the same suffix, *e.g.*, NEPOTISM).

equilibrium: *i.e.*, aequilibrium, *equal balancing*, from the adjective **aequilibris, aequus**, *equal*, and **libra**, *a pair of scales*.

estimator: for **aestimator**, agent noun of **aestimare** (80), *one who sets a value, an appraiser;* cf. ESTEEM, 42.

excursus: *a running out, a digression*, especially where an author runs beyond the limit and appends a further exposition of some topic treated in his work.

exordium: the *laying of the warp* for weaving, from **exordiri**, *begin to weave*. **Exordiri** was generalized as *begin;* so **exordium** became any *beginning, an introduction* to a discourse.

factor: *a doer* or *maker*, agent noun of **facere**, *do* (80).

farrago: *a mixed cattle feed* (**far, farr-is**, *spelt, coarse grain*);* hence *a medley*. From both nouns and verbs derivative nouns were sometimes made in -āg-o(n) and -īg-o(n). Cf. **lumbago, virago,** and **vertigo,** below, also **imago,** IMAGE, 31.

finis: *boundary, limit, end.*

focus: *a fireplace, a center of fire, a meeting place, e.g.,* of light rays.

forceps: *a pair of tongs;* **formus,** *warm* (cf. **fornax,** FURNACE), and **cap** from **capere**. *"Hot-takers"* were tongs; then pincers in general.

formula: *a little form*, diminutive of **forma** (68).

forum: the Roman *market place*, perhaps originally merely *an outdoor space* (cf. **foris,** *a door,* **foras** and **foris,** *out of doors*).

frustum: *a piece*. We have limited the word mainly to *a piece* of a geometrical solid, of a cone, a pyramid, etc.

fulcrum: *a support*, particularly, in Latin, *a bedpost*, from **fulcire,** *prop;* hence *a point of support.*

fungus: *a spongy plant, a mushroom;* for 'sfungus,' (Grk. σφόγ-γος). Cf. **spongia** and the English derivative SPONGE.

generator: *producer*, agent noun (80) of **generare,** *produce*. Cf. **gignere** (root gen), *beget*.

genius: the personification of vital or productive strength; then *a guardian spirit*. As a tutelary spirit of a person or place, it has the plural **genii**; as applied to persons of innate ability, GENIUSes. The root is that of **gignere** (gen), *beget*. See **genius loci,** 59.

genus: *race, breed, kind,* like **genius** made from root **gen, gignere;** pl. **genera.**

gladiator: *swordsman,* from **gladius,** *sword,* formed like agent nouns of first conjugation verbs; then *one who fought* in the public combats (80, end).

gladiolus (pl. -i): *a little sword,* diminutive of **gladius** (68). Applied as early as Pliny to the sword lily.

herbarium: *a collection of plants;* from **herba,** HERB, the adjective was **herbarius,** as a noun, *botanist;* the neuter, **herbarium** (71).

hiatus: *an opening,* action noun from **hiare,** *open* the mouth (88). **Hiatus** in poetry, then, is a succession of vowels keeping the mouth open.

honorarium: adj. from **honor** (101), *i.e.,* **honorarium donum,** once *a gift* made on one's appointment *to a post of honor;* used now of a *fee for services* rendered.

horror: *a bristling* of hair, action noun of **horrere,** *bristle, stand on end* (81). There may have been also in Latin a reference to the dreadful appearance of a bristling beast.

humus: *ground* or *soil.* From this is **humilis,** HUMBLE, *i.e., down on the ground.* Cf. also **homo** and **humanus.**

ibex: the name in Latin, as adopted into English, of a kind of *goat,* or *chamois.*

ignis fatuus: *foolish fire.* **Fatuus,** perhaps lit. *smitten;* then *silly.*

impetus: *a flying* or *falling upon, an impulse* (cf. **impetere, in +** **petere,** *fly* or *rush upon, attack*).

incubus (Late): *what lies upon one;* hence *oppressive weight, nightmare.* The corresponding verb is **incubare** (incubatus rare), *lie on,* from which we have INCUBATE; then INCUBATOR.

index: *a pointer* or *indicator,* from **dic-,** *show,* as in **indicare,** *point out,* **dicere,** *say.* Pl. INDEXES; Lat. pl., especially in mathematics, **indices.**

inertia: *inactivity,* abstract noun (74) from **iners, inertis,** INERT, *i.e.,* **in + ars, artis,** *not having skill;* therefore *indolent.*

insignia (pl.), distinctive *marks,* pl. of **insigne,** originally neut. of the adjective **insignis,** *marked, having a mark* (**signum**) *upon* (**in-**) *one.*

insomnia: *sleeplessness,* from **insomnis,** *sleepless,* **in-,** *not,* and **somnus,** *sleep.*

intercessor: *a go-between,* agent noun of **inter-cedere, -cessus,** *go between, interpose,* Eng. INTERCEDE.

interregnum: *between reigns,* the *interval* between the death of a king and the choosing of his successor; the acting ruler for the time being **interrex.**

janitor: *doorkeeper.* **Janus** with his two faces looking in and out was god of the door, and **janua** the *door* itself; **janitor** is made with the agent suffix exactly as we have made 'porter.' Cf. JANUARY (216).

lacuna: *opening, hole* (cf. **lacus,** LAKE). We use **lacuna** particularly of *a gap in a line* of a manuscript, where words have been omitted or erased.

languor: *faintness,* noun of condition (81) from **languere,** *be faint.*

larva: *a ghost, a mask;* related to **lares,** tutelary divinities of the household. This stage in an insect's development is suggestive of the mask.

lemur: The pl. **lemures** was the Latin name of ghosts of the dead. This kinsman of the monkey is a "ghost" only from his going about at night.

lens: *a lentil* (LENTIL, Fr. 'lentille,' being the Lat. **lenticula,** diminutive of **lens**). Lens has been applied first to a double convex piece of glass because of its having the shape of the bean-like lentil seed; then to pieces of differently shaped surfaces.

liberator: agent noun (80) of **liberare,** *set free* (**liber**).

lictor: *binder,* as if an agent noun from the root **lig** in **ligare,** *bind.* The officers who walked before a Roman magistrate seem to have been called lictors either from their binding into bundles the rods which they carried or from binding those who offended against the dignity of the magistrates.

literati (usually in pl.): *lettered, men of letters, scholars,* **litteratus** from **littera,** 107. (Commonly with one *t* in English.)

locus (pl. **-i**): *place;* now used as a mathematical term designating the place where a point or line may be under certain conditions.

Lucifer: *light-bearer,* **lux, lucis** + **ferre;** a name of Venus as the morning star. But the church fathers, reading in Isaiah, 14 : 2 of the king of Babylon compared to the morning star, and regarding Babylon as symbolic of the powers of evil, mistook

Lucifer for Satan, and the error was given further currency by Dante and Milton.

lumbago: *pain in the loins,* **lumbus** meaning *loin.* See **farrago** above.

Magi: plural of **magus,** a word of Persian origin and applied to the members of a priestly caste of ancient Persia. The wise men who visited the infant Jesus are often called the **Magi.**

mamma: a child's reduplicative word for *mother* [1]*; the breast* (cf. MAMMAL, *nourishing young from the breast*). The English word (spelled also 'mama') may have come partly through Fr. 'maman.'

mica: *a crumb, a grain* of salt or other mineral. The word has possibly been influenced in meaning by **micare,** *glisten,* with which it is not connected etymologically.

militia: *warfare, troops,* from **miles, militis,** *a soldier;* we use it only as *troops.*

minutiae: **minutia,** an abstract noun (74), from **minutus,** *small* (pf. pple. of **minuere,** *diminish*), *i.e., smallness.* The plural **minutiae** was used for *small things, trifles, minor details.*

moderator: *manager, director,* agent noun from **moderare,** or **moderari,** *regulate* (80); **modus,** *measure,* there being originally an -es stem giving **moder-are** (156). Cf. **modes-tia,** 74. We apply the word especially to the presiding officer of certain assemblies.

momentum: *i.e.* **mo(vi)mentum,** action noun of **movere,** *move* (90), and in English the *force of motion* in a moving body. In Latin **momentum** applied also to a particle which turned the scales, from which we have MOMENT, either as *a small part of time* or as *import, i.e.,* a weight to turn the scales of events.

monitor: *adviser,* agent noun of **monere,** *advise* (80).

moratorium: neuter of the adjective **moratorius** (102), from **morator,** *one who causes delay* (**morari,** *delay*). A modern use of **moratorium** is to denote the *period of delay* allowed for meeting a financial obligation.

---

[1] Varro, quoted by the grammarian Nonius (81, 4), **Cum cibum ac potionem buas ac pappas vocent, matrem mammam, patrem totam:** *Since they [infants] call food and drink bua and pappa, their mother mamma, their father tota.* See **papa** below. Properly such words are Indo-European rather than Latin, a kind of universal child-language. See Jespersen, *Language,* pp. 154–160.

motor: *a mover*, agent noun of **movere** (80), *move* (**mo[vi]tor**).

nasturtium: for **nastortium**, *nose-twister;* **nasus**, *nose*, and -**tortium**, -**turtium** from **torquere**, **tortus**, *twist* (cf. TORMENT, 90, TORTURE, 87). The pungent odor of the flower is supposed to cause the nose-twisting.[1]

nausea: *seasickness*, Grk. 'nausia' (ναυσία), (cf. **navis**, *ship*, **nauta,** *sailor*); extended then to similar sickness not due to the sea.

nebula: *a mist, a little cloud.*

nucleus: for 'nuculeus' (like -ulus, 68), a diminutive of **nux, nucis,** *a nut, a little nut, the kernel of a nut, a core, the inner part* of a thing.

odium: *hatred* (cf. **odi,** *I hate*, 82).

omen: a term of Roman augury which we have taken to refer to any *sign of future events.*

onus: *a burden* (cf. ONEROUS and EXONERATE; also **onus probandi,** 59).

opus: *work*, a musical *work*, one of a series of pieces.

pabulum: *food*, especially the *feed* of animals, *fodder* (cf. **pascere,** *feed*). But even the Romans used the word figuratively, like our 'mental pabulum.'

pallor: noun denoting condition (81), from **pallere,** *be pale.*

papa[2]**:** a child's imitative word asking for its food, spelled also **pappa** (cf. **pappare,** *eat pap*). The Eng. PAP is of like origin, and is likewise used in some sections for *father.*

pastor: *a feeder*, agent noun of **pascere,** *feed* (80); the *feeder* of a *flock*. Cf. REPAST from **pastus,** *food.*

peninsula: for **paeninsula,** *i.e.*, **paene-insula,** *almost an island.*

plebs: We have adopted this name of the common people of ancient Rome; its original meaning was *the crowd.*

pollen: *fine flour, fine dust, dust* on the anthers of flowers.

possessor: *owner, one who sits by* or *before* a thing as his own, agent noun (80) of **possidere,** *sit before, own* (144, **pro**).

precursor: for **praecursor,** *forerunner*, agent noun of **praecurrere,** *run before.*

---

[1] Pliny, *Natural History*, 19, 8, 44, § 155, **Nasturtium nomen accepit a narium tormento.**

[2] Included here as a Latin transfer because it underwent no change in French. Cf. **mamma** and Note.

premium: for **praemium,** *profit, reward;* made from **prae-emere,** *take* or *buy first;* a **premium** is what one gets before others.

professor: *one who speaks publicly,* agent noun of **profiteri, professus** (80), **pro** with **fateri,** *declare;* a **professor** *speaks before his class.*

prospectus: *a looking forward,* action noun of **prospicere, prospecere,** *look forth* (144, **pro**); a **prospectus** enables us to *see beforehand* a work that has not yet developed.

pupa: *a girl* or *doll,* fem. of **pupus,** *a boy; the undeveloped child; a chrysalis.* See PUPIL, 202.

pus: referring to matter from a sore, the word is related to PUTRID, and PUTREFY.

rabies: *madness.* Through the French the same word became RAGE. Cf. RABID.

radius: *a rod, spoke* of a wheel (42).

ratio: *a reckoning, relation,* action noun of **reri, ratus,** *think, calculate* (85). See 42, REASON.

rector: *ruler, guide,* agent noun of **regere,** *rule* (80).

regalia (pl.): *things pertaining to a king,* neut. pl. of the adjective **regalis,** from **rex, regis,** *king* (98); *the trappings* suggestive of royalty.

regimen: *guidance, direction, prescribed rule,* action noun of **regere,** *rule* (89).

residuum: *remainder,* from **residere,** *sit back* (cf. RESIDENCE, 41). The English form of the word, taken from the French, is RESIDUE.

rostrum: *the beak* of a bird, and then of a ship, *i.e., the curved end of the prow.* The platform from which addresses were delivered to the people in the Roman Forum was ornamented with beaks of ships taken from the Antians 337 B.C., and for this reason it was called **rostra,** *the Beaks.* We now use the singular for the speaker's platform. **Rostrum** is for **rod-trum** (147) from **rodere,** *gnaw, peck* (cf. RODENT).

saliva: *spittle,* of the same origin as the English 'slime.'

sanatorium: neuter form of the adjective **sanatorius** (102), *health-giving;* **sanare,** *heal,* **sanator,** *healer* (80).

sanctum: *a holy place.* The noun is the neuter of the pf. pple. of **sancire,** *fix as a sacred thing, ordain;* then *dedicate.* We use also the phrase **sanctum sanctorum,** *holy of holies.* Cf. SANCTION, SANCTIMONY (79), and on the same root SACRED.

scintilla: *spark* or *little spark,* a diminutive form, but '**scinta**' does not occur. We have also as derivatives SCINTILLATION and SCINTILLATE (128).

scrofula: **Scrofa** means *a breeding sow;* the diminutive **scrofula** should mean *a little pig.* It was used in the plural for a swelling of the glands of the neck, possibly on account of a playful comparison of these to little pigs. Or the rough uncleanly appearance of the scrofulous skin may have suggested the hide of a sow.

sculptor: *a cutter* or *engraver,* agent noun of **sculpere,** *carve* (80).

sector: From **secare, sectus,** *cut,* the Cl. Lat. **sector,** agent noun, was *one who cuts.* In Late Lat. **sector** was used to translate the Grk. 'tomeus' ($\tau o\mu\epsilon\dot{v}s$) as a mathematical term designating the part of a circle between two radii. As a military term it is applied to a part of the front on the firing line.

series: *row,* from the verb **serere,** *bind together.* Cf. ASSERT, and DISSERTATION. **Asserere (sibi),** *join to oneself, claim, declare one's own, declare,* ASSERT. **Dissertatio,** *arrangement in series* (**dis-,** *separately,* for consideration), *discussion.*

serum: *whey;* from the watery part of milk the word was applied to the watery part of other things, *e.g.,* of blood.

simulacrum: *a likeness, an image* or *phantom,* action noun of **simulare,** *imitate* (92).

sinus: *a curve, fold, a bay* or *gulf;* hence *a cavity* (cf. SINUOUS, *curving in and out);* INSINUATE (**in-sinuare**), *bring in by winding ways.*

species: *a look, appearance,* from **specere,** *look at.* It then becomes the particular thing to be looked at, or *the kind* which is distinguished from all the others. See also **specie,** 56.

specimen: *a sign, an example,* literally, *the mark* by which a thing is *seen* or recognized (**specere,** 89), and hence that which exhibits such marks.

spectator: *a looker-on,* agent noun of **spectare,** *behold* (80); **spectare,** frequentative of **specere,** *look at* (130). Cf. **spectrum** and SPECTRE (93).

spectrum: *an appearance* or *vision,* from **specere,** *look at;* the *series of colors* observed when light is separated by refraction. Cf. SPECTRE 93.

speculator: *scout, explorer,* agent noun of **speculari** (80). The verb was made from **specula,** *a watchtower* (from **specere,** *look at*). The modern **speculator** is a financial scout or watcher.

splendor: *brightness,* action noun of **splendere,** *shine* (81).

sponsor: *a promiser, i.e., a surety* or *bondsman,* agent noun of **spondere,** *promise* (80).

squalor: *filthiness* (81); **squalere** meant *be stiff* or *rough;* then *be stiff with dirt.*

stamen: *warp, thread; i.e.,* in the upright loom, the *standing* thing, from **stare,** *stand* (89). As a botanical term, the **stamen** is a "threadlike" part of a flower. Since the threads make the firm texture of cloth, we use the plural **stamina** to denote firmness or strength.

status: *standing, i.e., condition* or *position,* action noun from **stare,** *stand* (88).

stimulus (pl. -i): *a goad, incentive.*

stratum (pl. -a): *that which is spread out,* neut. pf. pple. of **sternere,** *spread;* so it became *a bedcover* or *a bed,* and in general, *a layer.* For *a lower layer* we use **substratum.** Cf. STREET, 8.

stupor: noun of condition (81), **stupere,** *be stunned* (cf. STUPID, 112).

tedium: for **taedium,** *weariness;* **taedet,** impersonal, *it wearies* (82).

terminus: *a boundary line,* so TERM is a *limited* time or a *limited* word (cf. also DETERMINE, Lat. **determinare,** *fix a limit*).

tiro: *a newly levied soldier, a recruit;* hence any *novice.*

toga: *a covering,* particularly the *outer garment* of the Roman citizen in time of peace; from root of **tegere,** *cover* (157). A special ornamented **toga** was worn by magistrates; hence our expression "senatorial toga." The word seems to have given our colloquial TOGS, and its derivative TOGGERY.

torpedo: *a crampfish* or *numbfish,* a kind of eel which gives an electric shock producing numbness; the original meaning was *numbness,* **torpere,** *be numb.* The word comes to be applied to things which in some way resemble this fish, a kind of fireworks or a submarine cartridge.

torpor: from **torpere,** *be sluggish,* a verbal noun to denote a *condition of inactivity* (81).

tremor: *a trembling*, action noun (81) of **tremere**, *tremble, quiver.*

tribunal: at Rome, a raised *platform* on which were the seats of the magistrates; formed like adjectives in **-alis** (98), from **tribunus,** a TRIBUNE, *i.e.*, in very early times, the chief officer of the TRIBE, **tribus**, originally a *district*, designating one of the three original groups of the Roman people. From **tribus** was made **tribuere,** "*divide into districts,*" *apportion, assign*, (with **ad-**) ATTRIBUTE; and from the verb again **tributum**, *the allotted (tax)*, TRIB- UTE.

tuber: *a bump* or *knob*, particularly on the *root* of a plant; of the same origin as **tumor.** Also see TUBEROSE, 202.

verbena: in Latin usually plural, *foliage* or *branches.*

vertebra (pl. **-ae**): *a joint, something to turn on*, from **vertere**, *turn;* then specifically, a *joint* or *bone of the spine* (92).

vertex (pl. **vertices**): *a turning point*, from **vertere**, *turn;* the *point* about which a thing turns, the *top.* See **vortex**, another form of the same word.

vertigo: *a turning* or *whirling around*, particularly *dizziness*, from **vertere**, *turn*, with **-igo(n).** See **farrago**, above.

vesper: *evening* or the *evening star;* we use the English plural VESPERS for an *evening religious service.*

victor: *a conqueror*, agent noun of **vincere**, *conquer* (80).

villa: *a country home*, for '**vic(es)la**' (69), from **vicus**, *village.* See VILLAIN, 197.

vinculum: *a bond, a fetter*, noun of means, **vincire**, *bind* (91); now particularly as a mathematical sign binding together certain quantities.

violator: agent noun (80) of **violare**, *injure, outrage.*

virago: *a manlike woman;* an extended form of '**vira**,' said to have been an old word for *woman*, a feminine of **vir**, *man;* for **-ago** see **farrago**, above.

virus: *slime;* then a *poisonous liquid.* Cf. VIRULENT, 106.

viscera: *entrails*, plural of **viscus, visceris.**

vortex (pl. **vortices**): *a turning point, a whirlpool* (see **vertex**).

53. A number of Latin adjectives appear unchanged in English, sometimes as adjectives, often as nouns. Such are the following:

aliquot: *several, some,* from **alius,** *some* or *other,* and **quot,** *how many.* In English it applies to a number that evenly divides another, as 'an ALIQUOT part.'

anterior: made from the adverb (preposition) **ante,** *before,* on analogy of the double comparatives **posterior, interior.**

bonus: *good;* and what is received in addition to that ordinarily granted is particularly *good.*

complex: *folded together,* **com-,** *together,* and the root of **plicare,** *fold.*[1]

decorum: *suitable,* (neut.) *that which is suitable;* **decorus** being the adjective from **decor,** action noun of **decere** (81), *be fitting.* Cf. DECORATE, DECORATION.

desideratum: *a thing desired,* pf. pple. of **desiderare.** DESIRE represents a French modification of the same verb (cf. 173b).

duplex: *twofold;* **duo,** *two,* and the root of **plicare,** *fold.*[1] Cf. DUPLICATE.

emeritus: pf. pple. of **emereri,** *earn one's pay completely* (e-).

indecorum: *what is not suitable,* neuter of **indecorus** (see **decorum**).

integer: *whole,* literally, *untouched,* **in-,** *not,* and **teg,** a form of the root **tag**[2] of **tangere,** *touch; a whole number,* **numerus integer,** *untouched* as compared with one that has been *broken, i.e.,* a FRACTION (**frangere, fractus,** *break*). Through OF **integer** became ENTIRE.

interior: a double comparative form like **exterior** (54); **in-ter-ior,** Eng. 'inner.'

junior: *younger,* comparative of **juvenis;** a shortened form for **juvenior.**

major: *greater,* comparative of **magnus;** as a noun, an *army officer* next above a captain.

maximum: *greatest,* neuter superlative of **magnus,** *great.*

medium: *middle* place or thing, neuter of **medius,** *middle.* It is used also of a *middle* person, *e.g.,* an intermediary between the living and the dead.

---

[1] Another explanation of the element -**plex,** -**plix,** connects it with the root **plak,** occurring in **plangere,** *strike,* Grk. 'plakē' (πλάκη), *a stroke. One-stroke* (**simplex**), *two-stroke* (**duplex**), etc. for *one-time, two-times,* etc. See Walde, *Et. Wb.,* **duplex.**

[2] Nom. -**ger** for older '-gros,' where -**tag**- would become -**teg**-, according to 149.

memorandum (pl. -a): *what must be remembered,* neuter of **memorandus,** gerundive of **memorare,** *bring to remembrance.*

minimum: *least,* superlative from the root **min** (cf. **minor**); **-mus** is a superlative suffix, as in **primus** and **ultimus.** MINIM is another spelling of the same word, denoting a very small note in music, or a very small measure (one-sixtieth of a drachm).

minor: *smaller,* used as a comparative of **parvus,** *little,* but from the root **min** which appears in DIMINISH; as a noun, a **minor** is yet *too little* to be legally a citizen.

minus: *less,* neuter of **minor,** q.v.

miser: *wretched,* describing the unfortunate who has nothing but money.

modicum: **Modicus,** from **modus,** *measure* (97; see MODE, MOOD, 45), meant *of proper measure, moderate. Proper measure* suggests *small measure,* and the adjective came to mean *small* or *trifling.* Its neuter **modicum** comes to us as a *small quantity.*

multiplex: *manifold;* **multus,** pl. **multi,** *many,* and the root of **plicare,** *fold.* See **duplex** and Note above.

neuter: *neither; neither gender.* In a wider sense, we have NEUTRAL, NEUTRALITY, NEUTRALIZE. The word is **ne,** *not,* with **uter,** *which of the two?*

par: *equal.* We use it especially of equality of monetary exchange, equality of market price and actual value.

pendulum: *hanging,* a *hanging* weight, neuter of **pendulus,** from **pendere,** *hang* (121).

plus: *more,* used as comparative of **multum,** *much.*

posterior: *after, hinder,* comparative of **posterus,** itself a comparative of **post,** *after.*

prior: *earlier,* comparative of an O. Lat. **pri,** *before;* **primus,** *first,* is its superlative. With the meaning *superior,* **prior** became a noun, the title of a superior officer of a religious order.

redivivus: *living again, restored.*

referendum: *what must be referred, i.e., carried back* (**re-ferre**), neuter of **referendus,** gerundive of **referre;** particularly the *carrying back* of a question to the sometimes sovereign people.

senior: *older,* comparative of **senex,** *old* (base **sen-**).

simile: a *like thing,* neuter of **similis** (cf. SIMILAR); the root is also in Eng. 'same.'

sinister: *left, on the left side.* The Roman augur in taking the auspices, sat facing the south, his left hand toward the east, the region of light and good fortune; **sinister** therefore in this connection regularly meant *favorable, good.* The Greek seer faced the north in a similar ceremony and the left for him was the unfavorable region. **Sinister** further applied to what was done with the left hand and came to mean *awkward, wrong, bad.* Either from this sense or from the Greek point of view in the auspices, the word in Latin sometimes meant *unlucky* or *evil,* and with this meaning only came into English.

ulterior: *farther;* a double comparative, **ul-ter-ior, ul-** being the same as we find in **ille (ollus),** *that, on that side;* **ulterior** is *more and more on that side.*

ultimatum: *coming last,* pf. pple. neut. of **ultimare,** *be at the end.* The verb was made from the superlative adjective **ultimus** (128). Cf. **ulterior.**

vacuum: an *empty space,* neuter of **vacuus,** *empty.*

To this list may be added the names of the months **September, October, November, December** (216).

54. The following nouns and adjectives also show the Latin nominative form, but have come indirectly, *i.e.,* through French into English. Cf. **52, N.**

color: originally *a covering* (see 31).

exterior: comparative of **exter** or **exterus,** *outside.* This is a double comparative, since **exter** itself is a comparative of **ex,** *out.* Cf. Eng. 'outer.'

honor: the same in meaning (AF '[h]onour').

inferior: *lower,* a double comparative; **inferus** (older **infer**), *lower.*

labor: *toil* for wages.

minister: *servant,* a double comparative from the same **min-** which appears in **minus;** hence one *"more smaller"* or *of low degree,* as **magister,** MASTER, is literally *"more greater"* (45).

murmur: an imitative word, repeating a syllable in imitation of the sound designated.

odor: the Fr. 'odeur,' *odor.*

rumor: OF 'rumour,' Lat. **rumor(em),** *noise, hearsay.*

senator: a member of the **senatus,** *i.e.,* the *company of old men,* from **senex,** *old, old man* (70). Cf. **senior** and SENILE.

superior: *upper,* comparative of **superus,** the adjective being made from the adverb (preposition) **super,** *up, above.*

vapor: *steam, vapor.*

55. Of adverbs and prepositions we have the following:

alias: *otherwise, at another time* or *place,* adverb from **alius,** *other* (probably accusative pl. or genitive sing. form); a law term but very common in giving assumed names of criminals; it is used also as a noun, meaning an assumed name.

alibi: *elsewhere,* **alius** + **bi** (as in **ibi, ubi**). We make it a noun to apply to one's establishing proof that he was elsewhere when a certain offence was committed.

extra: *beyond, i.e., beyond* the ordinary or necessary. The Latin adverb (preposition) itself is for **extera,** a case form of **exter (exterus),** *outer,* comparative of **ex** (see **exterior**), as it occurred in the phrase **ex extera parte,** *on the outer side.* However, **extra** as an English adjective, or noun, as in 'EXTRA work,' 'all the EXTRAS,' is probably an abbreviation of EXTRAORDINARY (144), and we find the adopted word only in compounds like **extra-**CURRICULAR, **extra**-SCIENTIFIC.

gratis: *freely, without pay,* a contraction of **gratiis** (as in Plautus and Terence), ablative pl. of **gratia,** *thanks, favor;* hence *out of favors, by way of kindness.*

instanter: Latin *urgently,* English *immediately,* an adverb made from **instans, instantis,** pres. pple. of **instare,** *stand on, at,* or *by.* To stand by indicates one's interest; then the urgency of the case, and the need for immediate action. Cf. INSTANT, under SIMULTANEOUS, 205.

interim: *meanwhile,* the preposition **inter,** *between,* with **-im,** in origin an accusative pronominal form. It has become a noun in English to denote an intervening time.

item: *likewise, also;* formerly used to introduce each separate article of an enumeration. A division or paragraph beginning with the word came to be called an **item.**

non: *not,* as a prefix; *e.g.,* **non**-CONDUCTOR, **non**-COMBATANT.

tandem: *at length, i.e., after a long time.* The English use is only a pun on the Latin meaning from a university student's saying of two horses harnessed one in front of the other that they were harnessed **tandem**. Then came the **tandem** bicycle, and later the **tandem** plane.

verbatim: *word for word*, a Low Latin adverb made from **verbum**, *word*. In like manner we have **literatim**, *letter for letter*, and have made **seriatim**, *by series;* all after the form of **gradatim**, *step by step*, from **gradus**, **paulatim**, *little by little*, from **paulus**, etc.

56. Again we have preserved from an earlier time certain inflectional forms of nouns, pronouns, and adjectives, such as the following:

folio: abl. case of **folium**, *a leaf*. In old documents reference was made by page as **in folio**; from the constant use of this case it was adopted as an English word. So also we have made **quarto, octavo**, and **duodecimo**.

limbo: **Limbus**, *a border*, was used by the church fathers in the phrase **limbus patrum** to designate the place bordering hell, where the Old Testament saints had their abode. The ablative was taken from **in limbo patrum**, and all the more easily since the Italian word is 'limbo' from the accusative **limbum** (47).

nostrum: *our own*, neuter of the possessive adjective **noster**. As *a medicine which is ours* it is *known only to us;* it is therefore a patent and particularly a quack medicine.

numero: See abbreviation **no.** (60).

omnibus: *for all*, dat. pl. of the adjective **omnis**, *all;* the vehicle is so called from being intended *for all* classes of people. Much more common now is the use of BUS, the last syllable only of this dative. An 'OMNIBUS bill' seems to have place *for all* measures.

proviso: abl. sing. neut. of the pf. pple. of **providere**, taken from the law phrase **proviso quod**, *it being provided that;* the participle is in ablative absolute relation with the **quod** clause.

quorum: In commissions issued to certain justices in England was formerly the expression **Quorum aliquem vestrum ... unum esse volumus**: *Of whom we wish some one of you to be one*, where the presence of one or more of these justices was necessary for the transaction of business. From this expression the first word came to have its present use.

rebus: *with things,* the abl. pl. of **res,** *a thing,* the sentence in such a puzzle being expressed not with words but *with things.*

requiem: *rest,* acc. of **requies,** and the first word of an antiphon used in the mass for the dead, **Requiem aeternam dona eis, Domine:** *Grant them eternal rest, O Lord.*

specie: abl. sing. of **species** (52), once written **in specie,** *in actual form, i.e., minted metal coin* as contrasted with paper money.

via: *by the way,* abl. sing. of **via;** used for *by way of.*

vim: *force, energy,* acc. sing. of **vis.** The accusative may have come into use from its common occurrence in school Latin (*e.g.,* **per vim**).[1]

57. The following verb forms are used mostly as nouns in English:

affidavit: *he made an oath,* 3 pers. sing. perf. of a Low Latin word, **affidare, ad-fidare,** *pledge* (Lat. **fidere,** *trust*), state an oath (**fidem dare**); as a noun it comes to mean a *statement under oath.*

ave: *Hail!* imperative 2 pers. sing. of **avere,** *be* or *fare well;* used for **Ave Maria** the first words of the angel Gabriel, addressing the Virgin (Luke 1 : 28); used also to introduce a prayer to her; hence the song of Annunciation, or such a prayer.

caret: *(it) is lacking,* 3 pers. sing. pres. of **carere,** the sign indicating an omission.

caveat: *let him beware,* 3 pers. sing. pres. subj. of **cavere,** *be on one's guard.* As an English noun it is first a legal notice warning one not to act until the opposing party is heard; then in a more general way, a *warning.* Cf. **caveat emptor,** 61.

deficit: *it is wanting,* 3 pers. sing. pres. of **deficere,** *fail, be wanting* (**de-facere**). Cf. Eng. 'make off' for 'get away.' So **deficit** becomes a *shortage.*

exit: *he goes out,* 3 pers. sing. pres. of **exire;** a stage direction, pl. **exeunt,** *they go out.* **Exit** however has become a noun denoting either one's passing out or the way by which he goes.

fiat: *let it be done,* 3 pers. sing. pres. subj. of **fieri.** As a noun it is a form of order from a source of final authority; as an adjective

---

[1] If we follow a suggestion in NED that the word may be of "imitative or interjectional origin," it must of course be omitted here, unless indeed the interjection be an echo of **per vim.**

it applies to what is based only on an authoritative order, as 'fiat money.'

habitat: *it dwells,* 3 pers. sing. pres. of **habitare;** we use it for the region where a plant or animal naturally *lives.*

ignoramus: *we do not know;* 1 pers. pl. pres. of **ignorare;** originally a law term written on a bill when the evidence was not found sufficient for proceeding with the action; now as a noun applied to any person distinguished for his ignorance (**gno,** *know,* 223; **in-gno,** 153).

imprimatur: *let it be printed,* 3 pers. sing. pres. subj. pass. of **imprimere,** *permission to publish* granted by a censor; hence, in general, *approval* or *sanction.*

innuendo: *by nodding,* abl. gerund of **in-nuere,** *nod at* or *toward;* once used as a law term in quoting a statement at first made definite *by a nod.* One's statement "He was there," accompanied by a nod toward the plaintiff, appears in the record as "He stated that he (**innuendo** the plaintiff) was there," where ordinarily we should say "meaning" or "referring to"; hence **innuendo** became an *indirect reference* or *insinuation.*

interest: *it makes a difference, it concerns,* 3 sing. pres. of **interesse,** literally, *be between.* From *it concerns* the verb means *it is to one's advantage,* and as an English noun it easily becomes *profit,* especially a *share* in a business or the *premium* paid for the use of money. We have it also as a verb, and INTERESTS appears as a double 3 pers. sing.[1]

mandamus: *we order,* 1 pers. pl. pres. of **mandare;** as a legal term, a writ issued by a court directing the performance of a public duty, or issued by a superior court directing certain action in a lower court. Cf. COMMAND, 196.

memento: *remember,* 2 pers. sing. imperative of **meminisse;** so *a token for remembering,* a "remember me."

placebo; *I shall be pleasing,* 1 pers. sing. future of **placere;** the opening anthem of the vespers for the dead, named from the

---

[1] Low Latin, however, used the infinitive **interesse** in the sense of *usury,* and an old verb in English was 'interess.' Skeat (Dictionary) regards the English verb INTEREST as made from the pple. INTERESS'D by confusion with the noun **interest.** Again the *-t* has been explained as added from the *-t* of 'debt.'

first word, Psalm 116 (Vulgate 114): 9, **Placebo Domino in regione vivorum,** *I shall be acceptable to the Lord in the land of the living.* The word is also applied to a medicine of no efficacy, given to please the patient.

posse: *be able,* infinitive; in Mediæval Latin as a noun, *power;* particularly **posse comitatus,** *the power of the* COUNTY, including all whom the sheriff might summon into service; hence *a force with legal authority.*

propaganda: The verb **pangere,** root **pag,** meant *fasten.* **Propagare,** *fasten down, set out,* was used of setting out plants; so *to extend a growth, generate,* PROPAGATE. We use it also of the extension of doctrines. A committee of cardinals established in 1622 by Pope Gregory XV for supervising foreign missions was called **Congregatio de propaganda fide,** *The Committee for Propagating the Faith.* This has been abbreviated to the one word, an abl. fem. of the gerundive.

quietus: from Med. Lat. **quietus est,** *he is freed* (from a debt); so *a discharge, a final settlement, an ending* (QUIET, 202).

recipe: *take,* 2 pers. sing. imperative of **recipere,** *receive.* From being the first word of a Latin prescription, it came to mean a prescription, and commonly now a formula for preparing food.

tenet: *he holds,* 3 pers. sing. pres. of **tenere;** *one's doctrine.*

veto: *I forbid,* 1 pers. sing. pres. of **vetare;** hence a *prohibition,* especially the act of one department of a government in forbidding what another department has ordered. For example, it was the word used by the Roman tribunes in opposing measures of the senate.

58. Both noun and verb forms are sometimes disguised by a change of spelling:

CREED: for **credo,** *I believe,* the first word of the Apostles' Creed, as also of some others. **Cre(d)-do, cor(d)** (228), *heart* + *-do, put,*[1] *put one's heart* or *confidence in a thing.*

DEBENTURE: for **debentur,** *(they) are due,* 3 pers. pl. pres. passive of **debere,** *owe,* since such a written statement of debt began in

---

[1] In **-do, -ditus,** of **credo, condo, perdo,** we have the Latin representation of a root meaning *put* (Grk. 'thē,' $\theta\eta$), but naturally there was some confusion between such words and compounds of **do, dare,** *give.*

its Latin form, it is said, with the words **Debentur mihi,** *There are due to me.*

DOMINIE: formerly spelled **domine,** voc. of **dominus,** *master,* title of a pastor of the Dutch Reformed Church, extended sometimes to other ministers.

DIRGE: for **dirige,** imperative sing. of **dirigere (di-regere),** *direct,* as the first word of a funeral antiphon beginning **Dirige, Domine, Deus meus, in conspectu tuo viam meam,** *Direct, O Lord, my God, my way in thy sight* (Psalm 5 : 8).

EFFIGY: while this seems to represent the Fr. 'effigie,' Lat. **effigies,** *form, image* (**effingere,** root **fig,** *make out, fashion*), yet the common expression "in effigy" was earlier written **in effigie,** where **effigie** was not the French form, but the Lat. abl. sing.

FACSIMILE: shortened from **factum simile,** a *thing made like, an exact copy.*

FACTOTUM: from **facere totum,** *do-all,* one employed to *do all* kinds of things, or *a servant* having charge of all his master's affairs.

IMPROMPTU: for **in promptu,** *in readiness,* adopted in its combined form through the French, with the meaning of *offhand,* or *extemporaneous(ly).* Cf. PROMPT, 154.

PARSE: for **pars,** *part.* In the days of the Latin study of grammar, the question put to the student was **Quae pars orationis?** *What part of speech?* Answering this question became PARS-ing, and the verb was spelled PARSE.

PLAUDIT: for **plaudite,** imperative pl. of **plaudere,** *applaud.* At the close of a Latin play an actor appeared on the stage and announced the end of the performance by calling out, **Plaudite,** *applaud!* In English the final *e* seems to have been regarded as a silent vowel, then dropped.

POULTICE: for **pultes,** the plural of **puls, pultis,** *a pap* or *pottage,* with *-ce* for an ending probably to give the word the appearance of being French.

PREMISES: for **praemissas,** *i.e.,* **praemissas sententias,** *aforesaid statements* (lit. *sent before,* **praemittere**), an expression used in legal documents to refer to the first statements as to the parties to a transaction, or to avoid repetition of property description already given. It was then extended to apply to the property itself. PREMISES in logic, and household PREMISES are thus originally the same. From this plural, a singular PREMISE has been made.

PULSE: for **puls,** a *pap* or *pottage* (see POULTICE); then the word becomes the name for the ingredients of the pottage, *i.e.,* beans, peas, etc.

QUERY: for **quaere,** *ask,* imperative sing. of **quaerere,** introducing a subject of inquiry, *Ask* —, *i.e., There is question;* hence a *question.*

SEPTUAGINT: **septuaginta,** *seventy.* The SEPTUAGINT translation of the Hebrew scriptures into Greek is so called because it is said to have been made by *seventy* persons (or by seventy-two persons in seventy-two days, according to tradition). Another story is that the translation was sanctioned by the Jewish Sanhedrin of seventy-one members. It has been assigned to a date of about 275 B.C., under Ptolemy Philadelphus of Egypt.

STYLUS: The correct Latin spelling was **stilus,** originally a *pointed stick* or a *stalk* of a plant; then the *instrument* used *for writing* on a waxen tablet. In the latter sense we have adopted the word, and the spelling with *y* is not altogether our mistake. The derived word is STYLE, of writing; then of other things.

VAGARY: for **vagari,** *to wander about,* pres. infinitive; so a *wandering* of thought or a *freakish scheme.* 'Vagrant,' *wandering,* is naturally associated with **vagari,** but is probably a Germanic word, influenced in spelling by the Latin word rather than derived from it.

CHAPTER II

LATIN WORDS AND PHRASES BORROWED IN ENGLISH

59. Apart from the Latin words that have come over to us and been fully naturalized, many others have preserved their Roman citizenship at the same time that they render regular and valuable service to the language of their adoption.[1] Such are the following words and phrases,[2] so familiar to us from our daily reading:

ab initio: *from the beginning,* **initium,** *a going in* from **in-ire.**

ad captandum: *for catching, i.e., for catching* popular favor.

addendum (pl. **addenda**): *a thing (things) to be added,* neut. gerundive of **addere.**

ad finem: *to the end.*

ad hoc: *with reference to this; with regard to this* particular thing.

ad infinītum: *to the unlimited, endlessly;* **in-,** *not* + **finitum,** pf. pple. of **finire.**

ad interim: *for the meantime, meanwhile* (see **interim,** 55).

[1] Latin words thus adopted follow English and not Roman pronunciation. Thus *c* and *g* are hard before *a, o, u,* soft before *e* and *i, ti* + a vowel is 'sh-,' etc., as in English. We say for **me judice,** 'me judisee,' not 'may yudikĕ'; **viva voce,** 'vi-va vo-see,' not 'weewa wo-kĕ.' However, in college circles the Roman pronunciation of certain phrases is often heard: **cum laude,** 'coom lou-de' (*ou* as in *out*); **alma mater,** 'ahlma mahter.' Every separate vowel (or diphthong) makes a separate syllable and the Latin rule of accent should be observed: words of only two syllables are accented always on the first, those of more than two, on the syllable next to the last if that is long, otherwise on the third from the end. A syllable is long if it has a long vowel or if its vowel is followed by two consonants. Thus **ad valō′rem, corrigen′dum, pro tem′pŏre.** For the guidance of readers not familiar with Latin accent, long vowels determining accent are marked in the following list.

[2] Some of the phrases, of course, are quite modern.

ad libitum: *according to one's pleasure;* **libitus,** *pleasing,* pf. pple. of the impersonal **libet,** *it pleases.*

ad litteram: *to the letter, i.e., exact* or *exactly.*

ad nauseam: *to sickness, to a sickening degree;* **nausea** is literally *seasickness* (52).

ad rem: *to the matter, to the point* or *purpose.*

ad summam: *to the (full) sum, on the whole, in short.*

ad unguem: *to the nail, to the utmost nicety,* since the ancient sculptor gave the finishing touch to his work with the finger nail, and the joiner likewise thus tested the fit of a joint.

ad valōrem: *according to value.*

a fortiōri [1]: *from the stronger* (comparative of **fortis,** *brave, strong*); a form of argument proceeding from the stronger statement to the weaker.

agenda: *things to be done,* neut. pl. of the gerundive of **agere,** *do.*

alma mater: *fostering mother;* **almus,** *nourishing,* from **alere,** *nourish* (suffix -mo-s). In ancient Rome it was applied to goddesses, especially Ceres and Cybele; now to the college from which one graduates.

alter ego: *other I, one's other self, confidential friend.*

ante bellum: *before the war,* especially in the United States, *before* the Civil *War.*

a posteriōri [1]: *from the latter* (see **posterior,** 53); a form of argument proceeding from effect to cause, inductive reasoning.

a priōri [1]: *from the former* (see **prior,** 53); a form of argument proceeding from antecedent to consequent, from cause to effect, deductive.

aqua vitae: *water of life,* a name for distilled spirits, brandy, or whiskey.

arbor vitae: *tree of life,* name of an evergreen shrub.

argumentum ad hominem: *argument (directed) at the man, i.e.,* directed at one's opponent rather than at the question.

ars gratia artis: *art for the sake of art.*

benedicite: *bless ye, praise ye,* imperative pl. of **benedicere.** It is the first word of a canticle of the English Church, and so names the canticle.

[1] The ablative of comparatives commonly ended in *-e,* occasionally in *-i.*

bona fide: *in good faith;* hence *real* or *genuine.*

casus belli: *occasion for war;* **casus,** *occurrence,* from **cadere,** *fall* (88).

cave canem: *beware of the dog;* words sometimes inscribed on the door or threshold of a Roman house.

ceteris paribus: *other things being equal;* abl. abs.

commūne bonum: *the common good.*

confessio fidēi: *confession of faith,* a statement of creed.

corrigendum (pl. **corrigenda**): *a thing* (*things*) *to be corrected,* neut. gerundive of **corrigere,** *correct.*

cui bono: *for good to whom? for whose profit?* "It was a Roman lawyer's maxim who held that when you were at a loss to tell where the responsibility for a crime lay, your best chance was to inquire who had reaped the benefit of it." [1]

cum grano salis: *with a grain of salt.*

cum laude: *with praise; with honor* in a college class.

de facto: *from the fact, actual;* the noun **factum** is the pf. pple. of **facere,** *do;* the 'de facto government' is the government actually functioning. Cf. **de jure.**

Dei gratia: *by the grace of God.*

de jure: *from legal right,* as opposed to **de facto,** q.v.

dele: *erase,* imperative sing. of **delere,** *erase, destroy;* used by proof readers (see **d.,** 60). Cf. our derivative DELETE (from pf. pple. **deletum,** 132), and the adj. IN-DELIBLE, *not to be erased* (116).

de novo: *from the new, anew.*

Deo volente: *God being willing.*

deus ex machina: *a god from a machine,* a device introduced into the Greek theatre for carrying a god on or off the stage, often to relieve a tangle of the plot.

Deus vobiscum: *God* (*be*) *with you,* or (sing.), **Deus tecum.**

dies irae: *the day of wrath,* judgment day.

dramatis persōnae: *persons* or *characters of the drama.* See PERSON, 45. (**Drama** was borrowed from Greek, meaning a *doing, action.*)

ecce Homo: *behold the Man,* the words of Pilate to the Jews at the trial of Jesus, John 19 : 5. See also 66.

editio princeps: *first edition* of a book.

---

[1] Fowler and Fowler: *The King's English,* p. 35. See Cicero, *Pro Milone,* 12, 32; *Pro Roscio,* 30, 84.

e pluribus unum: *out of many one, one (composed) of many* (see 62 end).

ergo: *therefore.*

errātum (pl. **-a**): *error*, neut. pf. pple. of **errare**, *wander, make a mistake.*

et: *and.*

et tu Brute: *Thou too, Brutus?* According to tradition the words of Julius Caesar when he discovered Brutus among the assassins; hence it may refer to any friend turned enemy.

ex cathēdra: *from the chair, i.e., from the chair* of the bishop; hence *with official authority;* **cathēdra**, originally Greek.

excelsior: *higher, loftier* (see 64).

exceptis excipiendis: *things excepted that ought to be excepted*, pf. pple. and gerundive of **excipere** in abl. abs.

ex officio: *from the office, by virtue of one's office.*

ex parte: *from the part; i.e., from one side only.*

ex pede Herculem: *from the foot Hercules;* "from the sample you may judge the whole." There was a story that Pythagoras, by comparing the length of the stadium of Hercules at Olympia with the ordinary Greek stadium of 600 feet, calculated the length of Hercules' foot and from that his height.

ex post facto: *from what is done afterward*, applied especially to a law enacted after the offence which it concerns has been committed.

ex tempore: *from the time, i.e., without preparation, extemporaneously.*

facile princeps: *easily first;* **princeps** from **prim-us** and **cap-** of **capere**, *i.e., taking first* place.

fecit: *(he) made (it);* used on works of art, the artist's name being inserted as subject.

fiat lux: *let there be light*, Genesis 1 : 3.

finis: *the end.*

fraus pia: *a pious fraud*, a deception intended for a good purpose.

genius loci: *the genius of the place;* the protecting *genius of the place*, growing out of the notion of a **genius domus** or **genius familiae**, the tutelary *divinity of the house* or *family;* now applied also to the spirit of a community or institution. See Vergil, *Aeneid*, 5, 95; cf. **genius**, 52.

gloria in excelsis (Deo): *glory (to God) in the highest;* Luke 2 : 14.

gloria Patri: *glory to the Father.*

gradātim: *step by step, gradually,* adverb from **gradus,** *step,* Eng. GRADE.

habeas corpus: *you may have the body,* a writ for delivering a person from prison.

homo sapiens: *discerning man, man* as a *thinking* animal; the *"genus man,"* i.e., **genus homo.**

in absentia: *in absence.*

in articulo mortis: *in the moment of death* (see ARTICLE, 68).

in esse: *in being, in actual existence;* a mediæval use of **esse,** *to be,* as a noun.

in extenso: *in extended* form, *in full.*

in extrēmis: *at the last, in the hour of death.*

in fieri: *in being made, in* the process of *being made;* Med. Lat. **fieri,** *to be made,* as a noun.

in fine: *in the end, in short.*

infra: *below,* used in references in books.

in limine: *on the threshold, at the outset.*

in loco parentis: *in the place of a parent.*

in medias res: *into the midst of things;* so (as place where) **in mediis rebus,** *in the midst of things.*

in memoriam: *in* or *for the memory* of one.

in nubibus: *in the clouds,* i.e., merely under consideration.

in pace: *in peace.*

in perpetuum: *forever, in perpetuity.*

in posse: *in the possibility, potentially;* a Mediæval Latin phrase with **posse,** *to be able,* as a noun (cf. **posse,** 57, **in esse, in fieri**).

in propria persōna: *in one's own person,* or simply *in person.*

in re: *in the matter,* introducing a statement of the subject of a letter or document; also simply **re.**

in situ: *in position;* e.g., of parts of a ruined structure left in their proper place.

in statu quo: *in the situation in which* a matter was before; also **in statu quo ante.** So the nominative has been adopted, **status quo.**

inter nos: *between us.*

in toto: *on the whole, entirely.*

ipse dixit: the Latin version of the Greek phrase used by the disciples of Pythagoras [1]; *he himself said* (it), *i.e.*, the master himself has spoken and discussion is superfluous; a dogmatic assertion.

ipsissima verba: *the very words*, an exact quotation; **ipsissima**, a superlative formation from the pronoun **ipse**; **ipsissimis verbis**, abl., *in the very words*.

ipso facto: *by the very fact, in the very nature of the deed.* Cf. **ipso jure**, *by the law itself.*

Jupiter pluvius: *Jupiter of the rain*, the god that dispenses the rain; used now only in playful reference to rainy weather.

lapsus linguae: *a slip of the tongue;* sometimes **lapsus pennae**, *a slip of the pen.*

lapsus memoriae: *a slip of memory.*

lares et penātes: These were household gods, guardians of the home. The **lares** were tutelary divinities, presiding over a particular locality, and among the Romans were commonly protectors of the home. The **penātes** were properly guardians of the inner house (cf. **penitus**, *within*). To go through the inmost part was **penetrare**, from which we get PENETRATE; -**trare** as in **in-trare**, ENTER (cf. **trans**, *going over;* hence *across*).

laudātor temporis acti: *praiser of the past time;* one who lauds the good old times as contrasted with the present. Horace uses the phrase in *Ars Poetica*, l. 173.

lex non scripta: *law not written, unwritten law.*

loco citāto: *in the passage cited*, used in references in books.

locum tenens: *holding a place, i.e.,* for some one else, a deputy (cf. LIEUTENANT, 29).

Magna Charta: the *Great Charter*, the charter of English liberties which King John was forced to sign in 1215.

magna cum laude: *with great praise, with great honor* in a college class (cf. **cum laude**); so **maxima cum laude**, *with greatest distinction*, also **summa cum laude**, *with highest distinction.*

magnum opus: *a great work*, one's masterpiece.

materfamilias: *mother of a family;* **familias**, an old gen. sing. form.

me judice: *I (being) judge, in my judgment.*

membra disjecta (disjecta membra): *scattered parts*, especially of a ruined building.

[1] Quoted by Cicero, *De Natura Deorum*, 1, 5, 10.

memorabilia: *things worthy to be remembered;* neut. pl. of **memorabilis,** from **memorare,** *remember* (116).

mirabile dictu: *wonderful to tell;* the adjective from **mirari** (116); so **mirabile visu,** *wonderful to see.* The pl. **mirabilia** has come to us through the Fr. 'merveille' as MARVEL.

modus operandi: *manner of operating,* gerund of **operare.**

multum in parvo: *much in little.*

mutatis mutandis: *things being changed that ought to be changed, the necessary changes being made,* pf. pple. and gerundive of **mutare** in abl. abs.

ne plus ultra: *no more beyond, the utmost perfection.*

nil: *nothing,* shortened form of **nihil.** Cf. ANNIHILATE, **annihilare (ad-nihil,** 128) *reduce to nothing;* NIHILism, *"nothingism,"* a program or doctrine looking to the destruction of the social organization. **Nihil** from **ne-hilum,** *not a thread, not a bit.*

nolens volens: *unwilling, willing, whether one wills or not.* Cf. Eng. 'willy nilly,' for 'will he, nill he' ('ne-will he' = *will he not).*

non compos mentis: *not sound of mind.* We have also **compos mentis. Non compos mentis** has been sadly twisted into NINCOMPOOP.

non est: *it is not, it is non-existent.*

non sequitur: *it does not follow;* an unwarranted conclusion.

novus homo: *a new man,* one who rises to distinction through his own efforts rather than from prestige of his family.

obiit: *he (she) died;* used in old epitaphs.

onus probandi: *the burden of proving, responsibility for proof.*

pari passu: *with equal step,* in like measure, in proportion.

particeps criminis: *a sharer of the crime;* **pars, partis,** with **cap-** of **capere,** *take,* PARtaker (PART-taker).

passim: *everywhere,* literally *scattered far and wide;* adverb from **passus,** pf. pple. of **pandere,** *spread out, scatter.*

paterfamilias: *father of a family* (see **materfamilias**).

Pater noster: *our Father; the Lord's prayer,* so called from these first two words. Also the *rosary* by which the prayer is said. The change of meaning becomes rather striking as the expression is applied to a kind of fishing tackle and to a London street; the fishing line **(pater noster)** having hooks attached at intervals like the beads of the rosary; and **Pater Noster Row** so called possibly from the number of rosary and prayer-book makers doing business on that street.

pater patriae: *father of (his) country,* applied especially to Cicero.[1]

pax tecum: *peace (be) with you;* also pl. **vobiscum.**

per: *through, by;* often used before an agent's signature, following his use of his principal's name.

per annum: *by the year, for (each) year.*

per capita: *by the heads, for (each) person.*

per centum, per cent.: *by the hundred, on (each) hundred.*

per contra: *on the contrary,* on the opposite side of the account.

per diem: *by the day;* then *wage* or *allowance* for each day.

per saltum: *by a leap, all at one jump;* **saltus,** action noun of **salire,** *leap* (88).

per se: *by itself, in its own power.*

persōna grata: *a welcome* or *acceptable person;* negative, **persōna ingrata** or **persōna non grata.**

pollice verso: *the thumb turned (down);* when a gladiator after winning the contest in the arena looked to the spectators for a signal whether he should kill his opponent, the turning of the spectator's thumb toward his breast meant death (cf. 66); **pollice presso,** *the thumb pressed* (in the palm) signified that the man's life should be spared.

pons asinōrum: *the bridge of asses;* the proposition in geometry over which to lead the stupid beginner was like leading an ass over a bridge. This particular proposition was the fifth of the first book of Euclid, that if a triangle has two sides equal, the angles opposite these two sides are equal.

post hoc ergo propter hoc: *after this, therefore on account of this;* the treatment of an event as the effect of a preceding one merely on the ground of its later occurrence.

post mortem: *after death.*

prima facie: *on the first view;* applied to evidence that is convincing at first view, and is valid unless disproved.

pro bono publico: *for the public good,* or *for the state prospering* (like **pessimo publico facere,** Livy, 2, 1, 1).

[1] *Pro Sestio,* 57, 121; Juvenal, 8, 244; used also of Marius, Trajan, and others.

pro et con: for **pro et contra,** *for and against;* often '**pro** and **con.**'

pro rata: for **pro rata parte,** *according to a calculated part, i.e.,* in proportion; **reri,** *think, reckon,* pf. pple. **ratus.** Cf. RATE, RATIO, RATIONS. We have also the English verb PRORATE, made from the phrase.

pro tempore: *for the time, for the time being.*

quasi: *as if, as it were,* or *in a certain sense.*

quid pro quo: *something for something, an equivalent* or *substitution.*

quod erat demonstrandum: *which was to be shown or proved;* **demonstrare,** *show.*

quod erat faciendum: *which was to be done;* **facere,** *do* or *make.*

quondam: *formerly, one time.*

rara avis: *a rare bird; a wonderful thing.*[1]

reductio ad absurdum: *reduction to the absurd;* the proof of a proposition by showing the absurdity of its contradictory opposite.

requiescat in pace: *may he (she) rest in peace;* an old form of epitaph.

res judicāta: *a matter judged, a case* already *decided.*

semper fidēlis: *always faithful.*

sic: *so, thus;* often written parenthetically after a quoted word or phrase which seems quite unreasonable yet is given exactly as it was used.

sine die: *without day; without* appointed *day* for reconvening when a body adjourns.

sine qua non: *without which not; what is essential, an indispensable condition;* the fem. relative agrees with **res,** *thing,* understood.

speculum vitae: *mirror of life.*

status quo: *the situation in which* the matter formerly was. See **in statu quo.**

stet: *let it stand;* 3 sing. subj. of **stare,** *stand;* used in proof reading to restore what has been deleted (cf. **dele**).

sub judice: *under the judge;* hence *still in question,* not yet decided.

sub poena: *under penalty* (written also **subpoena**); a writ requiring a person's appearance in court within a specified time under penalty for failure to do so. The Latin form of such a writ began with the words **sub poena.**

---

[1] Cf. Juvenal, *Satires,* 6, 165; **Rara avis in terris, nigroque simillima cygno,** *A rare bird on earth and very like a black swan.* In Horace, *Satires,* 2, 2, 26, it refers to the peafowl.

sub rosa: *under the rose, i.e., in strict confidence.* We do not know the origin of the phrase. It has been observed that from Egyptian mythology the younger Horus, whose emblem was the rose (or lotus-flower?), was represented in art as a child having his finger in his mouth, and that when this was regarded as a sign not of childishness but of secrecy, he became a god of silence. That this was the origin of the expression **sub rosa** is very doubtful.

sui generis: *of its own kind,* of a class to itself, *unique.*

sui juris: *of one's own right.*

summum bonum: *the highest good.*

supra: *above;* used in references in books (cf. **infra**).

tabula rasa: *a scraped tablet, a clean slate.*

Te Deum: *Thee God,* an ancient hymn of thanksgiving beginning with the words **Te Deum laudamus,** *We praise thee (O) God.*

terminus ad quem: *the end to which, the end toward which* one aims. So **terminus a quo** is *the end from which, i.e., the starting-point.*

terra firma: *firm* or *solid earth.*

terra incognita: *an unknown land.*

tertium quid: *a third something,* something intermediate between two opposites or resulting from the union of two opposing forces; something neither mind nor matter.

toga virīlis: *the manly toga* (52); the toga assumed by the Roman youth when he became of age.

tu quoque: *thou also,* implying that the case of the one to whom it is addressed is quite the same as that of his rival or opponent.

ultima Thule: *farthest Thule,*[1] the land farthest north — it may have been Iceland, some say one of the Shetland Islands. Figuratively, it signifies any far-off mystical place or some unattainable goal.

ultra: *beyond,* as adverb (preposition) probably for **ultra parte** (cf. **extra**), from the adjective which gives **ulterior,** q.v. We use it in compounds, like ULTRA-fashionable, ULTRA-violet. Cf. **ne plus ultra.**

usus loquendi: *usage of speech* (Cicero, *Orator,* 48, 160.)

ut: *as,* occurs in book references like **ut supra,** *as above,* **ut saepe,** *as often.*

vade mecum: *go with me, one's constant companion;* a book or other article constantly carried with one.

[1] Juvenal, 15, 112; Tacitus, *Agricola,* 10.

vae victis: *woe to the vanquished!* After the sack of Rome by the Gauls under Brennus, 390 B.C., as the ransom money was being paid, so Livy says, there was heard the cry intolerable for Romans, **vae victis!** [1]

varia lectio: *a different reading,* in texts of literary works; pl. **variae lectiones.**

variōrum: *of different (men);* a **variōrum** edition of a work is one with notes or readings of various editors, **cum notis variōrum.**

versus (Low Lat. for **adversus**): *against* (see 60, **vs.**); from legal phraseology.

via dolorōsa: *way of sorrow;* the way traversed by Jesus from Pilate's court to the place of crucifixion.

vice versa: *the succession being turned,* the terms being interchanged.

vis inertiae: *the power of inertia,* the power of matter to resist change.

vox populi: *the voice of the people.* See also 61.

60. Many of our most common abbreviations represent Latin words:

@: for **ad,** *at,* in giving a price.

A.B.: **Artium Baccalaureus,** *Bachelor of Arts* (see BACHELOR, 202).

A.C.: **Ante Christum,** *before Christ.*

A.D.: **Anno Domini,** *in the year of (our) Lord.*

ad lib.: **ad libitum,** *at pleasure* (59).

aet. or **ae.:** **aetate** or **aetatis,** *in age* or *of age;* formerly used in giving one's age.

A.M.: **Anno Mundi,** *in the year of the world;* used in older church or Biblical chronology.

A.M.: **Ante Meridiem,** *before midday.*

A.M.: **Artium Magister,** *Master of Arts.*

A.U.C.: **Ab Urbe Condita,** *from the founding of the city,* literally, *from the city founded;* or **Anno Urbis Conditae,** *in the year of the city founded;* used in giving dates from the founding of Rome, 753 B.C.

ca. (also **cir.** and **circ.**): **circa,** *about;* especially in giving approximate dates.

[1] Livy, 5, 48, 9.

cf.: confer, *compare,* imperative of **conferre.**

cwt.: centum-weight, *hundred-weight,* a hybrid formation (207).

d. (written δ in proof reading): **dele,** *destroy, erase* (59); or **deleatur,** *let it be destroyed, erased.*

d.: denarius, *a penny,* in English money.

D.D.: Divinitatis Doctor, *Doctor of Divinity.*

D.D.D.: **Dono Dedit Dedicavit,** a form for the dedication of a book, meaning (the author) *has given and dedicated for a gift;* or **Dat Donat Dicat,** *He gives, presents, dedicates.*

D.G.: **Dei Gratia,** *by the grace of God.*

D.V.: **Deo Volente,** *God being willing.*

e.g.: exempli gratia, *for the sake of example, for example.*

et al.: et alii (aliae), *and others;* also **et alibi,** *and elsewhere.*

etc.: et cetera, *and other things,* commonly read *"and so forth."*

et seq. (also **et sq.,** pl. **et seqq., et sqq.**): et sequens, et sequentes, or **et sequentia,** *and the following, and what follows.*

et ux.: et uxor, *and wife.*

fec.: fecit, *he (she) made* (this), used in signing works of art, the artist's name being inserted as subject.

h.e.: hoc est, *this is;* in explanations, like **i.e.**

H.J.: **Hic Jacet,** *here lies;* or **H.J.S., Hic Jacet Sepultus,** *here lies buried;* found on old tombstones.

ib. or **ibid.:** ibidem, *in the same place, i.e., in the same* work; used in giving additional references to the same literary work.

id.: idem, *the same* (author); used in giving additional references to the same author.

i.e.: id est, *that is,* in adding an explanation.

I.H.S.: **In Hoc Signo** (see **In hoc signo vinces,** 61); also **In Hac (Cruce) Salus,** *in this (cross) safety.*

I.H.S.: **Iesus Hominum Salvator,** *Jesus, Savior of Men.* However, the abbreviation I H S was originally only the first three letters of the Greek word for Jesus (IHΣΟΥΣ), but with their adoption into Latin, and with the Latin aspirate represented by the same character as the Greek long *e* (H), these Latin words were substituted as the meaning of the letters. Similarly they are said to stand in German for 'Iesus Heiland Seligmacher,' *Jesus, Savior, Sanctifier,* and have even been worked back into Greek as 'Iēsous Hēmeteros Sōtēr' ('Ιησοῦς Ἡμέτερος Σωτήρ), *Jesus, our Savior.*

Imp.: Imperator, *Emperor.*

inf.: infra, *below;* in references in a book or document.

in loc.: in loco, *in place, in a* specified *place;* used in references.

I.N.R.I.: Iesus Nazarenus Rex Iudaeorum, *Jesus of Nazareth, King of the Jews,* the Latin inscription on the cross of Christ.

i.q.: idem quod, *the same which, the same as.*

£: *i.e.,* **L,** for **libra,** *pound,* English money.

lb.: libra, *pound.*

l.c. (also **loc. cit.** or **in loc. cit.**): **(in) loco citato,** *in the place cited;* used in references to books.

lib.: liber, *book.*

Litt.D.: Litterarum Doctor: *Doctor of Literature.*

LL.B.: Legum Baccalaureus, *Bachelor of Laws.* See BACHELOR, 202.

LL.D.: Legum Doctor, *Doctor of Laws.*

M.: Meridie, *at midday, at noon.*

M.D.: Medicinae Doctor, *Doctor of Medicine.*

N.B.: Nota Bene, *note well.*

no.: numero, *in number,* abl. sing. of the noun **numerus.**

nol. pros.: nolle prosequi, *not to wish to prosecute,* a form of record indicating that a plaintiff discontinues a suit, or an attorney a prosecution. The abbreviation has even been made into an English verb NOL-PROS.

non seq.: non sequitur, 59.

ob.: obiit, q.v. 59.

op.: opus, *a work,* a single musical composition (52).

per cent.: per centum, q.v. (59). The sign % is a modification of Pc as a further abbreviation of **per cent.**

Ph.B.: Philosophiae Baccalaureus, *Bachelor of Philosophy.* See BACHELOR, 202.

Ph.D.: Philosophiae Doctor, *Doctor of Philosophy.*

pinx. (also **pnxt.** or **pxt.**): **pinxit,** *he (she) painted (this);* used in signing paintings, the artist's name being inserted as subject.

P.M.: Post Meridiem, *after midday, afternoon.*

pro tem.: pro tempore, q.v. 59.

prox.: proximo (mense), *of* (lit. *in*) *next month.*

P.S.: Post Scriptum, *written afterward.*

Q.E.D.: Quod Erat Demonstrandum, q.v. 59.

Q.E.F.: Quod Erat Faciendum, q.v. 59.

Q.E.I.: **Quod Erat Inveniendum,** *which was to be found.*

q.v.: **quod vide,** *which see;* imperative of **videre.**

℞: **Recipe,** *take;* used on prescriptions (see 57).[1]

R.I.P.: **Requiescat In Pace** (59), *Let him (her) rest in peace.*

s.: **solidus,** *shilling,* English money (see SOLDIER, 202).

sc.: **scilicet,** *i.e.,* **scire-licet,** *it is permitted to know, you may under-stand, to wit,* or *being understood,* introducing an explanation or a term to be supplied.

sc. (also **sculp.** or **sculpt.**): **sculpsit,** *he (she) carved* or *sculptured* this; used in signing pieces of sculpture, the artist's name being inserted as subject.

seq. (pl. **seqq.**): **sequentes** or **sequentia** (see **et seq.,** above).

st.: **stet,** q.v. 59.

S.T.D.: **Sacrae** (or **Sanctae**) **Theologiae Doctor,** *Doctor of Sacred Theology* (cf. **D.D.**).

sup.: **supra,** *above;* in references in books.

s.v.: **sub voce** (or **verbo**), *under the word;* in references to word lists or dictionaries.

ult.: **ultimo (mense),** *of* (lit. *in*) *last month.*

ux.: **uxor,** *wife.*

v.: **vide,** *see,* imperative sing. of **videre.**

var. lect.: **varia lectio,** 59; for plural, **vv. ll.**

viz.: **videlicet,** *i.e.,* **videre-licet,** *it is permitted to see* (cf. **sc.**), *to wit, namely.* The z was originally not the letter but a sign indicating an abbreviation, as in *oz.* for *ounce.*

vs. or **v.:** **versus,** *against.*

&: for **&,** *i.e.,* **Et,** *and.*

61. Certain Latin phrases and sentences, some of them having attained the dignity of proverbs, find their way into our common reading. We know the origin of some; others, occurring in Latin authors, may even there have been already proverbial; and still others are mere foundlings whose origin is of no great consequence. We may note the following:

---

[1] It is also said that this ℞ was made from ♃ used as a symbol of Jupiter, and was placed at the head of a prescription to secure the favor of the god that the compound might be effective.

Ab ovo usque ad mala: *From the egg even to the apples, i.e.*, from the beginning to the end of the Roman dinner, as in Horace, *Satires,* 1, 3, 6.

Ad astra per ardua: *To the stars through difficulties.* So we find **Per angusta ad augusta,** *Through straits to honors,* and note the more common expression of the same sentiment in the state motto of Kansas, 62.

Ars longa, vita brevis: *Art (is) long, time short,* or, according to Longfellow, "Art is long and time is fleeting" (*Psalm of Life*). In its Greek form the saying was attributed to the physician Hippocrates [1]; Seneca thus quotes him in *De Brevitate Vitae,* 1, 1.

Aut Caesar aut nullus: *Either Caesar or nobody,* motto of Caesar Borgia; "all in all or not at all."

Ave Caesar, morituri te salutant: *Hail Caesar, those who are about to die salute thee,* the greeting of the gladiators to the Emperor Claudius Caesar just before they engaged in combat, as told by Suetonius, *Life of Claudius,* 21, 6.

Beati possidentes: *Blessed (are) they that possess;* "possession is nine points of the law."

Bis vincit qui se vincit in victoria: *Twice does he conquer who conquers himself in the victory.* Given among maxims of Publilius Syrus, a writer of mimes (dramatic dialogues), of the first century B.C.

Carpe diem: *Seize the day; enjoy the present;* Horace, *Odes,* 1, 11, 8, has the line, **Carpe diem, quam minimum credula postero,** *Enjoy the day, trusting the morrow as little as possible.*

Caveat emptor: *Let the buyer beware* (since the bargain is binding); a law phrase which may easily occur in other than legal language.

Cogito, ergo sum: *I think, therefore I am;* called the basis of the philosophy of the French philosopher Descartes (1596–1650).

De gustibus non est disputandum: *About tastes there must be no disputing;* and we say, "There is no accounting for tastes."

Delenda est Carthago: *Carthage must be destroyed;* now meaning *The fight must be carried to a finish.* The words are said to have been used by Cato the Elder to close every address he made to the Senate, Carthage being Rome's rival and bitter enemy.

---

[1] *Aphorism* 1: Ὁ βίος βραχύς, ἡ δὲ τέχνη μακρή.

De mortuis nil nisi bonum: *About the dead nothing except good;* said to have come in its Greek form from Diogenes Laertius; attributed also to Solon and to Chilo. Any of the sages might have said it.

Dictum sapienti sat est: *A word to the wise is sufficient.* It occurs in Plautus, *Persa*, 4, 7, 19, and in Terence, *Phormio*, 3, 3, 8. Quoted also as **Verbum sapienti sat est.**

Diem perdidi: *I have lost a day;* said to have been the exclamation of the Emperor Titus at a dinner when a day had passed without his doing some good deed. Suetonius, *Life of Titus*, 8, 1.

Docendo discitur: *One learns by teaching;* so **Docendo discimus,** *We learn by teaching.* Seneca, *Epistles*, 7, 8 says **Dum docent, discunt,** (*Men,*) *while they teach, learn.*

Dulce et decorum est pro patria mori: *Sweet and fitting it is to die for one's country.* Used by Horace in *Odes*, 3, 2, 13.

Dum tacet, clamat: *While it is silent, it speaks out;* motto of the Woodmen of the World, adapted from Cicero's words, when in his first oration against Catiline (21), he makes the very silence of the senators a testimony against the traitor, **Cum tacent, clamant.**

Dum vita est, spes est: *While there's life, there's hope.*

Dum vivimus, vivamus: *While we live, let us live;* found in a mediæval collection of proverbs (Inscriptiones Gratuli).

Dux femina facti: *A woman the leader of the deed;* Vergil, *Aeneid*, 1, 364. Cf. the French 'Cherchez la femme.'

Eripuit caelo fulmen, mox sceptra tyrannis: *He wrested the lightning from the sky, then the sceptres from tyrants;* an inscription by Turgot for the Houdon bust of Benjamin Franklin. The same inscription was used on two Franklin medals (1784 and 1786).

Errare humanum est or **Humanum est errare:** *To err is human.* Cf. Cicero, *Philippics*, 12, 2, 5: **Cujusvis hominis est errare,** *It is (natural) for any man to make a mistake.*

Esse quam videri: *To be rather than to seem;* in Sallust's *Catiline*, 54, and Cicero's *De Senectute*, 26.

Exitus acta probat: *The outcome justifies the deeds;* Washington's motto. (Ovid, *Heroides*, 2, 85.)

Ex nihilo nihil fit: *Nothing is made out of nothing.* So Lucretius, 1,

265, **Res . . . docui non posse creari de nilo,** *I have taught that matter cannot be created from nothing.* Cf. also Harvey's law: **Omne vivum ex vivo,** *Every living* (*thing*) *from a living* (*thing*).

Festina lente: *Make haste slowly;* the Latin form of a Greek proverb, a favorite saying of Augustus Caesar. (Suetonius, *Life of Augustus,* 25, 4; σπεῦδε βραδέως.)

Finis opus coronat: *The end crowns the work.*

Fortuna caeca est: *Fortune is blind* (Cicero, *De Senectute* 15, 54).

Fortuna fortes juvat: *Fortune aids the brave;* quoted as a proverb in Terence's *Phormio,* 1, 4, 26. Of like meaning is **Animum fortuna sequitur,** *Fortune follows courage,* and **Audentes fortuna juvat,** *Fortune aids the daring.*

Homo sum, humani nihil a me alienum puto: *I am a man, nothing* (*of the*) *human do I regard as foreign to me.* Terence has this in *Heauton Timorumenos,* 1, 1, 25.

Iacta alea est: *The die is cast.* Thus Julius Caesar, as he crossed the Rubicon, announced his decision to break with Pompey and begin civil war. (Suetonius, *Life of Julius,* 32.)

In hoc signo vinces: *In this sign thou shalt conquer;* the motto of the Emperor Constantine. He is said to have had a vision of a fiery cross in the sky and under the cross these words, or their Greek equivalent, a vision which led to his conversion to Christianity.

In medio tutissimus ibis: *You will go safest in the middle* (course); in Ovid, *Metamorphoses* 2, 137 (without **in**).

Laborare est orare: *To labor is to pray;* the motto of the Benedictine monks.

Magna est veritas: *Great is truth;* also with the addition **et praevalet,** *The truth is mighty and it prevails,* in the Vulgate, III Esdras, 4 : 41.

Mens sana in corpore sano: *A sound mind in a sound body.* This occurs in Juvenal, *Satires,* 10, 356.

Ne moveas Camarinam [1]: *Don't disturb Camarina, i.e.,* "Let well enough alone"; "don't bring on trouble by trying to get rid of trouble." Camarina, a lake in Sicily near the town of the same name, was a source of malaria to the people, who were warned by the Delphic oracle, however, not to drain it. They drained

---

[1] The Greek Μὴ κίνει Καμάριναν.

it and made it possible for the enemy to pass over its bed and plunder the town.

Ne sutor supra crepidam: *Let not the cobbler (judge) above his last.* In a painting made by the great Greek artist Apelles, an error in the shoe latchet was detected by a cobbler, who thereupon presumed to criticize the legs also. The saying is the Latin of Apelles' reply: "Stick to your last." (Pliny, *Natural History*, 35, 36 (10), 22, **ne . . . judicaret.**)

Nil desperandum: *Nothing must be despaired of,* "Never despair," Horace, *Odes*, 1, 7, 27; motto of the Earl of Lichfield.

Non omnis moriar: *I shall not all die* (Horace, *Odes*, 3, 30, 6).

Nulla dies sine linea: *No day without its line.* Pliny, *Natural History*, 35, 36 (10), 22, says that it was the custom of Apelles never to let a day be so busy that he should not by drawing a line practice his art, and from this came the proverb.

Nulla fides fronti: *No trust in the countenance;* also **Ne fronti crede,** *Do not trust the face.* Cf. *Macbeth* I, 4, 11–12, "There is no art to find the mind's construction in the face."

Nullum quod tetigit non ornavit: *Nothing which he touched did he fail to adorn;* Dr. Samuel Johnson's epitaph on Oliver Goldsmith.

Omnia mutantur: *All things change;* Ovid, *Metamorphoses*, 15, 165, says **Omnia mutantur, nihil interit,** *All things change, nothing dies.* To Lotharius (Lothair I), a German emperor of the ninth century, has been attributed the sentence, **Omnia mutantur, nos et mutamur in illis,** *All things change, we also change with (in) them;* quoted sometimes as **Tempora mutantur,** *Times change,* etc.

Omnia vincit Amor: *Love conquers all things;* also said of **Labor,** *labor,* and of **Veritas,** *truth.* (Vergil, *Eclogues*, 10, 69; *Georgics*, 1, 145.)

O tempora! O mores!: *O the times! O the customs!* Cicero's exclamation in the first oration against Catiline (1), as he presents the conditions of the time of his consulship.

Palma non sine pulvere: *No palm without the dust;* "No reward without the struggle." Cf. Horace, *Epistles*, 1, 1, 51.

Palmam qui meruit ferat: *Let him who has won the palm bear it;* the motto of Lord Nelson, also of the Royal Naval School of England. The line comes from a Latin poem by John Jortin.

Poeta nascitur, non fit: *The poet is born, not made;* or with less truth, **Orator fit, poeta nascitur,** *The orator is made, the poet is born.*

Possunt quia posse videntur: *They are able because they seem to be able;* "They can because they think they can"; said of rowers in the boat race in Vergil, *Aeneid,* 5, 231.

Potior est qui prior est: *He is preferred who is earlier;* "First come, first served." Cf. Terence, *Phormio,* 3, 2, 48, **Ut potior sit qui prior est,** *That he may be preferred who is first.*

Principia, non homines: *Principles, not men.*

Quot homines, tot sententiae: *How many people, so many opinions* (Terence, *Phormio,* 2, 4, 14).

Salus populi suprema est lex: *The welfare of the people is the supreme law.* Cf. motto of Missouri, 62.

Senex bis puer: *An old man twice a child;* also in the plural, **Bis pueri senes.**

Si monumentum requiris, circumspice: *If you seek a monument, look around;* epitaph of the architect Sir Christopher Wren in St. Paul's Cathedral in London, the church itself being his own great work. Cf. motto of Michigan, 62.

Sic transit gloria mundi: *So passes the glory of the world.*

Similia similibus curantur: *Likes are cured by likes;* the motto of homeopathy as stated by its founder Samuel Hahnemann.

Sit tibi terra levis: *Be the earth light on thee, may the earth rest lightly on thee;* addressed to the dead, an old epitaph.

Summum jus summa injuria: *Greatest right, greatest wrong;* the utmost enforcement of law may result in injustice.

Tempus fugit: *Time flees, i.e., Time flies.*

Timeo Danaos et dona ferentes: *I fear the Greeks even when bringing gifts;* the enemy are not to be trusted even when they seem friendly (Vergil, *Aeneid,* 2, 49).

Varium et mutabile semper femina: *A fickle and changeable thing always is woman.* (Vergil, *Aeneid,* 4, 569–570.)

Veni, Vidi, Vici: *I came, I saw, I conquered;* the laconic expression of Julius Caesar, following his victory over Pharnaces, king of Pontus, at Zela, B.C. 47 (Plutarch, *Life of Julius Caesar,* 50). Suetonius gives these not as Caesar's words, but as an inscription displayed in his triumphal procession (*Life of Julius,* 37, 2).

Vox populi, vox Dei: *The voice of the people, the voice of God.*

62. Many states of the American Union have Latin mottoes:

Arizona: **Ditat Deus:** *God enriches.*

Arkansas: **Regnant populi:** *The people rule.*

Colorado: **Nil sine numine:** *Nothing without the divine will.*

Connecticut: **Qui transtulit, sustinet:** *He who transplanted, sustains.*

District of Columbia: **Justitia omnibus:** *Justice to all.*

Idaho: **Esto Perpetua:** *Let her be eternal.*

Kansas: **Ad astra per aspera:** *To the stars through difficulties.*

Maine: **Dirigo:** *I direct.*

Maryland: **Scuto bonae voluntatis tuae coronasti nos:** *With the shield of thy good will hast thou crowned us.*

Massachusetts: **Ense petit placidam sub libertate quietem:** *With the sword she seeks peaceful rest under liberty.*

Michigan: **Si quaeris peninsulam amoenam, circumspice:** *If you seek a pleasing peninsula, look around.* Cf. **Si monumentum** etc. in the preceding section.

Missouri: **Salus populi suprema lex esto:** *The safety of the people shall be the supreme law.*

New Mexico: **Crescit eundo:** *It increases by going;* it grows as it goes (Lucretius, 6, 341). Vergil (*Aeneid*, 4, 175) says of Rumor, **Vires acquirit eundo,** *It gains strength as it goes.*

New York: **Excelsior:** *Higher.*

North Carolina: **Esse quam videri:** *To be rather than to seem* (see 61).

South Carolina: **Animis opibusque parati. Dum spiro spero:** *In spirit and resources prepared* (Vergil, *Aeneid*, 2, 799). *While I breathe I hope.*

Virginia: **Sic semper tyrannis:** *Thus always to tyrants.*

West Virginia: **Montani semper liberi:** *Mountaineers always free.*

Wyoming: **Cedant arma togae:** *Let arms give place to the toga.* (Cicero, *De Officiis*, 1, 22, 77; *In Pisonem*, 30, 73). See **toga,** 52.

United States: **E pluribus unum:** *From many one,* or *One of many;* one government of many states. Vergil's *Moretum*, 104, in describing the mixture of ingredients of a dish prepared, says, **Color est e pluribus unus.**

63. Colleges and universities often use Latin mottoes to express their aims or purposes. Many others could be added to the following list:

American University: **Pro Deo et Patria:** *For God and Native Land.*

Amherst: **Terras irradient:** *Let them illumine the lands.*

Arizona, University: **Sursum:** *Upwards.*

Brown: **In Deo speramus:** *In God we hope.*

Bryn Mawr: **Veritatem dilexi:** *I have loved the Truth.*

Catholic University of America: **Deus lux mea:** *God my light.*

Chicago: **Crescat scientia, vita excolatur:** *Let knowledge increase, let life be perfected.*

Cincinnati University: **Juncta juvant. Alta petit:** *Union is strength* (lit. *things joined together help*). *It seeks the heights.*

Clark: **Fiat lux:** *Let there be light.*

Columbia: **In lumine tuo videbimus lumen:** *In thy light shall we see light* (Psalm 36 : 9).

Dartmouth: **Vox clamantis in deserto:** *The voice of one crying in the wilderness* (Matthew 3 : 3).

Delaware, University: **Scientia sol mentis est:** *Knowledge is the sun of the mind.*

Denver University: **Pro scientia et religione:** *For science and religion.*

Duke: **Eruditio et Religio:** *Learning and Religion.*

Emory University: **Lex, Lux:** *Law, Light.*

George Washington: **Deus nobis fiducia:** *God our trust* (lit. *for us*).

Georgia, University: **Et discere et rerum exquirere causas:** *Both to learn and to investigate the causes of things.*

Goucher: **Gratia et Veritas:** *Grace and Truth.*

Harvard: **Veritas. Christo et Ecclesiae:** *Truth. For Christ and the Church.*

Illinois, University: **Labor omnia vincit:** *Labor conquers all things.* See Oklahoma, University.

Indiana, University: **Lux et Veritas:** *Light and Truth.* See Yale.

Johns Hopkins: **Veritas vos liberabit:** *The truth shall make you free.* Cf. Tennessee, University.

Michigan, University: **Artes, Scientia, Veritas:** *Arts, Science, Truth.*

Missouri, University: **Salus populi:** *Safety of the people.* Cf. motto of the State of Missouri in the preceding section.

Nebraska, University: **Litteris dedicata et omnibus artibus:** *Dedicated to literature and all the arts.*

North Carolina, University: **Lux, Libertas:** *Light, Liberty.*

North Dakota, University: **Lux et Lex:** *Light and Law* (cf. Emory University).

Northwestern: **Quaecumque sunt vera:** *Whatsoever things are true* (Philippians 4 : 8).

Notre Dame: **Crux spes unica:** *The cross the only hope.*

Oklahoma, University: **Labor omnia vincit:** *Labor conquers all things* (see Illinois, University).

Oregon, University: **Mens agitat molem:** *Mind moves the mass.*

Pennsylvania, University: **Litterae sine moribus vanae:** *Literature without character is vain.*

Pittsburgh: **Veritas et Virtus:** *Truth and Virtue.*

Princeton: **Dei sub numine viget:** *It flourishes under the will of God.*

South Carolina, University: **Emollit mores nec sinit esse feros:** *Makes gentle the character and does not allow it to be unrefined* (Ovid, *Epistles from Pontus,* 2, 9, 48).

Southern Methodist University: **Veritas liberabit vos:** *The truth shall make you free* (cf. Tennessee, University).

Tennessee, University: **Veritatem cognoscetis et veritas vos liberabit:** *Ye shall know the truth and the truth shall make you free* (John 8 : 32).

Texas, University: **Disciplina praesidium civitatis:** *Instruction the safeguard of the state.*

University of the South: **Ecce quam bonum:** *Behold how good* (Psalm 133 : 1).

Vermont, University: **Studiis et rebus honestis:** *For studies and noble achievements.*

Washington: **Per veritatem vis,** *Through truth power.*

Wellesley: **Non ministrari sed ministrare:** *Not to be ministered unto but to minister* (Matthew 20 : 28; Mark 10 : 45).

Yale: **Lux et Veritas,** *Light and Truth* (see Indiana, University).

64. The use of Latin titles for works of English literature has been common from John Gower to the present time. The title used may be a well-known Latin phrase or it may

be of the author's making.   The following rather random
list will illustrate:

Annus Mirabilis (Dryden), *The Wonderful Year*, a poem giving
the remarkable events of the year 1666.

Apologia pro Sua Vita (Cardinal Newman), *A Defense of His Own
Life*.

Aratra Pentelici (Ruskin), *Plowshares of Pentelicus;* six lectures on
sculpture, delivered at the University of Oxford, 1870.

Astraea Redux (Dryden), *Astraea Returned;* Astraea was the goddess
of Justice who, following the Golden Age, left the earth on
account of the wickedness of men.

Auspex (Lowell), *The Diviner, i.e., Observer of the Birds* (AUSPICES,
202).

Carmen Triumphale (Southey), *Song of Triumph*.

Confessio Amantis (John Gower), *The Confession of a Lover*.

De Profundis (Mrs. Browning, also Oscar Wilde and others), *Out
of the Depths* (Psalm 130 : 1).

Dei Sponsa (Patmore), *The Bride of God*.

Desideria (Wordsworth), *Longings*.

Dominus Mea Illuminatio (Blackmore), *The Lord My Light*.

E Tenebris (Oscar Wilde), *Out of the Darkness*.

Excelsior (Longfellow), *Higher*.

Ex Ore Infantium (Francis Thompson), *Out of the Mouth of Babes*
(Psalm 8 : 2).

Fors Clavigera (Ruskin), *Fortune with the Nail;* referring to an
Etruscan design representing Atropos fastening a nail into a
beam with a hammer; also to Horace, *Odes*, 1, 35, 17–20.

In Memoriam (Tennyson, also Mary Lamb, Edwin Arnold, and
others), *In* or *For Memory*.

Laus Deo (Whittier), *Praise to God*.

Lux Est Umbra Dei (Symonds), *The Light Is the Shadow of God*.

Magna Christi Americana (Cotton Mather), *Great Works of Christ
in America*.

Magna Est Veritas (Patmore), *Great Is Truth* (61).

Mari Magno (Clough), *On the Great Sea*, or "Tales on Board."

Memorabilia (Browning), *Recollections* (*things worthy to be remembered*).

Morituri Salutamus (Longfellow), *We About to Die Salute.* See 61, **Ave Caesar,** etc.

Mors Benefica (Stedman), *Kindly Death.*

Munera Pulveris (Ruskin), *Gifts of the Dust* (Essays on Political Economy); referring to Horace, *Odes,* 1, 28, 1–4.

Nosce Teipsum (Davies), *Know Thyself.*

Pater Filio (Bridges), *Father to Son.*

Pro Patria (Thomas Moore), *For the Native Land.*

Qua Cursum Ventus (Clough), *Where the Wind (Guides) Their Course.*

Qui Laborat Orat (Clough), *Who Labors Prays.* Cf. **Laborare est orare,** 61.

Religio Laici (Dryden), *The Religion of a Layman.*

Religio Medici (Sir Thomas Browne), *The Religion of a Physician.*

Sartor Resartus (Carlyle), *The Tailor Retailored.*

Simplex Munditiis (Ben Jonson), *Simple in Neatness* ("Of unadorned neatness," Horace, *Odes,* 1, 5, 5).

Solvitur Acris Hiems (Clough), *Severe Winter Is Melting Away* (Horace, *Odes,* 1, 4, 1).

Super Flumina Babylonis (Swinburne), *By the Rivers of Babylon* (Psalm 137 : 1).

Sursum Corda (Mrs. Browning), *Lift up Your Hearts* (lit. *Upward hearts*).

Tempora Acta (Lytton), *Times Past.* Cf. **laudator,** etc., 59.

Via Crucis (F. Marion Crawford), *The Way of the Cross* (A Romance of the Second Crusade).

Virginibus Puerisque (Stevenson), *For Girls and Boys.* — Horace, *Odes,* 3, 1, 4, **Virginibus puerisque canto,** *I sing for girls and boys.*

Since translations become so well known we might include such titles as **Quo Vadis** (Sienkiewicz), *Whither Goest Thou?* and **Mare Nostrum** (Ibáñez), *Our Sea,* (*i.e.,* the Mediterranean. Cf. Caesar, *Gallic War,* 5, 1, etc.).

65. Songs are often known by Latin titles, frequently the first word or phrase, if the song originally was written and sung in Latin. The title may also be transferred to the music. Such are these:

Ave Maria, *Hail Mary* (see **Ave,** 57), an anthem with various musical settings used in the church from a very early period.

Dies Irae, *The Day of Wrath,* a Latin hymn of the thirteenth century, set to music by Mozart, Gounod, Verdi, and others.

Lux Benigna, *Kindly Light,* music by Dykes for Cardinal Newman's hymn *Lead Kindly Light.*

Magnificat, *Doth Magnify,* a hymn beginning **Magnificat anima mea Dominum,** *My soul doth magnify the Lord,* a version of Luke 1 : 46–55, used in the vesper service of the Western Church from about A.D. 500.

Miserere, *Have Mercy, i.e.,* **Miserere mei, Domine,** *Have mercy on me, O Lord,* the beginning of Psalm 51. The musical composition for the Good Friday service of the Sistine Chapel is by Gregorio Allegri (d. 1640).

Salve Regina, *Hail Queen,* the title of an old Catholic hymn to the Virgin, beginning **Salve Regina Misericordiae,** *Hail, Queen of Mercy.*

Stabat Mater, *The Mother Was Standing (i.e.,* the Mother of Jesus), the beginning of a hymn accredited to Jacobus de Benedictis (1300), the music by Haydn, Rossini, and others.

66. Certain great paintings we know by their Latin titles; such are:

Angelus: the work by Millet representing two peasants who, hearing the bell, pause to recite the **Angelus.** This was a form of devotion commemorating the Annunciation, beginning **Angelus Domini nuntiavit Mariae,** *The angel of the Lord announced to Mary.*

Beata Beatrix, *Blessed Beatrice,* by Rossetti; Dante's Beatrice, made, however, as a portrait of the painter's wife.

Ecce Ancilla Domini: *Behold the Handmaid of the Lord* (Luke 1 : 38), the Annunciation, by Rossetti.

Ecce Homo: *Behold the Man,* the presentation of Christ to the people by Pilate (John 19 : 5). This has been painted by various artists, as Correggio, Guido, Titian, Murillo, Van Dyck, Rembrandt.

Mater Dolorosa, *The Sorrowing Mother,* representing Mary in sorrow for the sufferings of her son; notably the painting by Titian.

Muscipula, *The Mousetrap,* by Joshua Reynolds (cf. **-cipula,** 121 end).

Noli Me Tangere, *Touch Me Not:* words of Jesus to Mary Magdalene (John 20 : 17), in the scene painted by Correggio; also by Titian.

Pollice Verso, *The Thumb Turned* (59), by J. L. Gérôme.

Salvator Mundi, *The Savior of the World,* by Antonello da Messina.

Sibylla Palmifera, *The Sibyl Carrying a Palm,* Rossetti's painting illustrating his sonnet of that name.

Venus Verticordia, *Venus, Turner of Hearts,* also by Rossetti.

CHAPTER III

WORD FORMATION IN LATIN

67. For an understanding and appreciation of the relationship existing between Latin derivatives in English, it is necessary to observe the relationship that existed between their originals in Latin. In this chapter, therefore, will be given the chief features of Latin word formation as illustrated in our derivatives.

The simplest element common to a group of related words is called a *root*. From such an element numbers of words were made by the use of prefixes and suffixes. **Ag-** was a root meaning *do;* add suffixes **-ent, -tus** (or **-tum**), **-ilis, -tio(n), -tor,** and we have **agens** (**agent-is**), **actus** (or **actum**), **agilis, actio(n), actor;** Eng. AGENT, ACT, AGILE, ACTION, ACTOR — primary derivatives. To some of these other suffixes were added: **act + ivus, actu + alis** (Late Lat.), **agili + tas, act-ivi + tas;** Eng. ACTIVE, ACTUAL, AGILITY, ACTIVITY — secondary derivatives. Again, a new verb stem was formed to make **agitare,** *keep doing, move repeatedly, disturb,* giving **agita-tus, agita-tio(n), agita-tor,** Eng. AGITATE, AGITATION, AGITATOR. Prefixes helped make other words giving us COGENT (123), REAGENT, REACT, INACTIVE, COGITATE. With such means of word-building in mind, we may consider (I) the formation of nouns, (II) the formation of adjectives, and (III) the formation of verbs.

I. THE FORMATION OF NOUNS

A. NOUNS MADE FROM OTHER NOUNS

68. Diminutives were formed by using the suffixes **-(u)lus, -olus** (after a vowel), and **-culus,**[1] the derivative usually

[1] *I.e.,* **-cu-lu-s, -co-lo;** originally two diminutive suffixes.

following the gender of the word from which it was made. The English ends in -ULE or -CLE (but sometimes uses the Latin word).

animal, *animal,* **animalculum,** *a little animal,* an ANIMALCULE or **animalculum.**

artus, *a joint,* **articulus,** *a little joint, a point,* a small member of a sentence, ARTICLE. Cf. the ritualistic phrase, "the hour and ARTICLE (*i.e.,* point) of death." The verb, **articulare,** was *to divide one's speech into its members,* utter each little member distinctly, ARTICULATE.

auris, *ear,* **auricula,** *little ear, the flap of the ear,* AURICLE, a division of the heart.

avus, *grandfather,* **avunculus,**[1] *a little grandfather,* perhaps originally as a term of affection, *grandpapa;* then *a mother's brother,* becoming through the French, UNCLE. It has also been suggested that he was called **avunculus** because, while of the same degree of kinship to his sister's children as their grandfather (**avus**) was, he had less authority.

calx, *a stone* (used as a counter in gaming), **calculus,** *a little stone,* likewise a counter for reckoning; Eng. **calculus** (52), and CALCULATE (128).

capsa, *box,* **capsula,** *a little box,* CAPSULE.

corpus, *body,* **corpusculum,** *a little body,* CORPUSCLE.

cutis, *skin,* **cuticula,** *little skin,* CUTICLE.

forma, FORM, **formula,** *a little form,* Eng. **formula.**

gladius, *sword,* **gladiolus,** *a little sword, a sword lily,* **gladiolus.**

globus, *a ball,* GLOBE, **globulus,** *a little ball,* GLOBULE.

granum, a GRAIN, **granulum,** *a little grain,* a GRANULE.

manica, used in pl. **manicae,** *a long sleeve, gauntlet, handcuff,* from **manus,** *hand;* **manicula,** OF 'manicle,' Mid. Eng. 'manycle,' later MANACLE.

pars, partis, a PART, **particula,** *a little part,* PARTICLE.

rivus, *a stream,* **rivulus,** *a little stream,* RIVULET. This English word

---

[1] Nouns in **-on-** (3rd decl.), adding **-culus** made derivatives in **-unculus,** *e.g.,* **carbo(n), carbunculus,** 202. This combination suffix is found in a few nouns of other stems.

is a double diminutive, combining the Latin form with the suffix -(*l*)*et*.[1]

scrupus, *a sharp stone*, **scrupulus**, *a little sharp stone*, from which SCRUPLE, 202.

venter, *belly*, **ventriculum**, (*little*) *stomach*, also VENTRICLE of the heart, evidently from its shape.

69. Simple **-lus** appears as the diminutive suffix in **castellum** from **castrum**, *a fortified place* (pl. **castra**, *camp*), as if '**caster-lum**,' *a little fortified place*, a CASTLE; so **cerebr-um**, **cerebellum** for '**cereb(e)r-lum**'; **corona**, '**coron-la**,' **corolla**; **libra**, *a balance*, '**lib(e)r-la**,' **libella**, a LEVEL (202); **liber**, *book*, '**liber-lus**,' **libellus**, *a little book*, a LIBEL. (See 148.)

70. The suffix **-atus** (Eng. **-ATE**) denotes office.

consul, *consul*, **consulatus**, *the office of consul, consulship*, and so CONSULATE.

magister, MASTER (45), *officer*, **magistratus**, *an office*, a MAGISTRACY (thus distinguished from MAGISTRATE); Lat. **magistratus** was used both of the office and of the officer.

pontifex, **pontificis**, *the chief priest*, PONTIFF (202), **pontificatus**, *pontiff's office*, PONTIFICATE.

senex, **senis**, *an old man*, **senatus**, *the office of the old man, the group of senators*, SENATE.

tribunus, a TRIBUNE, **tribunatus**, *tribuneship;* so TRIBUNATE.

triumvir, *one* of a board *of three men*, **triumviratus**, *the board of three*, TRIUMVIRATE. The word **trium-vir** was made as a nom. sing. from the gen. pl. **trium-virorum** as a compound.

71. Many nouns in **-ius, -ium, -arius, -arium, -orium,** made from other nouns are evidently but gender forms of adjectives (101, 102). They denote place or position, or as adjectives, meant *pertaining to, having to do with*. Most of these in English end in **-Y** (**-ARY**), or **-ium** may be lost and if *c* (*t*) or *g* precedes, the English has **-CE** or **-GE**.

---

[1] This diminutive suffix seems to have originated from the addition of the OF '-et' ('-ete') to words in -*l* representing Lat. **-ellum** or **-ale**.

adversus, *turned against, opposed to,* **adversarius,** *opposing,* AD-
VERSARY.

aestus, *tide,* **aestuarium,** *a place subject to the tides,* (*e* for *ae*) an
ESTUARY.

antiquus, *ancient,* **antiquarius,** *concerned with the ancient,* an ANTI-
QUARY.

apis, *a bee,* **apiarium,** *a place for bees,* an APIARY.

aqua, *water,* **aquarium,** *a place for water,* an AQUARIUM.

artifex (**artific-**), *a doer of art* (**ars, artis** + **facere**), **artificium,** *work
of the artist, skill,* ARTIFICE.

auditor, *a hearer,* **auditorium,** *place of the hearer* (52).

augur, *a diviner,* **augurium,** *the work of an augur,* AUGURY.

auspex (**auspic-**), *a prophet,* **auspicium,** *the prophet's divination,*
AUSPICES (pl.) 202.

avis, *a bird,* **aviarium,** *a place for birds,* an AVIARY.

calendae (**Kalendae**), the CALENDS, *the first day of the month,* **ca-
lendarium,** *what pertains to the beginning of months;* hence CAL-
ENDAR.

calva, *a skull,* the head with hair (and scalp) removed, from **calvus,**
bald. So **calvaria,** also *skull,* or in ecclesiastical Latin, *the place
of a skull,* CALVARY, the place of the crucifixion of Christ; a
translation of 'Golgotha,' the Greek rendering of an Aramaic
word for *skull.*

collega, *a comrade,* a COLLEAGUE (**con-legere,** *choose*), **collegium,** *a
gathering of colleagues,* a COLLEGE.

dies, *day,* **diarium,** *an allowance for a day, what belongs to a day,* a
DIARY.

emissus, *sent out* (pf. pple. of **emittere**), **emissarius,** an EMIS-
SARY.

factor, *a maker;* **factorium** should be a place for making things,
and it is in this sense that we have FACTORY. The Lat. **factorium,**
when used at all, was *an oil-press,* and the Med. Lat. **factoria**
was *a treasury.* Our word, like Fr. 'factorie,' returns to the
proper meaning of **factor** and **facere.**

granum, a GRAIN, **granarium** (or pl. **-ia**), *a place for storing grain,* a
GRANARY.

herba, an HERB, **herbarium,** *a place for* specimens *of plants, a collection of* dried *plants,* an **herbarium.**

hospes, hospitis, *a guest,* **hospitium,** *a place for guests,* a HOSPICE. Cf. HOSPITAL.

lapis, lapidis, *a stone,* **lapidarius,** *one having to do with stone,* a LAPIDARY.

liber, *book,* **librarius,** *one dealing with books, bookseller* (cf. LIBRA-RIAN), **librarium,** *a place for books,* a LIBRARY. **Liber** was originally the *inner bark* of a tree, used in an early time for writing tablets. Cf. **codex,** 52.

merx, mercis, *merchandise,* with **com-, commercium,** *getting merchandise together* for exchange, COMMERCE.

minister, *a servant* (54), **ministerium,** *the work of a servant,* MINISTRY (for 'ministery').

natator, *a swimmer* (**natare,** *swim*), **natatorium,** *a place for swimming,* adopted into English.

nota, *a note,* **notarius,** *one who writes notes* or *documents,* a shorthand writer, *a secretary,* a NOTARY.

sal, *salt,* **salarium,** *a soldier's money for providing salt,* SALARY.

semen, seminis, *seed,* **seminarium,** *a place for seed, a nursery for plants;* then a place for cultivating minds ("teaching young ideas to shoot"), a SEMINARY.

servus, *a slave,* **servitium** (on analogy of stems in -t), *a slave's work,* or *position, slavery,* SERVICE.

vicis (gen.), *a change, a turn;* **vicarius,** *taking another's place,* VICARIOUS; as noun, VICAR, holding a benefice under another officer or as deputy.

B. NOUNS MADE FROM ADJECTIVES

72. Quality nouns were formed in Latin with the suffix -tat (nom. -tas for -tats), which became French '-té' ('-tet,' 168), English -TY; in most instances *i* precedes the suffix (140, N. 1):

acerbus, *bitter,* **acerbitas,** ACERBITY.

aequalis, EQUAL, **aequalitas,** (*e* for *ae*) EQUALITY.

aequus, *level,* EQUAL, *fair,* **aequitas,** (*e* for *ae*) EQUITY. Cf. **iniquus** (**in** + **aequus**), *unfair,* **iniquitas,** lit. *unfairness,* INIQUITY.

aeternus (for **aevi-ternus,** *age-long*), ETERNAL, **aeternitas,** (*e* for *ae*) ETERNITY.

alacer, *eager, quick,* alacritas, ALACRITY.

amoenus, *pleasant,* amoenitas, (*e* for *oe*) AMENITY.

antiquus, *ancient,* antiquitas, ANTIQUITY.

asper, *rough,* asperitas, ASPERITY.

assiduus, *persistent* (ad-sidere, *sit down to* a thing), assiduitas, ASSIDUITY.

atrox, atrocis, *horrible, savage,* atrocitas, ATROCITY.

avidus, *eager, greedy,* aviditas, AVIDITY.

benignus (cf. bene, bonum; gen-, gn-, gignere, *beget*), *good-natured, kind,* benignitas, BENIGNITY.

brevis, *short,* brevitas, BREVITY.

celeber, *renowned,* celebritas, CELEBRITY (extended in English to apply to a celebrated person).

civilis, *belonging to a citizen* (civis), civilitas, CIVILITY.

comis, *friendly,* comitas, *friendliness,* COMITY.

debilis, *weak* (de-habilis, *un-*ABLE, 114), debilitas, *weakness,* DEBILITY.

declivis, *sloping down,* declivitas, DECLIVITY.

dignus, *worthy,* dignitas, DIGNITY (43).

facilis, *easy* (do-able, facere, *do*), facilitas, *ease,* FACILITY. An old (adverb) form was facul, appearing in facultas, *ability to do,* FACULTY. In like manner from difficilis, older difficul, we have difficultas, DIFFICULTY. (Our DIFFICULT evidently borrows its *t* from the noun.) The oldest sense of FACULTY in English seems to have been *a branch of learning,* facultas serving in Mediæval Latin to translate Aristotle's 'dynamis' (δύναμις), *power,* used with that meaning. So it came to mean a department of a university, and now the corps of teachers of the institution.

familiaris (familia, 99) *belonging to the family,* familiaritas, FAMILIARITY.

gravis, *heavy, severe,* GRAVE, gravitas, GRAVITY.

heres, heredis, HEIR, hereditas, HEREDITY.

honestus, *honorable,* HONEST, honestas (for honestitas), *honorableness,* HONESTY. (Neut. stem hones-, cf. modestus, 74.)

humilis, *lowly* (humus, *the ground*), humilitas, HUMILITY.

immunis, *exempt from service* (in, *not* + munus, *service*), immunitas, IMMUNITY.

levis, *light,* levitas, LEVITY.

liber, *free*, libertas, LIBERTY.

loquax, loquacis, *talkative*, loquacitas, LOQUACITY.

majus, *greater*, (-es stem) majestas, *greatness*, MAJESTY.

mendax, mendacis, *lying*, mendacitas, MENDACITY.

necesse (neut.), *unavoidable* (ne + ced-, *"no way to go"* [?]), necessitas, NECESSITY.

pauci (pl.), *few*, paucitas, *fewness, scarcity*, PAUCITY.

posterus, *later*, posteritas, *later time*, POSTERITY.

qualis, *of what kind*, qualitas,[1] QUALITY.

quantus, *how much*, quantitas,[1] QUANTITY.

rapidus, *swift* (rapere, *snatch away*), rapiditas, *swiftness*, RAPIDITY.

sanus, *sound, whole*, SANE, sanitas, *saneness*, SANITY.

securus, *free from care* (202), *safe*, securitas, SECURITY.

simplex, simplicis, *single*, SIMPLE, simplicitas, SIMPLICITY.

universus (uni-versus, *turned into one*), *all together, general*, universitas, *a whole, a corporation*, UNIVERSITY (with possibly, in modern usage, some reference to its dealing with the whole field of knowledge).

unus, *one*, unitas, UNITY.

utilis, *useful*, utilitas, *usefulness*, UTILITY.

vicinus, *of the (same) village* (vicus), *neighboring*, vicinitas, *proximity*, then *neighborhood*, VICINITY.

virilis, *manly*, virilitas, VIRILITY.

73. In the case of adjectives in -ius, second declension, e (varied from o of the stem) is used before the suffix -tat- and accordingly appears in the English word, thus:

anxius, *distressed*, ANXIOUS, anxietas, ANXIETY.

pius, *dutiful; dutiful to the gods*, PIOUS, pietas, PIETY.

proprius, *one's own, characteristic, suitable*, PROPER, proprietas, PROPRIETY; the older meanings of *ownership* and *peculiarity* are obsolete. Cf. PROPERTY, 30.

sobrius, SOBER, *not drunk*, sobrietas, SOBRIETY.

socius, *sharing*, as noun *ally, fellow* (sequi, *follow*, 157), societas,

---

[1] From the Greek adjectives 'poios' (ποῖος), *of what kind*, and 'posos' (πόσος), *how much*, Aristotle coined the philosophic terms 'poiotēs' (ποιότης), and 'posotēs' (ποσότης), *of-what-kind-ness*, and *how-much-ness*, which Cicero translated qualitas and quantitas.

fellowship, SOCIETY; cf. ASSOCIATION, made from **associare** (85), **ad + socius**, *join to as a partner.*

varius, *different*, VARIOUS, **varietas**, VARIETY.

Likewise, **satis**, *enough*, **satietas**, SATIETY.

74. Abstract nouns were also made with the suffix **-ia**, Eng. -Y:

controversus (**contro-** like **contra-**), *turned against*, **controversia**, CONTROVERSY.

contumax (**contumac-**), *insolent* (**con-tumere**, *swell up*), **contumacia**, CONTUMACY.

efficax (**efficac-**), *accomplishing* (**efficere**, *accomplish*), **efficacia**, EFFICACY.

fallax (**fallac-**), *deceitful* (**fallere**, *deceive*), **fallacia**, FALLACY.

infamis (**in + fama**), *not (well) spoken of* (**fari**, *speak*), INFAMOUS, **infamia**, INFAMY.

memor, *mindful*, **memoria**, MEMORY.

miser, *wretched*, **miseria**, MISERY.

modestus (neut. stem **modes-**; cf. **moderator**, 52; **modus**, o-stem, *measure*), *moderate*, MODEST, **modestia**, MODESTY.

perfidus, *faithless* (**per + fides**, 144), **perfidia**, PERFIDY.

victor, *conqueror*, **victoria**, VICTORY.

Also from the noun **nomen** with negative **in-**, **ignominia**, *(having) no name, disrepute*, IGNOMINY. (Cf. INFAMY, above.) For **i-gno-** cf. **cognomen**, 52. From **concors** (**concord-**), *having hearts together*, and **discors** (**discord-**), *having hearts apart*, came **concordia** and **discordia**, both of which are shortened in English, CONCORD and DISCORD. Similarly, **vigil**, *watchful*, **vigilia**, *a watch, a guard*, Eng. VIGIL. **Inertia**, from **iners** (142), has been adopted as an English word. The noun **custos, custodis**, *guardian*, gave **custodia**, CUSTODY; and from **famulus**, *a servant*, **familia**, *the whole group of servants;* then the whole *household* and retinue[1]; FAMILY. Of like formation with the above is **injuria**, INJURY (**in-** not,

[1] Cf. Caesar, *Gallic War*, I, 4, **Omnem suam familiam ad hominum milia decem.**

and **jus, juris,** *a right*) with the corresponding adjective **injurius.** **Gratia,** from **gratus,** *pleasing,* following such words as those given in 75, 76, below, became GRACE in English (176).

75. Adjectives with stem in -nt, including many present participles, formed quality nouns with this suffix -ia, the -tia appearing in English as -CE or -CY [1] (176):

absens, *being away,* ABSENT, **absentia,** ABSENCE.

abundans, *overflowing,* ABUNDANT, **abundantia,** ABUNDANCE.

arrogans, *claiming* (*too much*) *for oneself* (123), ARROGANT, **arrogantia,** ARROGANCE.

clemens, *gentle, mild,* **clementia,** CLEMENCY.

constans, *standing together, standing firm,* CONSTANT, **constantia,** CONSTANCY.

continens, *holding together, restraining* (*oneself*), **continentia,** CONTINENCE.

diligens (di + **legere,** *choose apart* from others), *esteeming, careful in choosing,* DILIGENT, **diligentia,** DILIGENCE.

efficiens, *accomplishing,* EFFICIENT, **efficientia,** EFFICIENCY.

elegans (like the pple. **eligens**), *choosing, tasteful,* ELEGANT, **elegantia,** ELEGANCE.

frequens, *repeated,* FREQUENT, **frequentia,** FREQUENCY.

indigens (for **indu-,** old prefix = **in-,** 144, and **egere,** *need*), *lacking,* INDIGENT, **indigentia,** INDIGENCE.

magnificus (comparative and superlative on a stem **magnificent-**), *great-doing,* MAGNIFICENT, **magnificentia,** MAGNIFICENCE.

negligens (**nec-legere**), *unheeding,* NEGLIGENT, **negligentia,** NEGLIGENCE. See RELIGION, 32.

patiens, *suffering, enduring,* PATIENT, **patientia,** PATIENCE.

perseverans, *continuing strictly* (cf. **per-severus,** *very strict*), PERSEVERing, **perseverantia,** PERSEVERANCE.

[1] Latin words ending thus had the accent on the antepenult. The influence of Greek abstract nouns in -*ia* introduced into Latin was toward accenting the Latin word as -i'a. The variation in accent accounts for the variation in English endings, for regularly the form '-ntia would give Fr. '-nce,' English -*nce,* while -nti'a would become Fr. '-ncie,' Eng. -*ncy.* Cf. also -a'ria and -ari'a, the former like **-arius** giving Eng. -*ary,* the latter becoming the suffix -*ery* or -*ry.*

petulans, *attacking (in jests;* cf. **petere,** *rush at*)*, insolent,* PETULANT, **petulantia,** PETULANCE.

providens, *foreseeing,* PROVIDENT, **providentia,** PROVIDENCE.

prudens (contracted from **providens**), PRUDENT, **prudentia,** PRU-DENCE.

76. Following the analogy of stems in **-t (-nt),** a few adjectives in **-us,** second declension, used **-tia (-i-ti-a)** in making the corresponding noun, Eng. -CE (-ICE).

avarus, *desirous* (cf. **avere,** *long for*), **avaritia,** AVARICE.

justus, *righteous* (**jus,** *right*), JUST, **justitia,** JUSTICE.

malus, *bad,* **malitia,** MALICE.

notus, *known* (**noscere,** *know*), **notitia,** NOTICE, *i.e., knowledge.*

77. Similar to the above, but strictly coined words (203), are a number of English nouns in -ACY made either purely on analogy (cf. FALLACY, EFFICACY, CONSTANCY), or else from Med. Lat. **-atia (-acia).** Such are these:

accuratus (**ad-curare, cura,** *care, devote care to*), *done with care,* so ACCURACY, but Lat. **accuratio.**

confoederatus (**con** + **foedus, foederis,** *agreement*), *bound together by agreement;* from this CONFEDERACY (Late Lat. **confoederatio**).

effeminatus (**ex-, ec** + **femina,** *woman*), *made feminine,* EFFEMINACY, Lat. **effeminatio.**

intimatus (**intimare**), *made known,* from **intimus,** *inmost* (superl., cf. **interior,** 53), INTIMACY. Our adj. INTIMATE follows more closely the meaning of **intimus.**

luna, *moon,* **lunaticus,** LUNATIC (97), LUNACY.

obstinatus (**obstinare,** *be determined*), OBSTINATE, OBSTINACY.

supremus, *highest,* SUPREME, SUPREMACY (Fr. 'suprématie') following PRIMACY from **primus,** for which there was a Low Lat. **primatia.**

78. Nouns of quality were often made with the suffix **-tudo(n), -tudin-, i** preceding the suffix (140, N. 1), Eng. -TUDE (Fr. '-tude'). This corresponds in meaning to English '-ness':

altus, *high*, altitudo, ALTITUDE.

amplus, *large, spacious*, AMPLE, amplitudo, AMPLITUDE.

beatus, *happy, blessed*, beatitudo, BEATITUDE.

fortis, *brave, courageous*, fortitudo, FORTITUDE.

lassus, *weary*, lassitudo, LASSITUDE.

latus, *wide*, latitudo, LATITUDE (201).

longus, LONG, longitudo, LONGITUDE (201).

magnus, *great*, magnitudo, MAGNITUDE.

multus, *much*, pl. *many*, multitudo, MULTITUDE.

pulcher, *beautiful*, pulchritudo, PULCHRITUDE.

quietus, QUIET, quietudo (for 'quietitudo'), QUIETUDE.

servus, *slavish*, as noun *slave*, servitudo, SERVITUDE.

similis, *like*, similitudo, SIMILITUDE.

sollicitus, *wholly moved* (sollus, *whole;* ciere, citus, *stir*), *anxious*, SOLICITOUS, solicitudo, SOLICITUDE.

solus, *alone*, SOLE, solitudo, SOLITUDE.

turpis, *shameful*, turpitudo, TURPITUDE.

vicis (gen. of a noun, no nom.), *interchange* (cf. adv. vicissim, *in turn*), vicissitudo, *change of fortune*, VICISSITUDE.

79. Nouns were sometimes formed from adjectives or other nouns with the suffix -monia or -monium, Eng. -MONY:

acer, acris, *sharp*, acrimonia, ACRIMONY.

mater, matris, *mother*, matrimonium, MATRIMONY.

parcus, *sparing, frugal*, parcimonium (and parsimonium; cf. parsus, pf. pple. of parcere, *spare*), *economy;* PARSIMONY.

pater, patris, *father*, patrimonium, PATRIMONY.

sanctus, *sacred*, sanctimonium, SANCTIMONY.

testis, *witness*, testimonium, TESTIMONY.

So also from the root of alere, *nourish*, alimonium, ALIMONY. In fact the double suffix -mon-ia, -io, indicates a lost verbal adjective in -mon (Grk. -μων).

C. NOUNS MADE FROM VERBS

80. From verb stems nouns were made denoting the agent; their suffix was -tor or -sor, varying in the same way as in the pf. pple. (147). The English form is the same as the Latin nominative (52, N.).

augere, auctus, *cause to grow, increase,* **auctor,** Eng., earlier spelling, AUCTOR and AUTOR; since about 1550, AUTHOR.

audire, auditus, *hear,* **auditor,** AUDITOR.

debere, debitus, *owe,* **debitor,** becoming Eng. DEBTOR (cf. DEBT, 175).

invenire, inventus, *come upon, find,* **inventor,** INVENTOR.

jurare, juratus, *swear;* the Latin noun was **jurator,** *a swearer,* but French had a shorter form 'jureur,' and English has followed that, although with Latin spelling, JUROR.

narrare, narratus, *tell,* NARRATE, **narrator,** NARRATOR.

opprimere, oppressus, OPPRESS, **oppressor,** OPPRESSOR.

orare, oratus, *speak* (**os, oris,** *mouth;* hence *use the mouth*), **orator,** ORATOR.

procurare, procuratus, *exercise care* (**cura**) *for,* **procurator,** *a manager* or *superintendent,* especially as agent for another, PROCURATOR; shortened also into PROCTOR. **Procuratio** (85), *management* (as an agency), was represented in Low Lat. by **procuratia** which became Eng. PROCURACY, shortened into PROXY.

protegere, protectus, *cover over,* PROTECT, **protector,** PROTECTOR.

transgredi, transgressus, *go across,* TRANSGRESS (*cross over the line*), **transgressor,** TRANSGRESSOR.

tueri, tutus (*safe, i.e., looked after*), *look at, look after, defend,* **tutor;** the TUTOR becomes a guardian or a private instructor.

The corresponding agent suffix in English is *-er;* a Latin verb once fully adopted into English may be treated as a native word and make its agent noun in *-er;* thus we have CORRUPTer, CONSUMer, DEFENDer, DESERTer, EXPLORer, while the Latin nouns are **corruptor, consumptor, defensor, desertor, explorator.**

Some nouns in **-tor** were apparently made from other nouns, as **gladiator,** from **gladius,** *sword.* We may assume either that from **gladius** a verb was made which did not survive in Latin, and **gladiator** was its agent noun, or that forms in **-a-tor** were so common that such words were made merely from analogy, as in English we make words like *mouser, hatter, tinner,* with no corresponding verbs.

81. Nouns in -or were derived from verbs to name the act or condition. Here again the English word is the same in form as the Latin nominative (52, N.).

ardere, *be on fire, burn,* **ardor,** ARDOR.

candere, *be bright, shine,* **candor,** *brilliancy, purity of mind,* CANDOR.

clamare, *shout, cry out,* **clamor,** CLAMOR.

errare, *wander, go astray,* **error,** *wandering,* ERROR.

favere, *be well-disposed, befriend,* **favor,**[1] FAVOR.

fervere, *boil, be agitated,* **fervor,** FERVOR.

furere, *rage, be mad,* **furor,** FUROR.

humere, *be moist,* **humor,** *liquid,* HUMOR (see 33).

liquere, *flow, be liquid, be clear,* **liquor,** first *fluidity;* then *a liquid,* LIQUOR.

rancere (only in pres. pple. **rancens**), *stink,* **rancor** (Late), *a foul odor;* hence *an offensive sort of spite* or *grudge,* RANCOR. Eng. 'rank' in the sense of *rancid* is due to a confusion, 'rank' meaning properly *of coarse thick growth.*

rigere, *stiffen, be rigid,* **rigor,** *a stiffening,* RIGOR.

tenere, *hold fast,* **tenor,** *a steady course,* later *the meaning of a law;* so TENOR, the *meaning* or *drift* of a statement; also the part in music which *holds* the dominant note, the part of the chief male voice.

terrere, *frighten,* **terror,** TERROR. Note the twofold meaning of the noun in English as in Latin, the feeling and the object or cause of that feeling; one's TERROR at the approach of a robber, himself a TERROR to the neighborhood.

tumere, *swell,* **tumor,** *a swelling,* TUMOR.

valere, *be strong,* **valor,** *worth, value.* Worth in battle is bravery, *i.e.,* VALOR. VALUE is a fem. pple. of Fr. 'valoir' from **valere.**

vigere, *be lively, thrive,* **vigor,** *liveliness,* VIGOR.

82. A considerable number of second declension neuters in -ium, made from verbs, denote action or result. The

---

[1] In the expression "curry favor" we have an entirely different word, a distortion of 'favel.' 'Favel' was an old name for a horse, *i.e.,* a *fallow horse,* once regarded as a symbol of hypocrisy.

suffix appears usually as -Y in English; but we may use the Latin word, or we may drop the ending; then if *c* (*t*) or *g* precedes, we have -CE or -GE:

colloqui (com-loqui), *speak together*, **colloquium**, *conversation*, COL-LOQUY.

facere, *do*, with **bene** (cf. **beneficus**), **beneficium**, *well-doing, an ecclesiastical favor*, a BENEFICE. BENEFIT came by way of the French from Lat. **bene-factum**, as PROFIT from **profectum** (**proficere**, *make progress, be advantageous*).

facere, *make*, with **os**, **oris**, *mouth*, **orificium**, lit. *mouth-making*, ORIFICE.

facere, *do*, with **ops**, **opis**, *means of help*, **officium**, *a rendering of service*, OFFICE.

gaudere, *rejoice*, **gaudium**, *a rejoicing, an object producing joy*, GAUD and its doublet JOY (170). Cf. GAUDY, 210.

loqui, *speak*, with **solus**, **soliloquium**, *a speaking alone*, SOLILOQUY.

mederi, *heal*, **re-medium**, *a healing again*, a REMEDY.

odisse, *hate*, **odium**, *hatred*, Eng. **odium**.

pendere, *weigh*, with **stips**, **stipis**, *gift*, **stipendium** (for 'stipipendium'), *a weighing out of one's pay*, STIPEND.

praejudicare, *judge beforehand*, **praejudicium**, *a judging beforehand*, (*e* for *ae*) PREJUDICE.

refugere, *flee back*, **refugium**, *a fleeing back, a place to flee back to*, a REFUGE.

studere, *be eager*, **studium**, *interest*, STUDY.

subsidere (sub-sedere), *settle down*, SUBSIDE, **subsidium**, *a settling down, staying by* (to furnish aid), *reserve troops, help*, SUBSIDY.

83. These are not far removed from some of the nouns in 71, if we observe the verbal idea in the latter:

artificium (artifex), *art-doing*: **facere**, *do*.

auspicium (auspex), *bird-watching*: **specere**, *watch*.

collegium (collega), *a group of those chosen together*: **legere**, *choose*.

hospitium (hospes), *an entertaining of* (*being in power over*) *strangers* (see **hospes** under HOST, 202): **posse** (pot-esse), *be able*.

servitium (servus), *doing a slave's work*: **servire**, *be a slave*, SERVE.

84. Action nouns were also formed in -io(n); Eng. -ION:

condicere, *talk over together, agree upon;* **condicio,** *agreement, terms,* written later **conditio** (176); then erroneously associated with **condo, conditus,** *put together;* CONDITION then means *terms of agreement,* and, in general, *situation.*

contingere (root **tag**), *touch,* **contagio,** *a touching,* CONTAGION.

legere, *collect,* **legio,** *a gathering, a levy of soldiers;* hence a LEGION.

oblivisci (-sc- 131), *forget,* **oblivio,** *a forgetting* or *a being forgotten,* OBLIVION.

opinari, *think, suppose,* **opinio,** *a supposition,* an OPINION.

optare, *choose,* **optio,** *a choosing, a choice,* an OPTION.

rebellare, *wage war again* (**bellum**), said of the conquered, *renew hostilities,* **rebellio,** *a revolt,* REBELLION.

regere, *direct, rule, mark out the boundary lines;* **regio,** *the boundary line,* the *section* so marked off, REGION.

suspicere, sub-specere, *look at from underneath, look askance* or *secretly at,* **suspicio,** *a looking askance,* SUSPICION.

85. A far more common suffix for action nouns was -tio(n), -sio(n), showing the same variation (-sio) as in the pf. pple.[1] (147); Eng. (also Fr.), -TION, -SION:

aberrare, aberratus, *wander away,* **aberratio,** *a wandering away,* ABERRATION.

abluere, ablutus, *wash away* (cf. LAUNDRY, 202), **ablutio,** ABLUTION.

accedere, accessus, *approach, be added,* **accessio,** ACCESSION.

aestimare, aestimatus, ESTIMATE, **aestimatio,** (*e* for *ae*) ESTIMATION (see ESTEEM, 42).

afficere, affectus, (**ad-facere,** *do to*), *treat,* AFFECT, **affectio,** AFFECTION, both as a state of body and as an attitude of mind, the one bad, the other good.

agere, actus, *do,* ACT, **actio,** ACTION.

agitare, agitatus, *drive about,* **agitatio,** AGITATION.

altercari, altercatus, *take the other side* (as if from 'altercus,' from **alter,** *other*), *dispute,* **altercatio,** ALTERCATION.

augere, auctus, *increase,* **auctio,** *an increase* of price or bids, AUCTION.

avertere, aversus, *turn away,* **aversio,** AVERSION.

---

[1] Really two suffixes, -t- (as of the pf. pple.), and -io (84).

cavere, cautus, *be on one's guard,* cautio, CAUTION.

comprehendere, comprehensus, *grasp,* comprehensio, COMPRE-HENSION.

concludere, conclusus, *shut together, close,* conclusio, CONCLUSION.

conficere, confectus, *make* or *put together,* confectio, *a putting together;* CONFECTION becomes practically a CONCOCTION, *a cooking together* (coquere, COOK).

confundere, confusus, *pour together, mix,* confusio, CONFUSION.

constituere, constitutus, *establish,* constitutio, CONSTITUTION.

construere, constructus (136), *build together,* constructio, CONSTRUC-TION.

contrahere, contractus (cf. 146), *draw together,* contractio, CON-TRACTION.

conversari, conversatus, *turn* (*back and forth*) *with, keep company with,* conversatio, CONVERSATION.

definire, definitus, *set a limit to* (finis), definitio, DEFINITION.

desperare, desperatus, *be hopeless* (spes), desperatio, DESPERATION.

dicere, dictus, *say,* dictio, DICTION.

dissolvere, dissolutus, *loose apart, break up,* dissolutio, DISSOLU-TION.

distinguere, distinctus, *mark for separation,* DISTINGUISH, distinctio, DISTINCTION.

dividere, divisus, *break apart,* DIVIDE, divisio, DIVISION.

dominari, dominatus, *be master* (dominus), dominatio, DOMINATION.

edere, editus, *give out, publish,* editio, EDITION.

educare, educatus, *bring up, rear,* educatio, EDUCATION.

eloqui, elocutus, *speak out,* elocutio, ELOCUTION.

erudire, eruditus (e + rudis, *rough, bring out of the rough*), *polish, instruct,* eruditio, ERUDITION.

exsequi, exsecutus, *follow out, follow to the end,* ex(s)ecutio, EXECU-TION.

fingere, fictus, *fashion, make,* fictio, FICTION.

imitari, imitatus, IMITATE, imitatio, IMITATION.

imprimere, impressus (old form of pres. stem pres-), *press upon,* IMPRESS, impressio, IMPRESSION.

inquirere, inquisitus, *search for,* INQUIRE *into,* inquisitio, INQUISI-TION.

inscribere, inscriptus, *write upon,* INSCRIBE, inscriptio, INSCRIPTION.

invenire, inventus, *come upon, find,* inventio, INVENTION.

legare, legatus, *send as ambassador,* legatio, LEGATION.

liberare, liberatus, *set free* (liber), liberatio, LIBERATION.

manere, mansum, *remain, abide,* mansio, MANSION (*abiding place*).

mittere, missus, *send,* missio, *a sending,* MISSION.

movere, motus, MOVE, motio, MOTION.

munire, munitus (older form, moenire, moenia, *walls*), *wall off, fortify,* munitio, *means of defence,* MUNITION, *i.e.,* materials for warfare, AMMUNITION.[1]

mutare, mutatus, *change,* mutatio, MUTATION.

nasci, natus, *be born,* natio, *a birth, a group of like birth,* NATION.

noscere, notus, *become acquainted with,* notio, NOTION.

occupare, occupatus, *lay hold of* (ob-capere, p. 187 N.), occupatio, OCCUPATION.

orare, oratus, *speak* (*use the mouth,* os), oratio, ORATION; PERO-RATION, *a speaking through, the close of a speech.*

partire, partitus, *divide into parts* (pars), partitio, PARTITION.

pendere, pensus, *weigh, weigh out* money, *pay,* pensio, *payment,* PENSION.

percipere, perceptus, *take wholly* (per-capere), PERCEIVE, perceptio, PERCEPTION.

petere, petitus, *fly at, attack, seek, ask,* petitio, *a request,* PETITION.

probare, probatus (probus, *good*), *test,* PROVE, probatio, PROBATION.

reri, ratus, *reckon, calculate,* ratio, RATION (42).

respirare, respiratus, *breathe back, exhale,* respiratio, RESPIRATION.

restituere, restitutum, *restore,* restitutio, *restoration,* RESTITUTION.

salutare, salutatus, *wish health to* (salus), *greet,* salutatio, SALU-TATION.

secare, sectus, *cut,* sectio, *a cutting, a division,* a SECTION.

secedere, secessum, *go apart, withdraw,* secessio, SECESSION (145).

stare, status, *stand, stop,* statio, *a standing place,* STATION.

superstare ('superstitus,' not used), *stand* (*in awe*) *over,* superstitio, SUPERSTITION.

tradere, traditus, *give over, hand down,* traditio, TRADITION.

tueri, tuitus, *look at, look after,* tuitio, TUITION; so INTUITION, *looking* (*directly*) *into* a thing. Cf. tutus, TUTOR, 80.

---

[1] AMMUNITION from Fr. 'amunition,' probably made by mistaking 'la munition' for 'l'amunition.'

vertere, versus, *turn*, versio, VERSION.
videre, visus, *see*, visio, VISION.

86. This suffix with the first conjugation **a, -atio**, was used even in Latin with no corresponding verb, as **constellatio** (**com** + **stella**), *a group of stars*, CONSTELLATION; **tabulatio**, *flooring, i.e., putting in the form of a table* (**tabula**), TABULATION, just as **tabula** from meaning *a plank*, came to mean also *a list*. However, we find pf. pple. forms **constellatus** and **tabulatus** (107). The suffix is often used in English to form nouns from non-Latin verbs as 'botherATION,' 'flirtATION,' 'organizATION' (211).

87. Many action nouns were made to end in **-tura, -sura** (corresponding to the phonetic change of the pf. pple., 147); Eng. -TURE, -SURE:

aperire, apertus, *open*, **apertura**, APERTURE.
armare, armatus, *furnish with arms*, **armatura**, *armor or an armed force*, ARMATURE, *protective armor;* the English word is extended in use to a protective covering as of plants, and to the piece of soft iron between the poles of a magnet to protect against the dissipation of magnetic force.
capere, captus, *take, seize*, **captura**, CAPTURE (as noun; then verb).
censere, census, *estimate, judge*, **censura**, *judgment*, CENSURE.
colere, cultus, *cultivate*, **cultura**, CULTURE.
conicere, conjectus, *throw together*, "*put two and two together*," **conjectura**, CONJECTURE.
findere, fissus, *split*, **fissura**, *a split*, FISSURE.
frangere, fractus, *break*, **fractura**, *a break*, FRACTURE.
jungere, junctus, *join*, **junctura**, JUNCTURE.
nasci, natus, *be born*, **natura**, NATURE.
pingere, pictus, *paint*, **pictura**, *a painting*, PICTURE.
premere, pressus, PRESS (**pressare**, 130), **pressura**, PRESSURE.
scribere, scriptus, *write*, **scriptura**, *a writing*, SCRIPTURE.
stare, supine **statum**, *stand*, **statura**, STATURE.
struere, structus, *build*, **structura**, *a building*, STRUCTURE (see CONSTRUE, 136).

temperare, temperatus, *regulate*, temperatura, TEMPERATURE.
texere, textus, *weave*, textura, TEXTURE.
tingere, tinctus, *dye*, TINGE, tinctura, *a dyeing*, TINCTURE.
tondere, tonsus, *shear*, tonsura, TONSURE.

But from **uti, usus**, the noun **usura**, *use, i.e., use of money*, becomes Eng. USURY.

Observe that **litteratura**, *letters*, LITERATURE, is made without a corresponding verb, although **litteratus** was used. Cf. **literati** (52).

88. Another group of action nouns consists of those of the fourth declension in **-tus, -sus**, corresponding in phonetic change with the pf. pple. (147), and identical in (nom.) form with it; in English the last syllable usually has been dropped or survives as silent -E (163):

advenire, *come to, arrive*, adventus, ADVENT.
apparare (ad-parare), *make ready*, apparatus, *preparation, equipment*, Eng. apparatus (adopted).
appetere (ad-petere, *fly toward*), *seek after*, appetitus, APPETITE.
aspicere (ad-specere), *look at*, aspectus, ASPECT.
audire, *hear*, auditus, AUDIT, an examination of accounts originally with a *hearing* of the parties concerned.
cadere, *fall*, casus, CASE; *what befalls one, a happening;* in grammar, a form that *falls* away from the nominative; then extended to the nominative itself. A graphical representation of declension by the upper right-hand quadrant of a circle showed the vertical radius as nominative, other radii *fell* from this or were *slanting* (**obliqui**), OBLIQUE CASES. Casus, a translation of Grk. 'ptōsis' (πτῶσις), *a falling*.
canere, *sing*, cantus, CANT (with reference to its sing-song tone); with **ad-** accentus, ACCENT.
censere, *assess, reckon*, census, Eng. census (adopted).
circumire, *go around*, circu(m)itus, circuitus, *a going around*, CIRCUIT.
congredi, *come together, meet*, congressus, *a meeting*, CONGRESS.
consentire, *feel together, agree*, consensus, Eng. consensus (adopted).
convenire, *come together*, conventus, *assembly*, CONVENT.

egredi, *go out,* **egressus,** EGRESS.

evenire, *come out, happen,* **eventus,** EVENT, *i.e., outcome.*

habere, *have, keep (oneself), be in a certain condition,* **habitus,**
condition, HABIT (cf. COSTUME, CUSTOM, 48).

labi, *slip,* **lapsus,** *a slip,* LAPSE.

progredi, *go forward,* **progressus,** PROGRESS.

prospicere, *look forward, look into the distance,* **prospectus,** PROSPECT;
prospectus has also become English (52).

recedere, *go back, withdraw,* **recessus,** RECESS.

sentire, *feel, understand,* **sensus,** SENSE.

tangere, *touch,* **tactus,** TACT, *i.e.,* skill in *touching* or *handling.*

transire, *go across,* **transitus,** TRANSIT; we use it for passage in
general, for passage of a heavenly body across a field, and for
an instrument that measures horizontal angles in surveying.

uti, USE, **usus,** USE.

89. Nouns denoting means or results of acts have as their
suffixes -men, -mentum, -bulum, -culum, -brum (-bra),
-crum; and sometimes -trum; Eng. -MEN, -MENT, -BLE, -CLE,
-C(H)RE, -TER (-TRE).

Nouns in -**men:**

acuere, *sharpen* (**acus,** *a needle*), **acumen,** *that which is sharpened,*
Eng. acumen.

fluere, *flow,* **flumen,** *that which flows, river;* FLUME (OF 'flum').

levare, *lighten,* **levamen,** *that which lightens,* figuratively as *consola-*
tion, literally in English, LEAVEN (OF 'levain').

regere, *rule, guide,* **regimen,** *a direction of affairs,* Eng. **regimen** (52).

specere, *look at,* **specimen,** *that by which a thing is seen or distin-*
guished, Eng. specimen (52).

90. Nouns in -**mentum** (89):

arguere, *make clear* (ARGUE), **argumentum,** *means of making clear,*
ARGUMENT.

armare, *furnish with arms* or other *equipment,* **armamenta** (pl.),
implements, ARMAMENT.

caedere, *cut,* **caementum,** for 'caed(s)mentom,' *pieces of stone cut*
but unfinished, (*e* for *ae*) CEMENT.

complere, *fill out,* COMPLETE, **complementum,** COMPLEMENT and COMPLIMENT, the *fulfilling* of a courteous act (Ital. 'complimento'); COMPLEMENT was also formerly used in this sense.

condire (accessory form of **condere,** *put together,* see CREED, 58 and Note), *preserve, pickle,* **condimentum,** CONDIMENT.

deterere, *rub away,* **detrimentum,** *damage,* DETRIMENT.

docere, *teach,* **documentum** (doci-, 149, end), *means* or *example for teaching,* DOCUMENT.

emoliri, *accomplish,* **emolumentum** (emoli-, 149, end), *attainment, profit,* EMOLUMENT.

experiri, *try, test,* **experimentum,** EXPERIMENT.

fervere, *boil,* **fermentum** (for 'fervimentum'), FERMENT.

firmare, *make firm,* **firmamentum,** *a strong support, the fixed sky,* FIRMAMENT.

fovere, *warm,* **fomentum** (for 'fovimentum'), *a warm lotion;* from this a verb was again made, **fomentare** (128), giving Eng. FOMENT.

frangere (root frag), *break,* **fragmentum,** *a piece broken off,* FRAGMENT.

impedire, *hinder* (*catch* or *entangle the feet,* **in** + **pes, pedis,** *foot*), **impedimentum,** IMPEDIMENT (see EXPEDITE, 202).

increscere (-cre-sc-ere, 131), INCREASE, **incrementum,** INCREMENT.

instruere, *build in, construct,* **instrumentum,** *means for constructing,* INSTRUMENT.

linere, *smear,* **linimentum,** *something to smear on,* LINIMENT.

monere, *warn, remind,* **monumentum** (or **moni-,** 149, end), *a reminder,* MONUMENT.

movere, *move,* **momentum** (for 'movimentum'), MOMENT and **momentum** (52).

nutrire, NOURISH (186), **nutrimentum,** NUTRIMENT.

ornare, ADORN (ad-ornare), **ornamentum,** ORNAMENT.

pingere (root **pig**), *paint, color,* **pigmentum,** PIGMENT.

regere, *rule,* **regimentum,** *government,* REGIMENT; formerly used of the orderly government, much like **regimen;** now of a government body of troops.

secare, *cut,* **segmentum** (sec-mentum), SEGMENT.

sedere, *sit,* **sedimentum,** *a settling,* SEDIMENT. (Cf. the hybrid settleMENT.)

tegere, *cover,* **tegmentum, tegimentum,** or **tegumentum** (149, end), TEGUMENT.

temperare, *mix properly, regulate,* **temperamentum,** TEMPERAMENT. Cf. DISTEMPER (OF 'destemprer'), a disturbing of the proportion of humors controlling one's temperament (HUMOR, 33).

testari, *bear witness, make a will,* **testamentum,** *a will,* TESTAMENT.

torquere, *twist,* **tormentum** (**torq-**), *an instrument for hurling or twisting,* or *of torture,* TORMENT.

vestire, *clothe,* **vestimentum,** VESTMENT (OF 'vestement').

Apparently from the noun **linea,** LINE, came **lineamentum,** LINEAMENT; from the adj. **rudis,** *unskilled,* **rudimentum,** RUDIMENT; and from the interjection **la,** a cry of sorrow, **lamentum,** LAMENT.

91. Nouns in -bulum, -bula, -culum (89):

currere, *run,* **curriculum,** *a race course,* Eng. **curriculum** (52).

fari, *speak, tell,* **fabula** (fem.), FABLE. (An abbreviated variant of this is FIB.)

mirari, *wonder at,* **miraculum,** *something to be wondered at,* MIRACLE.

orare, *speak,* **oraculum,** *a speaking, a divine announcement* or *prophecy,* ORACLE.

pascere (**pa-sc-ere,** 131), *feed,* **pabulum,** Eng. **pabulum** (52).

perpendere, *suspend carefully, let hang down,* **perpendiculum,** *plumb line;* with adj. suffix, PERPENDICULAR (99).

receptare, *receive* (cf. **recipere,** and 130), **receptaculum,** RECEPTACLE.

spectare, *look at,* **spectaculum,** *something to be looked at,* SPECTACLE.

stare, *stand,* **stabulum,** *a standing-place,* STABLE; but **obstare,** *stand in the way,* **obstaculum,** *a hindrance,* OBSTACLE.

vehere, *carry, convey,* **vehiculum,** *a conveyance,* VEHICLE.

vincire, *bind,* **vinculum,** *a bond,* Eng. **vinculum** (52).

vocare, *call,* **vocabulum,** *name,* VOCABLE (cf. VOCABULARY, and 71).

92.
When *l* occurs in either of the two syllables just preceding the suffix, **-brum** and **-crum** are used instead of **-bulum** and **-culum** (155); **-brum** (fem. **-bra**), however, is not restricted to this use:

fulcire, *prop up,* **fulcrum,** Eng. **fulcrum** (52).

sepelire, *bury,* **sepulcrum** or **sepulchrum** (p. 187 N.), SEPULCHRE.

simulare, *make like*, simulacrum, *a likeness, an image*, Eng. simulacrum (52).

vertere, *turn*, vertebra, *a joint*, Eng. vertebra (52).

93. Nouns in -trum (89):

cad-, meaning uncertain, possibly *cut, cut off, fence off*, castra (cad-
trum, 147), *enclosure, camp;* CHESTER, etc. (8).

claudere, *shut in*, CLOSE (167), claustrum (claud-trum, 147), *enclosure*, CLOISTER, 31.

monere, *warn*, monstrum (mon- with suffix -es, *i.e.*, 'monestrum'),
a warning, an omen, an evil omen, something dreadful, MONSTER.

rodere, *gnaw*, rostrum (rod-trum 147), *a beak*, rostrum (52).

specere, *look at*, spectrum, *a vision* or *apparition*, SPECTRE (cf.
spectrum, 52).

II. THE FORMATION OF ADJECTIVES

A. ADJECTIVES MADE FROM NOUNS

94. The suffix -osus denoting *full of, endowed with, given
to*, appears in English usually as -OUS,[1] sometimes -OSE.

ambitio, AMBITION (*a going around*, 145), ambitiosus (for 'ambi-
tionosus'), AMBITIOUS.

bellicus, adjective from bellum, *war* (97), bellicosus, *warlike*,
BELLICOSE.

calamitas, CALAMITY, calamitosus (for 'calamitatosus'), CALAMI-
TOUS.

callum (or callus), *hard skin*, callosus, *hard-skinned*, CALLOUS.

copia, *abundance*, copiosus, COPIOUS.   (Co + ops, opis, *resource;
a gathering of resources*).

fama, FAME (*talk*, fari, *speak*), famosus, *talked of*, FAMOUS.

fastidium, *loathing, squeamishness*, fastidiosus, *disdainful*, FASTI-
DIOUS.

genus, generis, *race, birth*, generosus, *of (noble) birth, having qualities in keeping with noble lineage*, GENEROUS.

[1] According to 160, 162, 167, -ōsum became -ōs(u), then *-ous;* *-ose*
is directly from Latin but the final *-e* is after the fashion of the French
(163).   The suffix involves od- of odor; hence lit. *smelling of*.

gratia, *favor,* GRACE, **gratiosus,** *showing favor,* GRACIOUS (176).

ingenium, *inborn quality* (**in** + **gen,** *inborn*), *ability,* **ingeniosus,** INGENIOUS.

injuria (**in** + **jus,** 74, end), *not right, wrong,* **injuriosus,** INJURIOUS.

insidiae (pl.), *ambush* (**in-sedere,** *sit in* a place), **insidiosus,** *as if in ambush;* hence *deceitful,* INSIDIOUS.

invidia, ENVY (*a looking on;* so the adj. **invidus,** ENVIOUS, 144, **in-,** and **invidere,** *look on with envy*), **invidiosus,** *hateful,* INVIDIOUS.

jocus, a JOKE, **jocosus,** JOCOSE.

luxuria, LUXURY, **luxuriosus,** LUXURIOUS.

monstrum, *an evil omen* (93), then a MONSTER, **monstrosus,** MON-STROUS.

mos, moris, *custom, habit,* **morosus,** *given to some* (*disagreeable*) *habit,* MOROSE (cf. MORAL, 98).

nervus, *a tendon, sinew,* NERVE; also the *string* of an instrument or bow; **nervosus,** *sinewy, vigorous;* somewhat changed in meaning is our NERVOUS. Cf. **enervare, -atus,** *take out* (**e-**) *the sinews, unnerve,* ENERVATE.

odium, *hatred,* **odiosus,** *hateful,* ODIOUS.

officium, *service* (202), OFFICE, **officiosus,** *courteous, obliging;* but our word OFFICIOUS has come to mean *too ready to offer one's services.*

onus, oneris, *a burden,* **onerosus,** *burdensome,* ONEROUS.

perfidia, *faithlessness,* **perfidiosus,** PERFIDIOUS.

pernicies, *ruin* (**per** + **nex,** *slaughter,* **pernecare,** *kill outright*), **per-niciosus,** PERNICIOUS.

religio, RELIGION (32), **religiosus** (for 'religionosus'), RELIGIOUS.

ridiculum, *a jest* (**ridiculus,** *laughable,* **ridere,** *laugh,* 91), **ridicu-losus,** RIDICULOUS.

studium, *zeal, interest,* **studiosus,** STUDIOUS.

sumptus, *expense* (**sumere,** *take to one's self* or *for one's own use*), **sumptuosus,** SUMPTUOUS.

superstitio, SUPERSTITION (85), **superstitiosus** (for 'superstitio-nosus'), SUPERSTITIOUS.

suspicio, SUSPICION (84), **suspiciosus** (for 'suspicionosus'), SUS-PICIOUS.

verbum, *word,* **verbosus,** *wordy,* VERBOSE.

victoria, VICTORY, **victoriosus,** VICTORIOUS.

viscum, *mistletoe,* **viscosus,** *sticky,* since birdlime was made from mistletoe berries; VISCOUS.

vitium, VICE, **vitiosus,** VICIOUS (176).

With u before the suffix: **voluptas,** *pleasure,* **voluptuosus,** VOLUPTUOUS.

With i before the suffix: **cura,** *care,* **curiosus,** *careful, inquisitive,* CURIOUS; later in our objective sense of *exciting attention.* Also **labor,** LABOR, **laboriosus,** LABORIOUS.

95. Many Latin adjectives in **-us, -ius,** have followed those in **-osus,** and taken the suffix **-ous** (**-ious**) upon coming into English, *e.g.:*

abstemius, *temperate,* ABSTEMIOUS: lit. *keeping away from intoxicating drinks,* **abs** + root appearing in **temetum,** *strong drink,* a root originally meaning *be stupefied* or *choked.*

arduus, *steep, difficult,* ARDUOUS.

dubius, *doubtful, uncertain* (Late, **dubiosus**), DUBIOUS; **du-o,** *two,* and **b** probably representing the same root as gave **fu-i** and Eng. 'be,' *being two;* hence *uncertain.*

indigenus (Late Lat.; **indu,** 144, **in-** + **gen**), INDIGENOUS (cf. **indigena,** *one born in a country*).

industrius (**industria,** *industry*), INDUSTRIOUS.

ludicrus (or **-cer, ludus,** *play*), *sportive,* LUDICROUS.

nefarius (**nefas,** *not right,* 156), *wicked,* NEFARIOUS.

noxius (later **noxiosus; noxa,** *harm*), *harmful,* NOXIOUS. Cf. **obnoxius,** *liable to* (*harm*), *subject to penalty;* hence *blameworthy* and *offensive,* OBNOXIOUS.

odorus, *emitting an* ODOR (Lat. **odor**), ODOROUS.

prosperus, *according to one's hope* (**pro** + **spes**), PROSPEROUS.

sedulus (cf. **sedulo,** *i.e.,* **se dolo,** *without cunning*), *diligent,* SEDULOUS. If derived from **sedere** (121), cf. ASSIDUOUS, 122.

spurius, *not genuine,* SPURIOUS.

strenuus, *active,* STRENUOUS.

varius, *spotted, motley,* VARIOUS.

From **via,** *way:* **de-vius,** *out of the way,* DEVIOUS.

    im-per-vius, *having no way through,* IMPERVIOUS.

    ob-vius, *across one's way,* OBVIOUS.

    prae-vius, *before on the way,* PREVIOUS.

96. The suffix was further extended when adjectives of quite different formation added also -ous and appeared in English with the two suffixes (204), thus:

illustris (luc- of lux, lucere), *in the light, distinguished,* ILLUSTRIOUS.

salubris (salus, *health*), *healthful,* SALUBRIOUS.

scurrilis (scurra, *buffoon,* 100), *buffoonlike,* SCURRILOUS.

somnifer (somnus, *sleep;* fer-, *bear*), *sleep-producing,* SOMNIFEROUS.

The wide extension of this suffix may be explained in part by the readiness of Late or Mediæval Latin to modify the classical word by adding or substituting -osus. Then, when -ous had become common, it was added to words of non-Latin origin, as murderous, wond(e)rous, and even AS 'rihtwis' was altered to righteous.

97. Again, denominative adjectives were made both in -icus and -ticus, Eng. -IC and -TIC:

aqua, *water,* aquaticus, *relating to* or *living in water,* AQUATIC.

civis, *citizen,* civicus, *pertaining to the citizen,* CIVIC.

classis, *a calling* or *summoning* of citizens; a CLASS, military or naval (*fleet*), classicus, *pertaining to the (first) class;* hence CLASSIC (cf. Eng. slang CLASSY).

domus, *home,* domesticus (on a neut. stem domes-; cf. modestia, 74), *belonging to the home,* DOMESTIC.

erratus, *a wandering,* erraticus, *wandering about,* ERRATIC.

fanum, *a temple;* then as if from 'fanatum,' "*templed,*" fanaticus, *inspired by the divinity of the temple,* FANATIC.

luna, *moon,* lunaticus, *affected by the moon, moon-struck,* LUNATIC.

lympha, *water* (of the same origin as 'nymph,' *a water deity*), lymphaticus, *affected by water, distracted* (cf. "water on the brain"), LYMPHATIC. But this use of LYMPHATIC is obsolete; the word now means *watery* or *relating to* LYMPH.

nauta, *sailor,* nauticus, *pertaining to sailors,* NAUTICAL (204).

populus, PEOPLE, publicus, PUBLIC. Poplicus (for 'populicus,' cf. O. Lat. poplus) seems to have been altered to publicus through association of populus and pubes, *the youth, the grown young men* or *citizens.*

rus, *country,* rusticus, *countrylike,* RUSTIC.

98. Very common to give the meaning *pertaining to* was the suffix -alis, Eng. -AL:

annus, *year,* **annalis,** *pertaining to the year,* ANNALS (pl.), *records of the years.* Cf. ANNUAL, 41, 'yearly.'

artificium, *handicraft* (**artifex,** 71, *craftsman,* **ars** + **facere,** *art working*), **artificialis,** ARTIFICIAL.

astrum, *star,* **astralis,** *relating to the stars,* ASTRAL.

bestia, BEAST, **bestialis,** *like a beast,* BESTIAL.

caput, capitis, *head,* **capitalis,** *pertaining to the head* or *to life;* also CHIEF, CAPITAL. Cf. 35. Note that also from **caput** is CAPITOL, the Lat. **Capitolium,** the temple of Jupiter on the Tarpeian Mount (Capitoline Hill); hence the *head* government building of a state or country.

cardo, cardinis, *hinge,* **cardinalis,** *serving as a hinge, essential* (cf. 'pivotal'), CARDINAL. See also 202.

caro, carnis, *flesh,* **carnalis,** *belonging to the flesh,* CARNAL. Cf. CHARNEL, 42.

casus, *a fall* (88), *what befalls, an occurrence,* **casualis,** *merely happening,* CASUAL.

Ceres, *goddess of agriculture, grain,* **cerealis,** *pertaining to grain,* CEREAL.

conju(n)x, conjugis, *wife* or (less often) *husband* (**conjungere,** *join together;* **jugum,** *yoke*); **conjugalis,** *relating to marriage,* CONJUGAL. Cf. **maritus,** *husband,* from which **maritalis,** MARITAL.

corpus, corporis, *body,* **corporalis,** *pertaining to the body,* CORPORAL. CORPORAL as the name of a military officer is a different word, as different as the *head* from the *body,* being a corruption of Fr. 'caporal' from Ital. 'caporale,' made from 'capo,' *head* CHIEF. Lat. **caput.**

duo, *two,* **dualis,** *consisting of* or *relating to two,* DUAL.

fatum, *the thing spoken* (**fari, fatus,** *speak*), *prophecy, destiny, death,* **fatalis,** *death-bringing,* FATAL.

flos, floris, FLOWER, **floralis** (in **floralia,** *flower garden*), *consisting of flowers,* FLORAL. The Romans used the adjective as from **Flora,** the goddess of flowers, **Floralia** being her festival.

gradus, *step,* GRADE, **gradualis,** *by steps,* GRADUAL.

initium, *beginning* (**in-ire,** *go into*), **initialis,** *relating to the beginning,* or *serving as a beginning;* we use it also as a noun for an INITIAL letter.

judicium, *judgment, court,* **judicialis,** *relating to court,* JUDICIAL (cf. JUDGE, 30).

latus, lateris, *side,* **lateralis,** *pertaining to the side,* LATERAL.

lex, legis, *law,* **legalis,** *by* or *of the law,* LEGAL (see LOYAL, 43).

liber (adj.), *free,* **liberalis,** *belonging to freedom, characteristic of free men,* LIBERAL. Cf. GENEROUS.

litus, litoris, *shore,* **litoralis,** *belonging to the coast,* (litt-) LITTORAL.

manus, *hand,* **manualis,** *pertaining to the hand, held in the hand* (*handbook,* 39, 40), MANUAL; also *done by the hand,* as 'MANUAL labor.'

mors, mortis, *death,* **mortalis,** *subject to death,* MORTAL. We use it also in an active sense, *causing death,* as 'MORTAL combat.'

mos, moris, *custom,* **moralis,** *pertaining to manners,* MORAL; but the plural **mores,** *customs,* or *habits,* became *character,* and the adjective means *in accordance with* (*good*) *character.* We have also taken from the French the noun MORALE, *morality,* but evidently confusing this in meaning with Fr. 'moral,' denoting *moral condition* as to confidence and ready obedience.

municipium, *a city which had the privileges of Roman citizenship,* from **munus,** *office* and **capere,** *receive;* **municeps,** *one who takes office* or *duties;* **municipalis,** *pertaining to a* **municipium,** *belonging to the town,* MUNICIPAL. Cf. MUNICIPALITY; also IMMUNE, IMMUNITY, 72.

murus, *wall,* **muralis,** *belonging to the wall,* MURAL, *on the wall.*

natura, NATURE, **naturalis,** *according to nature,* NATURAL.

navis, *ship,* **navalis,** *belonging to ships,* NAVAL.

nomen, nominis, *name,* **nominalis,** *relating to a name,* NOMINAL (*in name only*).

norma, *a carpenter's square, a rule* or *standard* (NORM), **normalis,** *according to rule,* NORMAL.

numerus, NUMBER (174), **numeralis,** *designating number,* NUMERAL.

ordo, ordinis, *rank,* ORDER (OF 'ordre' for 'ordne'), **ordinalis,** *denoting order,* ORDINAL.

pes, pedis, *foot,* **pedalis,** *pertaining to the feet,* PEDAL.

plus, pluris, *more,* **pluralis,** *relating to more than one,* PLURAL.

princeps, principis, *chief;* **principalis,** *of the chief,* PRINCIPAL. It

seems to have been under the influence of this word that the
noun **principium**, *a beginning*, or *what is fundamental* (Fr. 'prin-
cipe'), became PRINCIPLE in English.

ratio, rationis, REASON (170), **rationalis,** *reasonable,* RATIONAL (cf.
42).

sensus, *feeling, sensation,* **sensualis,** *endowed with feeling, belonging
to the physical senses,* SENSUAL.

vox, vocis, VOICE, **vocalis,** *uttered with voice,* VOCAL (also VOWEL, OF
'vouel').

99. When *l* occurs in either of the two syllables next
preceding the suffix, regularly the suffix is **-aris,** Eng. -AR,
instead of **-alis,** Eng. -AL [1] (155):

angulus, *corner,* **angularis,** *having corners,* ANGULAR.

anulus, *a ring,* **anularis** (less correctly spelled **annularis**), *pertaining
to a ring,* ANNULAR, *ring-shaped* (ANNULAR eclipse).

capillus, *hair,* **capillaris,** *hairlike,* CAPILLARY (as if -arius, 101).
'CAPILLARY attraction' is so called from the fact that this molec-
ular force affecting the surface of liquids is easily observed in
fine, hairlike tubes.

collum, *neck,* **collaris,** *worn on the neck,* neut. **collare,** COLLAR.

consul, Eng. consul, **consularis,** *pertaining to a consul,* CONSULAR.

familia, FAMILY, **familiaris,** *belonging to the family,* FAMILIAR.

insula, *island,* **insularis,** *relating to an island,* INSULAR.

joculus, *a little joke,* diminutive of **jocus, jocularis,** JOCULAR.

luna, *moon,* **lunaris,** *pertaining to the moon,* LUNAR.

miles, militis, *soldier,* **militaris** (earlier also **militarius,** 101), MILI-
TARY.

mola, *millstone,* pl. **molae,** *mill,* **molaris,** *pertaining to grinding at
the mill,* MOLAR.

oculus, *eye,* **ocularis,** OCULAR.

particula, *a little part* (68), **particularis,** *having to do with little parts,*
PARTICULAR.

perpendiculum, *a plumb line* (perpendere, *weigh* or *suspend care-*

---

[1] However, from **linea,** a LINE, we have both **linealis** and **linearis,**
LINEAL and LINEAR; and from **glacies,** *ice,* the adjective was **glacialis,**
GLACIAL (but the French has furnished us also a form in *r* as a noun,
GLACIER). **Labialis,** LABIAL, was Late Latin.

fully), **perpendicularis**, *according to the plumb line,* PERPEN-
DICULAR.

populus, *people,* **popularis,** *belonging to the people, favored by the
people,* POPULAR.

regula, *a straight stick, ruler* (cf. **regere,** *rule*), **regularis,** REGULAR.

salus, salutis, *safety,* **salutaris,** *contributing to safety,* SALUTARY (as
if from -arius, 101).

seculum (for **saeculum**), *a generation, the times,* **secularis,** *belonging
to the times,* and in ecclesiastical Latin, *worldly, temporal,* SECULAR.

singuli, *one by one,* **singularis,** *applying to one, unique,* SINGULAR.

sol, *sun,* **solaris,** *of the sun,* SOLAR.

vulgus, *the common crowd,* **vulgaris,** *belonging to the common people,*
VULGAR, as 'VULGAR Latin,' or *belonging to the lower class* and
hence *coarse.*

100. Adjectives in **-ilis,** Eng. -ILE (less often -IL), have
much the same meaning as those in **-alis** and **-aris:**

civis, *a citizen,* **civilis,** *relating to citizens* or *to the state,* CIVIL; also
characteristic of a citizen, as 'CIVIL behavior' (cf. CIVILITY).

gens, gentis, *a clan,* **gentilis,** *belonging to the clan, i.e., one's own
clan,* GENTLE; or *belonging to the* foreign *tribe,* GENTILE. See
also GENTEEL, 43.

hostis, *enemy,* **hostilis,** *after the manner of the enemy,* HOSTILE.

juvenis, *young, youth,* **juvenilis,** *pertaining to the young,* JUVENILE.

puer, *boy,* **puerilis,** *boyish,* PUERILE.

servus, *slave,* **servilis,** *pertaining to slaves, slavish,* SERVILE.

vir, *man,* **virilis,** *manly,* VIRILE.

101. Denominative adjectives were very commonly made
with the suffix **-arius,** Eng. -ARY.[1] Some such adjectives,

---

[1] But from **grex, gregis,** *a flock,* **gregarius** has followed the adjectives in -OUS (94) and given us GREGARIOUS; **gregarius** meant *belonging to the flock,* or *of the common herd;* our derivative is *disposed to go
in flocks.* From **refringere, refractus,** *break in pieces,* was **refractarius,**
but Eng. REFRACTORY on analogy of adjectives in -torius below (102);
disposed to break in pieces suggests *hard to handle.* Cf. Eng. "*go to
pieces*" for *display temper.* The suffix -arius, represented in French
by 'ier,' came thence into English as -EER in a number of coined
words, AUCTIONEER, ENGINEER, MOUNTAINEER, PROFITEER, etc. Note
also that PRIMARY and PREMIER (Fr.) are doublets from **primarius.**

having become nouns, have been mentioned above (71). Other examples are these:

arbiter, arbitri (52), *judge, umpire,* **arbitrarius,** *done by arbitration,* also *of one's own will as an umpire,* ARBITRARY.

auxilium, *aid,* **auxiliarius** (also **auxiliaris**), *rendering aid,* AUXILIARY.

contra, adverb (prep.), *against,* **contrarius,** *being over against,* CONTRARY.

elementum, *first principle,* ELEMENT, **elementarius,** ELEMENTARY.

epistula, epistola, *letter,* **epistolarius** (also **epistolaris**), EPISTOLARY.

honor, HONOR, **honorarius,** *relating to honor, done* or *bestowed as an honor,* HONORARY. Cf. **honorarium,** 52.

judicium, *judgment, court,* **judiciarius,** *belonging to the courts,* JUDICIARY.

legio (84), LEGION, **legionarius,** *belonging to the legion,* LEGIONARY.

littera, LETTER (169), **litterae,** *literature,* **litterarius,** LITERARY.

merces, mercedis, *hire, pay,* **mercenarius** (earlier **mercennarius** for 'merced-narius'), *serving for hire,* MERCENARY. This -**narius** must have been taken from forms in **n**-stem + **arius** (cf. **ordinarius** below).

necesse (adj.), *unavoidable* (72), **necessarius,** NECESSARY.

ordo, ordinis, *rank, order,* **ordinarius,** *of the (usual) order,* ORDINARY. **Ordinarius** as a noun was *an overseer* maintaining order, *e.g.,* the centurion of the first rank; so Eng. ORDINARY may be an officer.

proprietas, *one's own quality* or *character* (73); also *ownership;* **proprietarius** (for 'proprietatarius'), *belonging to one as his own,* PROPRIETARY. As applied to medicines, cf. **nostrum** (56).

secundus (adj.), *following* (**sequi,** *follow*), SECOND (the French spelling), **secundarius,** *of second class,* SECONDARY.

subsidium, *reserve troops* (**sub-sidere,** *sit down in hiding*), *support, assistance,* **subsidiarius,** *belonging to the reserve,* SUBSIDIARY. Cf. SUBSIDY, 82.

tempus, temporis, *time,* **temporarius,** *lasting but for a time,* TEMPORARY.

veterinus, *draught animal, beast of burden* (lit. *yearling, year-old,* from **vetus,** *old;* cf. **veteranus,** 103); **veterinarius,** *having to do with work animals,* VETERINARY.

voluntas, *free will,* **voluntarius** (for '**voluntatarius'**), *of one's free will,* VOLUNTARY.

102. Adjectives of like meaning were often formed with the suffix **-ius** (Eng. -Y) added to agent nouns in **-tor, -sor** (80). When once the combination suffix **-torius** (**-sorius**) had become common, it may have been used to make such adjectives with no conscious reference to the agent noun. We have, for example:

auditor, *a hearer,* **auditorius,** *pertaining to the hearer* or *hearing,* AUDITORY.

consolator, *one who consoles,* **consolatorius,** *serving for consolation,* CONSOLATORY.

contradictor, *one who replies,* **contradictorius** (Late Lat.), *saying the opposite thing,* CONTRADICTORY.

cursor, *a runner,* **cursorius,** *pertaining to the runner* or *to running,* CURSORY, *i.e., after the fashion of one running;* hence *hasty.*

declamator, *public speaker, declaimer,* **declamatorius,** *belonging to declamation,* DECLAMATORY; similarly formed, EXCLAMATORY.

desultor, *one who leaps down* (**desilire, desultus**), particularly a rider in the circus games or in battle who leaped from one horse to another; **desultorius** thus gives us DESULTORY for leaping first to one thing then to another with no definite aim.

explanator, *explainer,* **explanatorius** (Late Lat.), *serving to explain,* EXPLANATORY.

gladiator, Eng. gladiator (80), **gladiatorius,** (with added -AL suffix, 98) GLADIATORIAL.

notor, *one who knows,* **notorius,** *making known* (not classical as adjective); Med. Lat., *well-known,* NOTORIOUS, *known to the public.*

peremptor, *a destroyer* (**perimere, per** + **emere,** *take away completely, destroy*), **peremptorius,** *destructive;* then *final* or *decisive,* PEREMPTORY.

praedator, *a plunderer* (**praeda,** *booty,* PREY, 224 *get,* **praedari,** *plunder*), **praedatorius,** *plundering,* (*e* for *ae*) PREDATORY.

senator, Eng. senator, **senatorius,** (with added -AL suffix, 98) SENATORIAL.

transitor, *one who goes over,* **transitorius,** *passing away,* TRANSITORY.

103. Denominative adjectives were also made with the suffix -anus, Eng. -AN or -ANE [1], meaning *belonging* or *pertaining to;* thus:

germen, germinis, *offshoot,* **germanus,** probably for 'germ(i)nanus,' *kindred, brother,* GERMANE.

homo, hominis, *man,* **humanus,** perhaps for 'hom(i)nanus' (old form **hemo,** and probably related to **humus,** *soil,* since man is **terrae filius,** "of the earth, earthy"), *pertaining to man;* hence both HUMAN and HUMANE.

meridies, *midday,* **meridianus,** *pertaining to midday; (a line) marking the middle of the day,* MERIDIAN. **Meridies** was made by dissimilation (155) from an older **medidies, (medius)** *middle of the day.*

mons, montis, MOUNTAIN, **montanus,** appearing in TRAMONTANE, and ULTRAMONTANE. The simple adjective, coming through the French, became our noun MOUNTAIN, from which we have made also MOUNTAINOUS (94).

mundus, *earth,* **mundanus,** *of the earth,* MUNDANE.

pagus, *a district,* **paganus,** *belonging to the country district,* not of the religious group of the city; hence PAGAN.

Roma, ROME, **Romanus,** ROMAN. Thus many ancient and modern proper adjectives have been made: 'Sicilian,' 'American,' 'African,' 'Christian,' 'Carthaginian,' 'Indian.'

silva, *forest,* **silvanus,** also written **sylvanus,** *forestlike,* SYLVAN (or SILVAN).

urbs, *city,* **urbanus,** *of the city,* URBAN, or *characteristic of the city people, i.e., courteous, polite,* URBANE. Cf. SUBURBAN, SUBURB, 143.

vetus, veteris (adj.), *ancient, of the old time,* **veteranus,** *belonging to those of the old time;* especially of soldiers who had served a long time, VETERAN.

Very common is **-i-anus,** a combination of **-anus** with the **-io-** suffix used for making clan names (originally patronymic), as

---

[1] The suffix varies somewhat in words coming through the French (Ch. IV): **capitanus,** CAPTAIN (36); **certus,** *sure,* **certanus,** CERTAIN; **montanus,** MOUNTAIN, see above; **medius,** *middle,* **medianus,** MEAN (MEDIAN); **sacristanus** (Low Lat. **sacrista,** *sacred utensils*), SACRISTAN, SEXTON; **super,** *above,* **superanus,** OF 'soverain,' SOVEREIGN (28).

Julius, Julianus; whence -ianus makes adjectives from many proper nouns not in -io-; *e.g.*, **Ciceronianus,** Ciceronian, **Christianus,** Christian.

104. Like **-anus** in meaning is the suffix **-inus,** Eng. -ine, sometimes -in:

aquila, *eagle*, **aquilinus,** *eagle-like*, aquiline, now especially of a nose that is like the eagle's beak. **Aquila** itself, meaning the *dark brown* bird (**aquilus**), became OF 'aigle,' and Eng. eagle.

asinus, *ass*, **asininus,** *from an ass*. The Latin adjective was used literally, but the noun, like ours, was applied to the animal's human counterpart and with this meaning we have received the adj. asinine.

canis, *dog*, **caninus,** *belonging to a dog*, canine.

columba, *dove*, **columbinus,** *pertaining to a dove;* columbine we now apply particularly to a garden plant, perhaps from the resemblance of the spurs of its flowers to the beak of a dove.

divus (adj.), *belonging to a deity*, (noun) *a god*, **divinus,** divine.

equus, *horse*, **equinus,** *pertaining to horses*, equine.

femina, *woman*, **femininus,** feminine.

Latium, Eng. Latium, **Latinus,** *belonging to Latium*, particularly, lingua **Latina,** *the language of Latium*, Latin.

libertus, from **liber,** with the pf. pple. suffix -tus (-to-), *set free;* hence *a freedman;* **libertinus,** *a freedman;* now *one free of all restraint*, or *given to licence*, is a libertine.

mare, *sea*, **marinus,** *belonging to the sea*, marine.

sal, *salt*, **salinum** (as neut. noun or with **vas,** *vessel*, supplied), *a salt-cellar;* so saline. Note that our noun is the same as **sal,** with a suffix -*t*.

sup-, original form of **sub, supinus,** *downward, lying on the back*, supine. As a grammatical term (**verbum**) **supinum,** the supine (verb), is the "*verb lying flat on its back*," perfectly inactive by reason of having no signs of voice, mode, person, or tense — the absolute verb.

After *i* of the stem we find **-enus,** perhaps by dissimilation of vowels, *i-e* for *i-i;* **alius,** *another*, **alienus,** *belonging to another, foreign*, alien.

105. Of this group are properly feminine nouns in **-ina**, a word like **ars** being understood: **discipulus,** *a pupil,* **disciplina** (for **discipul-ina**), (the art) *that relates to pupils,* DISCIPLINE; **doctor,** *a teacher,* **doctrina,** *teaching,* DOCTRINE. Here, too, we place **genuinus,** *innate, natural,* GENUINE, not made directly from **genus,** *race,* but coming from the same root, **gen** (cf. **gignere,** *beget*).

106. Some denominative adjectives were formed with the suffix **-(u)lentus, -(o)lentus,** Eng. **-(U)LENT, -(O)LENT,** with the meaning *disposed to, abounding in,* etc.:

corpus, *body,* **corpulentus,** *developed in body,* CORPULENT.

fraus, fraudis, *deception,* **fraudulentus,** *cheating,* FRAUDULENT.

ops, opis, *means, resources,* **opulentus,** *blessed with resources,* OPULENT.

pestis, *plague,* **pestilentus,** *plague-bringing,* PESTILENT (cf. PESTILENCE, 33).

somnus, *sleep,* **somnulentus** or **somnolentus,** *given to sleep, drowsy,* SOMNOLENT.

trux, trucis (adj.), *wild, rough,* **truculentus,** *disposed to be wild,* TRUCULENT.

turba, *uproar,* **turbulentus,** *boisterous,* TURBULENT. See TURBID, 113.

virus, *poison,* **virulentus,** *full of poison,* VIRULENT.

vis, *force,* **violentus,** *employing force,* VIOLENT.

107. Denominative adjectives in **-atus,** Eng. **-ATE,** were made on the analogy of perfect passive participles of denominative verbs (128). In the same way English adjectives, quasi-participles, are formed in *-ed* while no corresponding verb is in use (*e.g.,* 'long-haired,' 'moneyed,' 'storied'):

deliciae, *pleasure,* **delicatus,** *addicted to pleasure, weak,* DELICATE.

dens, dentis, *tooth,* **dentatus,** *toothed,* DENTATE.

fortuna, FORTUNE, **fortunatus,** *favored by fortune,* FORTUNATE.

gradus, *step, degree,* Low Lat. **graduatus,** *having taken a degree;* as noun, GRADUATE.

laurea, for laurea corona, *a laurel wreath*, laureatus, *crowned with a laurel wreath*, LAUREATE. See BACHELOR, 202.

littera, LETTER (169), litterae, *literature*, litteratus, *lettered, educated*, LITERATE; negative ILLITERATE, *unlettered*. Cf. literati, 52.

penna (pinna), *wing, feather*, pennatus, *winged*, pinnatus, *feathered*, PENNATE, *winglike*, PINNATE, *featherlike*. See 12, pinna, N.

serra, *a saw*, serratus, *saw-shaped* or *saw-toothed*, SERRATE (also SERRATed, 125).

108. An old adjective suffix, originally participial, carrying the notion of *pertaining to*, was -no-, nom. -nus. Combining with other suffixes it furnished a number of words in -ernus, -urnus: from nouns in -ter, fraternus, maternus, paternus; from exter(ior), infer(ior), etc., externus, infernus, internus, supernus; nox, noctis, nocturnus (cf. Grk. 'nuktōr,' νύκτωρ, *by night*); diurnus, probably on analogy of nocturnus (dies, *day*, diu, *by day*); tacitus, taciturnus. Most of these words have come to us with the added suffix -AL (cf. ver-n-alis, VERNAL, from ver, *spring;* also 204): FRATERNAL, MATERNAL, PATERNAL, EXTERNAL, INFERNAL, INTERNAL, SUPERNAL, DIURNAL, NOCTURNAL. But we have also the noun NOCTURN, *a night service* of the early church, and the French form NOCTURNE, *a piece of music* suitable to the quiet of the night. Taciturnus also gives us TACITURN. From the adv. modo, *just now*, modernus (Late), *belonging to the time just now*, becomes Eng. MODERN. Modo was the ablative of modus, *measure*, originally *in* or *with measure, only*, etc.; so as applied to time, it came to signify *just now*.

109. The suffix -ensis meaning *originating in*, or *belonging to*, was used to make adjectives from many place names and from a few other nouns. Coming through Old French as '-eis,' it became Eng. -ESE and has been widely extended in modern formations (hybrids, 207), as ChinESE, SiamESE, JohnsonESE. It appears in:

amanuensis, a-manu + -ensis, *pertaining to a "servant from the hand"* (52).

FORENSIC, **forum,** the public *market-place;* the Latin adjective was **forensis,** to which we have added -IC (97, 204).
See also HORTENSE, 213.

110. Adjectives signifying *consisting of, like, belonging to,* were made with the suffix **-eus,** sometimes with a combination suffix **-ac-eus, -an-eus,** all passing over to other groups in English, usually in -EOUS (-ACEOUS, -ANEOUS, 94), sometimes in -EAL (98):

corpus, corporis, *body,* **corporeus,** *bodily, consisting of flesh,* CORPOREAL.

creta, *chalk* (**terra creta,** *sifted earth,* **cernere, cretus,** *sift*), **cretaceus,** *chalklike,* CRETACEOUS.

funus, funeris, a FUNERAL, **funereus,** *belonging to a funeral,* FUNEREAL.

ignis, *fire,* **igneus,** *fiery,* IGNEOUS.

miscellus (adj.), *mixed* (**miscere,** MIX [1]), **miscellaneus,** *mixed, of all sorts,* MISCELLANEOUS.

os, ossis, *bone,* **osseus,** *consisting of bone,* OSSEOUS.

sanguis, sanguinis, *blood,* **sanguineus,** *bloody,* SANGUINE (as if from -inus, 104); for meaning see 41.

sponte (abl., defective noun), *free will,* **spontaneus,** *of one's own accord,* SPONTANEOUS.

sub terra, *under earth* (cf. 143), **subterraneus,** *underground,* SUBTERRANEAN (as if **-an-e-an-us**).

111. In **-tus** like third conjugation participles (**ductus**) are:

astus, *cunning, craftiness,* **astu-tus,** *endowed with cunning,* ASTUTE.
jus, *right,* **jus-tus,** *righted, in accordance with the right,* JUST.
robus (**robur, robor**), *strength,* **robus-tus,** *powered, equipped with strength,* ROBUST.

Here possibly belong also two adjectives in **-itus:**

fortuitus, *occurring by chance,* FORTUITOUS (cf. **fors, fortis,** *chance,* and the *u*-form of stem in **fortuna,** FORTUNE).

---

[1] The Latin pf. pple. was **mixtus,** which came into English as MIXT; then MIXED, which implied a present MIX (cf. 132).

gratuitus, *done as a favor*, GRATUITOUS (cf. **grates, gratus,** etc.;
analogy with **fortuitus** may account for the Latin word, unless
there was also a stem **gratu-**). Cf. also **liber-tus,** 104.

B. ADJECTIVES MADE FROM VERBS

112. Many adjectives formed from verbs show the suffix
-i-dus, Eng. -ID.[1] They denote a quality implied or a tendency expressed in the verb:

acere, *be sour,* **acidus,** *sour,* ACID (cf. **acer,** *sharp*).

arere, *be dry,* **aridus,** *dry,* ARID.

candere, *be white,* **candidus,** *white, clear,* CANDID.

fervere, *boil, glow,* **fervidus,** *glowing, hot,* FERVID.

florere, *bloom* (flos, FLOWER), **floridus,** *flowery, blooming,* FLORID.

fluere, *flow,* **fluidus,** *flowing,* FLUID.

frigere, *be cold,* **frigidus,** *cold,* FRIGID.

horrere, *bristle, shudder* (*at*), **horridus,** *bristling,* HORRID.

humere, *be moist,* **humidus,** *moist,* HUMID.

languere, *be faint,* **languidus,** LANGUID.

liquere, *be fluid,* **liquidus,** *flowing,* LIQUID.

livere, *be blue,* **lividus,** *bluish,* LIVID.

lucere, *shine* (cf. **lux,** *light*), **lucidus,** *shining, bright,* LUCID.

pallere, *be pale,* **pallidus,** PALE (OF), PALLID.

placere, *please,* **placidus,** *pleasing;* hence *peaceful,* PLACID.

rabere, *be mad,* **rabidus,** *mad,* RABID.

rapere, *snatch,* **rapidus** (*snatching away*), *hurrying on,* RAPID.

rigere, *be stiff,* **rigidus,** *stiff,* RIGID.

sordere, *be black, be dirty, be base;* **sordidus,** *dirty, base,* SORDID.

squalere, *be stiff* with dirt, *be filthy,* **squalidus,** SQUALID.

stupere, *be stunned,* **stupidus,** *struck senseless,* STUPID.

tepere, *be lukewarm,* **tepidus,** TEPID.

timere, *fear,* **timidus,** *disposed to fear,* TIMID.

torpere, *be sluggish,* **torpidus,** *benumbed,* TORPID (cf. TORPEDO, 52).

torrere, *parch, bake,* **torridus,** *parched,* TORRID.

turgere, *swell,* **turgidus,** *swollen,* TURGID.

[1] In a number of instances such an adjective may have been parallel
with the verb rather than derived from it, *e.g.,* **florere** and **floridus** both
from **flos; lucere** and **lucidus** both from **lux.** See 113.

valere, *be strong,* **validus,** *strong,* VALID.

vivere, *live,* **vividus,** *lifelike, animated,* VIVID.

113. Several such adjectives seem to have been made from roots that did not survive in Latin verbs or were suggested by certain nouns, as:

limpidus, *clear, transparent,* LIMPID.

luridus, *pale yellow* (the noun is **luror**), LURID.

morbidus, *sickly, disposed to disease,* MORBID; **morbus,** *disease.*

solidus, *solid,* from **sollus,** *whole, complete, compact,* SOLID.

turbidus, *disturbed;* **turba,** the *bustling disorder* of a crowd (often *the crowd* itself); *disorder* in general. We apply the adjective TURBID particularly to disturbed and muddy water.

vapidus, *having emitted* VAPOR, **vapor;** *having lost its spirit,* or *strength,* VAPID.

114. Adjectives denoting originally a passive capacity were formed by adding -ilis to the verb root, Eng. -ILE:

agere, *move, drive,* **agilis,** *easily moved;* then *quick to move,* AGILE.

docere, *teach,* **docilis,** *capable of being taught,* DOCILE.

facere, *do,* **facilis,** *easy to do, ready, easy of access,* FACILE.

frangere (root **frag**), *break,* **fragilis,** *breakable,* FRAGILE.

habere, *hold,* **habilis,** *that may be held, easily managed, suitable* or *apt,* ABLE (OF).

115. Adjectives in -tilis, -silis, usually correspond to the pf. pple. forms in -tus, -sus, having the same phonetic change (147), Eng. -TILE, -SILE:

ducere, ductus, *lead,* **ductilis,** *that may be moved* (*led*) or *hammered,* DUCTILE.

ferre, *bear, produce,* **fertilis** (active in its force, and made as if we had 'fertus'), *productive,* FERTILE.

fodere, fossus, *dig,* **fossilis,** *dug out, dug up,* FOSSIL.

mittere, missus, *let go,* **missilis,** *that may be hurled,* MISSILE (**missile telum**).

repere, reptus, *creep,* **reptilis,** *creeping,* REPTILE; if **serp** is another form of the root **rep**, then SERPENT, **serpens,** is a doublet of REPTILE.

texere, textus, *weave*, textilis, *woven*, TEXTILE.

versari, versatus, *turn oneself about, be busy* or *engaged*, versatilis, *movable, readily turning from one thing to another*, VERSATILE.

volare, volatum, *fly*, volatilis, *flying, swift, easily passing away*, VOLATILE.

Probably from the pres. pple. of utor, utens, *using*, was utensilis (for utent-tilis, 147), *fit for use*, pl. utensilia, *materials* or UTENSILS; Med. Lat. utensile, UTENSIL.

116. Of like meaning with these are the large number of adjectives formed from verbs by means of the suffix -bilis. English follows the French which reduced -bil-em to -BLE (159, 160):

admirari, ADMIRE, admirabilis, ADMIRABLE.

affari (ad-fari), *speak to*, affabilis, *that may be spoken to*, AFFABLE.

arare, *plow*, arabilis, *that can be plowed*, ARABLE.

corrigere (regere), *make straight*, with in- incorrigibilis, *that cannot be corrected*, INCORRIGIBLE of persons. Cf. incorrectus, *uncorrected*, INCORRECT.

credere, *believe*, credibilis, *believable*, CREDIBLE.

durare, *endure, last*, durabilis, *lasting*, DURABLE.

honorare, *honor*, honorabilis, *bringing* or *gaining honor*, HONORABLE.

horrere, *bristle, shudder (at)*, horribilis, *dreadful*, HORRIBLE.

intelligere (intellegere, 150), *discern*, intelligibilis (intellegibilis), *easily discerned*, INTELLIGIBLE.

miserari, *pity*, miserabilis, *pitiable*, MISERABLE.

movere, *move*, mobilis (for mov[i]bilis), *movable*, MOBILE.

noscere, *know* (no-sc-ere, 131), nobilis, *well-known, deserving to be well-known*, NOBLE.

numerare, *count*, ENUMERATE; in-numerabilis, *uncountable*, IN-NUMERABLE.

placare, *quiet, appease*, placabilis, *ready to be appeased*, PLACABLE.

probare, *approve*, probabilis, *that may be approved* as correct, PROBABLE.

solvere, *loosen*, SOLVE, solubilis (solv-), *that may be solved* or *dissolved*, SOLUBLE.

stare, *stand*, stabilis (active in force), *capable of standing*, STABLE.

terrere, *frighten*, terribilis (active in force), *such as to cause fright*, TERRIBLE.

tolerare, *bear, endure*, tolerabilis, *endurable*, TOLERABLE.

tractare, *manage*, tractabilis, *manageable*, TRACTABLE. The verb is frequentative of trahere, tractus, *draw* (130).

venerari, *reverence*, VENERATE (venus, veneris, *love*), venerabilis, *worthy to be reverenced*, VENERABLE (41).

volvere, *turn, roll*, volubilis (active in its force, and volu- = volv-), *rolling*, especially referring to words, VOLUBLE.

117. This suffix is sometimes joined to the perfect passive participle stem, thus:

admittere, admissus, *allow to come to* a place, ADMIT, admissibilis (Late Lat.), ADMISSIBLE.

comprehendere, comprehensus, *grasp, understand*, comprehensibilis, *understandable*, COMPREHENSIBLE.

corrumpere, corruptus, *break to pieces, destroy*, CORRUPT, corruptibilis (Late Lat.), CORRUPTIBLE.

defendere, defensus, *smite down*, DEFEND (DEFENDANT, 30), defensibilis, DEFENSIBLE.

destruere, destructus, *pull down*, DESTROY, destructibilis (Late Lat.), DESTRUCTIBLE.

flectere, flexus, *bend*, flexibilis, *that may be bent*, FLEXIBLE.

plaudere, APPLAUD, plausus, plausibilis, *deserving applause; pleasing*, PLAUSIBLE.

118. It is well to observe that true Latin formations of this class have in English -ABLE, when coming from first conjugation verbs, otherwise -IBLE [1] (or occasionally -BLE, when -bilis was added directly in the Latin word); that non-Latin words have adopted regularly -ABLE, as in the preceding paragraphs we have used *believ*ABLE, and *understand*ABLE, alongside CREDIBLE, and COMPREHENSIBLE. We even make such English adjectives from nouns, as well as

[1] From capere, *take*, however, we have CAPABLE, representing Late Lat. capabilis (116), which had the same meaning as capax, *able to hold* or *receive*, and possibly from the latter adjective the *a* was taken over for the second syllable.

from verbs: COMFORTABLE, FASHIONABLE, OBJECTIONABLE, SEASONABLE, along with laughABLE, unthinkABLE, workABLE. (An exception in spelling is gullIBLE, 211.) From Latin verbs fully adopted into English we make the adjective in -ABLE, regardless of the Latin conjugation: **dependere**, DEPEND, did not furnish a Latin adjective '**dependibilis**,' but from DEPEND as an English word we have DEPENDABLE; from **movere, mobilis**, we get MOBILE, but from MOVE, we make MOVABLE.

119. Verbal adjectives denoting tendency or inclination were made with the suffix **-ac(i)**, nom. **-ax (-ac-s)**. The English derivative passes over to the -OUS (-osus) group (94) and ends in -ACIOUS:

audere, *dare*, **audax**, *daring*, AUDACIOUS.

capere, *take*, **capax**, *capable of receiving*, therefore *large*, CAPACIOUS.

efficere, EFFECT, **efficax**, *that can produce an effect*, EFFICACIOUS.

fallere, *deceive*, **fallax**, *deceitful, deceptive*, FALLACIOUS.

loqui, *talk*, **loquax**, *talkative*, LOQUACIOUS.

perspicere, *see through*, **perspicax**, *able to see through*, PERSPICACIOUS.

pugnare, *fight*, **pugnax**, *fond of fighting*, PUGNACIOUS.

rapere, *snatch*, **rapax**, *ready to snatch* things, RAPACIOUS.

sagire, *perceive keenly* (cf. **sagus**, *prophetic*, **praesagire**, PRESAGE), **sagax**, *keen-witted*, SAGACIOUS.

tenere, *hold*, **tenax**, *holding fast*, TENACIOUS.

vivere, *live*, **vivax**, *lively*, VIVACIOUS.

vorare, *swallow whole, devour*, **vorax**, *swallowing greedily*, VORACIOUS.

120. The suffix **-tivus, -sivus**, seems to have arisen from the addition of **-ivus** to the pf. pple. stem; Eng. -TIVE, -SIVE (147). Adjectives thus formed express tendency, or a quality implied in the verb:

aboriri, abortus, *begin amiss* (**ab-**), *miscarry*, **abortivus**, *born prematurely*, ABORTIVE.

accusare, accusatus, *call to account*, ACCUSE, **accusativus** (30), ACCUSATIVE.[1]

---

[1] The Lat. *accusativus* was something of a mistranslation of the Greek name of the case. The Greek 'aitia' (αἰτία) meant *cause* or

adoptare, adoptatus, ADOPT, **adoptivus** (for 'adoptativus'), ADOPTIVE.

agere, actus, *drive, do,* **activus,** *ready to act,* ACTIVE.

capere, captus, *take, catch,* **captivus,** *taken prisoner,* CAPTIVE.

colligere, collectus, *gather,* COLLECT, **collectivus,** *taken together,* COLLECTIVE.

dare, datus, *give,* **dativus,** *pertaining to giving,* and with **casus,** CASE, understood, DATIVE.

demonstrare, demonstratus, *point out, show,* **demonstrativus,** DEMONSTRATIVE.

fugere, fugitum, *flee,* **fugitivus,** *fleeing, runaway,* FUGITIVE.

imperare, imperatus, *put (a duty) on, command* (**in** + **parare,** *prepare,* 149, N. 2), **imperativus,** *of command,* IMPERATIVE.

indicare, indicatus, *declare,* **indicativus,** *declaring,* INDICATIVE.

lucrari, lucratus, *gain,* **lucrativus,** *profitable,* LUCRATIVE.

nasci, natus, *be born,* **nativus,** *related to* or *connected with one's birth,* NATIVE.

nominare, nominatus, *name,* **nominativus,** *having to do with naming,* and with **casus,** CASE, understood, NOMINATIVE.

pati, passus, *suffer,* **passivus,** *capable of suffering,* PASSIVE.

praerogare, praerogatus, *ask before,* **praerogativus,** *asked before* (others), *i.e., asked first* for an opinion or a vote and thus specially favored; hence as a noun (*e* for *ae*) PREROGATIVE.

vocare, vocatus, *call,* **vocativus,** *pertaining to calling,* and with **casus,** CASE, understood, VOCATIVE.

vovere, votus, *promise solemnly, vow,* **votivus,** *promised with a vow,* VOTIVE.

Similarly from **festum,** *a holiday,* and **furtum,** *stealing, theft* (**fur,** *thief*), adjectives were made, **festivus,** *suited to a holiday,* FESTIVE, and **furtivus,** *characteristic of one stealing, secret,* FURTIVE.

121. Verbal adjectives in **-ulus** denote tendency. These also pass over to the -OUS (-osus) group (94) and show in English the double suffix -ULOUS:

bibere, *drink,* **bibulus,** *drinking freely,* BIBULOUS.

credere, *believe,* **credulus,** *ready to believe,* CREDULOUS.

---

responsibility; its adj. 'aitiatike' (αἰτιατική), *pertaining to that which is caused* or *affected,* was the name for the case of the object, and this the Romans translated as **accusativus.**

garrire, *chatter,* **garrulus,** *chattering,* GARRULOUS.

pendere, *hang,* **pendulus,** *hanging,* PENDULOUS (cf. **pendulum,** 53).

queri, *complain,* **querulus,** *disposed to complain,* QUERULOUS.

tremere, *shake,* TREMBLE (Med. Lat. **tremulare**), **tremulus,** *trembling,* TREMULOUS.

With these may be compared nouns like **speculum, specula** (202, SPECULATE), **specere,** *look at;* perhaps **regula, regere,** RULE (42), and **tegula** (12), **tegere,** *cover.* **Discipulus,** *pupil,* DISCIPLE, points to a compound **dis-cipere,** which should mean *take apart, take up mentally,* as **praecipere,** *take up before* (pupils), gave **praeceptor,** *teacher,* PRECEPTOR. For **-cipulus,** cf. **mus-cipula,** *mouse-taker, mousetrap* (66). The traditional derivation of **discipulus** from **discere,** *learn,* gives no satisfactory explanation of the second element, though **discere** must have had an influence on the meaning.

122. Adjectives in -uus were made from certain verbs, expressing a quality implied in the verb; and these again take the -OUS (-OSUS) suffix (94), ending in English in -UOUS:

ambigere, *go about* (**amb-agere**), *hesitate, be uncertain,* **ambiguus,** AMBIGUOUS.

assidere, *sit at* or *by* (**ad-sedere**), **assiduus,** *sitting by* a thing, *busy with it,* ASSIDUOUS. Cf. ASSESS (**ad-sessus**), *sit by* as judge (of a fine or property value). The causative **sedare, sedatus,** *settle,* gives SEDATE.

congruere, *come together, agree,* **congruus,** *agreeing,* CONGRUOUS; also the negative, **incongruus,** INCONGRUOUS.

conspicere, *look at attentively,* **conspicuus,** *attracting attention,* CONSPICUOUS.

continere (**tenere**), *hold together,* **continuus,** *holding together,* CONTINUOUS (cf. CONTINENT, 123).

contingere, *touch* (**tangere,** root **tag,** in compounds **-tig-,** 149), **contiguus,** *touching,* CONTIGUOUS.

decidere, *fall off* (**cadere,** *fall*), **deciduus,** *falling off,* of trees whose leaves fall, DECIDUOUS.

miscere, MIX, with **pro-, promiscuus,** *mixed,* PROMISCUOUS.

nocere, *harm,* **nocuus,** *harmful,* NOCUOUS: more common, however, in the negative, **innocuus,** *harmless,* INNOCUOUS. From the same

root is NOXIOUS, 95. Cf. **innocens**, *not harming*, INNOCENT; also
nocentia, NUISANCE, 199.

perspicere, *see through*, **perspicuus**, *easily seen through*, PERSPICUOUS.

But from **mutare**, *change*, **mutuus**, *interchangeable*, *reciprocal*,
became Eng. MUTUAL (Fr. 'mutuel'), as in 98. The meaning war-
rants a MUTUAL friendship, but not "Our MUTUAL Friend."

123. A very large number of present participles come
into English as adjectives, often also as nouns, regularly
ending in -ANT from first conjugation verbs, -ENT from all
others (190):

abesse, *be away*, **absens** (ab-s-ens), ABSENT.

absorbere, *drink down*, *suck up*, **absorbens**, ABSORBENT.

abundare, *overflow* (**unda**, *a wave*), **abundans**, ABUNDANT.

accidere, *fall to* or *on* (**cadere**, *fall*), *happen*, **accidens**, ACCIDENT.

adjacere, *lie next to* (**jacēre**), **adjacens**, ADJACENT.

adolescere, *grow up*, **adolescens**, ADOLESCENT.

agere, ACT, **agens**, AGENT, *a doer*, *i.e.*, *one who acts* for another.

antecedere, *go before*, **antecedens**, *going before*, ANTECEDENT.

applicare, *attach to* (**ad-plicare**), *devote oneself to*, *steer toward*, APPLY
   (189), **applicans**, APPLICANT.

arrogare (**ad-rogare**), *ask for oneself*, *claim as one's own*, *claim too
   much*, **arrogans**, ARROGANT.

aspirare (**ad-spirare**), *breathe on* or *toward*, *aspire to*, **aspirans**,
   ASPIRANT.

cogere, (**co-agere**), *drive together*, *compel*, **cogens**, *compelling*,
   COGENT.

competere, *seek along with* others (cf. **competitor**, 52); also *agree
   with*, *be equal to*, **competens**, *qualified*, COMPETENT.

complacere, *be very pleasing*, **complacens**, COMPLACENT, often suggesting in English that one is pleasing to himself as well as to
   others, self-COMPLACENT.

componere, *put together*, **componens**, COMPONENT.

confidere, *trust fully*, **confidens**, CONFIDENT.

consequi, *follow up*, **consequens**, CONSEQUENT.

continere, *hold together*, **continens** (149), *holding in check*, CONTI-
   NENT; also *connected* or *continuous*, and as a noun, *a continuous
   body of land*, a CONTINENT.

contingere, *touch, affect, befall,* **contingens,** CONTINGENT; as an adjective, *touching on* certain things, therefore *dependent;* as a noun, *what falls to one's part, a quota,* especially of soldiers.

crescere (131), *grow,* **crescens,** *growing* (especially of the moon), CRESCENT.

currere, *run,* **currens,** *running,* CURRENT.

delinquere, *be wanting* (de-linquere, *leave*), *do wrong,* **delinquens,** DELINQUENT.

differre, *carry apart,* DIFFER, **differens,** DIFFERENT.

diffidere, *distrust* (dis + fidere, *trust*), **diffidens,** *lacking confidence,* DIFFIDENT.

eloqui, *speak out,* **eloquens,** ELOQUENT.

eminere, *stand out, be prominent,* **eminens,** EMINENT. Root **men, mon** (157), *project, jut out,* as in **mons,** *mountain* [1]*;* so also IMMINENT below.

evanescere, *vanish away,* **evanescens,** EVANESCENT.

expectare (ex-spectare), *look out for, await,* EXPECT, **expectans,** EXPECTANT.

extare (ex-stare), *stand forth, exist,* **extans,** EXTANT.

fluere, *flow,* **fluens,** *flowing,* FLUENT.

immanere, *abide in* (in-manere), **immanens,** IMMANENT.

imminere, *project over, be near at hand, be threateningly near,* **imminens,** IMMINENT (see EMINENT above).

incidere, *fall upon* (in-cadere), *fall to one's lot, occur,* **incidens,** INCIDENT.

incumbere, *recline upon,* **incumbens,** *resting on,* INCUMBENT, used of the duty resting on the man, and of the man resting on the position.

ingredi, *go into* (in + gradi, *step*), **ingrediens,** INGREDIENT.

inhaerere, *stick in, cling to,* **inhaerens,** (*e* for *ae*) INHERENT.

insistere, *stand on, press on, persevere, urge,* **insistens,** INSISTENT.

insolescere, *swell up, be haughty;* on the same root (without -sc-, 131) **insolens,** INSOLENT.

insurgere, *rise on* or *against,* **insurgens,** INSURGENT.

itinerari, *go on a journey* (iter, itineris), **itinerans,** ITINERANT.

latere, *lie hidden,* **latens,** LATENT.

---

[1] Cf. Goldsmith's description of the eminent preacher in the *Deserted Village:* "As some tall cliff that lifts its awful form," etc.

militare, *be a soldier* (**miles**), *make war*, **militans**, MILITANT.

oboedire, *give ear* (**ob**, *in front, facing*, + the same root as in **audire**, *hear*), OBEY, **oboediens**, (*e* for *oe*) OBEDIENT.

obsolescere, *grow old* (probably **ob-solescere**, *become accustomed*, from **solere**, 131), **obsolescens**, OBSOLESCENT.

parere, *bring forth, give birth to*, old participial form **parens**, as noun, PARENT (regular pres. pple. **pariens**).

posse, *be able* (**pot-esse**), **potens**, *able, powerful*, POTENT.

praevalere, *be strong before* or *above* another, **praevalens**, (*e* for *ae*) PREVALENT.

proficere, *make forward* (**pro-facere**), *advance, accomplish*, **proficiens**, PROFICIENT.

pudere, *make ashamed;* **pudet**, *it shames*, **impudens** (**in-**, *not*), *shameless*, IMPUDENT.

pungere, *pierce* (cf. **punctum**, POINT), **pungens**, *pricking*, PUNGENT.

quiescere, *become quiet*, **quiescens**, QUIESCENT.

regere, *rule*, **regens**, *ruling, acting as ruler* (**rex**), REGENT.

repellere, *drive back*, **repellens**, REPELLENT.

repugnare, *fight back*, **repugnans**, *fighting against*, REPUGNANT.

reticere, *be silent* (**re** + **tacere**, *be silent*), **reticens**, RETICENT.

revereri, *hold in awe*, REVERE, **reverens**, REVERENT.

rodere, *gnaw*, **rodens**, RODENT.

salire, *leap*, **saliens**, *leaping forward;* SALIENT, *jutting out, important*.

secare, *cut*, **secans**, SECANT, *cutting* (through the circle).

sonare, *sound*, **sonans**, SONANT. Cf. CONSONANT, *sounding with* (only with something else).

stagnare, *become a pond*, from **stagnum**, *standing water*, **stagnans**, STAGNANT.

stridere, *whistle, creak*, **stridens**, STRIDENT.

stringere, *draw tight*, **stringens**, *binding*, STRINGENT.

studere, *be zealous*, **studens**, *zealous, eager*, STUDENT.

tangere, *touch*, **tangens**, TANGENT, *touching* (the circumference).

torrere, *parch, roast, boil*, **torrens**, *boiling;* then *a boiling stream*, a TORRENT.

unguere, *smear, anoint*, **unguens**, UNGUENT; OINTMENT through the French is of the same origin.

vigilare, *watch* (**vigil**, *watchful*), **vigilans**, VIGILANT.

124. Perfect passive participles likewise become English adjectives, -atus, -itus, usually as -ATE, -ITE, and consonant stems (third conjugation) without the silent -e (cf. 163):

abicere (ab-jacere), abjectus, *cast off*, ABJECT.

abrumpere, *break off*, abruptus, *broken off*, ABRUPT.

adaequare, *make equal to*, adaequatus, *made equal to* (the demands), (*e* for *ae*) ADEQUATE.

concrescere, *grow together*, concretus, *grown together, hardened*, CONCRETE.

considerare, *look at attentively* (CONSIDER, 202), consideratus, *reflected on carefully*, CONSIDERed; then, transferred from the thing to the person, *giving careful thought*, CONSIDERATE.

definire, *set the limits of* (**finis**, *limit*), definitus, *with limits fixed*, DEFINITE; also FINITE, *limited*, and INFINITE, 141.

desolare, *leave completely* (**de-**) *alone* (**solus**), desolatus, *forsaken*, DESOLATE.

desperare, *be out of hope* (**spes**), desperatus, *despaired of, beyond hope*, DESPERATE. Cf. DESPERADO, 50.

exquirere (ex-quaerere), *seek out*, exquisitus, *sought out* (and therefore *better than the ordinary*), EXQUISITE.

intricare, *entangle* (cf. **tricari**, *cause difficulties*), intricatus, *tangled*, INTRICATE. Through French **intricare** has given us INTRIGUE.

obstinare, evidently **ob** + **stanare**, an **n**-stem formation from **stare**: *stand in the face of, face with firmness*, obstinatus, *determined*, OBSTINATE (cf. **destinare**, DESTINE).

occulere, *cover over, conceal*, occultus, *hidden*, OCCULT.

polire, POLISH (186), politus, *polished*, POLITE.

praecidere (-caedere), *cut before, cut off in front*, praecisus, *cut off, shortened*, (*e* for *ae*) PRECISE.

tacere, *be silent*, or *pass over in silence*, tacitus, *passed over in silence, kept secret*, TACIT.

temperare, *regulate, restrain oneself*, temperatus, *held in restraint, self-controlled*, TEMPERATE.

125. Since many English verbs are made from the Latin pf. pple. stem (128, 132), their participles in -*ed* sometimes furnish us adjectives which are really double participle forms:

abstrahere, *draw away*, **abstractus**, ABSTRACT, ABSTRACTed.
animare, *fill with breath, give life to*, **animatus**, ANIMATed.
deicere, *cast down*, **dejectus**, DEJECTed.
situare (Late Lat.), *place* (**situs**, *position*, SITE), **situatus**, SITUATed.
variegare, *make of various sorts*, **variegatus**, VARIEGATed.

126. The gerundive or future passive participle in the case of several verbs has become an English adjective form, often used as a noun. Ending in -andus, -endus, according as the verb is of the first conjugation or not, these forms appear in English in -AND and -END, and retain their meaning of obligation:

dividere, DIVIDE, **dividendus**, *that must be divided*, DIVIDEND.
legere, *read*, **legendus**, *that ought to be read*, LEGEND (202).
minuere, *make less*, **minuendus**, *that must be lessened*, MINUEND.
multiplicare, MULTIPLY (**multum** + **plicare**, 189), **multiplicandus**, *that must be multiplied*, MULTIPLICAND.
revereri, *stand in awe of*, REVERE, **reverendus**, *that should be revered*, REVEREND.
stupere, *be stunned*, **stupendus**, *to be amazed at*, STUPENDOUS.
subtrahere, *draw from under, take away*, **subtrahendus**, *that must be taken away*, SUBTRAHEND.
tremere, *quake, tremble at*, **tremendus**, *that should be trembled at*, TREMENDOUS.

Several gerundive forms are given in other lists: **addendum**, 59, **agenda**, 59, **corrigendum**, 59, **lavanda** in LAVENDER, 48, LAUNDRY, 202; also **amanda**, 213, **memorandum**, 53, **referendum**, 53.

127. When such words came through French, the ending was -AND regardless of the conjugation of the verb: from **reprimere**, REPRESS, **reprimenda** (fem.) was *a thing that ought to be repressed;* then through the Fr. 'reprimande,' came REPRIMAND; **vivenda** (Low Lat. **vivanda**, Fr. 'viande,' *meat*) (neut. pl.) from **vivere**, *things to be lived on*, likewise became VIAND. Cf. 190, 191.

III. The Formation of Verbs

A. VERBS MADE FROM NOUNS AND ADJECTIVES

128. Most Latin verbs derived from nouns or adjectives were of the first conjugation.[1] Their corresponding English forms have usually been made from the perfect passive participle in -atus, and accordingly end in -ATE (132):

aequus, *equal,* **aequare,** *make equal,* **aequatus,** (*e* for *ae*) EQUATE.

agger (**ad-ger-ere,** *bring to; material brought to a heap*), *a mound,* with **ex- exaggerare,** *heap up as a mound,* **exaggeratus,** EXAGGERATE.

alienus, *belonging to another* (**alius**), *foreign,* **alienare,** *make to belong to another,* **alienatus,** ALIENATE.

asper, *rough,* with **ex- exasperare,** *make rough, irritate,* **exasperatus,** EXASPERATE.

corium, *skin, hide,* with **ex- excoriare,** *take the hide off,* **excoriatus,** EXCORIATE.

crastinus, *belonging to tomorrow* (**cras**), **procrastinare,** *set forward to tomorrow,* **procrastinatus,** PROCRASTINATE.

cumulus, *a heap,* with **ad- accumulare,** *heap on* (one thing on another), **accumulatus,** ACCUMULATE.

decimus, *tenth,* **decimare,** *select by lot every tenth man* (for punishment), *kill every tenth man,* **decimatus,** DECIMATE.

dominus, *master,* **dominari,** *be master,* **dominatus,** DOMINATE.

donum, *a gift,* **donare,** *present as a gift,* **donatus,** DONATE.

fluctus, *a wave,* **fluctuare,** *move in waves,* **fluctuatus,** FLUCTUATE.

frustra, *in vain* (neut. pl. or abl. sing. used adverbially; for 'frudtra,' 147; cf. fraus, fraudis, FRAUD), **frustrari,** *disappoint, trick,* **frustratus,** FRUSTRATE.

germen, germinis, *sprout* (GERM), **germinare,** *produce sprouts,* **germinatus,** GERMINATE.

hiberna, *winter quarters,* **hibernare,** *spend the winter,* **hibernatus,** HIBERNATE.

iterum, *again,* an adverb, really a comparative (-ter-) on a pronom-

---

[1] The converse is also true: the great majority of first conjugation verbs were derivative.

inal stem (as in **i-tem**); **iterare**, *repeat*, **iteratus**, ITERATE. Very common with prefix, RE-ITERATE.

lacer, *bitten, mangled*, **lacerare**, *tear, mangle*, **laceratus**, LACERATE.

liber, *free*, **liberare**, *set free*, **liberatus**, LIBERATE.

littera (**litera**), LETTER (169), with **ob-**, *over against*, **obliterare**, *rub out the letters*, **obliteratus**, OBLITERATE.

locus, *a place*, **locare**, *place*, **locatus**, LOCATE.

miles, **militis**, *a soldier*, **militare**, *serve as a soldier*, **militatus**, MILITATE.

negotium (**ne**, *not* + particle **g** + **otium**, *leisure*), *business*, **negotiare**, *arrange as business*, **negotiatus**, NEGOTIATE.

nomen, **nominis**, *name*, **nominare**, *name*, **nominatus**, NOMINATE.

novus, *new*, with **re-** **renovare**, *make new again, renew*, **renovatus**, RENOVATE.

numerus, NUMBER (174), with **e-** **enumerare**, *count out*, **enumeratus**, ENUMERATE.

onus, **oneris**, *burden*, with **ex-** **exonerare**, *take away the burden*, **exoneratus**, EXONERATE.

opus, **operis**, *work*, **operari**, *work*, **operatus**, OPERATE.

radius, *the spoke* of a wheel (52), **radiare**, *send out from a center like spokes*, or *like rays of light*, **radiatus**, RADIATE.

repudium, from root of **pudere**, **pudet**, *it shames*, applied to what one is afterward ashamed of and therefore rejects; particularly it is a dissolution of marriage; **repudiare**, *reject*, **repudiatus**, REPUDIATE.

robor (**robur**, cf. **robustus**, 111), *a hard wood, e.g., oak;* then *strength;* with **com-** (**cor-**), **corroborare**, *strengthen*, **corroboratus**, CORROBORATE.

scintilla, *spark* (52), **scintillare**, *sparkle*, **scintillatus**, SCINTILLATE.

socius, *ally*, with **ad-** **associare**, *join to one as an ally*, **associatus**, ASSOCIATE.

stimulus, *a goad*, **stimulare**, *spur on*, **stimulatus**, STIMULATE.

stirps, *stock, stem*, with **ex-** **ex(s)tirpare**, *pluck out the stock, root out*, **extirpatus**, EXTIRPATE.

unda, *wave*, with **in-** **inundare**, *cover with waves*, **inundatus**, INUNDATE. Cf. ABUNDANT, 123.

vastus, *empty, waste*, with **de-** **devastare**, *lay waste*, **devastatus**, DEVASTATE.

ventulus, *a little wind*, diminutive of **ventus**, **ventilare** (for 'ventulare,' 149, end), *toss in the air, fan*, **ventilatus**, VENTILATE.

vestigium, *a track, trace*, VESTIGE, with **in-** **investigare**, *get on track of*, **investigatus**, INVESTIGATE.

129. A few verbs of other conjugations are made from nouns and adjectives, the derivative in English either following the Latin present stem or, through the French, ending in -ISH (186):

finis, *end*, **finire**, *end*, FINISH.

flos, floris, FLOWER, **florere**, *flower*, FLOURISH.

lenis, *mild*, **lenire**, *make mild* or *be mild*, pres. pple. **leniens**, LENIENT (123).

poena, *penalty*, (poen-, pun-) **punire**, *inflict a penalty*, PUNISH.

servus, *slave, servant*, **servire**, *be a servant*, SERVE.

vestis, *clothing*, with **in-** **investire**, *clothe*, INVEST.

See also **erudire**, ERUDITE from **rudis** (39, 'learned'), **expedire** (**impedire**), EXPEDITE (IMPEDE) from **pes** (202).

B. VERBS MADE FROM OTHER VERBS

130. Frequentatives or intensives, denoting repeated or intensified action, were made with a present following the pf. pple. stem of other verbs, ending in -to, -ito, sometimes in -tito,[1] and regularly of the first conjugation. The English form follows sometimes the present stem (pf. pple. of the simple verb), sometimes the pf. pple. stem of the intensive (132):

canere, cantus, *sing*, **cantare**, *keep singing;* then (like canere) *sing*, CHANT (cf. CANT, 42).

cedere, cessus, *withdraw, yield*, **cessare**, *yield fully*, CEASE (Fr. 'cesser'; cf. CESSATION).

convertere, **conversus**, *turn around*, **conversari**, *turn round and round;* hence *abide, be associated with*, CONVERSE (cf. CONVERSATION, 85).

dicere, dictus, *say*, **dictare**, *say repeatedly, pronounce*, **dictatus**, DICTATE.

---

[1] Adding -ito to the pf. pple. stem in -t-.

habere, habitus, *have,* **habitare,** *to have and to hold, dwell (in),* **habitat** (57).

haerere, *stick,* (as if pple. '**haesitus**' instead of **haesus**) **haesitare,** *stick fast,* **haesitatus,** (*e* for *ae*) HESITATE.

pellere, pulsus, *drive,* **pulsare,** *drive with blows, beat,* **pulsatus,** PULSATE.

resilire, *leap back* (**salire**), **resultare** (**re-saltare,** p. 187 N.; **resultus** was not used), *rebound* (cf. RESILIENT from **resiliens**), the *rebound* of an act is its after effect, its RESULT.

specere, *look at,* **spectare,** *look at attentively,* with **ex- exspectare,** *await,* EXPECT.

visere, visum, *look at, go to see* (from **videre,** *see*)*;* then, as if the supine had been '**visitum,**' **visitare,** *go to see,* VISIT. Like this, from **agere, actus,** came not '**actare,**' but **agitare,** *drive about,* AGITATE.

131. Many Latin verbs, among them a number of inchoatives (**inchoare,** *begin*), were formed from other verbs by adding **-sc-** to make a new present stem, the derived verb being of the third conjugation:

adolere, *increase,* **adolescere,** *grow up,* (from pres. pple.) ADOLESCENT.

alere, *nourish,* with **co- coalescere,** *grow together,* COALESCE.

candere, *shine* (cf. CANDOR, 81, CANDID, 112), with **in- incandescere,** *glow,* (from pres. pple.) INCANDESCENT.

creare, *form,* CREATE, **crescere,** *begin to be formed, grow,* (from pple.) CRESCENT.

fervere, *boil* (cf. FERVOR, 81, FERVID, 112), with **ex- (ec-) effervescere** (*begin to boil*), *boil out, boil over,* EFFERVESCE and EFFERVESCENT.

florere, *flower, flourish,* with **ex- (ec-) efflorescere,** *begin to bloom out,* (from pres. pple.) EFFLORESCENT.

132. The very common use of a perfect passive participle to make a present verb stem in English is easily explained from the fact that such a participle was first borrowed as an adjective (124), as, *e.g.,* the old and poetic CREATE from the Lat. **creatus.** Then on the analogy of English participles, it was felt that there should be a -*d* or -*ed* ending. This, once added, making CREATE*d*, implied a present CREATE, and the implication became sufficient excuse for the form. CREATE was not used as a present tense until the sixteenth century; in the fifteenth century the participle varied between CREATE and CREATE*d*, the former occurring occasionally even much later. Shakespeare wrote in *Midsummer Night's Dream*, 5, 1, 412:

> And the issue there create
> Ever shall be fortunate.

And in *King Henry VI*, Part II, 1, 1, 124–5:

> May he be suffocate
> That dims the honor of this warlike isle.

So Bacon, *Essay* 39:

> Except it be corroborate by custom.

133. In other conjugations also examples like the following could be multiplied, where English verbs show the Latin pf. pple. stem:

affligere (ad-fligere, *dash to the ground*), **afflictus,** AFFLICT.
agere, *do*, **actus,** ACT.
collabi, *fall together, fall in ruins*, **collapsus,** COLLAPSE.
complere, *fill up*, **completus,** COMPLETE (kept also as an adjective).
concoquere, *cook together*, **concoctus,** CONCOCT.
corrigere, *put right*, **correctus,** CORRECT.
eximere (ex + emere), *take out, remove*, **exemptus,** EXEMPT.
extorquere, *twist out*, **extortus,** EXTORT.
incendere, *set fire to, inflame*, **incensus,** INCENSE.
persequi, *follow up, pursue*, **persecutus,** PERSECUTE.

For pf. pples. becoming English adjectives, see 124, 125.

134. On the other hand, English verbs are made from the present stems of many Latin verbs, representing all conjugations (cf. 182):

annullare, ad + nullus, *bring to naught,* ANNUL.

condonare, *give as a present* (**donum**), *give one his debt; i.e., release from debt, release from punishment,* CONDONE.

conjurare, *bind together by an oath* (**jus, juris**), CON'JURE, or CON-JURE'.

contestari, *call to witness,* **testis,** *witness,* CONTEST.

deterrere, *frighten off,* DETER.

disputare, *think differently,* DISPUTE (137).

exaltare (**ex + altus**), *lift on high,* EXALT.

ferire, *strike,* with **inter** (through OF 'entreferir,' *exchange blows*), INTERFERE.

illuminare (**in + lumen, luminis**), *shed light on,* ILLUMINE and ILLUMINATE.

incurrere, *run into,* INCUR.

lamentari (**la-mentum,** 90, end), *wail,* LAMENT.

perturbare, *put thoroughly* (**per**) *into an uproar* (**turba**), *disturb greatly,* PERTURB.

revelare, *turn back* (**re-**) the VEIL (**velum**), *unveil,* REVEAL.

submittere, *send under, allow oneself* (**se**) *to undergo,* SUBMIT.

135. A perfect participle may come into English as an adjective (124) while its present stem makes an English verb with its own participle:

absolvere, absolutus, *release,* ABSOLVE, ABSOLVed, ABSOLUTE.

discernere, discretus, *distinguish between,* DISCERN, DISCERNed, DISCREET.

divertere, diversus, *turn aside,* DIVERT, DIVERTed, DIVERSE; also, adj. DIVERS.

offerre, oblatus, *bring forward* or *against,* OFFER, OFFERed, OBLATE, *carried against* or *crosswise, i.e., pushed out at the sides.*

requirere, requisitus, *seek after, need,* REQUIRE, REQUIRed, REQUI-SITE.

136. Again it is often the case that a Latin verb has furnished us two separate verbs, one from the present stem, the other from the perfect participle, thus:

conducere, conductus, *bring together,* CONDUCE, CONDUCT.

construere, constructus (orig. root **strugh,** cf. 146), *build together,* CONSTRUE, CONSTRUCT.

convincere, convictus, *refute, prove guilty,* CONVINCE, CONVICT.

evincere, evictus, *completely vanquish,* by evidence (so as to prove beyond doubt), EVINCE; or by judicial procedure (so as to dispossess of property), EVICT.

referre, relatus, *carry back,* REFER, RELATE.

refundere, refusus, *pour back, restore, give back,* REFUND, REFUSE.

repellere, repulsus, *drive back,* REPEL, REPULSE.

137. The same verb may come differently in different compounds:

remittere, remissus, *send back,* REMIT.
dimittere, dimissus, *send apart,* DISMISS.

disputare, disputatus,[1] *think apart,* or *differently,* DISPUTE.
amputare, amputatus (**am-, amb-**), *cut around, prune, cut off,* AMPUTATE.

emergere, *come forth* (**mergere,** *sink*) *come to the surface,* EMERGE. Cf. EMERGENCY, 202.
immergere, immersus, *cause to sink in, dip,* IMMERSE.

impedire, impeditus, IMPEDE (EXPEDITE, 202).
expedire, expeditus, EXPEDITE (202).

138. Of peculiar interest are the verbs COMPOSE, DEPOSE, EXPOSE, etc., often loosely cited as derivatives of Lat. **ponere;** -POSE, however, is neither **ponere** nor **positus.** The Greek 'pauo' (παύω) means *I stop,* and its noun 'pausis'

---

[1] **Putare** has been explained from **putus,** *pure,* as meaning *cleanse, prune, clear up, clear up an account, reckon, think;* or as possibly from a root meaning *cut;* then *prune,* etc. (See Müller, *Alt.-ital. Wb.;* Walde, *Lat. Et. Wb.*) **Deputare,** *cut off,* **deputatus,** gave Fr. 'député,' *one cut off, i.e., detached for special work,* Eng. DEPUTY.

($\pi a\hat{v}\sigma\iota\varsigma$) was represented in Latin by **pausa,** the Eng. PAUSE. From **pausa** was made **pausare** (128), *cease,* which in Low Latin meant also *cause to cease, make to rest,* becoming 'poser' in French and POSE in English. The Low Latin meaning of *cause to rest* (in a place) is practically *put* (in a place), and a confusion with **ponere,** *put, place,* especially with the participle **positus,** was not unnatural. But **ponere** was for **po-,** *aside* (145), + **sinere,** *allow, place* (cf. **situs,** SITE), **po-sinere** becoming **ponere,** while the participle remained **po-situs.** From **ponere,** therefore, but for this confusion, we should probably have "compone, depone, expone," exactly as we have POSTPONE, COMPONENT, DEPONENT, EXPONENT (123), and, through the French, COMPOUND and EXPOUND (154). The odd situation then is this: POSE is of Greek origin; COMPOSE, DEPOSE, EXPOSE, etc., have prefixes Latin, '-pose' Greek (through Latin); while COMPONENT, DEPONENT, EXPONENT, COMPOSITE, DEPOSIT, COMPOSITION, DEPOSITION, EXPOSITION, etc. are derived from Lat. **ponere, positus.**

IV. COMPOUNDS

139. While English is not so ready to combine native words for the making of new terms as it was in the time before its enrichment with foreign derivatives, yet our use of such words as 'airplane,' 'sight-seeing,' 'stronghold,' 'on-rushing,' 'broad-minded,' 'up-town,' shows that we have not forgotten how to simplify our expressions by the formation of compounds. By observing the method by which the Romans made their compounds we may understand more clearly certain derivatives which those compounds have given us. If we examine the English examples just given we find that 'airplane' and 'sight-seeing,' *i.e., a plane for the air,* and *seeing the sights,* present the first element in case relation to the second, the one a dative, the other an accusative; 'stronghold' is a single word but 'strong' is a modifier of 'hold'; so also the adverb 'on-' is a modifier of 'rushing'; in 'broad-minded,' while 'broad' is likewise a modifier of 'mind,' the addition of -ed gives a possessive meaning, "having a broad mind"; and in "an up-town street" we have as adjective modifier a prepositional phrase. The same classification will apply to most of our Latin compounds: Dependent, Descriptive, Possessive, and Prepositional, we may call them. These are together sometimes called Subordinating Compounds as distinguished from those few Coördinating Compounds which simply link together two words of equal rank. For example, the Romans added two and ten by saying **duodecim,** from which we have made the adjective DUODECIMAL; but our chief concern is with the groups named above, examples of which are given in the following paragraphs:

A. DEPENDENT COMPOUNDS

140. Illustrations of dependent compounds are:

aedificium [1] (**aedes** + **facere,** cf. **aedificare,** *build*), *house-making,* (with *e* for *ae*) EDIFICE (the result of *house-making*).

agricultura [2] (**agri cultura,** from **colere, cultus**), *cultivation of the field,* AGRICULTURE.

aquaeductus [2] (**aquae ductus**), *conveyance of water,* also *a conveyance for water,* (*e* for *ae*) AQUEDUCT.

belligerens (**bellum** + **gerere**), *war-waging,* BELLIGERENT. The compound verb in Latin, **belligerare,** *wage war,* transfers **gero**

[1] Following the common weakening of the unaccented vowel after the accent in the prehistoric period (149), the stem vowel of the first part of a compound was usually reduced to *i*. Sometimes the final stem vowel *a* or *o* (first or second declension) was dropped before a vowel, but *i* became the regular "composition vowel," introduced also into consonant stems and even written for *e* in **anticipare** (**ante** + **capere**), *take before,* ANTICIPATE (a kind of restoration of an original *i*, *i.e.,* 'anti').

[2] These are separable compounds, also called improper, since the first element preserves the case form and was sometimes written as a separate word.

to the first conjugation [1] and its participle should give, and earlier did give, 'belligerant,' but English now follows the form of the simple verb.

carnivorus (caro, carnis + vorare), *flesh-devouring*, CARNIVOROUS.

dentifricium (dens, dentis + fricare), *tooth-rubbing*, which as early as Pliny meant *tooth powder*, DENTIFRICE.

fumigare (fumus + agere), *produce smoke, smoke* (trans.), FUMI-GATE.

homicidium (homo + caedere, -cidere), *manslaughter*, HOMICIDE, 41; as applied to the person HOMICIDE represents **homi-cida**, *man-slayer, murderer*.

jurisdictio,[2] *declaration of law, legal authority*, JURISDICTION.

jurisprudentia,[2] *knowledge of law, the science of law*, JURISPRUDENCE.

legislator,[2] *proposer of a law, lawmaker*, LEGISLATOR (**ferre legem [ad populum]**, *bring forward a law*).

lucifer (lux, lucis + ferre), *light-bringing*, applied to the planet Venus, LUCIFER (52).

munificentia (munus + facere, -ntia, 75), *the making of presents*, MUNIFICENCE.

navigare (navis + agere),[1] *drive a ship, sail*, NAVIGATE.

omnivorus (omnis + vorare), *all-devouring*, OMNIVOROUS.

parricida (spelled also paricida). The first element here must have been originally '**pasos**' (Doric Grk. παός, for πασός), *a near relative*, **pas-i-caed-** becoming **paricid-a** (156), then associated with **pater,** as *slaying a father*, PARRICIDE.

participans (pars, partis + capere), pres. pple. of **participare** (123), from **particeps, participis,** *a partaker, part-taking*, PARTICIPANT.

satisfactio (satis + facere), *a doing enough, enough* to make amends; now also *enough* for one's own comfort, SATISFACTION.

solstitium (sol + -stitium, from **stare,** *stand*), *sun-standing*, SOL-STICE (23, 176), since at this point the sun seems to stop for turning back on its course.

somnifer (somnus + ferre), *sleep-bringing*, SOMNIFEROUS (96).

---

[1] When a verb is compounded with anything other than a preposition, the compound is of the first conjugation. Most such verbs, however, may have been made rather from compound nouns or adjectives, 128, as if, **navis + ag-ere**, '**navigus**,' **navigare**.

[2] See N. 2 on the preceding page.

terrificus (**terror** or **terrere** + **facere**, **-ficere**), *fear-making*, TER-RIFIC.

ventriloquus (**venter** + **loqui**), *one who speaks from the belly*, VEN-TRILOQUIST (Greek agent ending '-ist').

vituperare (**vitu-**, for **viti-** of **vitium**, + **parare**; cf. p. 187 N.), *make ready a fault, charge with a fault, blame*, **vituperatio**, VITUPERA-TION.

B. DESCRIPTIVE COMPOUNDS

141. Descriptive compounds are formed by uniting a word with an adjective or adverb modifier:

aequilibrium (**aequus** + **libra**), *equal scales, balancing weight*, (*e* for *ae*) EQUILIBRIUM.

beneficus (comparative and superlative on a stem **beneficent-**; **bene** + **facere**, **-ficere**), *well-doing*, BENEFICENT; likewise **bene-factor** and **malefactor**, *well-doer* and *evil-doer*, **bene** and **male** modifying the verbal idea of **factor**. Cf. also BENEDICTION and MALEDICTION, *well-saying* and *ill-saying*.

benevolens (**bene** + **velle**), *well-wishing*, BENEVOLENT.

biennium (**bi** + **annus**), **bi-** of like origin with **duo**, *two; a two-year period*. Cf. **triennium, quadrennium** (CENTENNIAL, 205).

dissonans (**dis** + **sonare**), *apart-sounding*, DISSONANT.

grandis + **loquens**, GRAND-*speaking*, GRANDILOQUENT.

infinitus (**in-** + **finitus**, pf. pple. of **finire**), *not ended, unending*, INFINITE.

inimicus (**in-** + **amicus**), *not friendly*, with suffix -AL (98), INIMICAL.

meridies, for **medi-dies** (155), **medi die**, *at midday*, kept in our abbreviations, **A.M.** and **P.M.**, 60.

paeninsula (**paene** + **insula**), *almost island*, (*e* for *ae*) PENINSULA.

privilegium (**privus** + **lex**), *private* or *individual law;* originally a law against or for an individual; then with the latter meaning, *a special right*, a PRIVILEGE.

semicirculus (**semi-** + **circulus**), *half-circle*, SEMICIRCLE.

veredictum (Low Lat.; **vere** + **dictum**), *truly said*. French made this 'verdit' and the English changed it to VERDICT to make the last syllable Latin again.

Of this class also are the verbs compounded with prepositions (more properly adverbs): **accipere, ad-capere**, *take to*, ACCEPT; **circum-venire (-ventus)**, *come around*, CIRCUMVENT; **dis-secare (-sectus)**, *cut apart*, DISSECT; **ex-cedere**, *go out* (and *beyond*), EXCEED; **in-fundere (-fusus)**, *pour into*, INFUSE; **trans-gredi (-gressus)**, *go across*, TRANSGRESS, etc.

C. POSSESSIVE COMPOUNDS

142. Possessive compounds are formed like the descriptive (adj. + noun), but they denote possession:

aequinoctium (aequus + nox), *the time that has* (days and) *nights equal*, (*e* for *ae*) EQUINOX (perhaps after OF 'equinoxe').

bipes, bipedis (bi- + pes), *two-footed*, BIPED. So also **quadrupes (-pedis)**, *having four feet*, QUADRUPED; **quadr-**, cf. QUADRANGLE below.

centipeda (centum + pes), *having a hundred feet*, CENTIPEDE.

iners, inertis (in + ars, 149), *having no art or skill;* hence *inactive*, INERT.

magnanimus (magnus + animus), *having a great soul*, MAGNANIMOUS.

multiformis (multus + forma), *having many forms*, MULTIFORM.

pusillanimis (pusillus + animus), *having a very little soul*, PUSILLANIMOUS.

quadrangulum, neut. of **quadrangulus (quadriangulus)**, *four-angled*, QUADRANGLE; **quadr-** in compounds for **quattuor**.

semestris, for **semenstris (sex + mensis + adj. suffix -tris)**, *of six months, semiannual;* **semestris cursus**, *a six months' course* in college. This expression we have borrowed from Germany, and omitting **cursus**, we make the noun SEMESTER, applying it often to half a school year even if that be but four or five months.

triangulum (tri- + angulus), *having three corners* or *angles*, TRIANGLE.

tridens, tridentis (tri- + dens), *three-toothed*, TRIDENT.

triremis (tri- + remus), a boat *having three* benches of *oars*, TRIREME.

unanimus (unus + animus), *having one mind*, UNANIMOUS.

unicornis (unus + cornu), *having one horn*, UNICORN.

uniformis (unus + forma), *having one form*, UNIFORM.

143. Prepositional compounds are preposition and noun combined:

abnormis, ab norma, *from the rule, departing from the rule,* with Eng. addition of -AL (98), ABNORMAL. So also **enormis, e norma,** *out of the rule, beyond the ordinary,* ENORMOUS (cf. 96).

aggregare, aggregatus, ad gregem, *(add) to the herd,* so *make up the total;* AGGREGATE. From **grex** also **congregare,** CONGREGATE, for *get the flock together* (**con-,** 144)*;* **segregare,** SEGREGATE, *separate the flock* (**se-,** 145). Cf. **egregius** below.

annihilare, annihilatus, ad nihil, *to nothing;* hence, *bring to nothing;* ANNIHILATE (128, 132).

egregius, e grege, *out of the herd, different from the common herd, exceptional.* But EGREGIOUS (95) in English is now used only with words of bad or uncomplimentary meaning, as 'EGREGIOUS blunder.'

exorbitare, ex orbita, *out of the* ORBIT, *get off the track;* pres. pple. **exorbitans;** 'EXORBITANT prices' are those which fly the track.

expectorare, expectoratus, ex pectore, *out of the breast, expel from the chest,* EXPECTORATE.

exterminare, exterminatus, ex termino, *from the boundary, drive from the boundary,* EXTERMINATE.

incarnare, incarnatus, in carnem, *into flesh, put into flesh,* IN-CARNATE.

intervallum, inter valla, *between the ramparts, the space between* the outer *breastworks* and the soldiers' tents; then *the space between two points,* and in English we extend it to time, INTERVAL.

perennis, per annum or **annos,** *lasting through the year* or *years* (with −AL, 98), PERENNIAL.

proconsul, pro consule, *for* or *instead of a consul,* an officer serving *in the place of consul,* or an *ex-consul* as governor of a province; Eng. **proconsul.**

proportio, pro portione, *according to one's share* (**portio,** PORTION), PROPORTION.

subjugare, subjugatus, sub jugum, *under the yoke (i.e.,* the spears placed for a conquered army to pass under), *send under the yoke*, SUBJUGATE.

suburbium: sub urbe, *beneath* or *close about the city*, SUBURB.

Compare also ABORIGINES (52), AMANUENSIS (52), DELIRIUM (52), DEVIOUS, IMPERVIOUS, OBVIOUS (95), ELIMINATE (202), PROFANE (202), PROSPEROUS (95), SUBTERRANEAN (110).

144. What we commonly call prepositions in Latin were originally and properly adverbs, and could therefore be used in composition with verbs and adjectives, making descriptive compounds (141). Such adverbs (prepositions) were thus used sometimes with their definite and literal meanings, sometimes figuratively, sometimes for emphasis or with intensive force. These uses may be seen in the following:

a, ab, abs, *away, from;* commonly **ab-; a-** before *m, p,* and *v;* **abs-** before *c* and *t;* see also **po-** (145):

> **a-vertere,** *turn away,* AVERT.
>
> **a-vocatio (a-vocare,** *call away), a calling away* (from one's business), AVOCATION.
>
> **ab-ducere, abductus,** *lead away,* ABDUCT.
>
> **abs-condere,** *hide away,* ABSCOND.
>
> **abs-tinere (tenere),** *hold off,* ABSTAIN.
>
> **ab-uti, abusus,** *use off* (from the proper purpose), *misuse,* ABUSE.

ad, *to, toward:*

> **ad-ducere,** *bring to, bring forward,* ADDUCE.
>
> **ad-optare,** *wish to* (oneself), *take to oneself by choice,* ADOPT.
>
> **ad-ventus (ad-venire),** *a coming to* a place, ADVENT.

In ADVANCE and ADVANTAGE, the *d* is a mistake, the prefix is not **ad-.** They both came from **ab-ante,** as if '**abantiare,**' '**abantaticum**' (177), *off before* or *ahead* of others. Then from the Fr. 'avancer,' 'avantage,' Middle English had 'avancen' and 'avantage,' later erroneously changed to 'ad-.'

ante, *before* (of time and space):

> **ante** + **cap-, anticipare, -atus,** *take beforehand,* ANTICIPATE (140 N.).

ante-cedere, *go before,* **antecedens,** *going before,* ANTECEDENT (123).

Often in modern formations and phrases, as **ante-bellum,** ANTEDATE.

circum, *around* (adv. acc. of **circus,** 52):

    circum-navigare, circumnavigatus, *sail a ship around,* CIR-CUMNAVIGATE.

    circum-scribere, *draw* a line *around,* CIRCUMSCRIBE.

com-, con-, co-, *with, together,* the same as the prep. **cum: com-** with labials, sometimes with vowels, and with *m* assimilated before *l* and *r;* **co-** regularly with vowels, *h,* and *gn;* elsewhere, **con-.**

    co-aevus, *having the age* (**aevum**) *together, contemporary,* (*e* for *ae*) COEVAL (98).

    com-(b)ustio (**comburere, combustus**), *a burning together, i.e., a burning up* (intensive), COMBUSTION. The simple verb was **urere; comburere** seems to have been formed to correspond to **amburere.**

    con-venire, *come together,* CONVENE.

contra, contro-, *against:*

    contra-dicere, -dictus, *speak against,* CONTRADICT.

    contro-versia (**controversus**), *a turning against* one (in discussion), CONTROVERSY. **Contro-** and **contra** seem to have been originally case-forms; **contro-** occurred only with a few derivatives of **vertere,** *turn.* Even 'controvertere' was not used and our CONTROVERT has been made by analogy.

In Old French the word became 'contre-' or 'cuntre-' and from this the English COUNTER- as it appears in words coming through the French (172); COUNTERMAND (**mandare,** *order*), COUNTERSIGN (**signare,** *set a mark on*); also in our own coined words like COUNTER-MOVEMENT, COUNTERPART.

de, *down* (*from*), *off, utterly* (*downright*); also with negative force or unfavorable meaning:

    debere (**de** + **habere**), *have a thing from* one; hence *owe;* **debitum,** DEBIT, DEBT.

    de-ferre, *carry away* or *forward,* DEFER.

    de-formis, *ill-formed* (**forma,** FORM), DEFORMed.

de-plorare, *weep for bitterly* (**plorare,** *weep*), DEPLORE.

de-scendere (**scandere,** *climb*), *climb down,* DESCEND.

de-secrare, *devote to a sacred purpose* (**sacer,** SACRED), has been taken into English as *divert from a sacred purpose,* DESECRATE, opposed to CONSECRATE (**consecrare**). More logical is the OF 'des-sacrer,' where the prefix is Lat. **dis-** (145), and the influence of the Old French word may account for the meaning in English.

de-spondere, *promise fully* (**spondere**), *promise fully to another, give up* (**animum,** *courage*); so DESPONDENCY (75) is *losing heart.*

de-tegere, detectus, *uncover,* DETECT.

e, ex(ec-), *out, from, completely* (cf. *out and out*); **ex-** before vowels and *h,* also before *c, p, g, s, t;* **ec-** becoming **ef-** before *f;* before other consonants, **e-**):

    ef-ficiens (**ec-** facere), *doing completely,* EFFICIENT.

    e-ventus (**e-venire,** *come out*), *outcome, what turns out* or *happens,* EVENT.

    expectare (**ex-spectare,** 130), *look out* (to the future) *for* (a thing), EXPECT.

    ex-tollere, *raise out from* (others), EXTOL.

extra, *outside, beyond* (55):

    extra-ordinarius, *beyond what belongs to the common order* (**ordo,** 101), EXTRAORDINARY.

    extra-vagans (**vagare,** *wander*), *wandering beyond* (the limit), EXTRAVAGANT.

in, *in, into, toward:*

    in-cisio (**caedere,** *cut,* **incidere, incisus**), *a cutting into,* INCISION.

    in-clinare (**clinare,** *lean*), *bend* or *lean,* INCLINE.

    in-vidiosus (94), from **in-vidus,** ENVIOUS, **in-videre,** *look upon grudgingly;* INVIDIOUS. ENVIOUS is the same word altered through the French.

The old form **endo, indu,** appears in **indigens,** INDIGENT (75), **indigenus,** INDIGENOUS (95).

In compounds coming through the French, **in-** became EN-; **ingenerare,** *implant,* or *produce,* has come to us as ENGENDER (174).

inter, *between, between times, at intervals:*

> **inter-mittere,** *leave off between times,* pres. pple. **intermittens,**
> INTERMITTENT.
>
> **inter-rumpere, -ruptus** (**rumpere,** *break*), *break in between,*
> *break off,* INTERRUPT.

In compounds coming through the French **inter-** became
ENTER-; from **inter** and **tenere** the French made 'entretenir'
and furnished us ENTERTAIN, *i.e.,* "*hold mutually*"; then used
for *maintain, provide for,* finally *provide with comfort, hospitality,*
or *pleasure.*

intra, *inside, within;* only in modern coined words, as INTRA-MURAL,
INTRA-STATE (206).

intro (adverb), *within, inside:*

> **intro-ducere,** *bring in,* INTRODUCE.
>
> **intro-spicere** (**specere,** *look, watch*), *look within,* from which we
> have made INTROSPECTION.

ob, *toward, against, across* one's way:

> **ob-durare,** *harden against,* **ob-duratus,** *hardened against* (an
> appeal), OBDURATE.
>
> **ob-longus,** *long crosswise,* OBLONG.
>
> **ob-trudere,** *thrust upon,* OBTRUDE.
>
> **ob-vertere,** *turn toward,* **ob-versus,** *turned toward one,* OBVERSE,
> *e.g.,* the face of a coin having the principal figure or inscrip-
> tion, the other being *turned back, i.e.,* REVERSE.
>
> **ob-viare, ob-viatus,** *meet on the way* (**via**), *meet to withstand,*
> OBVIATE (cf. OBVIOUS, 95).

per, *through, thoroughly* (*i.e.,* "*throughly*"), *wrongly, to the bad*
(pejorative use):

> **per-dere,** *destroy* (*put through,* see CREED, 58, and Note), **per-**
> **ditus, perditio,** *destruction,* PERDITION.
>
> **per-fidia** (**per-fidus,** *faithless,* **fides,** *faith*), *a violation of one's*
> *faith,* PERFIDY.
>
> **per-ire,** *pass away* (cf. Eng. 'fall through'), *go to the bad,*
> PERISH (186).
>
> **per-jurare,** *swear falsely,* PERJURE; like Eng. 'forswear.'
>
> **per-meare, per-meatus,** *pass through,* PERMEATE (132).
>
> **per-mittere,** *allow to go through,* PERMIT.

per-mutatio (**permutare**, *change completely*), *a complete change*, PERMUTATION.

per-vertere, *turn to the wrong*, PERVERT.

post, *behind, after:*

post-ponere, *place after*, POSTPONE.

post-scribere, *write after*, **postscriptum**, *written after*, POSTSCRIPT.

prae, *before, in front of* (becomes PRE- in English)*:*

prae-sidere (**sedere**, *sit*), *sit in front*, PRESIDE.

prae-texere, *weave before*, **praetextum**, *what is woven in front* (as a screen), PRETEXT.

Coined words in English, like Late Latin, have **prae-**, PRE-, meaning *before* in time, as PRE-EXISTENCE, PRE-SUPPOSE, PRE-WAR.

praeter, *beyond* (PRETER- in English)*:*

praeter-ire, *go beyond, pass by*, **praeteritum**, *passed by, past*, PRETERITE.

praeter-naturalis (Med. Lat.), *beyond the natural*, PRETER-NATURAL; from **praeter naturam**.

pro, prod- (before vowels), **por-**, *forth, in front, publicly, for:*

pro-ducere, *lead forth*, PRODUCE.

pro-spectus (**pro-spicere**, *look forward*), *a looking forward* or *forth*, PROSPECT, also **prospectus** (52).

pro-verbium, from **verbum**, *word, a word* (*used*) *publicly, a common expression* or *maxim*, PROVERB.

prod-igus (cf. **prodigere**, *i.e.*, **prod-agere**, *cast forth, squander*), *lavish, wasteful*, PRODIGAL, as if from **-alis**, 98 (cf. **prodiga-litas**, PRODIGALITY, 72).

por-tendere, *stretch forth* (to the future), *foretell*, PORTEND; so **portentum**, *sign, omen*, PORTENT.

pos-sidere (**por-sedere**), **possessus**, *sit before*, and by right of occupation *hold*, POSSESS.

retro (adverb), *backwards:*

retro-gradus (**gradus**, *a step*, **gradi**, *go, step*), *a going backwards*, RETROGRADE.

sub, sus- (**subs-**) before some words beginning with *c, p,* or *t, under, up* (*from under*), *in an underhand way:*

sub-dividere (Late Lat.), *divide under* (a division already made), SUBDIVIDE.

sub-icere, *throw under*, subjectum, *thrown under, subservient,* SUBJECT; (verbum) subjectum, the *word, statement* or *proposition, put down* as a foundation, a SUBJECT.

sub-ornare, *furnish secretly, procure in an underhand way:* then SUBORN.

su(b)s-pendere, suspendere, *hang under, hang up,* SUSPEND.

sub-scribere, *write under, write* one's name *under* an agreement, SUBSCRIBE.

sub-vertere, *turn up from below, turn upside down, overthrow,* SUBVERT.

subter, *below, underneath, secretly:*

    subter-fugium (Late, from subter-fugere, *flee secretly*), *secret flight, that to which one flees for escape,* SUBTERFUGE.

super, *over, above, excessive(ly):*

    super-ficialis (Late Lat.), *pertaining to the upper face* (super-ficies, facies, FACE, 149), *on the surface,* SUPERFICIAL.

    super-fluus, *over-flowing,* SUPERFLUOUS.

    super-intendere (in-tendere, *stretch toward, direct one's thought* or *energy toward*), *have the oversight of,* SUPERINTEND.

    super-lativus (latus, *carried*), *carried to excess,* SUPERLATIVE.

trans, tra-, *across, through,* possibly a participial form of -trare, *go across,* as in in-trare, *go into,* ENTER (Fr. 'entrer'):

    trans-ferre, *carry across, bring over,* TRANSFER.

    trans-gredi, trans-gressus, *go across* the lawful limit, TRANSGRESS.

    trans-lucere, *shine through,* translucens, TRANSLUCENT.

    tra-ducere, *lead across, lead along and expose to ridicule, dishonor,* TRADUCE.

145. Certain other adverbial prefixes are called inseparable, since they can occur only in composition. They are the following:

amb- (ambi-), *around:*

    amb-iguus (ambigere, amb + agere, 149), *a going around, going about in uncertainty,* AMBIGUOUS.

    amb-itio (amb-ire), *a going around* (to win favor), *the going around* of a candidate for office, AMBITION.

dis-, di- (before voiced consonants, 146), *apart*, also with negative force:

> **di-gerere, di-gestus,** *carry in different directions, distribute,* DIGEST.

> **dispergere, dispersus (dis-spargere,** *scatter*), *scatter apart,* DISPERSE.

> **dis-seminare, dis-seminatus (seminare,** *sow seed*), *scatter seed,* DISSEMINATE.

> **dis-similis,** *unlike,* DISSIMILAR (on analogy of adjectives in -aris, 99).

> **di-vulgare,** *spread abroad among the common crowd,* **vulgus,** DIVULGE.

> **dis-** sometimes became Fr. 'de-,' and thus appears as DE- in English:

>> DEFY from OF 'defier,' Low Lat. **diffidare (dis + fid-;** cf. **diffidere**); *renounce faith with, challenge to fight.*

>> DEPART, OF 'departir,' evidently from a Low Lat. **dis-partire,** for Lat. **dispertire,** *separate (and go) in different directions.*

in-,[1] *not:*

> **im-purus (in- + purus),** *not pure,* IMPURE.

> **in-eptus (in- + aptus),** *un-suited,* INEPT (149).

> **in-solubilis,** *that cannot be loosed* (**solvere,** *loose,* SOLVE), *not to be dissolved,* INSOLUBLE.

po-, *aside,* of the same origin as **ab,** Greek 'apo' (ἀπό); **ponere = po-sinere, po-situs** (138).

re-, red- (before vowels), *back, again:*

> **re-cordari,** *bring back to mind* (*i.e.,* heart, **cor, cordis**), RECORD. Cf. "learn by heart."

---

[1] In- is in origin the same as Eng. 'un-.' To be consistent we should use 'un-' to negative native words, and IN- to negative those of Latin origin: thus, 'un-ending,' IN-FINITE, **finitus,** *ended,* FINITE (**finire,** *end*); 'un-lawful,' IL-LEGAL (205); 'un-spotted,' IM-MACULATE, **maculare, maculatus,** *make spotted,* **macula,** *a spot.*

Yet a Latin word may have become so thoroughly English as to take *un-* for its negative. MEASURE is of Latin origin (**mensura**), but it may have an English suffix, MEASUREd, and the negative is unMEASUREd, alongside which is IMMENSE, pure Latin from the same source (**metiri, mensus,** *measure*). Cf. also unDIVIDed and INDIVISIBLE; unABLE, INABILITY, **inhabilis** (see **habilis,** 114).

re-currere, *run back, come in again*, RECUR.

red-emptio (redimere, redemptus, red-emere, *buy back*), *a buying back*, REDEMPTION.

se-, sed- (before vowels), *aside, away*. **Sine**, *without*, is an **n**-form from the same original:

se-cedere, *go apart*, SECEDE.

se-parare, se-paratus, SEPARATE (see COMPARE, 202).

sed-itio (ire, *go*), *a going aside* (for the purpose of revolt), SEDITION.

V. COMBINATIONS OF SOUNDS

146. Having now observed the adverbial prefixes in their effect on the meaning of words, we may well inquire next how they were attached and what consonant and vowel changes attended the process, what changes of pronunciation, in fact, naturally attend the union of two words or word elements of any class.

When the two English words 'cup' and 'board' are combined to make 'cupboard,' two changes of pronunciation occur: *p* is pronounced *b* through the influence of the *b* following, and the long *o*-sound of the second element is weakened because of losing its accent. 'Cupboard' becomes "cubbord," or "cubbrd." These are the changes that most frequently take place in the making of Latin words, the assimilation of consonants and the weakening of unaccented vowels.

When the Roman changed **ob-curro** to **occurro**, **direg-tus** to **directus**, he did exactly what we should have done if we had been dealing with 'OBCUR' and 'DIREGT,' at any rate what we have done in the case of many English words. The *d* of our past tense and perfect participle remains *d* in pronunciation when a vowel precedes the ending, as 'freed,' or when *b, g, l, m, n, r, s* (*z*), *v* precede, as 'rubbed,' 'dragged,' 'killed,' 'hemmed,' 'tanned,' 'feared,' 'used,' 'loved,' but becomes *t* in sound (and often written so), when *p, k, f, s* (*ss*) precede, as 'supped,' 'kicked,' 'snuffed,' 'kissed.' That is, certain consonants are pronounced with the vocal chords vibrant, others with the vocal chords completely inactive, or we have voiced and voiceless consonants, and the tendency is to make two consonants alike when they come together, either both voiced or both voiceless. This is assimilation. The English examples just given illustrate progressive assimilation, the influence of the first consonant going forward to change the second. Commonly in Latin the second consonant changes the first, or the assimilation is regressive as in the English word 'cupboard,' or in the rather common pronunciation of 'newspaper' with voiceless s (ss) on account of the following p, or the colloquial "haf-to" for 'have to.' So the Latin adds -tus to scrib- and makes not 'scribtus' but scriptus, but if -a is the added syllable it remains scriba; and we take over the words SCRIPT and SCRIBE already adapted to our local organs. In most words the change is made to another consonant pronounced with the same part of the mouth, as here b to p, another labial (lip sound), or agens, doing, but ac-tus, done, g (hard) changing to c another palatal.

147. Of much interest and of frequent occurrence is the very ancient development of an s-sound in the combination of two dentals dt, d(h)t, tt.[1] In Latin the result, most often observable in the perfect participle, was -ss-, which later became -s- if preceded by a long vowel or a diphthong[2]; e.g.,

---

[1] This change did not occur when t was merely doubled within the word, as in 'mito' with shortening of vowel (or 'mitito'?) becoming mitto, or litera, leitera in inscriptions) written as littera. Note also that tendere had two forms of pf. pple., tensus (tend-tus) and tentus (from confusion with the related tenere); hence for stretching to or straining toward, we have both INTENSE and INTENT.

[2] Lachmann's Law that a short root vowel is lengthened in the perfect participle when the root ends in a voiced consonant, but is not lengthened when the root ends in a voiceless consonant, would imply that -dt- in such a position always became -s-, which is not the case. See R. G. Kent, Lachmann's Law of Vowel Lengthening, Language IV, 3, 80 ff.

discutere, discut-tus, discussus, DISCUSS.
progredi, progred-tus (*dh-t*), progressus, PROGRESS.
sedere, sed-tio, sessio, SESSION.

applaudere, applaud-tus, applausus, APPLAUSE.
uti, ut-tus, usus, USE.
videre, vid-tio, visio, VISION.

In consonant combination:
respondere, respond-tus, responsus, RESPONSE.
vertere, vert-tus, versus, VERSE.
But -*dtr*- (-*ttr*-) became -*str*-, as rod-trum, rostrum (93).

The use of *s* in the perfect participle spread to other words that did not involve a *dt* or *tt*, *e.g.*, labi, lapsus, *slip*, Eng. LAPSE; spargere, sparsus, *scatter*, Eng. SPARSE, *scattering*.

148. Sometimes assimilation went further than merely changing one consonant to the same class as the other; the first consonant became the same as the other, *i.e.*, we have complete assimilation. So from corona with suffix -la, coron-la became corolla (69); from liber, liber-lus became libellus, Eng. LIBEL; from ster- (Eng. 'star,' Grk. 'astēr,' ἀστήρ, Eng. 'aster'), ster-la became stella (cf. STELLAR). This may be compared with our "gimme" for 'give me,' "leggo" for 'let go.' Compounds of prefix and verb may show complete assimilation; the final consonant of the prefix was often made the same as the initial consonant of the verb even though pronounced with an entirely different part of the mouth, as when dis-ferre became differre, sub-gestus, suggestus, ad-captus, acceptus, and gave us DIFFER, SUGGEST, and ACCEPT.

149. The second change in our word 'cupboard,' the weakening of the vowel in the unaccented syllable, occurs frequently in English and Latin alike. 'New-found-land' accented on the first syllable, becomes "Newfundland," or "Newfndlnd"; we preserve the accented -*or*- in 'histor'ical,' but 'his'tory,' for most of us, in the matter of pronunci-

ation, might as well be spelled "histery," if not "histry."
Now there was a very early period in the development of
the Latin language when every word had its accent on the
first syllable, and an altered pronunciation of the unstressed
second syllable we find represented in the spelling (cf. 159).
When in a later time the language settled down to the classical rule of accenting the penult if long, otherwise the antepenult, the vowel of the second syllable had become too
fixed in its quality ever to be restored.   Thus, **de-faciens**
became **deficiens**, and **de-factus, defectus; con-tangens** became **contingens; con-tenens** became **continens,** while **contentus** remained **contentus; con-caesus** became **concisus,** and
ex-claudo, excludo.   And along with FACILE, FACT, TANGENT,
TENANT, CAESURA, and CLAUSE, we have from the same
roots, DEFICIENT, DEFECT, CONTINGENT, CONTINENT, CONTENT,
CONCISE, and EXCLUDE.   In general it is true for Latin words
of the early period that in the unstressed syllable immediately following the original accent, *a* or *e,* followed by a
single consonant (except *r*), or by *ng,* changed to *i;* followed
by two consonants *a* became *e,* and *e* remained; while of the
diphthongs *ae* became *ī* and *au* became *ū* (sometimes *ō*).[1]
Before *r, a* became *e* and *e* remained: **in-paro, impero,**
prepare (a thing) *upon* (one), *order,* IMPERATIVE (120);
refero, *carry back,* REFER.   If, however, a compound was
made in the later time when the classical rule of accent
had been established, such a change did not occur: **recapi-
tulare,** *go over the headings,* and **infatuare,** *make a fool of,*
remained (**capitulum,** *little head,* **fatuus,** *foolish*) and became
English RECAPITULATE and INFATUATE.[2]   And in any period
long vowels were better able to hold their own, as **co-gnātus,**

---

[1] Strictly the change of *a* was first to *e* and then (about 230 B.C.) to *i,*
when a single consonant (except *r*) followed; *ae* (*ai*) likewise became first
ei then *ī, au* became *eu,* then *ū.*

[2] Other apparent exceptions to the statement given of such vowel
changes may be explained on the analogy of the simple verbs.   Cf.
praeparo, PREPARE, beside **impero.**

of the same stock, COGNATE, **accēdere,** *yield to,* ACCEDE. The *i* of the following syllable may originally have favored the use of *i* in the root syllable of a word like **recipio** as was evidently the case when the *ē* of **tēla,** *web* or *warp,* became *i* in **subtilis,** lit. *woven fine;* hence *delicate, nice,* SUBTLE.

The sound of unaccented *u* followed by *l* or *m* seems to have approached that of *i* (*ü*); the superlative meaning *best,* from which we get OPTIMIST (Greek agent suffix '-ist'), was at different times written **optumus** and **optimus;** we find **monumentum** and **monimentum, documentum** and **docimentum,** our MONUMENT and DOCUMENT; **ventulus,** *slight wind* (68), gave **ventilare,** Eng. VENTILATE.[1]

150. The following verbs illustrate assimilation and vowel weakening brought over in derived words:

ad-cadere, accidere, *fall to, befall,* **accidens,** ACCIDENT (cf. the coined word DECADENT, *falling down*).

ad-facere, afficere, affectus, *act upon, influence,* AFFECT (cf. FACT).

ad-gravare, aggravare, (p. 186, N. 2) **aggravatus,** *add to the weight of* (**gravis,** *heavy*), AGGRAVATE.

ad-ludere, alludere, *play at* or *toward, mention indirectly,* ALLUDE (to).

ad-nectere, annectere, annexus, *fasten on,* ANNEX.

ad-positus, appositus, *placed up to, suited to,* APPOSITE.

ad-quaerere, acquirere, *seek in addition,* ACQUIRE.

ad-rogare, arrogare, *ask* or *claim* (too much) *to* (oneself), **arrogans,** ARROGANT.

ad-sistere, assistere, *stand by,* ASSIST.

ad-spirare, aspirare, *breathe toward,* ASPIRE.

---

[1] Before a labial or *l* followed by another consonant (not *ll*) the un-accented *a* or *e* became *u* (earlier *o*): **ex-saltare, exsultare, exultare,** *leap vigorously,* EXULT; **impellere, impulsus,** *drive on,* IMPEL, IMPULSE (cf. **repellere,** 157); and even before a single labial this unaccented *a* was changed to a sound evidently intermediate between *i* and *u,* giving for example, **recipiens** and **occupans,** RECIPIENT, OCCUPANT, both from **capere;** possibly also **recuperare,** *take again,* RECOVER, RECUPERATE.

After *qu* (*c* in compounds) we have *a* becoming *u,* **quatere, quassus,** STRIKE (48, FRACAS), **concutere, concussus, concussio,** *a striking together,* CONCUSSION, **discussio,** *a shaking apart,* DISCUSSION, etc.

ad-tangere, attingere, *touch upon, reach,* ATTAIN (through French).

com-legere, colligere, collectus, *gather together,* COLLECT; also (through Old French) CULL, and COIL.

com-rumpere, corrumpere, corruptus, *break altogether, break down,* CORRUPT.

ex-(ec-)fundere, effundere, effusus (-fud-tus, 147), *pour out,* EFFUSE, adj. EFFUSIVE (120).

in-ludere, illudere, *play at, make sport with,* action noun **illusio,** ILLUSION.

in-premere (premere, 87), **imprimere, impressus,** *press in,* IMPRESS.

in-rigare, irrigare, irrigatus, *carry moisture to, wet,* IRRIGATE.

inter-legere, intellegere (intelligere), *pick out among things, discern, understand,* **intelligens,** INTELLIGENT.

ob-cadere, occidere, *fall* or *go down,* **occidens,** OCCIDENT (cf. LEVANT, 49), but action noun **occasio,** *a happening,* OCCASION.

ob-currere, occurrere, *run in the way,* OCCUR.

ob-ferre, offerre, *bring before one,* OFFER.

ob-mittere, omittere (apparently for 'ommittere'), *let go completely,* OMIT. (Possibly not **ob-,** but prothetic o-, cf. 180 N.)

ob-positus, oppositus, *placed over against,* OPPOSITE.

su(b)s-capere, suscipere, susceptus, *take under, undertake,* Med. Lat. **susceptibilis,** *ready to take,* SUSCEPTIBLE.

sub-currere, succurrere, *run under, run to help,* SUCCOR (through French).

sub-ferre, sufferre, *bear (up) under,* SUFFER.

sub-gerere, suggerere, suggestus, *carry under, supply,* SUGGEST.

sub-portare, supportare, *carry up to,* or *near,* in Low Latin *sustain,* SUPPORT.

sub-ripere, surripere, surreptus, *snatch away secretly,* **surreptitius,** *stolen, concealed,* SURREPTITIOUS (95).

151. Assimilation of consonants and sometimes vowel-weakening are to be noted also with inseparable prefixes:

dis-fundere, diffundere, diffusus (-fud-tus, 147), *pour forth, scatter,* DIFFUSE.

dis-spargere, dispergere, DISPERSE (145).

in-aequus, iniquus, *unfair,* INIQUITY (72).

in-(g)nobilis, ignobilis (153 end), *unknown, unworthy to be known,*
  IGNOBLE.

in-potens, impotens, *not able, not strong,* IMPOTENT.

in-religiosus, irreligiosus, *not religious,* IRRELIGIOUS.

152. When consonants were not easily united or assimilated, an objectionable combination could very simply be
remedied by the dropping of one of the sounds, and this the
Latin often did. The stem **part-** added *s* in the nominative,
and **part-s** became **pars,** and we have borrowed both PART
and PARSE (58). When **exag-** of **ex-agere (exigere)** added
the noun suffix **-men** (89), the result was **examen,** from
which came **examinare. Exigere** was *to drive out, force,
investigate, try out, weigh;* **examen,** *the tongue of the balance,*
an *indicator;* an EXAMINATION is *a weighing in the balance.*
Initial *gn-* was pronounced and written *n-* (cf. Eng. *know,*
223), as in '**gnotio,**' **notio,** NOTION. **Pris-mus** became **primus,**
first, but *s* stood easily with *t* and remained in **pris-tinus,**
early, original; hence PRIME and PRISTINE.

153. Commonly a consonant between two other consonants was dropped (not, however, in the combination of
prefix and verb); thus, the verb **extorquere,** *twist out,* furnishes us EXTORT because its participle from which our verb
is made (133), **extorqu-tus,** *i.e.,* **-torctus,** dropped the *c* and
became **extortus.** So the agent noun from **pasco (pa-sc-o)**
is **pastor** (52) for **pasc-tor.** But when the negative **in-** com-
bines with *gn-,* the combination is simplified to **ign-;** in +
gnorans, ignorans, IGNORANT.

154. The opposite process is to pronounce more consonants than we are etymologically entitled to (epenthesis,
174). The Romans took **red-em-** of **red + emere (redimere),** *buy back,* and formed a noun with the -tio suffix (85).
The effort to pronounce *m-t* generated a *p*-sound and they
said **redemptio** (Eng. REDEEM and REDEMPTION). As pf.
pple. of **promere (pro-emere),** *put forward,* **prom-tus** became
promptus, PROMPT; the variation between **tentare** and **tem-**

(p)tare, *try*, survives in TENTATIVE (120) and TEMPT. In like manner we have followed the French in changing hum(i)lem, to HUMBLE, and ten(e)rem to TENDER (174), and have made the Lat. cucumer- into CUCUMBER. In a number of words the full pronunciation of a final *n* developed a *d*-sound (excrescent *d*); hence we have from componere, exponere, COMPOUND, EXPOUND,[1] from sonus, SOUND.

155. As euphony and ease of pronunciation required successive consonants to be alike, often the same considerations tended to make unlike consonants in successive syllables. We have noted above the common use of -aris rather than -alis or -brum and -crum rather than -bulum and -culum as forms of suffixes when *l* preceded (99, 92), mor-alis, but mol-aris, oraculum, but fulcrum, etc. This shift we call dissimilation. Meridies was made from a locative medi die, *at the middle of the day;* the repetition of *d* was avoided by changing to meridies; otherwise we should be saying 'medidian' for MERIDIAN. 'Praestrigium' dropped an *r* and became praestigium, PRESTIGE (202). It was through dissimilation too that turtur, *a dove* (a word imitating the coo of a dove), changed *r* to *l* in the second syllable and gave Anglo-Saxon TURTLE(-dove), the kind of turtle whose voice may be heard in the land.[2] Similarly we have taken OF 'marbre,' Lat. marmorem (Mid. Eng. 'marbre'), and converted it into MARBLE; and from Lat. morus, *a mulberry tree*, with Eng. 'berry,' has been made not 'mor-berry' but MUL-berry.

156. One other euphonic change of Latin, accounting for a difference of spelling of certain related derivatives, is rhotacism, the change of *s* to *r* between vowels (Greek *r* is *rho*). The noun genus had originally two forms of stem,

---

[1] Other influences must have helped to add the -*d* to these verbs: Lat. -ponere became OF '-pondre' (174), and the Mid. Eng. 'expoune' had pf. pple. 'expound' (cf. 132).

[2] Song of Solomon, 2 : 12.

genos and **genes;** its declension in primitive times must have been '**genos, geneses,**' etc.; the final *-os* became *-us*, final *-es* became *-is*, and the *-s-* between vowels became *-r-*, and we know the word as **genus, generis.** So the verb, which might have been '**geneso,**' became **genero,** and we have in English both **genus** and GENERATE. Similarly **corpus, corporis,** was for '**corpos, corposis,**' the adjective not '**corposalis,**' but **corporalis.** But this same *s* in **corpusculum** is followed by a consonant and remains unchanged. We have thus CORPORAL and CORPUSCLE. From **rus,** *country,* we have RURAL and RUSTIC. The general statement of rhotacism, then, is that original *s* between two vowels was changed to *r*. Apparent exceptions are *s* for *ss,* as **causa** for '**caussa,**' CAUSE; *s* from *tt* or *dt* (147), as **fusus** for '**fudtus,**' FUSE; *s* initial in a compound, as **de-sistere,** DESIST; *s* in foreign words, as **rosa,** ROSE; *s* by analogy or as a mere archaism; **quaeso** for '**quaes-so**' on analogy of the perfect '**quaes-si,**' extended to **quaes-(s)i-vi,** pple. **quaes(s)itus** (probably after **petivi, -itus**), while **quaero** is a regular formation; thus we have **inquirere, inquisitus,** Eng. INQUIRE and INQUISITIVE.

VI. VOWEL GRADATION

157. The connection of certain related words in Latin and of their derivatives in English may be obscured by a variation of their vowel sounds. This variation, inherited from Indo-European times, and originally produced under the influence of accent, we call vowel gradation, or ablaut, the German name for vowel modification. It is sometimes a change of quantity, *i.e.,* of the time given to pronunciation, the vowel thus becoming stronger or weaker, as mentioned in 149; sometimes a change of quality, *i.e.,* of the vowel tone produced.

Ablaut series survive in English strong verbs: 'ride,' 'rode,' 'ridden'; 'spring,' 'sprang,' 'sprung.' Compare the classical derivatives 'biped' and 'tripod,' -ped and '-pod' being respectively Latin and Greek for the same word (*foot*). With such variations in mind it will not be difficult to see the relation between words like the following:

acer, *sharp, pointed;* Old Lat. **ocris** (Grk. ὄκρις), *a rugged hill:* ACRIMONY, MEDIOCRE (202).

datum, *given* (52); **donum,** *gift,* **donare,** *bestow as a gift:* DATE, DONATE.

divertere, *turn aside, go a different way;* **divortium,** *separation:* DIVERT, DIVORCE.

ferre, *bring;* **fortuna,** *what is brought:* CONFER, FORTUNE.

genuinus, *inborn;* **benignus,** *well born,* **cognatus,** *kin* (born with): GENUINE, BENIGN, COGNATE.

internecinus, *murderous* (**internecio,** *massacre,* **necare,** *kill*); **noxa,** *harm* (**nocere,** *harm*): INTERNECINE, NOXIOUS.

notio ('gnotio'), *a taking notice* (85), **cognitio,** *a becoming acquainted,* **recognitio,** *a knowing again:* NOTION, RECOGNITION.[1]

regere, *rule, i.e., direct;* **rogare,** *to direct oneself to, to turn or apply to* a person; hence *ask:* REGENT, INTERROGATE.

reminisci, *call to mind,* **mens,** *mind,* root **men-,** *think;* **admonere,** *give advice or warning to:* REMINISCENCE, ADMONISH.

repellere, *drive back;* in the pf. pple. the root was weakened from **pel** to **pl,** written **pul, repulsus:** REPEL, REPULSE.

seminarium, *a place for sowing seed* (71); **Saturnus,** *the god of sowing:* SEMINARY, SATURN.

sequi, *follow;* **socius,** *a follower, companion:* SEQUENCE, SOCIETY.

tegere, *cover;* **toga,** *a covering or garment:* TEGUMENT, toga (52).

terra, *dry land;* **torridus,** *dry and hot:* TERRESTRIAL, TORRID.

[1] The ablaut change is *gnō: gnă; gnă* becomes *gnĭ* by 149.

CHAPTER IV

FRENCH–ENGLISH FORMS OF LATIN DERIVATIVES

158. Had our borrowing been left to scholars and had it dealt directly with the literary language of the Romans, the forms of all our derivatives might have been accounted for in the chapter on Word Formation in Latin. Indeed, we have noted many words which we have received in practically if not actually their original forms. Yet another and a very large group bear the marks of their treatment, or mistreatment, in making their way through spoken Latin and spoken French. The peculiarities of common or Vulgar Latin as compared with the Classical, the development of this Low Latin into French, the modification of French words upon being received into English, and the uncertainties of English spelling when once a word had been adopted — these are subjects for philological works large and learned. The purpose of this chapter is merely to call attention to some important changes illustrated by our Latin-French derivatives, and thus to relieve in a measure the mystifying effect of the forms which some of these words have assumed.

In the declension of nouns six cases were entirely too many for the plain user of popular Latin. He confused them by mispronunciation and discarded those for which he felt no serious need, expressing the same relations by prepositional phrases. By the fifth century only two cases survived in the popular speech, the nominative and the accusative — or more properly an oblique case largely accusative. These were kept through the Old French period (600–1200), persisting fairly well through the thirteenth century. Then with the beginning of Modern French the simplifying process went one step further and in most instances reduced the cases from two to one. The accusative, or oblique case, by reason of its greater frequency came into general use and the old Latin declension had passed away.[1]

159. As to the forms of Latin words coming to us through spoken French, much is explained by the simple rule of Latin accent: words of two syllables were accented on the first, those of more than two syllables were accented on the penult if that was long, otherwise on the antepenult. Colloquial Latin of every period showed a tendency to suppress the short vowel of a syllable just before or just after the accent (cf. 149). People said 'poplares' for populares, 'vetranus' for veteranus, 'moblis' for mobilis, 'vinclum' for vinculum; and these people were as natural as those among us who say 'vetran' for 'veteran,' 'intrsting' for 'interesting,' even 'tolable' for 'tolerable,' or 'wheel-bar' for 'wheel-barrow.' This tendency of popular Latin, moreover, would be still greater in Celtic territory since Celtic languages had a stronger stress accent than the Latin.

160. Since it was the Latin accusative that furnished the French noun, we are especially interested in what happened to this case. Final *m*, which regularly marks the accusative singular, was but a feeble sound, as the elision of final syllables in -*m* would indicate, and as Quintilian expressly says.[2] **Tubam, porcum, hostem** from classical times must have tended toward 'tuba,' 'porcu,' 'hoste' with a nasal quality in the final vowel; then this short vowel following the accent was weakened or lost.

---

[1] A few examples remain of the nominative. The Lat. **ferus**, *wild*, became OF 'fiers,' adopted into English as FIERCE; **bellus**, *fair, beautiful*, OF 'bels' (with vocalized *l*, 179), became BEAU.

[2] *Institutiones Oratoriae*, 9, 4, 40.

I. Treatment of Vowels in Final Syllables

161. Final -*a* (left by the loss of -*m*) became -*e* (mute) in French, and remains as silent -*e* in English; we now omit this -*e*, however, if it is preceded by two consonants other than a mute and liquid combination (as *bl*).

Cl. Latin	Low Latin	Old French	English
crustam	crusta	cruste, crouste	CRUST (Mid. Eng. 'CRUSTE')
curam, *care*	cura	cure	CURE
famam	fama	fame	FAME
formam	forma	forme	FORM
gemmam	gemma	gemme	GEM (Mid. Eng. 'GEMME')
plumam	pluma	plume	PLUME
tabulam	tab(u)la	table	TABLE

162. Other final vowels than -*a* were very commonly lost and the French form was kept in English; thus:

Cl. Latin	Low Latin	French	English
arcum, *bow*	arcu	arc	ARC [1]
artem	arte	art	ART
frontem	fronte	front	FRONT
porcum, *pig*	porcu	porc	PORK
sermonem, *talk*	sermone	sermon	SERMON

Here again a mute plus liquid at the end made -*e* necessary, as in

duplum	duplu	double	DOUBLE

163. It then became the custom in English spelling to use the silent -*e* when the word stem ended in a single consonant preceded by a single vowel, regardless of the French; thus, we make DIVINE from later Fr. 'divin' (Lat. **divinum**), DUKE from 'duc' (Lat. **ducem**), although Middle English

---

[1] Also ARCH by confusion with OF 'arche' from Lat. **arca**.

had 'duc' and 'duk.' This rule of spelling was also extended
to words derived directly from Latin; thus:

Latin	English	Latin	English
cella, *room*	CELL	mulus	MULE (AS mul)
fanum	FANE	ovalis	OVAL
Faunus, a rural deity	FAUN	pactum	PACT
		pinus	PINE (AS pin)
lacus	LAKE (AS lac)	scriba	SCRIBE
merus	MERE		

II. Treatment of Vowels in Other Unaccented Syllables

164. The weakening or loss of unaccented vowels just
before or just after the accent, beginning from colloquial
Latin (159), continued during the time when French words
were in the making, as:

Cl. Latin	Low Latin	French	English
(baccalarem?)	baccalare	bachelier	BACHELOR (202)
hospitem, *guest* (202)	hosp(i)te	hoste (later hôte)	HOST
posituram	pos(i)tura	posture	POSTURE

165. An initial syllable had an advantage in its important
position, and its vowel might be pronounced even though
the accent followed on the second. In such a first syllable
a, e, ī, ū, were regularly kept; thus:

Cl. Latin	Low Latin	French	English
dūrare	durare	durer	(EN)DURE
mercedem, *reward*	mercede, *consideration*	merci (mercit)	MERCY
parentem (123)	parente	parent	PARENT
partire, *divide*	partire OF	departer	DEPART
rīpariam (ripa, *bank,* 26)	riparia	rivière (175 a)	RIVER

166. But in an initial syllable just before the accent, *ĭ*
became *e,* or often (before *l*) *a; o* and *ŭ* became *ou:*

Cl. Latin	Low Latin	French	English
bĭlancem, *having two plates*	bilancia	balance	BALANCE
cort + ensem (109; 45, COURTESY)	corte(n)se	courtois	COURTEOUS
mĭnutum (202, MINUTE)	minutu	menu	MENU (194)
nutrire	nŭtrire	nour(r)ir	NOURISH (186)

III. TREATMENT OF VOWELS IN ACCENTED SYLLABLES

Here we shall need to observe separately (*a*) open syllables (the vowel followed by a single consonant), and (*b*) closed syllables (the vowel followed by a consonant group):

167. (*a*) The general treatment of vowels in accented open syllables may be illustrated as follows:

Cl. Latin	Low Latin	French	English
clāvem, *key*	clave	clef	CLEF
cănem, *dog*	cane	OF chen, NF ken-il	KENNEL (202)
rēgem, *king*	rege	roi	ROY, ROYAL
brĕvem, *short*	breve	brief	BRIEF
spīnam, *thorn*	spina	OF espine (180)	SPINE
vĭam, *way*	via	voie (voi-age)	VOYAGE
hōram	hora	heure	HOUR
vōtum	votu	vœu	VOW
prŏbam	proba	preuve	PROOF
bŏvem, *ox, cow*	bove	bœuf	BEEF
pŏpulum	pop(u)lu	peuple	PEOPLE
pūrum	puru	pure	PURE
dŭos, *two*	duos	deux	DEUCE
clausum, *shut*	clausu	clos	CLOSE

168. The suffix -tāt- of quality nouns (72) became '-tet,' then '-te' (Mod. Fr. -té), and appeared in English as -TY; *e.g.*,

Cl. Latin	Low Latin	Old French	English
bonitatem	bonitate	bonte	BOUNTY
crudelitatem	crudelitate	cruelte	CRUELTY
fraternitatem	fraternitate	fraternite	FRATERNITY
puritatem	puritate	purte	PURITY

169. (*b*) The general treatment of vowels in accented closed syllables may be illustrated as follows:

Cl. Latin	*Low Latin*	*French*	*English*
carmen, *song*	**carm(i)ne** [1]	charme	CHARM
membrum, *limb*	**membru**	membre	MEMBER
īnsulam, *island*	**i(n)s(u)la**	OF isle (later, île)	ISLE
lĭtteram	**littera**	lettre	LETTER
co(h)ortem, cōrtem, *cohort*	**corte**	cour (OF cort)	COURT
pŏrtam, *gate*	**porta**	porte	PORT(AL)
pūrgo (purus + ago)	**purgo**	purge	PURGE
a(v)unculum (68)	**aunc(u)lu**	oncle	UNCLE

IV. Vowels Influenced by *y* (Consonantal *i*)

170. Within a word an *i* or *e* of Latin, followed by a vowel, became a *y*-sound, just as in English we pronounce 'Julia' as "Jul-ya." This *y* sometimes influenced the preceding consonant, and sometimes combined with the vowel of the preceding syllable; *e.g.*, **rationem** was pronounced "ratyo-nem," "ratsyone." The loss of the *t* and the combination of the *i* (*y*) with the *a* of the preceding syllable made 'raison,' Eng. REASON. The same *y*-sound developed also from *c* or *g* (cf. the pronunciation of 'car' and 'garden' as "kyar" and "gyarden"), and even the *c* of *cr* or *ct* affected the preceding vowel. The following are examples:

Cl. Latin	*Low Latin*	*French*	*English*
gaudia, *joys*	**gaudia** [1]	joie	JOY
memoriam, *memory*	**memoria**	memoire	MEMOIR
paria, pl. of **par,** *equals*	**paria** [1]	pair	PAIR
potionem, *drink*	**potione**	poison	POISON
pretium	**pretiu**	OF pris (prieis)	PRICE, PRIZE
sationem, *a sowing*	**satione**	saison (seison)	SEASON

[1] Classical Latin neuters shifted to masc. or fem. forms in Low Latin; then lost the final -*m;* **carmine** representing an acc. **carminem; gaudia** not the neut. pl. in Low Latin but representing **gaudiam.**

Cl. Latin	Low Latin	French	English
pacare, *appease, pacify*	pacare	payer	PAY
flagellum, *whip*	flagellu	OF flaiel	FLAIL
dignare, *count worthy*	dignare	OF degner, deigner	DEIGN
fructum	fructu	fruit	FRUIT
macrum, *thin*	macru	maigre	MEAGER
vindicare, *punish*	vindicare	OF a-vengier	AVENGE

171. An *i*-sound sometimes developed also before a nasal, as:

Cl. Latin	Low Latin	French	English
sanctum, *holy* (*ct*, 170)	sanctu	saint	SAINT
vanum	vanu	vain	VAIN
venam	vena	veine	VEIN

172. Here may be mentioned also the English development of Old French *o* into *ou* before a nasal with *t* or *d*. This French *o* represented either *o* or *u* of Latin, and our spelling with *ou* is found in general from the fourteenth century. The following are examples:

Cl. Latin	French	Anglo-Saxon	Modern English
abundare	OF abunder, abonder	(h)abunde	ABOUND
bon(i)tat-em	bonte(t)	bonte, bunte, bounte	BOUNTY
comit-em	compte AF counte		COUNT
contra (144)	OF contre, cuntre		COUNTER
font-em	font	fant (10)	FOUNT (also FONT)
mont-em	mont	munte, monte [1]	MOUNT
profund-um	profond		PROFOUND
rotund-um	OF rund, rond	rund(e), rond(e),	ROUND
son-um	OF son	sun(e), son(e)	SOUND (154, end)

[1] Borrowed again in the 12th century from Fr. 'mont.'

This change occurred also in words not French, as Lat. **pondus**, AS 'pund'; then POUND; and the native AS 'hund,' *hound*.

V. TREATMENT OF CONSONANTS

A. CONSONANTS DROPPED

173. (*a*) *T* and *d* after a vowel, becoming final by the loss of a syllable, were dropped, as:

Cl. Latin	Low Latin	French	English
mercedem, *reward*	**merced(e)**	merci (mercit)	MERCY
virtutem, *manliness* (**vir**)	**virtut(e)**	vertu	VIRTUE

(*b*) Consonants often disappeared between vowels:

Cl. Latin	Low Latin	French	English
crudelem	**crudele**	cruel	CRUEL
decidere, *fall down*	**decadere**	decaer	DECAY
magistrum (45)	**magistru**	OF maistre	MASTER
redemptionem (145)	**redemptione**	OF raençon, rançon	RANSOM
securum, *secure*	**securu**	OF seur, Fr. sûr	SURE (42)

(*c*) A consonant group might be simplified by dropping the first:

Cl. Latin	Low Latin	French	English
civitatem, *state*	**civitate, civtat(e)**	cité	CITY
dubitare	**dubitare, dub-tare**	douter	DOUBT (restoring Lat. *b*)
masculum	**masclu**	OF masle, Fr. mâle	MALE
periculum, **peri-clum**	**periclu**	peril	PERIL
subvenire, *come up, come to mind*	**subvenire**	souvenir	SOUVENIR

B. CONSONANTS ADDED

174. A consonant was often developed in the combination of other consonant sounds, a development called epenthesis (154), as *b* between *m* and *l* or *r*, and *d* between *l* or *n* and *r*.

Cl. Latin	Low Latin	French	English
cameram	camera, camra	chambre	CHAMBER
cinerem	cinere, cinre	cendre	CINDER
humilem, *lowly*	humile, humle	humble	HUMBLE
numerum	numere, numre	nombre (OF also numbre)	NUMBER
pulverem, *dust*	pulvere, pulre	poudre OF poldre, puldre	POWDER
rememorare	rememorare, rememrare	remembrer	REMEMBER
simulare	simulare, simlare	sembler	RE-SEMBLE
tenerem	tenere, tenre	tendre	TENDER

C. CONSONANTS CHANGED

175. (*a*) By assimilation, either partial or complete (146, 148), *e.g.*:

Cl. Latin	Low Latin	French	English
acrem, *sharp*	acre	aigre, vin-aigre (vinum, *wine*)	VINEGAR
debitam, *due* (f.)	debita, debta	dette	DEBT (restoring *b*)
duplum, *twofold*	duplu	double	DOUBLE
rotulam, rotulum, *little wheel*	rotula, rotlu	rolle	ROLL
subitum, *unexpected*	subitanu(m), subtan	soudain	SUDDEN
terminum, *limit*	terminu, termnu	termme, terme	TERM

Not far removed from such assimilation is the softening of *p* and *b* into *v* between vowels and before *r*,[1] as:

Cl. Latin	Low Latin	French	English
febrem	**febre**	OF fevre	FEVER
recuperare	**recup(e)rare**	OF recovrer	RECOVER
ripariam	**riparia**	rivière (26)	RIVER
tabernam, *shed, shop*	**taberna**	taverne	TAVERN

(b) Under the influence of consonantal *i* or *e* (*y*).

Examples given above (170) are **rationem** becoming 'raison' (Fr.), Eng. REASON; **potionem** becoming POISON; **pretium** becoming PRICE or PRIZE.

Other illustrations are:

Cl. Latin	Low Latin	French	English
ad + **propius**, *nearer*	**appropiare**	OF aprochier	APPROACH
calumniam,*false charge*	**calumnia**	OF chalange	CHALLENGE
caveam, *hollow*, CAVE	**cavea**	cage	CAGE
extraneum, *outer*	**extraneu**	OF estrange	STRANGE
salviam	**salvia**	sauge (179)	SAGE

176. The alteration of *t* to *s* before this *y*-sound had begun by the third or fourth century of this era. According to early grammarians **Titius** was pronounced as 'Titsius,' **etiam** as 'etsiam'; so **rationem** must have become 'ratsione' long before it became 'raison' (cf. Eng. -TION = "-shun," as in RATION). *C* was likewise softened before *e* and *i*, and from this change of pronunciation, *ci* from the seventh century was often written for *ti*, and so survives in many words; *e.g.*, **gratia, gratiosus** became GRACE, GRACIOUS; **pretium, pretiosus**, PRICE, PRECIOUS; **spatium, spatiosus**, SPACE, SPACIOUS; **vitium, vitiosus**, VICE, VICIOUS; **palatium** gave PALACE (but later PALATIAL), and **solstitium** SOLSTICE. Note also such differences of spelling as **ficticius** for **ficticius**

---

[1] Cf. the opposite change in **curvare**, *bend* (**curvus**), Low Lat. **curbare** OF 'courber,' Eng. CURB.

(from **fingere, fictus**, *mold, form*), Eng. FICTITIOUS; **nutritius** for **nutricius** (**nutrix, nutricis,** NURSE; **nutrire,** NOURISH), Eng. NUTRITIOUS.

(*a*) *C* and *g* at the beginning of a word before *a* occur as *ch* and *j* respectively, in:

Cl. Latin	Low Latin	Old French	English
carrum, *wagon*	**carreta** (dim.)	charete, (later, chariot)	CHARIOT
gambam (Late), *leg*	**gamba**	jambe	JAMB

The dialectal differences of French *c* and *ch*, representing Latin *c* before *a*, have been mentioned above (35). The change to *ch* must have come through this same *ky*-sound as suggested in 170: *ka*, then *kya*, became in sound "tcha," "cha" in central France, while hard *c* remained in the north (Picardy and most of Normandy). Similarly *g* became *j* in one dialect and remained hard *g* in the other.

(*b*) *Di* (= *d* + *y*), initial before a vowel, likewise became *j*; so:

Cl. Latin	Low Latin	Old French	English
diurnalem, *daily*	**diurnale**	journal	JOURNAL
sub + diurnare, *stay day after day, stay long*	**subdiurnare**	sojourner	SOJOURN

177. The Latin suffix -aticum seems to have changed in pronunciation to "-adigu"; then "adyu," "-adzhe," and was finally spelled -AGE; so **aetat-aticum** (**aetaticum?**), from **aetas,** *age,* Fr. 'âge,' Eng. AGE; **silvaticum** from **silva,** *forest,* Fr. 'sauvage,' Eng. SAVAGE. The suffix -*age* went back into Mediæval Latin as -**agium,** and its extension of use is illustrated not only in such French words as CARRIAGE (**carrus,** *wagon*), MARRIAGE (**maritus,** *a husband,* Low Lat. **maritaticum**), but also in bondAGE, breakAGE, FRUITAGE, PARSONAGE and other words of our own COINAGE.

D. OTHER CONSONANT CHANGES

178. *P* and *v*, following a vowel, left as final after the loss of a syllable, became *f*, as:

Cl. Latin	Low Latin	Old French	English
brevem, *short*	**brev(e)**	brief	BRIEF
caput, *head*	**cap(u)**	chef	CHEF (CHIEF, 44)

179. *L* before a consonant in many words was vocalized, *i.e.*, the written *l* disappeared leaving a *u*-sound which combined with the preceding vowel; then our later English often restored the Latin *l*:

Cl. Latin	Low Latin	Old French	English
ad + saltum, *a leap at*	**assaltu**	assaut	Mid. Eng. ASSAUT, (later, ASSAULT)
de-albare, *whitewash*	**dealbare**	dauber	DAUB (202)
falsam	**fall(i)ta**	faute	Mid. Eng. FAUT, (later, FAULT)
salsam, fem. pf. pple. *salted*	**salsa**	sauce	SAUCE

180. *S* initial before a consonant made a separate syllable 'es-' in Old French[1] and so came into English, as:

Cl. Latin	Low Latin	French	English
specialem, *belonging to a kind* (**species**)	**speciale**	especial	ESPECIAL
stabilire, *make stable*	**stabilire**	establir	ESTABLISH (186)
statum, *condition*	**statu**	estat	ESTATE (43)

[1] This use of what is called the prothetic vowel occurred occasionally as early as the second century after Christ, *e.g.*, **istudium, histudium,** and **estudium,** for **studium,** STUDY. Then when this vowel was dropped in the effort to restore the original form, the process was extended to perfectly legitimate initial syllables: **Hispania** became **Spania,** SPAIN; **historia, storia,** STORY. **Historia** was really a Greek work meaning *information gained by inquiry.* Cf. also SCALD for OF 'escalder,' Lat. **excalidare** (**calidus,** *hot*); and SHORT, probably from Low Lat. **excurtus** (7); also SCOUR, SCOURGE (202), SCAMP, SCAMPER (49).

181. It must be constantly kept before us that such changes as these belonged properly to the time when spoken Latin was becoming spoken French, and that many words came later into French, as into English, directly from the literary Latin. In some measure these newer French forms, also adopted into English, followed the model of the older words, but for the most part they do not conform to such principles as account for the modification of spoken words. Examples of words thus twice received into English through the French (popular words and literary words) have been given in 43. And one must not be surprised to find even in the older words many real or apparent exceptions to rules briefly and rather incompletely stated above, since the spoken word is ever subject to the influence of analogy and of dialectal peculiarities.

VI. Forms of Derived Verbs in English

182. Quite in line with the use of silent final *-e* in derivative nouns where in Latin the base ended in a single consonant preceded by a single vowel (163), and its omission elsewhere, is the usage in regard to English verbs derived from present forms of Latin verbs either directly or through the French (134). If here the root syllable ends in a single consonant preceded by a single vowel (except *-er*), the English verb has the silent final *-e*. As single consonants too we shall have to count *sc = s*, and *nc, ns;* and *v*, also *g* corresponding to Fr. *g-e*, in English must have *-e* following. Present stems in *-er* do not add *-e* in English: CONFER from **confero,** but INTERFERE from **ferio,** *strike* (134). So we have through the French:

Latin	French	English
accusare	accuser	ACCUSE
alterare	altérer	ALTER
citare	citer	CITE
com-initiare	commencer	COMMENCE

Latin	French	English
condensare	condenser	CONDENSE
judicare	juger	JUDGE
movere	mouvoir	MOVE
observare	observer	OBSERVE
provocare	provoquer	PROVOKE
revivere	revivre	REVIVE

And directly from the Latin:

Latin	English	Latin	English
accedere	ACCEDE	devolvere	DEVOLVE
adorare, *pray to, worship*	ADORE	inquirere	INQUIRE
		praescribere	PRESCRIBE
coalescere	COALESCE	producere	PRODUCE
collidere	COLLIDE	surgere	SURGE
deludere	DELUDE	transmutare	TRANSMUTE

183. But if the present stem of the Latin ends in two consonants (other than those mentioned), or in a single consonant preceded by a diphthong, no final *-e* is needed in English (cf. 163). A double consonant usually appears as single (but **addere**, ADD, and **errare**, ERR). Examples are:

Latin	French	English
affirmare	affirmer	AFFIRM
assignare	assigner	ASSIGN
concernere	concerner	CONCERN
defraudare	OF defrauder	DEFRAUD
importare	importer	IMPORT

Also:

Latin	English	Latin	English
abhorrere	ABHOR	dissentire	DISSENT
adaptare	ADAPT	distillare	DISTIL
admittere	ADMIT	laudare	LAUD
adornare	ADORN	respondere	RESPOND
comprehendere	COMPREHEND	succumbere	SUCCUMB

The root vowel was completely lost when **contra-stare,** *stand against,* and **re-stare,** *stop behind* or *stand still,* became Fr. 'contraster' and 'rester,' and then passed into English as CONTRA-ST and RE-ST.

184. From **cedere,** *go, yield,* we have CEDE, with compounds like **accedere** (**ad-**) above, **concedere,** *yield* (*go with one*), CONCEDE; **recedere,** *go back,* RECEDE; **secedere,** *go apart,* SECEDE; but the English spelling shifts in **procedere,** *go forward,* PROCEED, and **excedere,** *go out, go beyond,* EXCEED, which however were formerly written 'procede' and 'excede.'

185. **Reddere,** *give back,* became in Low Latin **rendere,** probably by analogy, since its opposite **prendere,** *take,* had the nasal. Through the French infinitive 'rendre,' came Eng. RENDER. From the pf. pple. **rendita,** *i.e.,* **pecunia rendita,** *money paid,* came Fr. 'rente,' Eng. RENT. **Tendere,** Fr. 'tendre,' also became TENDER, first as noun and then as verb. Several other infinitives coming through the French became English nouns; thus:

Latin	French	English
licere, *be permitted*	OF leisir (loisir)	LEISURE, Mid. Eng. leysir
manere, *remain*	manoir	MANOR, *abiding place*
mergere, *sink*	AF merger	MERGER
placere, *please*	OF plesir	PLEASURE, Mid. Eng. plesir
potere, Late Lat. for **posse,** *be able*	poer	POWER (28), see also posse, 57
rejungere, *join again*	rejoindre	REJOINDER
remanere, *stay back*	remaindre	REMAINDER

So also **minus nominare,** *name less,* OF 'mes-nomer,' became MISNOMER, *i.e., misnaming.* Cf. SOUVENIR, 173 *c;* also 57, **interest,** Note.

186. We have mentioned above (131) a group of Latin verbs whose present stems were made by the addition of -*sc*- to the stems of other verbs (sometimes noun stems), as **florere**, *bloom*, **florescere**, *begin to bloom*. A number of these, and others following merely by analogy, appear in French in the '-ir' conjugation (Latin fourth, -ire), with the -*sc*- addition giving certain forms in '-is-' or '-iss-,' from which such verbs in English end in -ISH.[1] Since the French pres. pple. shows the '-iss-,' it may be cited for comparison:

Latin	French	English
carus, *dear*	cher, cherissant, *hold dear*	CHERISH
complere, *fill up*	ac-complissant	ACCOMPLISH
demoliri, *destroy*	demolissant	DEMOLISH
finire	finissant	FINISH
florere, florescere	OF fleurissant	FLOURISH
nutrire	nourissant	NOURISH
perire	perissant	PERISH
punire	punissant	PUNISH
vanescere	OF vanissant	VANISH
vincere	OF veinquissant	VANQUISH

187. Some Latin compounds involving **facio**, *make*, transfer this verb in the form -**fico** to the first conjugation (p. 172, N. 1); then the infinitive -**ficare** with loss of *c* between vowels and the change of -**are** to '-er,' becomes in French '-fier' (173 *b*; 167), from which we have -FY. So:

Latin	French	English
amplificare (amplus + facere)	amplifier	AMPLIFY
clarificare (clarus + facere)	clarifier	CLARIFY
glorificare (gloria + facere)	glorifier	GLORIFY
pacificare (pax, pacis + facere)	pacifier	PACIFY
terrificare (terrificus, terror + facere)	terrifier	TERRIFY

[1] Some verbs not coming through the French in '-ir,' have -ISH in English on analogy of these; *e.g.*, DISTINGUISH, Fr. 'distinguer,' Lat. **distinguere**; PUBLISH, Fr. 'publier,' Lat. **publicare.**

Low Latin	French	English
certificare (certus + facere)	certifier	CERTIFY
nullificare (nullus + facere)	———	NULLIFY
simplificare (simplex, simplicis + facere)	simplifier	SIMPLIFY

188. Nouns, adjectives, and verb stems are used thus to make verbs in -FY. Other examples are: **deus,** *god,* DEIFY; **fortis,** *brave,* FORTIFY; **gratus,** *thankful,* GRATIFY; **justus,** JUST, JUSTIFY; **notus,** *known,* NOTIFY (not *make known* but *make to know*); **rectus,** *right,* RECTIFY; **signum,** SIGN, SIGNIFY; **species,** *a kind,* SPECIFY (*make the kind, indicate the particulars*); **testis,** *witness,* TESTIFY (**testificari**); **verus,** *true,* VERIFY.

On analogy and after the French, but without the Latin in -ficare, are **ramus,** *branch,* RAMIFY; **stupere,** *be stunned,* STUPEFY (**stupefacere**); and from Med. Lat. **exemplificare,** EXEMPLIFY (**exemplum,** EXAMPLE). CRUCIFY was made in like manner from **crucificare,** a Late Latin representation, or misrepresentation, of **cruci + figere,** *fasten to a cross.*

189. In the same way derivatives from the Latin **plicare,** *fold, wind together,* become French '-plier' and Eng. -PLY:

Latin	French	English
applicare (ad-plicare)	OF aplier (later, appliquer)	APPLY
multiplicare (multus + plicare)	multiplier	MULTIPLY
replicare	replier (later, repliquer)	REPLY

But COMPLY comes through Italian from **complere,** not from **complicare.** SUPPLY through French from **supplere,** *fill up,* is quite different from **supplicare,** *bend beneath, bow before,* SUPPLICATE. DEFY is OF 'defier,' Low Lat. **diffidare, dis-,** 145 (cf. **affidavit,** 57).

190. We should expect Latin present participles to appear in English in -ANT or -ENT according as their verbs were of the first conjugation or not, *e.g.*, CONSTANT from **constare,** CONSISTENT from **consistere.** And so they regularly do when they come directly from Latin. But the present participle in French ends in '-ant' regardless of the Latin conjugation represented (since '-ant' and '-ent' were pronounced alike in French) and this accounts for certain variations in English and for double forms, one from the Latin participle, the other from the French. The former is usually an adjective, the latter a noun: from **confidere,** CONFIDENT (Lat.) and CONFIDANT (Fr.); from **dependere,** DEPENDENT (Lat.) and DEPENDANT (Fr.); from **convenire,** CONVENIENT (Lat., *coming together;* hence *suitable*) and COVENANT (Fr., *an agreement*). So PENDENT and PENDANT, DESCENDENT and DESCENDANT. ASCENDENT was in use in an earlier time as an adjective, but ASCENDANT is now used for both noun and adjective, although not French, but made, Skeat says, "purely and foolishly on analogy of DESCENDANT, an honest French form." In both uses we have ATTENDANT (Fr.) from **attendere** (*stretch toward, direct the mind to*), and as nouns only, TENANT (Fr.) from **tenere,** *hold,* and LIEU-TENANT (29). **Valens,** from **valere,** *be strong,* has become VALIANT through the Fr. 'vaillant,' but remains Latin in PREVALENT (**praevalens**), *being of superior strength, prevailing.*

191. Similarly nouns in -NCE (75) may have -ANCE or -ENCE according as they follow French or Latin. From **sistere,** *stand,* we have RESISTANCE and PERSISTENCE; from **tenere,** *hold,* SUSTENANCE and CONTINENCE. The gerundive also, as has been said (127), may thus be transferred from -end- to -AND: **reprimenda,** Fr. 'reprimande,' Eng. REPRI-MAND, **vivenda,** Fr. 'viande,' Eng. VIAND.

192. Perfect passive participles in -atus (-atum), ended in -*e* (-*é*) in French: **appellatum, appellat(u),** 'apelle(t)', Fr. 'appelé,' spelled into English as APPELLEE, an old law term for one *appealed against,* corresponding to the active pple. APPELLANT or the agent noun APPELLOR (Lat. **appellator**).

From such a beginning in law terms, the suffix -EE has been widely extended, used for derivatives of Latin participles in **-tum** and **-itum** as well as **-atum**, added also to present verb stems and even to non-Latin words. Words thus formed serve as passives corresponding to agent nouns as active. The following are common:

COMMITTEE (AF pple. 'committe'): formerly *one commissioned* or *one to whom a matter is entrusted* (**committere**, *entrust*). About 1600 the word became collective, as we now use it.

debaucHEE (Fr. 'debauché'), *one led astray;* of uncertain origin.

DEVOTEE: coined in English from DEVOTE. Formerly DEVOTE was used as an adjective for *devoted, consecrated under a vow* (**devovere, devotus**).

DIVORCEE, or with the French distinction of masc. and fem., 'DIVORCÉ' and 'DIVORCÉE': *one divorced* (see 157).

EMPLOYEE: written also EMPLOYE after the French, and corresponding to 'employer.' Through French ('employer,' OF 'emplier') EMPLOY comes from Late Lat. **implicare** (189), *bend* or *direct upon* something.

PAYEE: *one to be paid,* as payer is *one to pay.* PAY, Fr. 'payer,' is Lat. **pacare** (170, 173 b), *appease, pacify* (**pax, pacis,** *peace*), and in Low Latin *pacify a creditor.*

REFEREE: *one to whom a matter is carried back* (**re-ferre**) for decision (Fr. 'referé').

REFUGEE: *one who flees for safety.* The French pple. is 'réfugié' ('se réfugier'). Cf. Lat. **refugium**, REFUGE (82), a place to which one *flees back* (**re-fugere**).

trusTEE: coined word from the Scandinavian word 'trust'; *one who is trusted.*

193. We have had occasion to mention the fact that words coming into English directly from Latin often assumed the same forms as those which came through Low Latin and French. It hardly need be added that the same is true of the suffixes given above in the chapter on Word Formation. Final -*a* becomes -*e* in **-ina, -tura, -sura,** giving -INE, -TURE, -SURE; **-tia,** with the *t* softened through the influence of *i*

(176) becomes -CE, and -ntia either -NCE or -NCY (Fr. '-nce,' '-ncie,' 75, N. 1); Lat. -bilis, -tilis, -culus, -crum, etc. become -BLE, -TLE, -CLE, -CRE, etc. and many a word in -AL, -ID, -MENT, -TION, -TOR, has never had any Low Latin or Old French experiences to rob it of an accusative -em or -um. The suffix -or we usually keep, preferring the Latin form to the French, but in our older books, often in works printed in England, -OUR is used following the AF '-our' (OF '-or,' '-ur') while -OUS has become a general ending to represent Lat. -osus. So, -tat- of abstract nouns (72), after its ending -em had been lost, came through OF '-tet' to Fr. '-té.' Once having been received as -TY in English, it is widely extended and no longer proves anything French in the history of a word. France set the fashions and we have followed them.

194. A number of modern French words of Latin origin have been adopted into English, preserving their French form and, in part at least, their French pronunciation. Such are the following:

ADIEU: 'à Dieu,' Lat. **ad Deum,** *To God* (I commend you). Cf. our 'Good-bye,' *God be with you.*

AMATEUR: Lat. **amator,** *a lover.* He studies art, music, etc. not professionally but because he is a lover of such things.

AMOUR: Lat. **amor,** *love; a love affair.*

APROPOS: *i.e.*, 'à propos,' **ad propositum,** *to the thing proposed* (**proponere,** *set forth*), *to the purpose,* suitable or suitably *to the matter in hand.*

AVOIRDUPOIS: a corruption of 'avoir de pois,' *to have weight,* Lat. **habere, de,** and **pensum (pendere,** *weigh*), OF 'peis,' then 'pois.'

BEAU: Lat. **bellus** (158, N.), *handsome, fine;* fem. BELLE, Lat. **bella(m),** *beautiful.*

BELLES-LETTRES: **bellus,** *beautiful,* **litterae,** LETTERS, *literature.*

CHAUFFEUR: Fr. 'chauffer,' *to heat,* is a made-over **calefacere,** *make warm* (cf. Eng. CHAFE, 202, and CHAFING-dish). The agent noun CHAUFFEUR meant *a fireman, a stoker.* The stoker has now been promoted to drive a car.

CHEF: same as CHIEF, Lat. **caput** (27, 44); the *head* (*cook*).

CORPS: Lat. **corpus,** *body; group* or *division*, as of the army (44).

DEPOT: Lat. **depositum** (43), *place to put things down.*

DETOUR: *a turning aside;* the French verb is 'détourner' (OF 'des-'), Lat. **di(s)** + **tornare,** TURN.

ÉLITE: pf. pple. of 'élire,' Lat. **eligere,** *choose,* Med. Lat. **electa,** *choice.* Cf. 'the ELECT.'

ENNUI: like ANNOY, from Lat. **in odio,** *in hatred* (202).

ÉTUDE: for OF 'estude' (180), Lat. **studium,** STUDY (82); *a composition* in music or other arts *for study or practice.*

FIANCÉ, fem. FIANCÉE (cf. 192): pf. pple. of 'fiancer,' *betroth, make a pledge,* OF 'fiance,' *a pledge,* Low Lat. **fidantia,** Lat. **fidentia,** *confidence,* all from Lat. **fidere,** *trust.*

LITTERATEUR: Lat. **litterator,** made from **littera,** pl. **litterae,** LETTERS, *literature,* with agent-noun suffix, *one devoted to literature* (cf. **gladiator,** 80, end).

LUCRE: Fr. 'lucre,' Lat. **lucrum,** *gain.*

MANŒUVRE: spelled also MANEUVER, Low Lat. **manu-opera** (43).

MÊLÉE: *a mixture* (44).

MENU: Lat. **minutum** (166, cf. MINUTE, 202); from *the little thing* this came to mean *detail;* then *a detailed list* particularly of food to be served.

NAÏVE: the fem. adj. from Lat. **nativus,** the French masc. being 'naïf.' Our use of this fem. form (rather than masc.) is perhaps due partly to the *v* of **nativus,** partly to analogy with 'naïveté.'

NÉGLIGÉ: *neglected,* pf. pple. (192) of 'négliger,' Lat. **negligere,** NEGLECT.

PARAMOUR: *i.e.,* 'par amour,' **per amorem,** *by* or *with love,* one *who assumes the place of lover.*

PERSONNEL: French spelled **persona** (45) as 'personne'; PERSONNEL, then, corresponds to **personalis** (98).

PROTÉGÉ (fem. -ÉE): *one protected,* pf. pple. (192) of 'protéger,' Lat. **protegere,** *shield one* (**tegere**) *in front* (**pro**), PROTECT.

RENAISSANCE: -ANCE, Lat. **-antia** (75), the verb 're-naître,' OF 'naistre,' going back to **nasci,** *be born;* hence *re-birth.*

RESTAURANT: *restoring,* pres. pple. of Fr. 'restaurer,' Lat. **restaurare,** RESTORE, *make strong again;* but the simple verb ('**staurare**') was not used.

SAVANT: pres. pple. of 'savoir,' *know; a knowing man;* it represents Lat. **sapiens** from which we have SAPIENT.

SEANCE: *a sitting;* -ANCE, Lat. -**antia** (75); OF 'seoir,' Lat. **sedere,** *sit.*

SOLITAIRE: Lat. **solitarius** (41, 'lonely'), *alone; a single diamond in a setting, or c game for a single player.*

SUITE: the same in origin as SUIT (30).

TABLEAU: diminutive of Fr. 'table,' Lat. **tabula,** TABLE.

CHAPTER V

CHANGES OF FORM AND MEANING

195. In many instances English words of Latin origin have undergone such changes of spelling or of meaning that in their present form and use they are effectively disguised. The queerness of their appearance or behavior may be an inheritance from their queer Latin originals or it may be the result of their later experiences. Many changes of form, as we have seen in the preceding chapter, were due to the French; for others our own English must be held responsible.

There are several processes by which in any language words may change their meaning. The following are very common.

196. Transference of a term to a new and often figurative application; *e.g.*, **clarus**, Eng. CLEAR, may apply to the sky and mean *bright*, to a statement and mean *intelligible*. GOVERNOR has come through the French from **gubernator**, *a pilot;* it may designate one who has never commanded a boat if only he guides the ship of state. **Mandare** was originally *give into one's hand* (**manus + dare**), but it easily came to mean *give one his task* or *duty, i.e.*, COMMAND. From **pomum**, *apple*, with -EL (Lat. dimin. **-ellus**), POMEL, now spelled POMMEL, should be *a little apple;* but we apply it to the knoblike projection on a saddle or the knob of a sword hilt. The use of this sword handle to beat one's opponent over the head gave us our verb POMMEL, but such punishment can now with equal propriety be administered with the fists. **Valva** in Latin was the *leaf* of a folding door; the VALVE in a pump or an engine is but another kind of door.

197. Sometimes the change degrades the meaning: **villanus,** a Low Latin form from **villa,** *a farmhouse,* was *a farm servant;* then *a serf.* As it came to us through the French, the boorishness of such a servant came into prominence till he became a *knave,* a *scoundrel, i.e.,* a VILLAIN. On the other hand, the new application of a term may lend it dignity, as when **minister,** *a servant,* becomes the chief officer of a church or a government representative in a foreign country.

198. The transfer is often from the physical or concrete to the mental or abstract: **apprehendere,** APPREHEND, was *take hold of,* but it meant also *grasp with the mind.* **Spiritus** was *a blowing* (**spirare**)*;* then *breath, soul,* SPIRIT; **incendere, incensus,** *set fire to;* then *rouse, stir* (with anger), INCENSE. **Mordere** was *to bite,* and MORSEL (formed as dimin. from **morsus**), *a little bite, i.e., a bit,* but REMORSE is a *biting of conscience* (24). **Informare** meant first *give shape to* (**forma**)*;* INFORM is *give shape to ideas.*

199. Less often the change is from the abstract to the concrete. From **cernere,** *sift, separate,* DISCERN, *judge,* **concernere** became *distinguish carefully, regard* (Med. Lat.). The word thus passed from the physical to the mental, but there is a return to the physical when our derived noun, CONCERN, from denoting a state of mind, is applied also to the object of our thought; from our feeling CONCERN for our business establishment, the establishment itself becomes the CONCERN. **Nocentia** (**nocere,** *hurt*), *guilt, transgression,* became through the French NUISANCE, applied to both things and persons. **Terror** is an inward state, but the man or beast that inspires the feeling becomes himself a TERROR (81). **Multitudo** is *many-ness,* number is abstract, but both the Latin word and the English MULTITUDE designate the very physical crowd itself.

200. A particular meaning may be generalized: CARRY we get from OF 'carier' which goes back to **carrus** (49,

CARICATURE), CAR, CARRIAGE, but has long ceased to suggest this special mode of transportation. The **circus** (52) includes much more than the original CIRCLE. A LESSON (Fr. 'leçon') now varies from an assignment in Latin to a practice in music, cooking, or flying a plane, but its original **lectio** (**lectionem**) was a *reading* (**legere**, *read*). PLUMBER is from **plumbum**, *lead*, but he no longer confines himself to this metal.

201. A general meaning may become specialized. CRESCENT was simply *growing* (123); then the *growing moon;* then this as a symbol of the Mohammedan religion. **Longitudo** and **latitudo** were simply *length* and *width*, but with the old conception of the earth as extending farther east and west than it does north and south, LONGITUDE and LATITUDE designated measurements in these directions respectively. LATITUDE in a figurative sense still has its broader meaning. PATENT from **patens, patentis**, *lying open*, means *exposed to view, evident*, but as a noun it became a *right* granted by the government for protection of an invention. The documents conveying this right were formerly called *letters patent* (**litterae patentes**), *i.e., an open letter*. **Sermo** (**sermonem**) was *talk, conversation* or *discourse;* we limit SERMONS to the pulpit as we have limited PULPIT to the church (45, PERSON).

202. In form or meaning the following words present some features of interest:

ABOMINATE: **abominari, abominatus** (128), from **ab** and **omen, ominis;** *turn away from the* (*evil*) *omen, turn from a thing as of ill omen.*

ACCORD: through Old French from Low Lat. **accordare, ad + cor, cordis,** *heart;* hence *bring one heart to another*, and thus *agree.* Or possibly from Low Lat. **corda**, Cl. Lat. **chorda** (Grk.), *the string* of a musical instrument, for **accordare** also means *to tune* an instrument. An ACCORDION, in either case, is supposed to produce harmony (-ION in imitation of CLARION, Low Lat. **clario, clarionis,** *clear sound*).

ADJUST: The OF 'ajuster,' or 'ajoster,' from which we get ADJUST, was Low Lat. **adjuxtare, ad-,** *to,* and **juxta,** *near, put side by side;* so *arrange.* **Juxta,** however, in the word was confused with **justus,** *right,* JUST; hence the French and English forms.

ADVISE: *to direct one according to what seems best;* through the French from **ad visum; videri,** *seem, seem good.*

AFFINITY: **affinitas,** quality noun (72) of the adjective **affinis, ad,** *near* and **finis,** *boundary, having adjoining boundary lines, bordering on, related to.*

AISLE: Lat. **ala,** *wing,* became Fr. 'aile,' the *wing* of a church; the -*s*- was probably introduced through the influence of ISLE (see below).

ALAS: Lat. **A lassum!** is *Ah, weary!* The Old French shortened it to 'a-las,' *Ah, wretched* (that I am)! Thus it was passed on to English as one word.

ALLEGE: Things are not what they seem. The etymologists show us that Lat. **allegare,** Fr. 'alleguer' would become Eng. 'alleague,' and ALLEGE is related to **allegare** in meaning only. In form it is traced to a late **ex-litigare,** *clear at law,* or to the hybrid **ex-ledigare,** Germ. 'ledig,' *free.*

ALLOW: OF 'alouer' ('allouer') from Lat. **allaudare (ad-laudare)** would mean *praise, approve;* from Low Lat. **allocare (ad-locare)** it should be *place, assign, admit.* The two Latin words produced one Old French form with their meanings confused or blended, as uses of the Eng. ALLOW illustrate.

ANCESTOR: The Lat. **antecessor** was *one going before* (**ante-cedere**)*;* this was made over into Fr. 'ancessour,' and so occurs in Middle English. Later a superfluous *t* was introduced.

ANGUISH: Through its various French spellings ANGUISH may be traced to Lat. **angustia,** *narrowness,* **angustus,** *narrow.* The narrowness of the breath passage expressed in **angere,** *choke,* suggests the suffering now designated by the word. 'Anger,' a Teutonic word, is of the same origin as these Latin words, since this emotion also was regarded as producing the physical effect of choking.

ANNOY: The OF 'enoier,' or 'anoier,' from the noun 'enoi,' 'anoi,' meant *vex, trouble;* the noun originally was made from the Latin phrase **in odio,** *in hatred.* To hold a thing in hatred was to be weary of it, vexed with it. The thing becomes an ANNOYANCE ('enoi'). This same noun, 'enoi,' is Mod. Fr. 'ennui' (194).

ANTIC: the same word as ANTIQUE (Lat. **antiquus,** *old*), *ancient.* What belongs to the old time is quaint or queer; thus ANTIC, as an adjective, came to mean *grotesque,* and as a noun *a fantastic trick* or *caper.*

APPRECIATE: As made from **ad + pretiare** (pretium, PRICE), this means *set a value on,* i.e., a proper value. Since Old French took **pretium** as 'preis' (170) and the verb as 'preiser,' it furnished us in APPRAISE a doublet of APPRECIATE. DEPRECIATE, from **de-pretiare,** is literally *lower the price.*

APPRENTICE: This word, coming from some French form representing the Low Lat. **apprenticius,** is a derivative of **apprendere,** i.e., **ad-prehendere,** *lay hold on,* and later APPREHEND, *learn.* The APPRENTICE is a *learner, one who apprehends.*

ARRIVE: The OF 'arriver,' from which we have ARRIVE, was the Low Lat. **arripare,** *get to the bank* (**ad + ripa,** *bank of a stream*). Originally the French word was used only of seamen and vessels. Cf. the English colloquial use of 'land,' when one "lands at the railway station."

AUSPICES: The Lat. **auspicium** is a shortened form of **avi-spicium,** from **avis,** *bird,* and **specere** (**-spicere**), *look into, watch* (cf. **augur,** 52, INAUGURATE inf.). The *bird-watching* was for discovering omens or signs from the gods as to the success of any undertaking. Hence favorable AUSPICES are favorable conditions for an enterprise.

BACHELOR: OF 'bachelier,' Low Lat. **baccalarius,** Med. Lat. **baccalaris.** Both the derivation and the changes of meaning are far from certain, but the following explanation, which has been suggested, is interesting: **bacca** was Low Lat. for **vacca,** *cow,* **baccalia,** *a herd of cows,* **baccalaria,** *a division of land* for keeping cattle, **baccalarius,** *a young countryman* who worked on such a farm under the tenant, *an inferior, a young or inferior soldier, a young unmarried man, any unmarried man, a younger member of a university, one with only an inferior degree.* Then somebody realized that it was not quite dignified to call a university man a farm hand or cowboy, and translated BACHELOR back to Latin as **baccalaureus,** that the young scholar might be crowned with the *laurel berry wreath*. BACCALAUREATE follows as our own coinage (107).

bankRUPT: a hybrid word since 'bank' is Teutonic for *bench* (a money changer's bench), while -RUPT is Lat. **ruptus, rumpere,** *break*. The bankrupt is *bank-broken*. The word, however, came from the Ital. 'banca rotta,' through the Fr. 'bankeroutte,' appearing in Middle English as bankeROUPTE; thus coming back to the Lat. **rupta,** which had changed to 'rotta' in Italian.

BIB: The Lat. **bibere,** *drink*, came into Middle English as 'bibben,' *to tipple*, and a BIB was *a drinking cloth*, now, however, for the child rather than for the tippler.

BISCUIT: This French word represents the Lat. **bis coctus,** *twice cooked* (**coquere,** *cook*), since it was formerly baked in an oven twice.

BUCKLE: *a little cheek;* **buccula** (**bucula**) was a diminutive of **bucca,** *the puffed out cheek*, applied also to the part of the helmet which covered the cheeks and mouth; through the Low Latin it became *a shield* (with its cheeklike curve) particularly *the boss* of a shield, from which the transfer to BUCKLE is easy.

BUGLE: The OF 'bugle' was *a wild ox;* Lat. **buculus,** *a bullock*, a diminutive from **bos,** *ox* (68). But the common use of the word has left us now nothing of the animal but the horn.

BULL: **Bulla** was *a knob*, particularly a leaden knob used as a seal; so *a seal* on an edict; then *the edict* itself, a BULL. Again **bulla** was *a bubble* and from it came Lat. **bullire** (EBULLITION), giving through the French, Eng. BOIL. As meaning *a jest* in the form of a contradictory statement ('Irish bull'), the word may still be derived from **bulla,** *a bubble*.

CANARY: The bird takes its name, of course, from the Canary Islands where it was found. The Lat. **insula Canaria,** according to Pliny,[1] was so named from its large dogs (**canarius** from **canis,** 101); or it may have been so called from its shape.

CANDIDATE: From **candere,** *be white*, was made the adjective **candidus** (112); from **candidus, candidatus** in participial form (107), as if *whitened*, meaning particularly *white-robed*. The **toga candida** was a brilliantly white garment worn by men who were seeking election to office (cf. **ambitio,** 145).

[1] *Natural History*, 6, 37 (32), 3.

CAPITULATE: Low Lat. **capitulum**, *little head*, from which we get CHAPTER (35), gave the verb **capitulare**, *divide into chapters* or *heads;* CAPITULATE thus meant to *arrange terms* of agreement *by heads;* then was restricted to submitting to such terms on the part of the vanquished.

CARBUNCLE: **Carbo, carbonis**, meant *a coal* (Eng. CARBON)*;* its diminutive **carbunculus** (for **carbon-culus**, p. 115, N.) was *a little (live) coal.* A CARBUNCLE, then, whether a gem or a boil, has the shape and the color of a little live coal.

CARDINAL: *like a hinge* (**cardo, cardinis**), that on which a thing turns; hence *of chief importance*, as the CARDINAL points, or CARDINAL virtues, also a *chief* or *leader* of the church, a member of the Pope's council. From this meaning CARDINAL denotes a *bright red* as the color of a cardinal's cassock and hat, and becomes the name of a kind of redbird.

CASH: According to the origin of the word, CASH should be kept in *a box*, Lat. **capsa** (68). The French modified **capsa** to 'casse,' extended it from the box to its contents, and passed it on.

CAULIFLOWER: *cabbage flower*, or rather *flowering cabbage*. The old form COLLYFLORY represented the OF 'col,' Lat. **caulis**, *cabbage*, with 'floris,' pple. of 'florir' ('fleurir'), from **florere**, *bloom*. The modern spelling restores the Lat. **cauli-** and makes the same change of **flor-** as we have in the noun FLOWER (26).

CHAFE: Our representation of OF 'chaufer' and Mid. Eng. 'chaufen' (cf. CHAUFFEUR, 194); thus the French had altered the Low Lat. **caleficare** ('calefcare'), the Classical **calefacere** (**calere** + **facere**), *make warm*, also *vex*. Cf. our expression "get hot" for *get angry*.

CHAPEL: Through the Old French this came from Low Lat. **capella**, *a (little) cape* or *hooded cloak* (cf. **cappa**, 12), according to Brachet, the **cappa**, or COPE, of St. Martin; it was then extended to mean a *sanctuary* containing relics. The custodians of St. Martin's cloak were called **capellani**, *i.e.*, CHAPLAINS.

CHARGE: The Old French like the Modern French verb was 'charger,' from the Low Lat. **carricare**, *load a car*, Lat. **carrus** (CARICATURE, 49). CHARGE suggests, therefore, *a carload*, *a burden*, whether of responsibility, duty, ammunition, or indebtedness. Cf. CARGO, 50.

CHERRY: While the Lat. **cerasus** came into Teutonic speech at an early period (5), the singular form which we use was a later borrowing. **Cerasum** (probably through Low Lat. **ceresia, ceresea**) became OF 'cerise.' The Middle English spelling with *ch-* must have come from the Norman French. The use of 'chiri' or 'chery,' and then CHERRY, beginning in English from the fourteenth century, was evidently due to mistaking the form in *-s* for a plural and dropping the *s* to make a singular. In exactly this way the Lat. **pisum** came over as PISE, PEAS(E), and then dropped the plural-sounding *s*. The form PEA has no more etymological right to its now undisputed place in the language than has "Chinee" for 'Chinese' or "Maltee" for 'Maltese.' We note also the Grk.-Lat. **cathedra** (**ex cathedra**, 59), *a seat*, which became Fr. 'chaire,' CHAIR, and by further alteration 'chaise,' *a sedan chair;* then *a vehicle* with such a seat. Adopted into English and regarded as a plural, it resulted in a singular SHAY. The "One-Hoss Shay" was faulty at least in its name. A certain Spanish wine was once called in English SHERRIS from the town Xeres where it was produced; then SHERRY was made as a singular. 'Xeres' is said to be a corruption of **Caesaris**, *i.e., Caesar's town.*

CITIZEN: CITY from **civitatem** has been given above (173*c*), the Fr. 'cité'; with '-ain' representing Lat. **-anus** (103), a man of the city was (OF) 'citeain,' becoming Mid. Eng. 'citesein.' The reason for the introduction of *s* or *z* is not clear, unless on analogy of DENIZEN, q.v.

CLIENT: **cliens, clientis,** *one who hears, one who listens* to another's advice, and is therefore under his protection or patronage, as a plebeian under the patronage of a patrician; another form of **cluens,** pres. pple. of **cluere,** *hear* (cf. **inclutus,** 225).

COAST: This is our spelling of OF 'coste,' Lat. **costa,** *a rib, a side.* The coast is the side of the continent. The French word also meant the *side of a hill;* hence the sled or the car may COAST down such an incline. With **ad,** Low Latin made the verb **accostare** and ACCOST is literally *get to the side of.*

COBBLEr: an English agent noun of COBBLE, which came through the OF 'cobler' from Lat. **copulare** (164, 175*a*), *bind together.* The "mender of bad soles" then is one who *fastens things together.* The Old French also had the noun 'cople,' which became

COUPLE, from **copula**, *a band* or *link* (**co-apere**, *join together*); a COBBLER is a COUPLer.

COHORT: The word meant first *an enclosed space* (**co** + same stem as in **hortus**, *a garden);* the COHORT was a company in the enclosure. See COURT, 28.

COIN: Since the piece of metal used as money was stamped by means of a wedge, the OF 'coin,' *a wedge,* meant also the *stamp;* then the *piece of money* itself. The word is a form of Lat. **cuneus**, *a wedge.* The wedge makes a corner; hence we have with another spelling COIGN.

COLPORTEUR: This French word (cf. 194) means *a neck-carrier,* 'col' + 'porteur,' Lat. **collum**, *neck,* **portator**, *carrier,* **portare**, *carry.* He carries his pack swung from his neck.

COMBINE: **com-binare** was made from **bini**, *two by two;* COMBINE is *to put together by twos,* or *join two things together.*

COMFORT: Through the Low Lat. **comfortare** the word meant first *make brave* or *courageous* (**fortis**), *strengthen.* Cf. ENCOURAGE, which is *to put heart into* (41).

COMPARE (-PARE, -PAIR): COMPARE is Lat. **com** + **parare**, from **par, paris**, *equal,* Eng. PAIR; hence *pair together, match.* APPAREL has the same root, having come (first as a verb) through the Old French ('a-parailler,' Low Lat. **ad pariculum**, dim. of **par**). It meant *put like with like.* Hence APPAREL suggests propriety of garb. Distinguished from these is PREPARE, **prae-parare**, where the verb means *make ready;* so *make ready beforehand.* Likewise SEPARATE, **se-parare**, is *make ready apart.* This **parare** also appears in **apparatus**, *a making ready for;* then *a device* or *contrivance.* **Re-parare** was *to make ready again,* and the English would probably have been spelled 'repare' (like PREPARE) but for the association of this word with IMPAIR, which represents OF 'empeirer,' from **in-** and **pejus, pejoris**, as if '**impejorare**,' *make worse.* Of still different origin is REPAIR, when one 'REPAIRS' to the next room; this is Late Lat. **re-patriare** (**patria**), *get back to one's native land.*

COMPILE: not *pile together,* although PILE is a good Latin word, being a round heap like *a ball,* **pila**. But COMPILE is the Lat. **compilare**, *snatch together* and *carry off, plunder.* It fortunately outgrew so sinister a meaning.

COMPLEXION: As an action noun of **complecti,** *twine together* (cf. **complex,** 53), **complexio** seems to have been the combination of the humors of the body (33) and became a constitution of skin, its color or appearance. Of like origin the fourth declension **complexus** has given us the noun COMPLEX, of a constitution more than skin deep, and modern physiological psychology may find again this connection between COMPLEXION and COMPLEX.

CONCLAVE: a room that may be locked up with *a key* (**clavis,** cf. also **clavus,** *nail,* and **claudo,** *shut up*). From the wide application of the Lat. **conclave,** meaning *dining room, animal cage,* etc., CONCLAVE became restricted to the apartments of the Vatican where the cardinals meet for the selection of a pope; then the body of cardinals in the CONCLAVE. The meaning again widens to any *secret and solemn assembly.*

CONSIDER: literally, *observe the stars,* Lat. **considerare, con,** *together,* **sidus, sideris,** *star* (cf. CONSTELLATION), possibly at first an astrological term. Such careful attention was then extended to other things than stars.

CONSTABLE: Through the OF 'comestable,' the word comes from the Lat. **comes stabuli,** *count of the stable;* **comes,** *a companion,* having passed over to apply to a court dignitary. From being *a master of horse, an equerry,* he has come to be *a peace officer.* See COUNT (below) and STABLE (91).

CONTEMPLATE: **contemplare,** *look at attentively* (**con-**), made from **templum,** *a place marked off* for augury; later a TEMPLE. CONTEMPLATION is such serious attention as befits the **templum.**

CONTROL: evidently from the OF 'contre-role,' *a duplicate roll.* ROLL comes through the French from **rotula,** *a little wheel* (**rota**). It was thus applied to a parchment *rolled up* (cf. VOLUME from **volvere**), and to the *list* written on such a parchment. As the COUNTER-ROLL was used to check or verify payments, it served to regulate; hence the meanings of *restrain* and *exercise authority over* (the verb probably being earlier in English than the noun). Adopted from French, RÔLE was the *register of actors,* from which it easily means the *part* an actor plays.

CONVEY: Low Lat. **con-viare,** *go on the way* (**via**) *with* (**con-**), *escort,* gave Old French the two forms 'conveier' and 'convoier,' both of which came into English, CONVEY, CONVOY. Note that

SURVEY (AF 'surveier') was made from **super-videre**, *look over*. Cf. PURVEY, 42.

COPY: Lat. **copia**, *a gathering of resources* (**co** + **ops**), *plenty*, *plenty* by way of multiplying an original; hence Med. Lat. **copiare**, *transcribe*, and our use of COPY.

COROLLARY: From **corolla**, *a garland* (52), the neut. adj. **corollarium** meant *a present of a garland, an additional gift* or *gratuity*. The COROLLARY under a proposition is an additional inference allowed.

COUNT: Lat. **comitem** (**comes**), *a companion:* **com-**, *with*, and -it- from **ire**, **itum**, *go, one who goes with another*.

COUNTRY: The Middle English, following the Old French, spelled it 'contree,' from Ital. 'contrada,' Late Lat. **contrata**, *i.e.*, **terra contrata**, *the land over against*, or perhaps, *spread out in front* as one comes from the city, Lat. **contra**, *against*.

COWARD: Through the French (OF 'cou-ard') the word goes back to the Lat. **cauda**, *tail*. It may originally have compared one to the bob-tailed animal, the rabbit, or to any animal that drops its tail in fear or turns its tail in flight. The -*ard* is a Teutonic suffix, seemingly depreciatory.

CRUISE: Following the Dutch 'kruis' in spelling, CRUISE was originally Lat. **crux**, **crucis**, *a cross*, and so called from the zigzag or criss-cross movement of such sailing.

CUBIT: Lat. **cubitus**, *a bend* (**cubare**, *lie down;* cf. RE-CUMBENT), applied particularly to *the bend of the elbow*, on which one reclines; then *the elbow*, and as a measure, the length from the elbow to the end of the middle finger, about a foot and a half. The ell of 'el(l)-bow,' the distance from either the elbow or the shoulder to the wrist, varied considerably in different countries. The AS 'eln' was originally the forearm; hence a CUBIT.

CULPRIT: It is said that in the court proceedings of the old time 'Culpable, prest,' *Guilty, ready*, in the statement of the case against the accused, signified, "Guilty, we are ready to prove it." In reports this was abbreviated to OF 'cul. prest' or AF 'cul. prit,' Lat. **culpabilis**, *guilty*, **praestus**, *ready*.

CURTAIL: The first part of this word is the Lat. **curtus**, *short;* the second, unfortunately, has no connection with *tail*, although the now obsolete CURTAL meant having a docked tail. The suffix was '-al' or '-all,' going back ultimately to a German source, and from the meaning of the word easily changed to spell 't-ail.'

DAME: From the French came this shortened form of **domina**, *lady*, fem. of **dominus**, *lord, master* (of *the house*, **domus**)*; similarly Sp. 'don' and 'doña.' Cf. also DOMINO (50) and DOMINATE (128).

DANGER: Through the French ('danger,' OF 'dongier') from a Low Latin form, probably **dominiarium**, belonging to **dominio**, the rule of the **dominus**, *master*. The authority of a feudal master spelled danger for his underlings. Also suggestive of the hard master was another form of this same **dominio**, when **dominionem** became **domnion** and OF 'donjon,' which we now spell DUNGEON.

DAUB: We have thus taken over the Old French spelling of Lat. **dealbare** (179), *whiten over* (**albus**), *whitewash*.

DEAN: **Decanus**, from **decem**, *ten*, with suffix **-anus** (103), was *a leader of ten* soldiers. The Latin word was later used for the *chief of ten* monks, and from this DEAN was applied to an officer of a cathedral or of a college.

DECIDE: **Decidere** (**de-caedere**) was *to cut off; to cut* (*cut the knot of*) a question was to *settle* it; **decidere** thus came to mean DECIDE.

DECREPIT: Lat. **de-crepitus**, *very old*, from **crepare**, *rattle, creak*, has been explained as literally *noiseless;* the DECREPIT then go about noiselessly, being too feeble to clatter around as they once did. But this explanation is quite uncertain; perhaps like an old vehicle they are *rattling down*. From **crepare** also we have through Old French CREVASSE or CREVICE, the *chink* or *cleft* made with *a rattling noise;* and DISCREPANCY is *a difference* of sound, *a different rattle*.

DELIBERATE: *to weigh in the balance*, since **deliberare** was made from **libra**, *a pound* (lb. 60) or *a pair of scales* (cf. PONDER, Lat. **ponderare**, from **pondus, ponderis**, *weight*). Similarly **pensare** (frequentative of **pendere**) meant *to weigh*, but also *to ponder;* and from the Fr. 'pensée' ('penser,' *think*), we have PANSY. So, Hamlet, 4, 5, 176, "and there is pansies, that's for thoughts."

DENIZEN: *one from within;* the Lat. **de + intus**, *from within*, became OF 'deinz.' Then was added '-ein' representing **-anus** (103), and from 'deinzein' (as if **de-intus-anus**) it was no long step to our DENIZEN.

DERIVE: The Latin is **derivare**, *drain off water*, **de**, *away*, and **rivus**, *a stream*. The DERIVATION of a word is *drawing it down stream* from its source.

DEXTERITY: *right-handedness;* **dexteritas**, from **dexter**, *skilful*, *i.e., right* (handed). Cf. **sinister** (53).

DILAPIDATED: **Dilapidare**, *squander* or *destroy*, was made from **di-**, *apart*, and **lapis, lapidis**, *a stone;* DILAPIDATed is literally *with the stones torn apart.*

DISMAL: OF 'dismal' was Lat. **dies mali**, *the evil days*, referring to the unlucky days in the mediæval calendar. When the origin of the word was lost sight of, the word *days* was added, "dismal days," and the term then passed to other things than days.[1]

DOZEN: The Lat. **duodecim** seems to have been altered in Low Latin to **dodece**, becoming then 'dotze,' 'doze.' With the suffix **-ena** (like **centena**), it became OF 'dozeine' and Eng. DOZEN.

DRILLING: As the name of a coarse cloth this word is unusual in that it has come from Latin by way of Germany and not France. The German 'Drillich' was corrupted from the Lat. **trilix, trilicis**, *three-threaded*, **tri-**, *three*, **licium**, *a thread;* and the English word is a corruption of the German.

EJACULATE: **jaculum**, *a javelin* (something *to throw*, **jacere**)*;* **ejaculari**, *shoot out* (as with a missile).

ELIMINATE: *put outside the threshold, put out of doors.* Its original **eliminare, eliminatus** was made from **e**, *out*, and **limen, liminis**, *threshold.*

EMANCIPATE: From **manu capere**, *to take by hand*, was made Lat. **manceps**, *one who acquires* property; then **mancipare**, *deliver* or *transfer* as property. **E-mancipare** was *to deliver* one *from* the power of the **paterfamilias** (59), and, in general, *to surrender from one's own authority*, EMANCIPATE.

EMERGENCY: Made after the fashion of nouns in **-entia** (75) from the verb **e-mergere**, EMERGE; **mergere** was *to sink*, and **e-mergere** *to come out* on the surface, "*sink out.*" An EMERGENCY is what appears on the surface suddenly and unexpectedly.

ENGINE: The Old French form was 'engin' for the Lat. **ingenium** (**in** + **gen**, root of **gignere**, *beget*), *inborn quality, genius;* then the *product of genius, an invention.* The word was shortened

---

[1] Skeat rejects this derivation, but see note s.v. in NED.

further to GIN, *a trap*, and again, meaning *machine*, in cotton-GIN.

ERA: apparently for **aera**, the pl. of **aes, aeris**, *bronze, money*. This plural was used for the counters in reckoning or the items of a computation and later (as a fem. sing.) of a point from which to reckon time; so *a period of time*.

ESCAPE: But for the disguise which the OF 'escaper' threw upon the word, we might see at once in this the Lat. **ex cappa**, *out of the cloak;* to ESCAPE is to *ex-cape* oneself (Skeat). The fugitive gets out of his cape in his haste (cf. SCAMPER, 49).

EXCRUCIATING: the Lat. **excruciare**, **ex**, *utterly*, and **cruciare**, *torture on a cross*, from **crux, crucis**, *a cross* (**crux**, 52). Cf. CRUCIFY, 188, end.

EXPEDITE: **Expedire, expeditus**, was from **ex**, *out*, and **pes, pedis**, *foot, get one's foot out, free one's movement*, and so *hasten*. The opposite verb was **impedire**, IMPEDE, *get one's foot in, entangle the feet, hinder*. The noun is IMPEDIMENT and the Roman **impedimenta** (*baggage*) may often have been *foot-entangling*.

FAIRY: The older spelling FAERY (cf. 'trickery,' 'witchery') suggests the early meaning of enchantment, *i.e.*, the practice of a FAY. FAIRY was then incorrectly applied to the FAY itself. FAY, Fr. 'fée,' Low Lat. **fata**, was a *goddess of fate*, **fatum** being FATE, literally *the thing spoken* (**fari**).

FARCE: This French word from Lat. **farcire**, *stuff*, meant *stuffing*, as the jests in a comedy; the FARCE is mere *stuff*.

FEMALE: Not related to MALE (**masculum**, 173 *c*), **femella** was dimin. of **femina**, *a little woman, young maiden*. **Femella** became OF 'femelle,' Mid. Eng. 'femele,' and has been altered to FEMALE merely by a false connection of the second syllable with MALE.

FENCE: a modification of DEFENCE, the OF 'defens' (Lat. **defensum**) or 'defense' (Late Lat. **defensa**), **defendere**, *ward off*. FENCE became the *act of defending* oneself; so FENCE with swords; or the means of protecting oneself or one's property, a FENCE.

FINE: **finis**, *limit, end* (cf. FINITE, 124, INFINITE, 141), used in Low Lat. for *a final agreement, an arrangement to end* a suit, often *a sum of money paid to end* trouble. So came our noun FINE, and the corresponding verb. Low Latin had also an adj. **finus**, applied to what is *ended, finished*, therefore, *perfect* or *excellent*

(FINE cloth, FINE health); to what is *cut* or *ground to the limit* of small particles (FINE meal); or to what is *very small* (a FINE point, FINE thread).

FISCAL: Lat. **fiscalis**, *relating to the public treasury*, **fiscus.** But **fiscus** was originally *a basket* woven of twigs and used as *a purse*. So **confiscare, -atus**, CONFISCATE, *lay by in a money-chest*, *i.e.*, *seize for the public treasury*. Cf. BUDGET, OF 'bougette,' dimin. of 'bouge,' from Lat. **bulga**, *a little bag* (Celtic in origin). From this also comes BULGE — a thing which purse or budget may or may not do.

FOREIGN: The *g* has even less excuse in this word than in SOVEREIGN, 28. The Mid. Eng. 'foreine,' OF 'forain,' represent Low Lat. **foraneus**, an adjective from **foras**, *out of doors*. Cf. 'outlander.'

FRONTISPIECE: From **frons, frontis**, FRONT, and **specere (-spicere)**, *behold*, Low Latin made **frontispicium** (71), *a looking at the forehead, face-looking*, the *façade* of a building[1]; then the illustration facing the title-page of a book. The connection in spelling or meaning with *piece* is unwarranted.

gamut: A combination of 'gamma,' the third letter of the Greek alphabet, and the Latin conjunction **ut.** It is said that Guido d'Arezzo, an Italian monk of the eleventh century, the first to designate the notes of the musical scale by the letters A to G, began his "great scale" from gamma-**ut**, from G as 'do,' since **ut** was formerly used for what we now call 'do,' and the scale began from the G of the lowest line of the bass staff. So the whole series of notes was called the gam**ut**. The story tells us further that d'Arezzo gave the common names to all the notes from certain syllables in a hymn to St. John the Baptist:

> **UT** queant laxis **RE**sonare fibris
> **MI**ra gestorum **FA**muli tuorum
> **SOL**ve pollutis **LA**biis reatum,
> Sancte Iohannes.[2]

---

[1] Milton, *Paradise Lost*, 3, 505–6:

> The work as of a kingly palace gate
> With frontispiece of diamond and gold
> Imbellished.

[2] *In order that thy servants may be able to celebrate the wonders of thy deeds with strength unhampered, remove the guilt from their polluted lips, Saint John.*

(*S* and *I* of the last line make *Si*, but originally the six syllables of the other lines seem to have named the six notes of a hexachord.)

GAUDY: The noun GAUD, less common than the adjective, is the Lat. **gaudium,** JOY, (cf. **gaudere,** *rejoice*). Thus joy finds expression in GAUDiness, or else GAUDiness increases happiness. Cf. 'gay' as applied to a person and to the colors of his clothes.

GIN (the drink): Lat. **juniperus,** JUNIPER, came into Old French as 'genevre.' In English as the name of a drink flavored with juniper berries, 'genevre' was altered to 'geneva,' evidently with the idea that the drink came from that city; 'geneva' was then contracted into GIN. The explanation of **juniperus** from **juvenis (junior),** *young,* and **parere,** *produce, making itself ever young, evergreen,* or *producing young* berries as others ripen, is interesting but hardly established. Another suggestion is **juni-per-,** *Juno's* PEAR (**pirum**).

GIST: The OF 'gist' was 3rd pers. sing. of the verb from **jacēre** meaning *lies* or *consists in,* and in its present use said to be from an Old French proverb, "Ie scay bien ou gist le lievre," *I know well where the hare lies, i.e.,* where the real point of the matter lies. Thus did **jacet** wander from its origin.

GLAND: The Lat. **glans, glandis,** was properly *an acorn.* The shape or size of a GLAND suggested the name.

HAUGHTY: Old French for **altum,** *high,* was spelled 'halt'; then 'haut' (179). With the derivative suffix '-ain' (Lat. **-anus**) another adjective was made, which in Middle English became 'hautein.' It seems that the abstract noun 'hautein-ness' was then divided 'hauti-ness' and *-gh-* was inserted on analogy of words like 'naughtiness'; from HAUGHTI-ness again HAUGHTY was made to correspond to 'naughty.' For meaning, cf. 'uppish.'

HEARSE: From the Lat. **hirpex, hirpicis,** this word is much changed in spelling, and more changed in meaning, for **hirpex** meant *a harrow.* OF 'herce' and Mod. Fr. 'herse' also mean *harrow,* and we preserve that sense in RE-HEARSE, *to harrow a thing over.* The change of meaning of the noun is thus given by Skeat: (1) a harrow, (2) a triangular frame for lights in a church service, (3) a frame for lights at a funeral, (4) a funeral pageant, (5) a frame on which a body was laid, (6) a carriage for a dead body.

HOST: The two Latin words **hostis**, *enemy*, and **hospes**, *host, entertainer of guests*, are not so far apart as their meanings would indicate. **Hostis** was *a foreigner*, therefore *an enemy*, and as applied to the army of the enemy, it became HOST, as in "Though an host should encamp against me," (Psalm 27:3), and is often used for *a very large number*. **Hospes**, for **hosti-pets**, *i.e.*, **hosti-potis** (*able*), must have signified *lord of the strangers, master of the feast* (**hospitium**, 83). **Hospes**, **hos(pi)t-em**, also became Eng. HOST. And **hostis** is itself the same in origin as *guest* (226).

IMMOLATE: **Immolare**, **immolatus** (128), from **in-** upon, and **mola,** *meal*, was *to throw meal upon*, *i.e.*, *sprinkle meal upon* the victim as part of the sacrificial ceremony. Then **immolare** meant *sacrifice*, a meaning retained in IMMOLATE.

IMPROVE: Under the influence of PROVE, APPROVE, REPROVE, etc. (from Lat. **probare**) this coined word has changed from its earlier spelling, 'emprowe' or 'improw,' from OF 'emprower,' 'prow' here going back to the **pro(d)-** of **prodesse**, *be of advantage*, the same PROW- as in PROWESS (OF 'prowesse'). IMPROVE thus means first *to turn to advantage*, as in "IMPROVE the opportunity"; secondly, *to make better*.

INAUGURATE: The augurs at Rome had the duty of interpreting the cries and flight of birds as signs of the success or failure of an undertaking. The name itself is probably a combination of **avis**, *bird*, with **gerere**, **au-ger** becoming **augur**, *dealing with birds* (cf. AUSPICES; also **augur**, 52). **Inaugurare**, then, from *consult the birds*, came to mean *conduct the formal ceremonies connected with beginning an enterprise*, particularly with the installation of an official.

INCULCATE: from **inculcare**, **inculcatus**, *i.e.*, **in** + **calcare**, *trample in, stamp in with the heel* (**calx**); but our word in the sense of *teach, impress upon*, has lost this suggestion of violence.

INDOLENCE: **Indolentia** from **indolens** (75) was properly *not grieving*, **in** + **dolere**. One's lack of grief becomes lack of concern, of ambition, and of energy.

INEXORABLE: *that cannot be prayed out of a purpose;* the negative with **exorabilis** from **ex-orare** (116), *gain by prayer*, literally, *pray out*.

INFANT: literally *un-talking*, **infans, in-**, *not* + **fans, fantis**, pres. pple. of **fari**, *speak*. As meaning *not capable of speaking for one-self, not of age*, it appears in INFANTRY (Fr. 'infanterie,' Ital. 'infanteria'), since a boy was a servant or attendant, and attend-ants of the knights were *foot-soldiers*.

INGENUOUS: The Lat. **ingenuus** (122), from the root of **gignere**, *beget*, meant *in-born, native;* then *freeborn*. Designating qualities belonging to the freeborn, it came to mean *noble, honorable, sincere*.

INOCULATE: **Oculus**, *eye*, was also *a bud* of a plant (cf. 'eye' of a potato), and **inoculare, inoculatus** (128), was *to bud* or *graft*. The change is easy to the medical sense of inserting infectious matter into the body to prevent disease.

INSECT: **in-secare, -sectus;** *cut into;* **insectum (animal)**, an animal that is *cut into* so that parts of the body are nearly severed, translating Grk. 'entomon' (ἔντομον) which we have in 'entomology.'

INSULT: **Insultare** is a frequentative (130; p. 187 N.) from **insilire, in** + **salire**, *leap*, and so should mean *keep leaping on*.

ISLE: This is the Old French alteration of **insula(m)**, *island*. It is to be noted that the *s* of 'island' was inserted from ISLE, whereas the two words have properly no connection except in meaning; 'island' is a native word, AS 'igland.'

ITALICS: ITALIC is Lat. **Italicus** from **Italia**, ITALY (97); this style of printed letters was devised by an Italian, Aldo Manuzio, about 1500.

JAIL: Low Latin, French, and English have combined thus to disguise the Lat. **cavea**, *a hollow place*, a CAVE. Low Latin cor-rupted **caveam** to **gabia** and made a diminutive **gabiola**, Old French changed this to 'gaiole' (173*b*), becoming Eng. GAOL; afterwards altered in spelling to JAIL.

JEOPARDY: There is little in the present form or use of JEOPARDY to suggest a *divided joke*, yet **jocus partitus** was the Late Latin original of the word. Old French made **jocus partitus** into 'jeu parti,' for a game with even chances; this involves a hazard, danger. 'Jeu parti' was easily changed to Mid. Eng. 'jupartie,' and this quite as easily respelled as JEOPARDY.

JEST: The Middle English spelling was the same with the OF

'geste,' meaning *a story, i.e., an account of exploits*, which could easily become laughable. The Latin was **gesta** (neut. pl.) or **res gesta**, pf. pple. of **gerere**, *do*.

JOVIAL: under the influence of **Jupiter**, *i.e.*, **Jou-pater**, *Father* JOVE; in astrology Jupiter was the happiest star of one's birth; its influence was said to give a cheerful disposition. Cf. MERCURIAL and SATURNINE.

KENNEL: The Mid. Eng. 'kenel' and the OF 'chenil' (167) indicate that an effort was made to construct an adjective from **can-is** with -ilis (100), *relating to a dog*.

LAUNDRY: properly LAUNDERY (-ERY, 75 N. 1), from LAUNDER, formerly *one who washes* (cf. LAUNDRESS). LAUNDER comes to us through the Low Latin and Old French from **lavandus**, gerundive of **lavare**, *wash* (cf. LAVE); see also LAVENDER, 48. The same root appears in ABLUTION; also in DELUGE from **diluvium**, and in ALLUVIUM, ALLUVIAL.

LEGEND: **Legere**, *gather*, when one gathered words from a page with the eye, meant *read*, gerundive **legendus**; **legenda**, *things to be read*, applying particularly to certain accounts of the saints which were to be read in the early church. These often included stories of miraculous events, and LEGEND was associated with the marvelous, the romantic, and the unhistorical.

LEVEE, LEVY: LEVEE is a respelling of the Fr. 'lever,' Lat. **levare**, *raise* (lit. *make light*, **levis**); from *a rising* in the morning it came to denote *a morning reception*. The pf. pple. fem. of the same French verb was 'levée,' which, as a noun denoting *something raised*, was applied to an *embankment raised* along a river (LEVEE), or to the *raising* of military troops (LEVY).

LEVEL: An older spelling was 'livel' like the Old French, Lat. **libella**, a diminutive of **libra**, *a balance* or *level* (69). **Libra** was also the word for *pound* (see **lb.** and £, 60).

LIBEL: **Libellus** was *a little book*, diminutive of **liber** (69); then *public announcement, a defamatory publication*, a LIBEL. See **liber**, 71.

LIVERY: The Fr. 'livrée,' of which LIVERY is the English spelling, is a participle of 'livrer,' DELIVER, going back through the Low Latin to **liberare**, *set free*. LIVERY, *the thing delivered*, was applied particularly to the special uniform delivered by a feudal lord to his attendants, and again to a stable where an allowance of feed was delivered for horses kept for hire.

MAINTAIN: Mid. Eng. 'maintenen,' Fr. 'maintenir' (so MAINTE-NANCE); made from Lat. **manu tenere**, *hold with the hand;* therefore *defend* or *support.*

MANIPULATE: This word has been coined according to 128 from Lat. **manipulus**, a MANIPLE, *a band of soldiers,* one of the three divisions of a cohort, in Caesar's time 100 to 120 men. The verb therefore signified *to direct movements* as of a band of soldiers. **Manipulus** from **manus**, *hand,* and the same root which appears in **plere**, *fill,* and **plenus**, *full,* was *a handful, a bundle of hay.* In ancient times the Romans are said to have used for a standard a pole with a bundle of hay fastened upon it; the men following this standard constituted the **manipulus**. If we do not accept this explanation, then the small division was but a *handful* of soldiers.

MAP: The Lat. **mappa** was *a napkin, a painted* or *colored cloth,* also a MAP. **Napa** was a Low Latin corruption of **mappa**, and this with our diminutive '-kin' made NAPkin.

MASS: AS 'maesse,' an alteration of **missa**, pf. pple. fem. of **mittere,** *let go;* it may have originated in the formula used for closing the church service, "**Ite, missa est**," *Go, it (the congregation) is dismissed.* **Missum** also became OF 'mes,' AS 'mes,' Eng. MESS, for *what is sent* or *placed* upon the dining table at one time.

MATRICULATE: **Matricula**, from which Late Latin made **matriculare, matriculatus**, was a diminutive of **matrix**, *a parent stock;* then *a public register.* The verb meant *to enroll on the public register,* and thus now *to admit* (or *be admitted*) *to college.*

MAXIM: Fr. 'maxime,' Lat. **maxima**, *i.e.,* **maxima sententia,** *greatest sentence* or *proposition.*

MEDIOCRE: MEDI- is **medius**, *middle;* -OCRE may be the Old Lat. **ocris** (cf. Grk. 'okris,' ὄκρις), *a rugged mountain* (another form of **acer**, *sharp,* 157). MEDIOCRE then means *half way up the mountain.*

MERCURIAL: an astrological term describing one born under the influence of the planet MERCURY (**Mercurius**), therefore *sprightly* and *fickle* like this Roman god. With the same idea we have MERCURY as the name of a chemical element. Cf. JOVIAL.

MINUTE: From **minutus**, *small*, the pf. pple. of **minuere**, *make small* (cf. **minor, minimus**), the fem. **minuta** in Low Latin was *a small part*. As *a small part* of an hour, or *a small part* of a degree of a circle, it became MIN'UTE, while our adjective from **minutus** is accented MINUTE'. The next further division of the hour or the circle, *i.e.*, the *second* small part, we call simply the SECOND, **secundus**, verbal adj. from **sequor**, *follow*.

MIRROR: Lat. **mirari**, *wonder at*, became Low Lat. **mirare** with the meaning *behold*. From this, or some derivative of it (probably 'miratorium,' OF 'miradoir,' 'mirour'), came MIRROR. The Low Latin meaning saves MIRROR from any suggestion of wonder and admiration which the Classical **mirari** might have left. MIRACLE is a related word (32).

MISCHIEF: MIS-, OF 'mes-,' Lat. **minus**, *less*, negative or depreciatory; CHIEF represents Lat. **caput** (44, 178); MISCHIEF is *the bad head* to which things come.

MISCREANT: MIS- (OF 'mes-') as above, Lat. **minus**, *less* or *not*, 'creant' the French pple. for Lat. **credent(em)**, *believing*, a MISCREANT being originally *an unbeliever* (cf. Ital. 'miscredente,' *heathen*). Similarly RECREANT is *one who believes again*, therefore changes his belief, especially one who gives up what he has contended for.

MOB: This is a reduction of the phrase **mobile vulgus**, *the changeable crowd*.

MOULT: Since the *l* does not belong in this word, we have in 'mout,' as it actually occurred in Middle English, the root of the Lat. **mut-are**, *change*. The *l* was introduced in the sixteenth century on analogy of words like FAULT (OF and Mid. Eng. 'faute'), which properly had the *l* (179).

MUSCLE: from **musculus**, a diminutive of **mus**, *a little mouse;* but even the Romans applied the same word to the mouselike fleshy parts of the body, also to a species of shellfish. In the latter meaning we commonly use the variant form MUSSEL.

NAVE: The OF. 'nave' from Lat. **navis**, *ship;* Low Lat. **nave(m)** was used for the *middle division* or *body of a church*, likening it to a ship.

NICE: Etymology may be dangerous to a word's reputation; NICE, which now means so much and so little, originally meant *ignorant*, being the Old French form of Lat. **nescius**, *not knowing* (cf. **ne-scire**). On its way from the Romans to us it became Old French for *lazy* as well as *dull*, and in Middle English *simple;* later *fastidious, delicate, exact.*

NOON: Lat. **nona**, *i.e.*, **nona hora**, *the ninth hour*, which, with the division of the day into twelve hours from sunrise to sunset, was about 3 P.M. When the church service held at that hour and called NONES was changed to midday, the meaning of **nona**, NOON, changed accordingly.

OFFICE: through the French from **officium**, a contraction of '**opifi-cium**,' *i.e.*, **ops, opis** + **facere** (**-ficere**), *help-making, service-rendering.*

OPPORTUNE: The adjective **opportunus**, made from **ob** and **portus**, *at* or *before the harbor*, suggests the timely arrival of one's ship.

OUTRAGE: not connected with 'out' or 'rage.' 'Outre' (for 'oltre') was the Old French rendering of **ultra**, *beyond;* -AGE the common suffix representing Lat. **-aticum** (177). The word therefore denotes *extremity* (*"beyond-ness"*) of wrong.

OVATION: When the Roman general returned to the city after an easy or unimportant victory, he was honored with an **ovatio**, properly *a shouting*, **ovare**, *shout, exult* (85); when he had gained a great and very significant victory, he was accorded a **triumphus**, TRIUMPH.

PALACE: One of the seven hills of Rome was the PALATINE, **Pala-tium** or **collis Palatinus**, possibly originally *a palisaded place* (**palus**, *a stake, palisade*). On this hill Augustus built his residence, as did also Tiberius and Nero. **Palatium** therefore from the Augustan period meant a *royal residence*, a PALACE (176).

PARBOIL: A French-English modification of **per-bullire**, BOIL *thoroughly*, **bulla**, *bubble*. By an early mistake the first syllable was connected with PART, and the word has thus come to mean *boil in part.*

PAVILION: The Lat. **papilionem** (nom. **papilio**) which French made into 'pavillon,' and English took over as PAVILION, meant originally *a butterfly*. On the same root as in **palpitare**, *vibrate*, PALPITATE (**pal-pi-**, reduplication, frequentative, or intensive); the butterfly is a "vibrator," and the spread out and flapping

sides of a tent suggested the butterfly wings, so that we know
PAVILION only as a tent.

PECULIAR, PECUNIARY: From **pecus**, *cattle*, was made **pecunia**,
wealth, since the wealth of the ancients consisted in cattle. But
with the change from reckoning values in terms of cattle to the
use of a simpler medium of exchange, **pecunia** became *money*.
From the same source, with different suffixes, **peculium** was the
property or *money* given by a father to a son, or by a master to
a slave, *to be his own*. With the suffix -arius (101) the one word
became PECUNIARY, the other with -aris (99), PECULIAR. Since
what is *one's own* and *personal* is *queer* to others, PECULIAR
becomes *strange*.

PEN: *a feather*, Lat. **penna** (OF 'penne'; cf. *feather* 223). The
name survived when the quill had passed.

PERFUME: The verb occurs in French as 'parfumer,' from Lat.
per + **fumare**, *smoke* (**fumus**, *smoke*, FUME), *smoke through and
through, fill with fumes*. (The noun is later.)

PESTER: a shortened form of 'impester,' OF 'empestrer,' *entangle*,
in + **pastorium**, which in Low Latin was *a fetter* with which
horses were staked out for *pasture*, (a word connected with
pascere, *feed*, and **pastor**, *a shepherd, a feeder*). To PESTER is
literally to *hobble*.

PILGRIM: earlier spelled 'pilegrim' and 'pelegrim,' coming through
the French with a shift from *r* to *l* in the first part (155) and of
n to *m* at the end, for the Latin word was **peregrinus**, *coming
from a foreign land;* the adjective being made from **pereger**, *one
going abroad, i.e.,* **per** + **ager**, one who travels *through the fields*.

PLOVER: The Latin adjective **pluvialis** from **pluvia**, *rain* (98),
came through Low Latin into Old French as 'plovier'; thence
into English as PLOVER, *rain bird*, since it was said to be found
most in the rainy season. (Cf. **Jupiter pluvius**, 59.)

POMEGRANATE: The Lat. **pomum granatum** (OF 'pome granate')
was *an apple full of seeds;* **granatum** in participial form (107)
from **granum**, *grain, seed*, was also used without **pomum** to mean
POMEGRANATE (see GRANADA, 215); the form GRENADE designates *a shell* filled with shot as a pomegranate with seeds.

PONTIFF: Lat. **ponti-fex**; **pons**, **pontis**, *bridge*, originally *path*,
facere, *make. A bridge-builder?* If so, he kept bridges in order

for the passage of religious processions.[1] *A path-maker?* If so, he either led the procession along a literal path, or had charge of the path between this world and the next.

PORCELAIN: Through the French this came from Ital. 'porcellana' and was applied to this kind of earthenware on account of its polished surface, which resembled the shell of the purple fish, called by this name. But the Ital. 'porcello' or 'porcella' is a diminutive of 'porco,' *a hog* (Lat. **porcum**), for the shape of the shell suggested *a little pig*, and thus connects for us PORK and PORCELAIN.

PORCUPINE: The name means *thorny pig*, Lat. **porcus**, *pig*, and **spina**, *a spine* or *thorn*. The Old French through which the English comes was 'porc-espin' (Sp. 'puerco espin' and Ital. 'porco spinoso').

PORPOISE: If there is anything in a name the porpoise is *a pig-fish.* The word comes to us from the OF 'porpeis,' for 'porc-peis,' representing Lat. **porcum-piscem**. For Italian and Spanish it is *a sea-pig*, 'porco marino,' 'puerco marino.' Somewhat like PORPOISE in its formation is GRAMPUS for **grandem-piscem**, *large fish*.

POST: From the feminine participle of **ponere**, *place*, **posita**, Late Lat. **posta**, came Fr. 'poste,' *a station*, which English borrowed as POST applied to the series of mounted men stationed at intervals for the rapid carrying of messages; hence POST OFFICE, POSTAL, etc.; to be distinguished from POST, *a pillar*, Lat. **postis**.

POSTHUMOUS: A mistake of spelling was made, this time by the Romans themselves. **Postumus** was a superlative of **post** (as **posterior** a double comparative, 53), applied to a child *late* born, particularly one born after the father's death. In this way the word was mistaken for a combination of **post** and **humus**, with the meaning *after* the father is laid *in the ground*. So we apply POSTHUMOUS to a work published after the author's death.

PREAMBLE: French gives us this noun from the Latin adjective

---

[1] Varro, *De Lingua Latina*, 5, 15: **A ponte arbitror, nam ab iis Sublicius est factus primum et restitutus saepe,** (They are so called) *I think, from pons, for by them the Pile Bridge was made at first and has been often repaired.*

prae-ambulus, *walking before,* **prae,** *before,* and **ambulare,** *walk* (cf. AMBLE, PERAMBULATE).

PRECIPICE: the Old French spelling of Lat. **praecipitium; praeceps (cap-ut), praecipitis,** *head foremost.* PRECIPICE is therefore *a place to go down headlong.* From **praecipitare, -atus,** we have the adjective PRECIPITATE, *headlong,* the verb PRECIPITATE, *hurl down headlong,* and in chemistry the noun PRECIPITATE for a substance *thrown down* from solution. Cf. SEDIMENT, 90.

PRECOCIOUS: from **prae-cox, prae-coquus,** or **prae-coquis,** *ripened too soon* (**coquere,** COOK or *ripen*). We may compare **prae-maturus,** *ripe beforehand,* PREMATURE, not to mention the Eng. "half-baked." The word **praecoquus** once made a journey around the Mediterranean and never looked the same again. As a name for an early-ripe fruit it was received into Greece as 'praikokia' (πραικόκια, pl.), it was taken by the Arabs as 'alburquq,' returned from Arabia to Spain as 'albaricoque,' appeared in France as 'abricot,' and crossed over to England to become APRICOT, helped, perhaps, in its transformation by **apricus,** *sunny, growing in the sun.*

PREDICAMENT: The Late Lat. **praedicamentum** (90) was made from **praedicare,** *declare in public, publish, declare,* PREDICATE; thus **predicamentum** meant *what is declared* or *predicated* and was used in Latin as a philosophic term to translate Aristotle's 'category' (κατηγορία, *assertion*). It thus came to mean *state* or *condition;* then particularly *an unpleasant situation.*

PREPOSTEROUS: **prae-posterus** (95), *before-after, before-behind, wrong end first.*

PRESTIGE: The Lat. **praestigium** has been explained from **prae-stinguere** in the sense of **exstinguere** (root stig), *put out with a point* or *goad,* but it comes rather from **praestringere,** *bind fast* (**oculos**), *blindfold, blind; i.e.,* **praestigium,** by dissimilation for 'praestrigium,' 155. In either case **praestigium,** *an illusion, a magician's trick,* refers to the blindness of the spectator, from which the Eng. PRESTIGE has been transferred to the blinding influence of one's position, pedigree, or past achievements.

PREVARICATE: The Lat. **praevaricari, praevaricatus,** meant *walk crookedly,* or *straddle.* Thus this polite form of lying is not altogether different from EQUIVOCATE, Lat. **aequivocus (aequus,** *equal, like,* **voc-,** *call), of like signification,* hence *ambiguous;* Low Lat. **aequi-vocare, -atus,** *speak ambiguously.*

PREVENT: **prae-venire, -ventum** (133), *come before;* literally (of time) in the older English, as "I prevented the dawning of the morning" (Psalm 119:147); but *what comes before* one may interfere with, *i.e.,* PREVENT his progress, this being a later meaning in Latin.

PROFANE: **Profanus, pro,** *before,* **fanum,** *a temple,* indicated what was *before,* or *outside the temple;* so the *secular* as opposed to the sacred; then also the *wicked.*

PUNCH: PUNCH, *to make a hole with an awl,* is an abbreviation of the noun PUNCHEON (OF 'poinson'), the Lat. **punctionem (punctio),** *a piercing,* PUNCTURE; then the shorter form was used as a noun. We have COMPUNCTION for the *prick of conscience,* the verb EXPUNGE, *strike* or *pierce out,* and from **punctum,** POINT, our coined word PUNCTUATE, *put the points in.* The root is **pug (pungere, pepugi),** the same as in **pugnus,** *fist,* **pugnare,** *fight;* but we must not apply this too far, for PUNCHing an opponent's head may be another matter, the same as PUNISH, from **punire.**

PUPIL: **Pupa** is *a girl* or *a doll.* Its diminutive **pupilla,** *little girl,* or *orphan girl,* meant also the *center of the eye* perhaps from the doll-like pictures contained therein. The masculine, **pupillus,** *little boy, orphan boy,* became *a schoolboy.* To add to the mixture of meanings, **pupa,** scientifically, is now *a chrysalis, the young girl* (or *boy?*) of an insect family, and through the French ('poupée'), **pupa** has become PUPPY (shortened also to PUP) as the little dog that takes the place of a doll, *i.e.,* a little pet dog. A diminutive of **pupa** is PUPPET, *a little doll* (worked by strings).

QUAINT: Other spellings of the old time were 'queint,' 'quoynt,' 'cwoint,' representing the OF 'coint,' made from Lat. **cognitum,** *known* (**cognoscere**). The change of English meanings seems to have been: *known, famous, remarkable, strange, odd.* The original meaning is kept in the compound AC-QUAINT (**ad + cognitum**).

QUARANTINE: This French word was made through the Low Latin from **quadraginta,** and designated *a period of forty days,* whether of the Lenten season, or of indulgence, or of holding a trader who came from an infected port.

QUARRY: **Quadrare** was *to square*, **quadratus**, *squared*, **quadratarius**, *a squarer, i.e., a stonecutter*. The Low Lat. **quadraria** was a *place for squaring stones*. This is the word which the Old French took over ('quarriere') and passed on to English to become 'quarrere' and later QUARRY.

QUIET, QUITE, QUIT: QUIET from **quietus**, *at rest*, the pf. pple. of **quiescere**, denominative from **quies, quietis** (see also COY, 42); QUIT introduced from French into English first as an adjective meant *at rest* (*from*), or *freed* (*from*), a meaning which survives in QUITCLAIM (**clamare**). The Old French form we have kept in the adverb QUITE, and the Old French verb, 'quiter' (later 'quitter') has given us QUIT. Thus to QUIT is *to be at rest from;* earlier it meant also *behave* or *conduct oneself*, as in the Biblical phrase, "Quit you like men." But our transitive verb QUIET is the Lat. **quietare**. Once more the same word appears in ACQUIT, made through Old French from **ad + quietare**, *set at rest, set free*.

QUINTESSENCE: From the sixth century B.C. or earlier the Greek philosophers were seeking an explanation of the universe, making various conjectures as to its original elements. The four elements thus assigned separately or in combination were earth, air, fire, and water. A fifth added to these (the ether) was called in Latin **quinta essentia**, *the fifth* ESSENCE (**essentia** as if from a pres. pple. **essent-** of **esse**, *be*). The QUINTESSENCE thus became the *final* and *pure essence*.

QUOTIENT: Lat. **quotiens** is an adverb meaning *how many times*. The final *t* in English is due to confusion with stems in -*nt:* if **patiens** gives PATIENT, why not **quotiens** QUOTIENT?

REAR: Lat. **retro-**, OF 'riere,' also Fr. 'arrière' for **ad retro**, *backward*, Eng. ARREARS.

RECALCITRANT: **Re-calcitrare** is *kick back* (**calcitrare**, *use the heel*, **calx, calcis**). The present participle became Eng. RECALCITRANT (123). We use in like manner *kick* and *kicker*.

REPINE: PINE here, also PAIN, are forms from Lat. **poena**, *punishment, suffering* (Grk. 'poinē,' *ποινή, requital, penalty*); apparently, to REPINE is *to suffer pain as one looks back* (**re-**).

REPREHEND: **Prehendere**, *seize*, compounded with **re-** was *to hold back*. To restrain the wrong-doer; then to reprove the wrong is to REPREHEND, and the wrong-doing itself is REPREHENSIBLE, *i.e.*, ought to be *seized and held back*.

RETALIATE: **Talio** in Roman law was a punishment of like for like, an eye for an eye, but probably not connected with **talis,** *such*. To give back like punishment was **retaliare, retaliatus,** RETALIATE.

RETORT: *a twisting back*, from **retorquere, retortus;** it may be *a reply twisted back* at an opponent; it may be *a twisted tube* in the laboratory.

REVEL: This Old French form is evidently the same as REBEL from the Lat. **rebellare,** *make war again* (**bellum,** 128). A REVEL (we have also the derivative REVELRY) involves the same confusion as REBELLION (84).

ROMANCE: The composite language of Gaul or France in the eighth to tenth centuries has been mentioned above as **lingua Romanica** (18). The adverb **romanice,** used in the phrase **romanice loqui,** became OF 'romans,' Eng. ROMANCE, Romance languages being descended from Latin. Then the term was applied to a fictitious story written in a Romance dialect and later to a story of adventure or love in any language.

ROSEMARY: a deceptive word since it has no connection with either a 'rose' or 'Mary.' The Lat. **rosmarinus, ros marinus** meant *sea dew* and the evergreen shrub was so called from some fancied connection with sea spray.

RUBRIC: **Ruber** meant *red* (cf. 'ruby'). We find the derived adjective only in the feminine **rubrica,** used for **terra rubrica,** *red earth*, particularly for coloring. So RUBRIC was a name for the part of a manuscript or printed page which was colored *red*, as, often in old works, the title-page and the headings.

RUMINATE: **Ruminari** (or -are), **ruminatus,** meant *chew the cud;* a RUMINANT is a cud-chewing animal. Figuratively, it meant *to ponder again, to work over in the mind* what has been thought of before.

SATIRE: The kind of literary composition which the Romans called **satira** or **satura,** is said to have been named from **lanx satura,** *a full dish*, a general mixture of fruits on a plate, or of ingredients in the food; hence *a medley* (**satur,** *full,* cf. **satis,** *enough*). Then without **lanx, satura** was *a medley* of composition, dealing often with the follies of society or the foibles of men.

SATURNINE: It was supposed in the study of astrology that the influence of the planet Saturn tended to a gloomy temperament. This adjective form has been made as if from 'Saturninus,' but the Latin adjective was **Saturnius**. Cf. JOVIAL, MERCURIAL.

SCOUR: The French have helped us to make SCOUR out of **excurare**, *give special care to*. The Latin verb, however, occurs only in the pple. **excuratus**.

SCOURGE: a French alteration of Late Lat. **excoriata** ('escourgée'), **corium**, *hide*, not that the whip takes the hide off as EXCORIATE would suggest (128), but the SCOURGE was a *strip of hide taken off*, **ex-coriata**.

SCRUPLE: **Scrupus** was *a sharp stone*, **scrupulus** *a little sharp stone*, such as gets into one's shoe and causes annoyance; hence *a source of anxiety, the annoyance of conscience*. But the tiny stone was used as a weight in medicine and we know it also as the twenty-fourth part of an ounce. Cf. **calculus**, 52.

SEARCH: This is our spelling of OF 'cerchier' from Low Lat. **circare**, a verb made from **circus**, *a circle*. To SEARCH is *to go round and round*.

SECRETARY: The original **secretarius** was one who could keep SECRETS. From **secernere**, *separate*, **secretum** was *a thing kept apart* from other people, a SECRET; **secretarium** was *a solitary place;* and from Low Latin through the French we have taken our word. Having lost sight of the original meaning we try to express the same thing once more by saying "private secretary."

SECURE: **Se-** or **sed-** was an old prepositional form meaning *without* (145; perhaps the same as the conjunction **sed**). With **cura** it makes **securus**, *i.e.*, **sine cura**, *without care*, and freedom from care implies freedom from danger.

SERGEANT: Our spelling of this word points at once to the Old French ('sergant,' 'serjant'), representing the pres. pple. **servientem** of **servire**, SERVE. When the verb had come into later French its participle was 'servant' (190), which the English likewise adopted. SERGEANT and SERVANT are therefore doublets.

SHAMBLES: This word came into Anglo-Saxon from Lat. **scamellum**, *a little bench* or *stool* (**scamnum**, *a step* or *bench*). That such a bench should be used for meat put on sale was rather an accident in the history of the word. From the *butcher's bench* it became a *slaughter-house.* (Cf. 'bank,' originally *a bench;* then the *money-changers' bench,* bankRUPT above.)

SINCERE: One explanation of **sincerus** is that **-cer-** is the same as **car-** of **caries,** *decay,* while **sin-** is **sine,** *without.* Another gives us **sin-** in **singuli,** *one by one,* **simplex,** *onefold;* and the **-cer-** (**cre-**) of **procerus,** *tall,* **crescere,** *grow.* Whether "*without decay*" or "*of singleness in growth,*" *i.e.,* "purity of nature," SINCERITY to the Roman meant *honesty* and *integrity* (cf. **integer,** *whole,* 53). The derivation sometimes given from **sine cera,** *without wax,* without bee's wax and therefore like pure honey, or without repairs made with wax on sculptured figures, is more interesting than trustworthy.

SOLDIER: It is no accident that SOLDER and SOLDIER are so much alike in appearance. From the Lat. **solidus,** SOLID, the verb **solidare** meant *make solid,* and from this (through the Old French) came SOLDER, *that which makes solid.* Now **solidus** (sc. **nummus,** *coin*) was a gold piece coined in the time of the Empire. And for a member of the army serving for money, the term **soldarius** was used in Low Latin; of this the Old French made SOLDIER and furnished it to us. SOLDER makes solid, and the SOLDIER serves for solid money. The Fr. 'sou' is a form of **solidus,** and we preserve the Latin word in the abbreviation **s.** in English money (60).

SOLEMN: Another and probably older form of **solemnis** (**sollemnis**) was **sollennis.** This seems to have been made from **sollus,** *whole,* + **annus,** *a year;* so *annual.* The adjective applied to what came every year, as a religious festival; hence *religious* and SOLEMN.

SPECULATE: From **specere,** *look at,* the Romans made **speculum,** *something to look into, a mirror,* and **specula,** *something to look from, a watchtower* (cf. 121). From **specula** the verb **speculor** meant *watch, observe;* hence SPECULATE (128), since our conclusions reached in a SPECULATIVE matter, or the chances taken by the financial **speculator,** depend on observations (cf. **speculator,** 52).

SPORT: The OF 'se desporter' was *to carry oneself apart* (Lat. **dis-portare**) from labor; so *to amuse oneself* (cf. AVOCATION, 144). As a noun DISPORT was shortened into SPORT, the amusement or the one who engages in it, and as an adjective SPORT applies to whatever pertains to him — clothes, make of cars, etc. Similarly SPITE has been made from DESPITE, OF 'despit,' Lat. **despectum,** *a looking down on others, contempt.* Cf. RESPITE, 42.

STATIONER: STATION is properly *a standing-place* (**stare,** *stand,* 85). A STATIONER was formerly the holder of such a stand for business, particularly for the sale of books. He sold also writing materials; hence the word STATIONERY, although there is nothing in the original word to indicate the character of business or wares.

STRAY: The Old French verb 'estraier,' which is responsible for our word (cf. ESTRAY), was made from Lat. **strata,** STREET (6); to STRAY is *to wander on the streets.* With the English prefix 'a(n),' *on,* we have ASTRAY.

SUFFRAGE: **suffragium,** *a vote,* perhaps originally *a roar of applause* at the choice of a candidate, **sub** with **frag-** as in **fragor,** *uproar* (**frangere,** *break;* cf. Eng. *"break loose"* used of noise).

SUPERCILIOUS: The Lat. **cilium** was *an eyelid,* **supercilium** *the eyebrow.* The lifting of the eyebrows was an ancient as well as a modern expression of haughtiness. Thus **superciliosus** meant *haughty,* SUPERCILIOUS (94).

SUPPLANT: **Supplantare** was to *put something under* (**sub-**) *the sole of the foot* (**planta**), and thus *trip one up.*

SURROUND: The Low Lat. **super-undare** (**unda,** *wave*), *to overflow,* seems to be the original of our word SURROUND (OF 'sor-onder'), the English form and meaning being due to a confusion with the word ROUND (Lat. **rotundus**).

TAILOR: That a TAILOR should be a *cutter* is perfectly proper. The agent noun (Fr. 'tailleur') was made from the verb (Fr. 'tailler') going back to Lat. **talea,** *a stick, a cutting* from a plant or bush. From the same source DETAIL refers to the cut-up parts, *i.e., minute account* of a matter; and RETAIL to the *small quantities* handled in sale. TALLY is of the same origin, *i.e., a cutting* of notches in a stick for a record; then the *record* kept by other means.

TANTAMOUNT: a combination of two words, Fr. 'tant,' Lat. **tantum,** *so much,* and Eng. 'amount,' *amounting to so much.* AMOUNT (OF 'amonter') represents **ad montem,** *to the mountain;* what approximates the mountain, piles up. Cf. PARAMOUNT ('par,'

Lat. **per**), of what comes *through to the mountain,* so reaches the height and is chief in importance.

TERRIER: From the Lat. **terra,** *earth,* the Low Latin made a noun **terrarium** (71), *a little hill of earth, a burrow.* Through the Old French this word came into English as TERRIER (-dog), *a burrow dog,* pursuing other animals into their burrows.

TEST: originally from Lat. **testa,** *a brick, a piece of earthenware,* seemingly connected with **terra** (**'tersa'**). Low Lat. **testa** was *a vessel,* and through Old French it came into English to designate a vessel used by the alchemists for trying their gold; hence *the refining process* of trial or examination.

TOILS: Like the second part of SUBTLE (149), TOIL, *a net,* comes from **tela,** for **'texla,'** from **texere,** *weave,* the French having modified **tela** to 'toile.' It was thus a woven snare for catching animals. As a diminutive of this the Fr. 'toilette,' Eng. TOILET, was *a little woven piece;* then *a cloth* for a dressing table; then the *table,* and the *act* or *mode of dressing.*

TRANCE: Fr. 'transe,' which in Old French meant *fright* or *swoon;* 'transir,' *shiver, be chilled, die;* literally, *pass over,* Lat. **transire;** cf. Eng. 'pass out,' also TRANSIT, 88.

TRANSOM: According to Skeat this is a corruption of **transtrum,** *cross beam,* that which *goes across* (**trans**) from wall to wall; cf. **-trum,** 93.

TRIVIAL: From the prefix, **tri-,** *three,* and **via,** *road,* the Romans used **trivia** for the *meeting place of three roads.* The corresponding adjective was **trivialis** (98), and what was found at the cross-roads was *commonplace;* therefore TRIVIAL.[1]

TUBEROSE: neither 'tube' nor 'rose,' but merely an adaptation of the Lat. **tuberosus,** an adjective (94) from **tuber,** *a swelling* or *protuberance.* PRIMROSE is also a misnomer, if those are right who regard it as a corruption of OF 'primerole,' Med. Lat. **primula** (68), *first little (flower).*

[1] Since it does not take three roads to make crossroads, it has been suggested that the use of **trivia** was due to the three-faced images of the goddess Diana (called also **Trivia**), set up at the crossing of two roads and representing her threefold nature, Luna in the heavens, Diana on the earth, Hecate in the lower world; in other words, that the cross-roads may have been named from the goddess, not the goddess from the crossroads. This, however, does not affect the meaning of TRIVIAL.

UMPIRE: Earlier the word was NUMPIRE but "a numpire" in pronunciation was like "an umpire" and the *n* was transferred to the article (like "an adder" for "a nadder," "an apron" for "a napron"). But the Middle English spelling was still different, 'nompere' (OF 'nomper'), for Lat. **non-par**, *not equal* (with the contestants); therefore *not on either side* of the contest and naturally *an unbiased judge.*

USHER: An USHER ought to be *a doorkeeper.* **Ostium** was *a door* (**os**, *a mouth*), and the adjective applying to one having to do with the door was **ostiarius** (101). **Ostiarium** became OF 'ussier' and Mid. Eng. 'uschere.' The USHER has now found other duties than keeping the door, as also has the **janitor** (52).

VEGETABLE: **Vegetare** meant *enliven, invigorate,* and the adjective in **-bilis** (116) was *enlivening,* but the French, through which our word has come, shows a meaning, *full of life, capable of growth.* **Vegetare** itself came from **vegetus**, *vigorous,* and this in turn from **vegere**, *excite.*

VERNACULAR: **Verna** was *a slave born in the house;* the word seems to have referred originally to the house rather than to the slave, and the adjective **vernaculus** meant *belonging to the household, domestic,* and so *native;* suffix **-ar-is**, 99.

VERSE: *a turning,* Lat. **versus**, from **vertere**, *turn* (88), *a turning back* to the next line.[1] A compound of the pple. **versus, proversus** (**provorsus**), *turned forward,* was shortened into **prorsus** or **prosus**, from which **prosa**, *i.e.*, **prosa oratio**, *straightforward* (unpoetic or unmetrical) *speech,* has given us PROSE.

VIE: from **invitare**, INVITE, a Middle English form being 'envien' (OF 'envier'). In gambling to INVITE was to *begin the game with a wager,* and to VIE with is to *contend* with as in a game.

---

[1] Some derive **versus**, *a furrow,* from **verrere**, *scrape, sweep.* A confusion of the two words would be easy.

CHAPTER VI

COINED WORDS AND HYBRIDS

I. Coined Words

203. In many instances an English word is of Latin origin, yet has not been derived from any corresponding Latin word. English and French people have used Latin material — prefix, base, suffix, parts of a compound — and made such words for their needs, perfectly good and serviceable members of our later language, but boasting no Roman pedigree. Their assumed originals are often as Latin as if they were found in the Latin dictionary, but the Romans lacked the occasion or the disposition to use them. Our freedom in such coinages is illustrated in words like 'interdenominational' and 'extraterritoriality,' not to mention the Elizabethan 'honorificabilitudinity.'

204. The building of new words by the use of additional suffixes is an easy and very common method. We have noted it already in our adjectives — those made with the suffix -ac(i)- add -ous (-osus); we make PUGNACIOUS but Latin had no '**pugnaciosus.**' From **secretum**, SECRET, we have SECRETARY, representing **secretarius**, but once having made SECRETARY a noun, we form another adjective with the -alis suffix, SECRETARIAL. *Daily* was **diurnus**, not '**diurnalis**' as the Eng. DIURNAL would imply; the Latin of PRIMEVAL was **primaevus**, *of the first age* (**aevum**), not '**primaevalis.**' **Fanum** gave **fan-at-ic-us**, but FANATIC became a noun and the adjective FANATICAL. **Membrum** with -anus (103) made what became a feminine noun **membrana**, *the covering of a* MEMBER, MEMBRANE, from which, as if add-

248

ing -osus, we have MEMBRANOUS. **Octogenarius,** *relating to eighty* (**octogeni,** *eighty each*), we have put into the group in -anus and made OCTOGENARIAN. As an adjective from **pater** to denote rank in the state, there was **patricius,** but now PATRICIAN (-anus). **Ratio(n)** adds -alis; then RATIONAL adopts a Greek verb suffix to give us RATIONALize, and the Greek agent suffix makes RATIONAList, to which we may add *-ic* whether Greek or Latin and get RATIONAListic. So **terra, terrestris,** Eng. TERRESTRI-AL; **caelum, caelestis,** CELESTIAL, but **equestris,** Eng. EQUESTRI-AN (-anus). **Vegetus,** *enlivening,* furnished **vegetare, vegetabilis,** VEGETABLE; while VEGET-ARI-AN (-arius, -anus) is of our own manufacture.

205. But the manufacturing process sometimes goes further than the shift or multiplication of suffixes, as we may see in some of the following words warranted by the needs of the time, not by derivation:

ACRID: from **acer, acris,** *sharp, sour,* on analogy of ACID (112).

ALLUVIAL: **alluere (ad-luere),** *wash against, wash to;* **alluvio,** *an overflow;* ALLUVIAL merely on analogy of adjectives in -alis (98).

AMBIDEXTROUS: as if from '**ambi-dexter-osus,**' literally *on-both-sides-righthanded* (Med. Lat. **ambidexter**).

AMELIORATE: With 'a-' (Lat. **ad**) and the Low Lat. **meliorare,** *make better* (**melior**), the French made 'ameliorer,' from which we have shifted to the Latin participial ending (132).

ANTEDATE: **ante,** *before,* DATE from **datum** (52).

ANTEDILUVIAN: From **diluere,** *wash away,* Latin had three nouns meaning a DELUGE, **diluvies, diluvium, diluvio.** The stem with -anus (103) and the preposition prefixed made ANTEDILUVIAN, *before the flood.*

AVIATION: **avis,** *a bird,* with the common -a-tio(n) of action nouns (85).

CAUDAL: If there had been a Latin adjective for **cauda,** *tail,* it would doubtless have been '**caudalis.**' The English word assumes such an adjective.

CENTENNIAL: There was no '**centennialis**' in Latin, and there was no noun '**centennium**' from which such an adjective could have been made. **Biennium** and **triennium** (**bi-**, **tri-** + **annus**), *a period of two (three) years*, suggested the Eng. QUADRENNIUM and MILLENNIUM, all of which might have adjectives in *-al;* by analogy with these came CENTENNIAL from the non-existent '**centennium.**'

CENTRIFUGAL: **centrum** (originally Greek), *a point*, particularly, of a pair of compasses, *the center of a circle;* **fugere**, *flee*, **fuga**, *flight;* then the common *-AL* for *-alis*, and *fleeing from the center* is CENTRIFUGAL.

CENTRIPETAL: formed like CENTRIFUGAL above, from the root of **petere**, *seek*, *center-seeking*.

COEFFICIENT: a pres. pple. form (123), as if from **co-efficere** (**ex-**, **ec-facere**), thus meaning *effecting with*, *producing an effect along with* something, as when 5 works with *x* in the expression 5*x*.

COINCIDE: *fall in with* (**in** + **cadere**, *fall*, **incidere**), as when two geometrical figures *fall in with* each other (Med. Lat.).

CONGENIAL: **genialis** relating to one's **Genius**: *relating to birth* (**gignere**, root **gen-**), as we say 'a GENIAL climate,' *i.e.*, one conducive to growth. It meant also *pertaining to social enjoyment* since the tutelary spirit called **Genius** along with growth furnished happiness. With **con-** it suggests *having a like Genius with others*, *i.e.*, of the same disposition or temperament with them.

CORONATION: **Coronare** was a derivative verb from **corona**, *crown* (128). '**Coronatio, -onis,**' *the crowning*, should have been a member in good standing of the large group of nouns mentioned in 85, but it was not.

CUNEIFORM: **cuneus**, *wedge*, and **forma**, *form;* but the Latin adjective does not occur.

DICTIONARY: **Dictio** from **dicere**, *say*, was *style of speaking*, DICTION. It might have made '**dictionarius**,' as **legio** made **legionarius**, but the Romans left to later times the making of the book and its name; Med. Lat. **dictionarius** (**liber**).

DISASTER: OF 'desastre,' Lat. **dis-** with sinister or negative meaning, and **astrum**, *star* (Grk. ἄστρον; see also ἀστήρ, 148, Eng. 'aster'), a DISASTER being due to one's unlucky star. Cf. our adj. 'ill-starred.'

DISINFECT: INFECT is from **inficere**, **infectus** (133), **in** + **facere**, *put in.* As *put in* or *dip into*, **inficere** came to be *dye, tinge*, not necessarily with any harm: a Roman boy might even be "infected" with his studies. But it could also mean *spoil* or INFECT. The compound with **dis-**, however, is purely modern, as indeed are many other words with this prefix, DISFIGURE, DISHONEST, DISINHERIT, DISLOYAL, etc. (145). Even DISMISS is not true to the Latin since **di-** was the form of this prefix before *m*, **dimittere.**

ENTITY: '**Ens, entis,**' is assumed as a pres. pple. of **esse** (as in **pot-ens,** *able-being*), and from this was made the Late Latin noun **entitas** (72), ENTITY, denoting *what actually exists, real substance*. With the negative we have NONENTITY.

FESTAL: The Latin adjective **festus,** with the original idea of *bright*, was applied to a holiday, since even for a Roman a holiday was happier than a work day. The neut. **festum** was *holiday;* English has added -AL (**-alis**). Cf. FEAST and FESTIVE (44, 120 end). By a combination of suffixes we have FESTIVAL.

FUNDAMENTAL: **Fundamentum,** from **fundare,** FOUND (90), in addition to the less usual FUNDAMENT, *foundation*, has furnished the very common adj. FUNDAMENTAL (98). The Greek agent ending then makes the hybrid FUNDAMENTALlist.

HORTICULTURE: seemingly as good Latin as AGRICULTURE (140), but a modern formation, **horti** + **cultura,** *cultivation of a garden.*

IDENTICAL: The best that Classical Latin can do for this word is to furnish its beginning in the pronoun **idem,** *the same*. From **idem** Low Latin, taking its cue from **identidem,** *again and again*, made **identitas,** *sameness*, IDENTITY. In English we use the two suffixes -ic-alis to make ourselves an adjective, following Med. Lat. **identicus.**

ILLEGAL: **Legalis** from **lex, legis,** is Latin. But instead of the negative adjective **in-legalis, illegalis** (Med. Lat.), the Roman would have used such a phrase as **contra legem.**

IMPECUNIOUS: *having no money* (**pecunia**). The negative word is manufactured; **pecuniosus** meant *having money*.

LABORATORY: In its earlier English form the word was ELABORATORY. **Elaborare** was *to work out* to the end; hence *work intently* or *incessantly*. With **audire, auditor, auditorium,** there might have been **laborare, laborator,** '**(e)laboratorium.**' But the Romans stopped with the LABORER (laborator) and the LABORATORY was left for the chemistry of the Middle Ages.

LEGACY: Mediæval Latin had legatia (77) but the Classical word was legatum, from legare, *appoint by a will;* it was primarily *appoint by law* (lex, legis), as also the legatus, LEGATE or ambassador, was appointed.

LOCOMOTION: MOTION *from a place;* a compound of locus and motio, action noun from movere. Likewise modern is LOCOMOTIVE; even motivus is only Mediæval Latin.

MALLEABLE: *"hammerable";* malleus, *a hammer, a mall;* malleatus, *hammered,* was used in Latin, but not 'malleabilis.'

MALNUTRITION: The MAL- of this and like words is French for the Lat. mal-us, *bad,* male, *badly.* From nutrire, *nourish,* nutrimentum (90) gave us NUTRIMENT; from nutrix, NURSE, came nutricius; hence NUTRITIOUS (176); NUTRITION assumes a 'nutritio' which was not used.

MANICURE: manus, *hand,* cura, *care; care of the hands;* French but not Latin.

MANUFACTORY: manu + factorium (71), *a place for making by hand,* which it is not. Manu + factura (87), MANUFACTURE, *hand-making.*

MEDIÆVAL: Aevum meant *eternity;* then merely *a long period, an age;* medium aevum, *middle age;* so with -AL (-alis), MEDIÆVAL (MEDIEVAL), *of the Middle Ages.*

MULTILATERAL: multus, *many* (pl.), with lateralis from latus, lateris, *side, having many sides;* (Med. Lat. multilaterus).

OMNISCIENT: The Latin compound meaning *all-knowing* was omniscius, and our word might have been 'omniscious' (95), but for the influence of the many present participles coming into English (123).

OSSIFY: os, ossis, *bone,* with -FY, for Fr. '-fier,' Lat. -ficare (187); this kind of compound occurs over and over, as CODIFY (CODE, codex), PETRIFY (petra, Grk., πέτρα, *rock*), SOLIDIFY (solidus, SOLID), etc. (188), with no Latin equivalents.

PLENIPOTENTIARY: A restoration of this word to Latin would be pleni-potentiarius, plenus, *full,* potens, *powerful,* or potentia, *power.* The compound occurs in Mediæval Latin.

PREDOMINATE: prae-, *before,* dominari, dominatus, *be lord* (domi-

nus), DOMINATE; '**praedominari**,' if it had been used, would have been *be lord over, prevail.*

PREHENSILE: **Praehendere**, or **prehendere**, was *to lay hold of.* With the suffix -**tilis** (-**silis**) (115) we have PREHENSILE, *adapted to taking hold of things.*

PROPENSITY: from **pro**, *forward*, and **pendere, pensus**, *hang;* so a *hanging forward* or *leaning toward, inclination.* The Latin word, however, was not '**propensitas**,' but **propensio** (85) and appeared earlier in English as PROPENSION.

QUADRILLION: From **mille**, *a thousand*, Italian had '**millione**' ('**milione**'), '-**one**' being an augmentative suffix, *a thousand thousand*, whence the Fr., and from that the Eng., MILLION. From this, with calm disregard for the important initial *m*, we have employed the prefixes **bi**-, *two*, **tri**-, *three*, also **quadr**-, *four*, and then the numerals **quint-us, sext-us**, etc., to make BILLION, TRILLION, QUADRILLION, etc.

RALLY: This is RE-ALLY (Fr. '**rallier**'), from **re** + **alligare, adligare**, *bind to* (*one*) *again.*

RAPTURE: **rapere, raptus**, *seize, snatch;* RAPTURE is a state in which one is *seized* (with emotion), *an ecstasy;* the word simply follows the form of CAPTURE, CULTURE, etc. (87).

REGICIDE: FRATRICIDE, PARRICIDE (140), MATRICIDE, HOMICIDE, — so the Romans have given us the *slayers of brother, father, mother,* and *man.* It was no fondness for royalty that kept them from adding '**regicida**,' *the slayer of a king.*

SIMULTANEOUS: From **momentum**, *a moment* (52), was made, at least in ecclesiastical Latin, **momentaneus** (110); similarly from INSTANT (**instans**, *pressing on*, as an urgent point of time; cf. **instanter**, 55) we have made INSTANTANEOUS, and from **simul**, *at the same time*, using a borrowed -*t*-, SIMULTANEOUS.

SOPORIFIC: *sleep-making*, **sopor**, *sleep*, -**ficus** from **facere**, *make.* The Latin word, however, was **soporifer**, *sleep-bringing* (**ferre**), and we have also SOPORIFEROUS.

SORORITY: From **frater**, *brother*, was formed **fraternus** (108), *brotherly;* then **fraternitas**, FRATERNITY. By a mechanical imitation — sister following brother — from **soror**, *sister*, SORORITY was made, as if there had been a Lat. '**sororitas**.'

STATEMENT: STATE from **stare**, *stand*, meant *a standing*, as also

ESTATE and STATUS (46). When STATE had come to be used as a verb the noun STATEMENT followed easily on analogy of the nouns in -mentum (90).

SUICIDE: cf. REGICIDE; sui, *of oneself,* caedere (-cidere), *kill;* a combination which a Roman would not have made.

SUPERANNUATE: a verb formed from super and annus, *above a year.* Earlier the form was SUPERANNATE (Low Lat. superannatus) for *living more than a year.* Now SUPERANNUATE is to retire or pension one who *has passed beyond the years* of active service, and we make it also an adjective and a noun.

TIMOROUS: From timor, *fear,* but Latin has no corresponding adjective in -osus (94).

TONSORIAL: The TONSORIAL artist should rather be "tonsorious" if he would be true to the barbers of Rome. The adjective from tonsor, *a shearer,* was tonsorius, not 'tonsorialis.'

TRAVESTY: literally *a change of clothing,* tra- (trans) indicating change. From vestis, *clothing,* vestire meant *clothe* (VEST, VESTURE, VESTMENT). The compound with tra- was not Latin but French ('se travestir') and the French pple. 'travesti' became Eng. TRAVESTY.

UBIQUITY: "*everywhereness.*" From the Latin adverb ubique, the noun has been formed on the analogy of nouns in -tas, -TY (72).

VACCINATE: The verb has no Latin counterpart, but VACCINE is Latin enough, vaccinus (adj.) from vacca, *cow* (104), since the serum for VACCINATION is obtained from cows.

VELOCIPEDE: a compound of velox, velocis, *swift,* and pes, pedis, *foot, swiftly propelled by the feet.*

VIADUCT: an English combination of via ducta, *a way constructed* (ducere).

VIVISECTION: vivus, *alive,* sectio, sectionis, *a cutting* (secare), *cutting what is alive, dissection of living animals.*

206. Another group of coined words consists of those made of Latin phrases, words in syntactical relation, like the Latin formations in 143; thus:

EXCULPATE: ex culpa, *from blame* (culpare, culpatus, *blame*)*;* Mediæval Latin had exculpatio which suggests an 'exculpare.'

EXHUME: **ex humo,** *out of the ground, take (a body) out of the ground.*

EXTEMPORARY: **ex tempore,** *from the time* (59), with -ARY, as if from -arius (101).

INTER: **in terram,** *into the earth,* i.e., *put into the earth* (Med. Lat. **interrare**).

INTERSTELLAR: **inter stellas,** *between the stars,* with suffix -AR (-aris, 99).

INTRAMURAL: **intra muros,** *within the walls,* with -AL (-alis, 98).

MANUSCRIPT: **manu scriptum,** *written by hand* (as one word, however, in Low Lat. **manuscriptum**).

NONDESCRIPT: **non descriptum,** *not described, that cannot be described.*

PERADVENTURE: **per adventuram (rem);** through the Fr. 'par aventure,' then back to the Latin, *through the thing coming upon one, through a mere happening, perhaps.*

PERFORCE: **per fortiam,** *by force.* The noun is a Low Latin formation from **fortis.**

PUNY: written *puisny* in *As You Like It* (III, 4, 46), representing the OF 'puis-ne,' Lat. **post natus,** *born after,* i.e., *younger,* and therefore *weaker.*

SINECURE: **sine cura,** *without care,* an ecclesiastical position *without the duty of caring* for souls; so any lucrative position without work or responsibility. A CURATE, however, Low Lat. **curatus** (from **cura,** 107), held a **curatum beneficium,** a BENEFICE *with the care of souls.*

SUBLUNARY: **sub luna,** with -ARY (-aris, 99), *under the moon;* hence *earthly.*

SUBMARINE: **sub mare,** *under the sea,* with adjective suffix -INE (-inus, 104).

SUPERSTRUCTURE: **super structura,** *a building above,* **struere,** build. (There was, however, a very rare Latin verb **superstruere.**)

Through the French we have ACHIEVE from '(venir) à chief,' i.e., **venire ad caput,** *come to the head, reach one's goal;* cf. 'a-head,' to ACHIEVE is *to get ahead.* The Fr. 'à gré' representing **ad gratum,** *according to what is pleasing,* became AGREE. Cf. also ADVISE (202), ANTEDILUVIAN (205), IMPROMPTU (58), INFURIATE (49), PRORATE (59), SUBPOENA (59).

II. Hybrids

207. Among coined words belong also hybrids, words made partly from one language, partly from another. Many such occur in English, but we are concerned here, of course, with those only which involve Latin words. Some of these also were Latin combinations; the Romans themselves made the mixture and we have adopted it. More often hybrids are of late formation, made in modern times in ignorance or in wilful disregard of the rights of the languages. This has been done in various ways: we may have (*A*) a Latin prefix + a non-Latin base; (*B*) a non-Latin prefix + a Latin base; (*C*) a Latin base + a non-Latin suffix; (*D*) a non-Latin base + a Latin suffix; (*E*) a compound of Latin and non-Latin elements. Examples of these groups are the following:

A. LATIN PREFIX + NON-LATIN BASE

208. ALlot: **ad,** *to,* and Eng. 'lot,' *assign one's lot* or *portion to* him.

ANTEroom: **ante,** *before,* and Eng. 'room,' *a room in front.*

BIgamy: **bi-,** *two,* and Greek '-gamia' from 'gamos' (γάμος), *marriage, double marriage.*

commingle: **com-,** *together* and Eng. 'mingle.'

compatriot: **com-,** *together,* Greek 'patriotes' (πατριώτης), Low Lat. **compatriota,** one who owes allegiance to the same country.

DEfile: **de,** *down (from)* and Eng. '-file.' The Middle English had a word 'defoulen,' coming from Old French and meaning *tread down,* but associated also with the Eng. 'foul.' There was also the Anglo-Saxon word 'fylan,' meaning *pollute,* the now obsolete 'file.' With these meanings the step from DEfoul to DEfile was easy.

DErange: (Fr. 'déranger') DE-, the OF 'des-,' Lat. **dis-,** *apart,* and 'range,' originally German, *set in order.* Cf. DISARRange.

Elope: **e,** *out,* and Dutch 'loopen.' The Dutch compound was 'ont-loopen,' *run away,* but the Latin prefix **e-,** being much more familiar than the Dutch 'ont-,' was substituted for it.

EMbody: 'em-,' *i.e.*, 'en-,' French for Lat. **in,** *in*, and Eng. 'body,' *put into a body, into bodily form.* Cf. INCARNATE (143).

EX-king: **ex,** *out*, and Eng. 'king'; so we use EX- with many words to denote *former*.

IMbed: **in,** *in*, and Eng. 'bed,' used only figuratively.

MALpractice: While coming into English through Mediæval Latin, 'practice' is Greek in origin, 'praktikos' (πρακτικός), *relating to doing;* the verb 'practice' seems to have been earlier than the noun. MAL- is Lat. **malus,** *bad.*

MIShap: If, as is very probable, this word was made on analogy of 'mischance,' the MIS- is in origin Lat. **minus** (cf. MISCHIEF, 202); 'hap' is Old Norse.

PERhaps: Lat. **per,** *through;* 'hap' as in 'MIShap'; the *-s* may have been added under the influence of the *s*-sound of PERCHANCE (CHANCE 43).

REly: **re-,** *back*, and Eng. 'lie,' *recline.* Strictly it should be spelled 'relie'; the change to '-ly' may have been due to analogy of APPLY, COMPLY, REPLY, etc.

SUBway: **sub,** *under*, and Eng. 'way.'

SUPERman: **super,** *above*, and Eng. 'man,' *a man above* ordinary men.

B. NON-LATIN PREFIX + LATIN BASE

209. AROUND: This 'a-' is a shorter form of 'an,' Middle English for 'on'; 'on round' meant *on a round.* ROUND is the OF 'roond' for Lat. **rotundum,** *round* (Eng. ROTUND), itself from **rota,** *a wheel.*

beCAUSE: 'be,' another form of the English preposition 'by'; the word was formerly written 'bi-cause.' CAUSE came through the French from the Lat. **causa.**

beLABOR: 'be-,' English prefix, meaning *for, on, over,* etc., making a verb transitive, and LABOR from Lat. **laborare.** *To work strenuously on one* is to beat him vigorously.

beSIEGE: Eng. 'be-,' as above, *around*, and SIEGE, going back through OF '(a)segier' and Low Lat. **assediare,** to Lat. **sedere,** *sit.* To beSIEGE the city was to *sit down by* it (AS 'besittan,' 23).

misCONSTRUE: 'mis-,' an English prefix denoting *amiss* or *wrongly,* and CONSTRUE from Lat. **con-struere,** *build together; put things together wrongly.*

unJUST: Eng. 'un-,' *not* (Lat. **in-**)*;* **justus,** *fair, right,* JUST.

C. LATIN BASE + NON-LATIN SUFFIX

210. APPENDICitis: **appendix, appendicis** (52); '-itis,' a Greek fem. suffix originally making an adjective in agreement with 'nosos' (νόσος), *disease.*

ARTless: Lat. **ars, artis,** *skill,* ART, and the English suffix '-less,' meaning *without,* AS '-leas,' *loose,* not the comparative *less.*

BRUTish: **Brutus** meant *stupid,* and in Late Latin designated an *irrational animal,* a BRUTE; '-ish' is English denoting *like.*

CLOSEness: CLOSE (Fr. 'clos') comes from the Lat. **clausus,** pf. pple. of **claudere,** *shut* (167)*;* '-ness' in English makes the abstract noun.

COMPANIONship: Through Old French and Low Latin COMPANION comes from **com-,** *together,* and **panis,** *bread;* COMPANIONS are those *who eat their bread together.* To this has been added the Eng. '-ship' denoting condition.

CORONer: **Corona,** a CROWN, gave the verb **coronare,** from which came the Late Lat. **coronator.** But instead of adopting this word, English has added to **coron-** the native agent suffix '-er.' The CORONer, *i.e.,* CROWNer, formerly was entrusted with the rights of the private property of the crown. From some Middle English verbs agent nouns were made in '-ier,' and COURTier is formed from French in the same way as CORONer from Latin (see COURT, 28).

DENTist: **dens, dentis,** *tooth,* and the Greek agent suffix '-ist' ('-istes,' -ιστης); DENTist taken literally into English is *a toother.* Similarly, ARTist, FLORist, HUMORist, and many others.

DUKEdom: DUKE, Fr. 'duc,' was Lat. **dux, ducis,** *a leader* (**ducere,** *lead*)*;* '-dom' is English expressing *jurisdiction,* and later *condition* or *state.*

FALSEhood: The Lat. **falsus,** pf. pple. of **fallere,** *deceive,* came to us through the OF 'fals' as FALSE; the Eng. '-hood' denotes *condition.*

GAUDy: GAUD is the Lat. **gaudium** (202); the English suffix '-y' denotes likeness or possession.

GRATEful: Lat. **gratus** is *pleasing;* **ingratus,** *unthankful,* we keep as INGRATE. To GRATE-, **gratus,** coming to us through the Old French, has been added the Eng. '-ful,' *i.e., full.*

LINen: The old noun was LIN from Lat. **linum,** *flax* (12); the English suffix is the same as in 'woolen,' 'golden,' etc.

PRINCEly: PRINCE from Lat. **princeps** (through French), *a chieftain,* and Eng. '-ly' meaning *like.* We may also say 'PRINCElike.'

PRINCEss: PRINCE as above; '-ess' the fem. ending, through Late Latin and French from Grk. '-issa' (-ισσα).

PUGILism: **Pugil, pugilis** was *a boxer,* on the same root as **pungere,** PUNCH (202), also **pugnus,** *fist,* **pugnare,** *fight;* '-ism' is from the Greek action noun suffix ('-ismos,' -ισμος).

TUBERCULOSis: TUBERCUL-, diminutive of **tuber,** *a swelling;* '-osis' is Greek (-ωσις), combining the 'o' of certain verb stems with an action suffix '-sis.'

VAPORize: Lat. **vapor,** *vapor,* or *steam;* with '-ize,' Greek '-izō' (-ίζω), a suffix forming denominative verbs in Greek.

VENTUREsome: VENTURE, a shorter form of Mid. Eng. 'aventure,' which now is ADVENTURE (from **ad-venturam,** cf. PERADVENTURE, 206), with Eng. '-some,' *like, possessed of,* or *given to.*

D. NON-LATIN BASE + LATIN SUFFIX

211. breakAGE: The Eng. 'break' has added -AGE, the French form of Lat. **'-aticum'** (177).

eatABLE: After the Latin form for making adjectives from verbs of the first conjugation, -A-BLE (-a-bilis) has been added to the English verb 'eat' (118). The Latin synonym is EDIBLE (**edere,** *eat*).

gullIBLE: The gull is not so stupid a bird as our use of the word would indicate. The name was formerly used of a young bird of any kind; perhaps it was only the young bird that was foolish. Having made it a verb, we combine this originally Celtic word with the -BLE (-bilis) to make an adjective (116, 118).

hindrANCE: the verb 'hinder' with -ANCE, Lat. -antia (75).

macadamizATION: the proper name 'Macadam' (John L.),' mac-,' Gaelic, 'Adam,' Hebrew, '-iz-,' the Greek suffix for denominative verbs (-ίζω), with the Latin action noun suffix (from first conjugation verb) -a-tio(n) (85).

merriMENT: 'Merry' came from Celtic; -MENT is Lat. -mentum (90).

murderOUS: Eng. 'murder' and the suffix -OUS, Lat. -osus (94).

oddITY: The Scandinavian 'odd' has here been treated as a Latin adjective, since -ITY is the Latin abstract noun suffix -(i)tat- (72).

parliaMENT: *a conference for parley;* the first element is Greek, the same as in 'parable.' In Low Latin the verb **parabolare** meant *to talk;* a modified form of this with Latin suffix -mentum gave parliaMENT (Fr. 'parlement'). ParliaMENT *talks* while CONGRESS *meets* (**congressus,** 88).

practiTIONER: The older word was 'practician' (cf. OPTICIAN), 'practice' being of Greek origin, -AN Latin (-anus); 'practician' must have suggested a spelling 'practition,' as if combining the Greek word with the Latin noun suffix -tio(n) (85). Then to such a Greek-Latin mixture was added the English agent noun suffix '-er.'

starvATION: From 'starve,' a native English word, meaning originally *die,* and then *die of hunger,* an action noun has been formed as if Latin (85) in -tio(n) from a first conjugation verb.

talkATIVE: Our English verb *talk* (as if with stem 'talk-a-') has taken the Latin verbal adjective suffix, -TIVE (120).

whimsICAL: 'Whim' is of Scandinavian origin; -ic and -al two Latin suffixes (97, 98). The -s- is perhaps from an earlier parallel form 'whimsey.'

withdrawAL: Latin neuter plurals in -alia (-alis, 98) came over through Old French to furnish an English suffix -AL for action nouns. This originally Latin suffix has been added to the English verb 'withdraw.'

wonderMENT: made after the fashion of action nouns in -MENT, Lat. -mentum (90), 'wonder' being the English verb.

E. COMPOUNDS OF LATIN AND NON-LATIN ELEMENTS

212. ALTImeter: Lat. **altus,** *high,* Grk. 'metron' ($\mu\acute{\epsilon}\tau\rho\upsilon$), *measure;* a *height-measuring* device.

asafŒTIDA: 'asa,' the Persian 'aza,' meaning *gum;* Lat. **foetidus** (**fetidus**), *stinking,* FETID; hence *stinking gum.*

autoMOBILE: 'Auto-' is Greek for *self* ('autos,' $\alpha\dot{\upsilon}\tau\acute{o}s$, intensive); MOBILE is the French form of the Lat. **mobilis** (116), from **movere,** MOVE; *self-moving.*

COMMONwealth: COMMON through the OF 'commun' represented the Lat. communis, com-, *with*, -munis, probably *bound by obligation* (munus) *with others*, and thus *belonging to all alike*. With this is united the Eng. 'wealth,' *i.e.*, *weal or good; the common welfare*, and so *the state*.

DICTAphone: DICTA- from dicere, dictus, *what has been spoken;* 'phone,' the Greek for *sound* or *speech* (φωνή). The instrument receives and turns again to sound things that have been said.

foreFRONT: the Eng. 'fore,' *coming first* (cf. Lat. pro); FRONT, Old French for Lat. frons (frontem), *forehead;* then *forward part*.

foreORDAIN: the Eng. 'fore,' as in foreFRONT, with ORDAIN, from the French (OF 'ordenir'), Lat. ordinare, *set in order* (ordo, ordinis), *arrange*.

HEIRloom: HEIR is the French representation of the Lat. heres (heredem); the Eng. 'loom' was *an implement* (particularly for weaving) or *a piece of furniture*.

monoPLANE: 'Mono-' is Greek for *only, single* ('monos,' μόνος), joined here with PLANE from Lat. planus, *level, flat*, planum, a PLAIN.

MOTORcycle: MOTOR, movere, *move* (52, 80); 'cycle,' Grk. 'kuklos' (κύκλος), *circle, wheel.*

MOTORman: MOTOR as in MOTORcycle, with Eng. 'man.'

MULTIgraph: *a manywriter, i.e.*, a machine for writing many copies; it should have been *'multiscribe'* or *'polygraph,'* according as it was Latin or Greek; but multus, *much, many*, is combined with 'graph,' Grk. 'graphō' (γράφω), *write*.

ostrich: a Latin-Greek compound. Our spelling is simple compared with Mid. Eng. 'oystryche,' OF 'ostruche,' but neither of these suggests at once the Latin original avis struthio, *ostrich bird*, 'strouthiōn' (στρουθίων) being a late Greek word for *ostrich*.

overPLUS: Eng. 'over' and Lat. plus, literally *over-more*. If we substitute Fr. 'sur' (Lat. super) for 'over,' we make the wholly Latin doublet SURPLUS.

PARtake: PART-take, pars, partis, and the Eng. (Scandinavian) 'take.'

PEDestal: The Lat. pes, pedis, *foot* and the Germ. 'Stall,' *stall or stand*, were united in the Ital. 'piedestallo,' which came to us through the Spanish as PEDestal.

petroleum: The Lat. **petra** is only an adopted Greek word (πέτρα), *rock;* **oleum,** oil. Petroleum is "*rock-oil.*"

purblind: The original meaning was pure-blind, pure from **purus,** with Eng. 'blind.' An old spelling 'poreblind' suggests a confusion with 'pore,' *look steadily,* as a possible explanation of the peculiar change of meaning, "*blind enough to go staring about.*"

sociology: Lat. **socius,** *companion, ally* (lit. *a follower,* **sequi,** *follow,* 157), with Grk. '-log-ia' from 'legō' (λέγω), *tell.* The science therefore *tells about comradeship,* or *association of people, i.e.,* society (**societas**).

spectroscope: Lat. **spectrum,** 52; '-scope,' the Grk. 'skopeō' (σκοπέω), *look at;* an instrument for *looking at the spectrum.*

tarpaulin: also tarpauling, *a covering treated with tar.* Tarpauling is for 'tarpalling'; pall, Lat. **palla** (10), *a robe* or *mantle* with Eng. 'tar' and suffix '-ing.'

television: 'tēle-,' (Grk. τῆλε), *far away,* with vision, **visio,** the action noun of **videre,** *see* (85).

televox: 'tēle-,' as in television (cf. also the purely Greek compounds 'telegraph,' 'telephone,' 'telescope,' 'telepathy'). Its combination with the Lat. **vox,** voice, serves to name a mechanical device receiving and responding to a message given by the voice over a telephone.

vitaphone: *life-sound;* Lat. **vita,** *life,* Grk. 'phone' (φωνή), *sound, voice, speech;* a rather inadequate name of a machine for reproducing speech along with moving pictures.

CHAPTER VII

DERIVATIVE NAMES

213. Many personal names in English are of Latin origin, sometimes genuine Latin, sometimes with French or English modifications; for example:

ALMA, fem. of **almus**, *cherishing, benign.*

AMANDA, *to be loved* (fem.), gerundive form from **amare**, *love.*

AMY: The Lat. **amata**, *loved*, pf. pple. fem. of **amare**, *love*, became Fr. 'aimée' (cf. 192), transferred thence to English as AMY.

ANTONY, Lat. **Antonius**, fem. **Antonia**, said to mean *inestimable* or *praiseworthy.* Spelled also ANTHONY and abbreviated to TONY.

AUGUSTUS, fem. AUGUSTA: **Augustus**, from **augere**, *increase*, meant *majestic*, AUGUST. With -inus (104) the name became **Augustinus**, AUGUSTINE, also shortened in English to AUSTIN.

BEATRICE: Italian, *one who makes happy* (**beatus**). The Latin form **Beatrix** uses the fem. agent suffix (cf. ADMINISTRATRIX, 52).

BELLE: the French form of Lat. **bella**(m), fem. of **bellus**, *beautiful.*

CALVIN: The Roman cognomen **Calvinus** was evidently made from **calvus**, *bald* (104).

CECIL, fem. CECILIA: Lat. **Caecilius**, derived probably from **caecus**, *blind.*

CELESTE: *heavenly;* a French form from **caelestis** (**celestis**), *pertaining to the heavens* (**caelum**), CELESTIAL.

CLARA: fem. of **clarus**, *bright.* CLAIRE is French.

CLARENCE: as if from '**Clarentius**,' formed from **clarens**, pres. pple. of **clarere**, *be bright.*

CLARIBEL: a compound of **clarus**, *bright*, and **bellus**, *beautiful; brightly fair.*

CLARICE: also from **clarus**, *bright, famous.* The Lat. suffix -ix (-icem) became '-ice' in Italian (cf. BEATRICE above) and CLARICE was formed with that suffix, perhaps to mean *making famous.*

CLARISSA: also from **clarus**; '-issa' seemingly the Greek fem. suffix (*-ισσα*; cf. PRINCESS, 210).

CLAUD, fem. CLAUDE, Ital. CLAUDIA: The Latin is **Claudius**, evidently from **claudus**, *lame*, though some have tried to be more complimentary and connect the name with **-clu-** of **inclutus**, *famous*.

CLEMENT: **clemens, clementis**, *gentle, mild*.

CONSTANCE: The Romans had both **Constans** and **Constantius**; **constans**, pres. pple. of **constare**, *stand firm*, CONSTANT; the fem. form **Constantia** has become CONSTANCE.

CORDELIA: made as if a fem. adj. form from **cor, cordis**, *heart; the lady with a heart*.

DRUSILLA: used as fem. of **Drusus**, said to have been taken from **Drausus**, the name of a Gallic chieftain, meaning *strong*.

EMILY: **Aemilius** was a name of uncertain origin. It may have been an Oscan word, though some have connected it with **aemulus**, *emulating*, others with the Grk. 'haimulos' (*αἰμύλος*), *wily, witty*. Its fem. **Aemilia** has become EMILY.

FELIX, fem. FELICIA: **felix**, *happy, fortunate*.

FESTUS: *joyful, having the holiday spirit*. Cf. FEAST, FESTAL, FESTIVE (44, 205, 120 end).

FLORA: **Flora** was the Roman goddess of flowers, from **flos, floris**, *a flower*.

FLORENCE: a fem. form (**Florentia**, the name of the city) made from the pres. pple. of **florere**, *bloom, flourish*, or else from **flora**, above.

GRACE: the French form of the Lat. **gratia(m)**, *favor*, GRACE (176).

HILARY: *gay, cheerful;* the Latin word is **hilaris** or **hilarus**, borrowed, however, from the Grk. 'hilaros' (*ἵλαρος*).

HORACE: Ital. 'Horatio,' Lat. **Horatius**, perhaps from **hora**, HOUR, *hour-keeping, prompt*.

HORTENSE: **hortensis**, *belonging to the garden* (**hortus**)*;* the Romans had the proper names **Hortensius** and **Hortensia**; HORTENSE (Fr.) should be *a garden woman*.

JULIUS, fem. JULIA: Vergil, in honor of Augustus, connected the name of the Julian gens with Aeneas's son Ascanius under the names Ilus and Iulus.[1] But a derivation found in poetry written

[1] *Aeneid*, I, 267–268.

by an ancient Roman in praise of his emperor can very safely
be rejected. We may regard more seriously the modern guess
that Iulus (Julius) was a combination of **Ju-**, the first syllable
of **Ju-piter**, *i.e.*, *Zeus-father*, or the *sky-father*, and the diminutive
suffix **-lus**. Besides JULIA, the Breton form of the feminine is
IOLA. With **-anus**, the name became **Julianus**, JULIAN, Fr.
'Julien,' and a diminutive fem. is JULIET ('Juliette').

JUSTIN: The Latin name was **Justinus** (104), from **justus**, JUST.

LAURA: *a laurel;* a fem. form made from **laurus**, *a laurel tree*.
Derivatives are LAURETTA, LORETTA.

LAURENCE or LAWRENCE: *laureled, crowned with laurel*. In Latin
there were two adjective forms, **Laurens** and **Laurentius**, both,
however, from the name of the Latin town **Laurentum**, which
itself may have been derived from **laurus**. The Italian form of
LAURENCE is LORENZO.

LEO, LEON: *a lion*. LEONA is evidently our homemade feminine;
the Latin feminine was **leaena**.

LETITIA: Lat. **laetitia**, *joy*.

LILLY, LILLIAN: possibly from **lilium**, *a lily;* LILLIAN as if from
'**liliana**' (103).

LUCIUS: fem. LUCIA (Ital., Sp.), LUCY, LUCINDA: from the root in
lux, lucis, *light* and **lucere**, *shine;* **Lucius** meant *of the day*, or
born at daybreak. With the suffix **-anus** (103) **Lucianus**, the
name of several saints, gave us LUCIAN (Fr. 'Lucien') and its
fem. **Luciana** may have encouraged the combination *Lucy Anne*.
Again, possibly from the form **Lucanus**, the name was turned
into Greek as 'Loukas' (Λουκᾶς) and has come to us as
LUKE.

LUCRETIA: perhaps from **lucrum**, *gain*, unless it involves the same
root as in LUCIUS.

MABEL: contracted from AMABEL, Lat. **amabilis**, *lovable* (116).

MARCUS, MARK: The name may be connected with **Mars** (cf.
MARTIN) or may mean *horseman* from Celtic 'marc,' *a horse*.
A diminutive is MARCELLUS.

MARTIN: From **Mars, Martis**, god of war, this assumes an adjective
in **-inus** (104), but the adjective from **Mars** was **martialis**,
MARTIAL (98).

MAURICE: *Moorish, dark;* made as if from '**Mauritius**,' but the adjective from **Mauri,** *the Moors,* was **Mauricus** (97); the name is also spelled Morris.

Max: shortened from Maximilian. The story is told that the Holy Roman Emperor Frederick III[1] combined the names of two great Romans, **Fabius Maximus** and **Scipio Aemilianus,** and made for his son the name Maximilian which has become common as Max, *i.e.,* the first syllable of **Maximus,** *greatest.*

Minerva: the name of the Roman goddess of wisdom and the arts; probably on the same root as **mens,** *mind,* and meaning *the thinker.*

Miranda: *one to be admired;* fem. gerundive form of **miror, admire.**

Nona: fem. of **nonus,** *ninth;* seems to have been first the name of the *ninth* child.

Nora: shortened from **Honora,** fem. of **honorus,** *honorable.*

Octavia: fem. of **Octavius,** probably originally from **octavus,** *eighth, the eighth* child.

Oliver (Fr. 'Olivier'), fem. Olive, Olivia: **oliva,** an olive or *an olive tree.*

Patience: the same as the common noun, **patientia,** from **patiens,** pres. pple. of **pati,** *suffer* (75).

Patrick: **patricius,** patrician (204) or *noble.* We keep the Lat. fem. **Patricia.**

Paul, fem. Pauline, Paulina: **paulus,** *little;* the feminine made with the suffix -ina (104).

Priscilla: a fem. diminutive from **priscus,** *ancient; elderly.*

Prudence: the same as the common noun, **prudentia (providentia),** *foresight* (75).

Rex: *king;* fem. Regina, *queen.* Cf. Roy, 167.

Rosa, Rose: **rosa,** a rose; other derivative English forms are Rosalie and Rosalind.

Rufus: **rufus,** *red.*

Silas: shortened form of **Silvanus,** a deity *of the woods* (**silva,** 103).

Silvester: Lat. **silvestris,** *belonging to the forest.*

Stella: **stella,** *a star.* The French form is Estelle (180).

Vera: fem. of **verus,** *true.*

Victor: **victor,** *conqueror,* agent noun of **vincere,** *conquer.*

Victoria: **victoria,** victory.

---

[1] King Frederick IV of Germany.

VINCENT: **vincens, vincentis,** pres. pple. of **vincere,** *conquer.*

VIOLA: the Latin word for VIOLET; VIOLET, from French diminutive, also becomes a personal name.

VIRGINIA: commonly regarded as an adjective from **virgo, virginis;** hence *maidenly.*

VIVIAN: as if from '**vivianus, viviana**' (103), *lively,* but the Latin adjective is **vivus,** *living.*

214. Geographical names furnish many illustrations of the world's indebtedness to Latin for significant terms. We Anglicize Latin names, or we adopt them as they have been delivered to us, or else we receive them through the medium of some other modern language. The following are examples:

ARGENTINA: a fem. adjective form (104) from **argentum,** *silver;* named for the silver displayed to explorers by the natives; however, it seems that this silver was not a product of the country but was brought from the mountains of Bolivia.

AUSTRALIA: It is said that when the old geographers imagined a continent in the southern hemisphere to balance the land of the northern, they referred to it as **Terra Australis incognita,** *the unknown land of the south.* After having for some time borne the name of 'New Holland' given it by the Dutch discoverers in 1664, the continent came to be called AUSTRALIA, as a new fem. adjective derived from **Australis,** thus receiving approximately the name provided before its discovery.

CANARY Islands: See CANARY, 202.

CAROLINA: the fem. adjective form (104) from **Carolus,** *Charles.* The name was first given by French settlers in honor of their king, Charles IX, but it was equally appropriate when the English got control of the section under their Charles I and Charles II.

CINCINNATI: Inasmuch as **Cincinnatus** once left his plow to become dictator of Rome, an American organization of officers who had fought in the Revolutionary War took for themselves his honorable name. From them this plural form of that name was given to the Ohio city.

FORMOSA: fem. of the adjective **formosus,** *beautiful, attractive of* *form* (**forma**). The island now called 'Taiwan' by the Chinese was named Formosa by Spanish navigators on account of the beauty of its scenery. A territory of Argentina also bears the name, presumably for a like reason.

GEORGIA: the form of a Latin adjective (fem.) from the name of George II; the name George is from the Greek for *farmer*.

ITASCA: In 1832 Henry R. Schoolcraft conducted a government expedition to the upper Mississippi and explored its sources. Having come upon the lake which seemed to be the real source, he asked the Reverend William T. Boutwell, a missionary accompanying the expedition, to furnish some Latin or Greek name expressing *the head* or *true source*. Boutwell said "**Verum caput**, or if you prefer, the noun **veritas**." In a few minutes Schoolcraft had taken the last two syllables of **veritas** and the first of **caput**, and declared the name should be ITASCA.[1]

LIBERIA: made from the Lat. **liber**, *free*, with the common fem. suffix of the names of countries. This *land of the free* was a colony founded in 1820 for freed slaves from the United States.

LOUISIANA: The suffixes are Latin, as if **-io-**, and **-anus** (103, end) had been added to the name of Louis XIV of France.

MARMORA: a fem. ending with **marmor**, *marble* (the proper adj. form in Latin is **marmorea**); *the marble sea*, or *the marble island*, from the marble quarries on the island.

MEDITERRANEAN: **medius**, *middle*, **terra**, *land*, with a doubling of the adj. suffix, as if **-terr-ane-anus** (103, 110), *the sea in the midst of the lands*. The Romans called it **Mare Internum**, *the Inner Sea*, or **Mare Nostrum**, *Our Sea*.

MONTANA: From **mons, montis**, *mountain*, the adjective was **montanus**, fem. **montana**; **Civitas Montana**, *the mountainous state*.

NOVA SCOTIA: *New Scotland*, the name applied to this peninsula by King James I. The ancient Latin name of Scotland was **Caledonia**.

PACIFIC: The Latin adjective is **pacificus**, *peace-making*, *peaceable*, from **pax, pacis**, *peace*, and **facere**, *make;* the ocean was so named by Magellan.

---

[1] For this rather remarkable explanation of the name, see W. W. Folwell, *A History of Minnesota*, Vol. I, pp. 114–115.

PENNSYLVANIA: **sylva,** another spelling for **silva,** *forest,* **silvanus** (**sylvanus**), *pertaining to the forest.* With the usual fem. ending of names of states and countries, Penn-SYLVANIA is the *Penn-wooded-country,* named in honor of William Penn and his father.[1]

PORTUGAL: **Portucalia** or **Terra Portucalensis** was the *land of the harbor of Cale,* this being the original name of the city now called Oporto ('O porto,' Lat. **illum portum,** *The Harbor*).

RUMANIA, ROUMANIA: also ROMANIA, *the country of the Romans,* since the people of this country thus proclaim their ancestry.

SUPERIOR: *higher* (54), the *higher* or *upper* lake.

TRANSYLVANIA: **Trans** + **sylvanus,** *the land beyond the forest.* See PENNSYLVANIA.

VIRGINIA: The adjective form was made from **virgo, virginis,** a VIRGIN (213), the name having been given to the state in honor of the virgin queen Elizabeth.

215. French, Spanish, Italian, and Portuguese geographical names accepted into English often become more interesting as we observe their Latin originals. The following are examples:

CHERbourg: a hybrid word, the first syllable a French modification of the Lat. **Caesaris;** 'burg' is a Teutonic word for *a fortified place;* hence *Caesar's castle.*

COLORADO: a Spanish pf. pple. masc. representing Lat. **coloratum,** *colored;* then in Spanish *red-colored;* probably applied to the state on account of the red-colored mountains.

DOMINGO: This Portuguese word for *Sunday* is the Lat. **Dominicus** (**-um**), an adjective from **dominus,** *master, lord* (97); hence *the Lord's Day;* and here apparently the *land reached on the Lord's Day.*

ECUADOR: Spanish for the Lat. **aequator,** EQUATOR, agent noun of

---

[1] Penn had suggested the name SYLVANIA. Others proposed Penn-SYLVANIA; whereupon Penn even went to King Charles to have the addition struck out, but the king refused to change it. "For I feared," said Penn, "lest it should be looked on as a vanity in me and not as respect in the king, as it truly was, to my father." (Amer. Encycl., *Pennsylvania.*)

aequare, *the line that makes equal, i.e.,* makes equal parts of the earth. The country is crossed by the equator.

FLORIDA: This adjective is Latin as well as Spanish, made from **florere,** *bloom,* **flos, floris,** a FLOWER (112), and it would seem to describe the state aptly as *flowery,* but Ponce de Leon gave the section that name in honor of his having landed there on Easter Sunday (March 27, 1513), the Spanish 'Pascua Florida,' *Feast of Flowers.*

FUNDY (Bay of FUNDY): The Port. 'Baya Fondo' is the *deep bay,* Lat. **fundus (-um),** *deep.*

GRANADA: seemingly *a pomegranate* (202), the Spanish pf. pple. fem. used, as also sometimes Lat. **granatum,** *seedy,* to mean *pomegranate* (**pomum,** *an apple full of seeds*). However, the Moors called the place 'Karnattah' (*hill of strangers?*) and GRANADA may have been at first a corruption of that name.

LABRADOR: The Port. 'lavrador' ('labrador'), *farmer,* is the Lat. **laborator,** *laborer.* It is said that when natives of that country were carried away to Lisbon as laborers, the new country was regarded as a source for slave labor, 'terra de lavradores,' *land of laborers.* Another explanation of the name is that John Cabot met a Portuguese farmer Fernandez who had been on a voyage on which he had seen what is now called Greenland: that Cabot's sailors discovering that coast later, called it the Labrador's land.[1]

MADEIRA: Portuguese for Lat. **materia,** *timber* (cf. MATERIAL). The name was applied on account of dense forests covering the island when it was discovered by the Portuguese in 1418.

MONTENEGRO: the Italian translation of the Slavic name meaning *dark mountain,* Lat. **montem nigrum.**

MONTEVIDEO: The story goes that when Magellan sailed up the Plata river he saw a hill rising behind the harbor and called out "monte-video," *i.e.,* **montem video,** *I see a mountain,* and thus gave the name to the country.

NATAL: The Port. 'dia de Natal' is the Lat. **dies natalis,** *the natal day,* the *birthday* (of Christ), *Christmas.* This part of the south African coast was discovered by Vasco da Gama on Christmas Day, 1497, and named by him **Terra Natalis.**

[1] *National Geographic Magazine,* XVII, 6, 364; XVII, 10, 587.

NEVADA: Spanish for *snowy*, corresponding to the Lat. **nivata,** pf. pple. form (107), the Latin, however, meaning *cooled with snow.* The name suggests the snow-covered mountains of the state.

PIEDMONT: The two French words 'pied' and 'mont' are the Lat. **ped(em)** and **mont(em),** or **pedem montis,** *foot of the mountain* (cf. Eng. 'foothills').

PROVENCE: This name of southeastern France is the French spelling of **provincia,** the region having become a Roman PROV- INCE in the second century B.C.

RIO GRANDE: The Latin represented in the Spanish name is **rivum grandem,** *great stream.*

RIVIERA: Italian meaning *coast*, particularly the coast of the Gulf of Genoa, Lat. **riparia,** neut. pl., *parts along the bank,* **ripa** (see RIVER, 26).

SALVADOR: Spanish spelling of the Lat. **salvator,** *savior*, the Span- iards thus naming the country in honor of Christ, the Savior. SAN SALVADOR, **Sanctus Salvator,** *Holy Savior.*

SARAGOSSA: When this Spanish town (the ancient Salduba) was made a military colony, the Romans named it **Caesarea Augusta,** of which SARAGOSSA is a Spanish corruption.

TRINIDAD: the Spanish form of the Lat. **trinitat(em),** TRINITY. There rise from the sea what appear from a distance to be three islands. As Columbus on his third voyage came near, he dis- covered that the three were one and the same land; hence an emblem of the TRINITY.

VERA CRUZ: the *True Cross*, Lat. **vera crux,** Cortez having named the place 'Villa Rica de la Vera Cruz,' *the Rich City of the True Cross.*

VERDUN: The French thus modified VERO-dunum (**Viro**-dunum), *man-hill;* **vir,** *man,* and 'dunum,' a Celtic word for *hill,* Eng. 'dune.'

VERMONT: The Fr. 'vert,' *green,* with 'mont,' *mountain,* would be Lat. **viridem montem,** *green mountain.*

216. The Roman year from which we have received the names of our months had originally, we are told, ten months. King Numa is credited with having changed the number to twelve. The old year began with March and the names of

the months were adjectives agreeing with the noun **mensis,**
month, expressed or understood.

MARCH, our representation of the Lat. **Martius,** *belonging to Mars,*
the Roman god of war.

APRIL, the adjective **aprilis,** probably **ap(e)rilis** (cf. 159), from
aperire, *open* (114), *the month of opening,* the *opening* of the earth
for the growth of vegetation.

MAY, from **Maius,** *belonging to Maia,* the root of whose name is the
same as appears in **magnus,** meaning *be strong, increase.* The
Grk. 'Maia,' (Μαîα), mother of Hermes (Mercury) is of different
origin (cf. **mamma,** 52).

JUNE, **Junius.** The claim which Juno makes in Ovid, *Fasti,* 6, 26,
that the name was given in her honor, is commonly allowed,
though some would connect it merely with the clan name
Junius.

JULY, **Julius.** This month was first called **Quintilis** (100), from
quintus, *fifth, the fifth month,* counting from March; but after
the death of Julius Caesar, the name was changed to **Julius** in
his honor and has come to us as JULY.

AUGUST, **Augustus.** In like manner this was the *sixth* month,
called **Sextilis** (100), from **sextus,** *sixth,* but in recognition of
the victories of Augustus Caesar the name was changed to
Augustus, AUGUST, in 8 B.C.

SEPTEMBER, OCTOBER, NOVEMBER, DECEMBER. These Latin
names we have kept, designating the *seventh, eighth, ninth,* and
tenth months of the old Roman year, the numerals **septem, octo,
novem,** and **decem** adding the adjective suffix -**ber.**

JANUARY. The adjective **Januarius** was made from **Janus** (101),
the name of an old Italian deity, the god of beginnings, having
charge of the door (**janua**), and, being literally two-faced, able
to look out and in at the same time. His month was the beginning of the new cycle of the sun after the winter solstice, and
with the reform of the calendar under Julius Caesar (B.C. 45),
became the beginning of the year.

FEBRUARY. On the fifteenth of this month the Romans celebrated
a festival called **Februa** or **Februalia,** *i.e., the feast of Purification,*
to free themselves from the sins of the whole year just closing.

Februum was a Sabine word for purification, and from this the adjective **Februarius** was made (101).

217. At the risk of trespassing on scientific territory we may just mention here the names of the signs of the Zodiac, those Latin names which still lend dignity to the introductory page of the patent medicine almanac. "Zodiac," from the Greek means *relating to animals,* referring to the animals pictured in certain constellations by the very lively imagination of the ancients. These constellations lie along a belt of the sky having the apparent path of the sun as its middle line, the twelve constellations or Signs of the Zodiac; however, five of the twelve have no proper place in a menagerie.

Aries, *the Ram*	**Scorpio,** *the Scorpion*
Taurus, *the Bull*	**Sagittarius,** *the Archer* (**sagitta,**
Gemini, *the Twins*	*an arrow*)
Cancer, *the Crab*	**Capricornus** (*goat-horned*), *the*
Leo, *the Lion*	*Goat*
Virgo, *the Virgin*	**Aquarius,** *the Water-bearer*
Libra, *the Balance*	**Pisces,** *the Fishes*

218. Freer than other names, less amenable to law than other derivatives, are those commercial or trade names which crowd our magazine pages, stare at us from the show windows, and speak to us from the billboards. Their Latin is sometimes picturesque, whimsical, unwarranted; many of them will pass away and come no more, a few may eventually have place in accepted English.

Some such words are genuine Latin though far removed from a Latin application: **Corona,** the *crown* of the typewriters; **Duplex,** *twofold* (53), whether razor blades, vacuum cleaners, or safety pins; **Lux,** the *light* which shines in the laundry; **Sanitas,** *wholesomeness,* even in a wall covering; **Velox,** the *swift* photographic paper; **Vertex,** the *vertical* file; not to mention the use of names of Roman mythology, as **Venus** pencils, **Vesta** batteries, and **Hercules** tires and overalls. Another group are Latin of a very recent coinage: ABSORBINE, a liniment name combining the verb with the suffix -ina; AQUA VELVA, the adjective evidently from the Eng. 'velvet,' denoting the *smoothness* of the shaving preparation; CELOTEX (**texere**), the *cell-woven* building material; CUTICURA, which *cares for the skin* (**cutis**) or *cures* it; RESINOL, **resina**, RESIN, and **oleum**, OIL, for salve or soap; STABILATOR, from **stabilis**, STABLE, a *steadier* of very Latin appearance; UNGUENTINE, an *ointment* (**unguentum**) with the -ina suffix; VICTROLA, a diminutive ending (68) combined with **victor**. Then there are the hybrids, which are always with us: CELLOglass or FLEXOglass, according as glass is CELL-made (**cella**) or FLEXIBLE (**flectere, flexus**); the DUofold pen; Orthosonic, a Greek and Latin *right-sounding* (**sonus**) radio; PEPSODENT, likewise linking Greek and Latin to connect *digestion* with *teeth* (**dens**); REXall remedies, *i.e.*, *king*-of-all; TANLAC, *bark-milk*, Teutonic *bark* and Latin *milk* (**lac**); and TARVIA, which puts even more than *tar* on the Latin *road* (**via**). So does the very practical and utilitarian business world look to Latin for striking and expressive names.

219. Naturally associated with our adopted Latin alphabet are the Roman numeral signs which we still preserve. One explanation of the signs I, V, and X has been that, as primitive Romans counted on their fingers, I was a single finger (cf. DIGIT for a single figure in Arabic notation, **digitus**, *finger*, 227), then II, III, IIII (as on old clocks), and the fingers separated from the thumb gave V; this doubled by joining the two hands made X. Whatever influence counting on the fingers may have had, the single stroke would naturally be used for one, and it is probable that V was merely the half of X, the Greek character adopted to denote 10. Of the Chalcidic form of the alphabet which was introduced into Italy, three characters were used by the Romans for numerals only: the *th*-sign ⊗ or ⊙ for 100, the *ch*-sign Ψ or ⊥ for 50, and the *ph*-sign ⅅ for 1000. The character ☉, written also C and C, was easily regarded as the first letter of **Centum.** The ⊥ denoting 50 came to be written L and the half of ⅅ was D, 500. And since from an early time M·P had been an abbreviation for **mille passus** (MILE, 6), the character ⅅ, written more freely ᴍ, in the second century of this era was identified with M as an abbreviation of **Mille,** a thousand.

These numeral signs were widely used in Europe even until the invention of printing in the fifteenth century, when for the most part they gave way to the Arabic figures which are now common.

Part III

COGNATE WORDS

CHAPTER I

COGNATE WORDS

220. The preceding chapters have dealt with English as borrowing from Latin, that neighborly disposition of our language to profit by association with that of the Romans. We must now add that these languages have been more than neighbors, that they are indeed blood relations. Far back in primitive times the ancestors of Romans and of Teutons, of Greeks also, of Hindus, Persians, Armenians, Slavs, and Celts, lived as one general people, probably in various groups and with different dialects of one general language. This great family, later to occupy the vast stretch of country from India to the most westward parts of Europe, we call the Indo-European family, and the language which they had in common, the Indo-European language. Where they lived originally, whether in southwestern Asia, as has long been thought, or in eastern or northern Europe, as some would have us believe, when, how, and why they migrated, are questions we are fortunately not called upon here to answer. But their kinship is abundantly proved in the words they have carried along from the common vocabulary of their old-time home.

221. We say **fero** means *I bear*, but the connection of **fero** and **bear** is more than identity of meaning. Our infinitive was formerly spelled 'ber-an'; **fer-** in Latin, **ber-** in English. Compare also **sed-ere** and **set**, or **corn-u** and **horn**. Such words are called cognates (*kin*), whereas the derived word in English actually takes over the Latin, as in INFER, SED-ENTARY, and CORN-ET (*a little horn*). Observe further that *f* of **fero**, and *b* of **bear** are both lip-sounds (labials), that *d* of **sedere** and *t* of **set** are both made with the end of the tongue just back of the upper teeth (dentals[1]), that *c* of **cornu** and *h* of **horn** (cf. *ch* of Scotch 'loch') are both made from the palate (palatals[2]). In each group are voiceless stops and voiced stops (146), while an expulsion of breath with these stops produced the Indo-European aspirates *ph*, *dh*, *kh*, etc. The phonetic value of these may be illustrated in such English words as 'uphold,' 'goodhearted,' 'packhorse,' while the corresponding fricatives *f*, *th* (θ), *h* (χ), of Latin and English words, were of later development.

222. Now such correspondences as we find in **fer-** and **bear**, corn- and **horn**, sed- and **set**, we must believe, are not accidental, especially when the same shifts of consonants are repeated in scores of words. They mean that certain Indo-European words came down through the centuries among a people finally settling in Italy as **fer-, corn-,** and **sed-,** while among a group settling in north Europe and eventually in Britain, these same words became **bear, horn,** and **set**. The alteration of original consonant sounds, as indicated here for English, belongs to what is called the first (Germanic or Teutonic) consonant shift.[3] The law of such regular consonant changes was set forth in the second edition of the first part of a German grammar published in 1822 by Jacob Grimm, the great German scholar, and has come to be known as Grimm's Law.[4]

---

[1] Strictly alveolars.

[2] 'Palatal' properly applies to sounds in which the breath obstruction is made by the middle part of the tongue with the hard palate (written below $\hat{k}$, $\hat{g}$, $\hat{g}h$); corresponding sounds in which the interference is made by the base of the tongue with the soft palate (**velum**) are called velars (less correctly gutturals; indicated here by *k, g, gh*).

[3] In the fifth century of this era occurred the second (High German) shift, which does not concern us here.

[4] A Danish scholar, R. K. Rask (1789–1832) and perhaps others before his time had observed the same thing. The law is Grimm's in that he was first to present it fully and scientifically.

For easy comparison of the English and the Latin representations of these Indo-European consonants,[1] they may be arranged thus:

	Ind.-Eur. Voiceless Stops	Ind.-Eur. Voiced Stops	Ind.-Eur. Voiced Aspirates
Labials:	p ⟨ Lat. p / Eng. f	b ⟨ Lat. b / Eng. p	bh ⟨ Lat. f-, -b- / Eng. b
Dentals:	t ⟨ Lat. t / Eng. th	d ⟨ Lat. d / Eng. t	dh ⟨ Lat. f-, -d-, (-b- if influenced by r)[2] / Eng. d

Palatals: $\hat{k}$	Lat. c	$\hat{g}$	Lat. g	$\hat{g}h$	Lat. h (g before or after consonant)[3]
Velars: k	Eng. h	g	Eng. c, k, ck	gh	Eng. g, y

In this table, underneath each sound indicated for a Latin word, will be found the corresponding sound of the English cognate, if there be one: f of **ferre** or **forare** (PER-FORATE), b of **bear** or **bore;** d of **sedere**, t of **set;** t of **tres**, th of **three;** c of **cornu**, h of **horn;** g of **ager**, c of **acre.** Cognates often have not the same but related meanings, as **ager** and **acre.**

223. Other examples are the following (listed in alphabetical order of the English):

[1] The voiceless aspirates are omitted here since they were extremely rare in Indo-European and fell together with other sounds in both the Latin and the Germanic group. The outline has been further simplified by omission of the labio-velars (k^w, g^w, g^wh), which would call for fuller treatment than this brief chapter should attempt.

f- means initial f; -b-, -d-, medial b, d.

$\hat{g}$ and g, also generally $\hat{k}$ and k, $\hat{g}h$ and gh, as the braces indicate, are not distinguished either in Latin or in English.

[2] Also -$dhlo$-, Lat. -$bulu$-.   [3] $\hat{g}h$, Lat. f before u.

flagrare: *black;* **flag-rare,** *burn,* Eng. FLAGRANT; **flag-** apparently
the same as Eng. *black* (as the result of burning).

edere: *eat; d,* remaining in **ed-,** becomes Eng. *t;* and the English
infinitive was once *et-*an, later *eat.*

patere: *fathom;* **pat-ere,** *lie open, lie stretched out;* the change of
p to *f* and *t* to *th* gives *fath,* with suffix, *fath*om, the *out-stretched*
(arms), *i.e.,* six feet.

penna: *feather.* **Penna** is for **pet-(s)na** (cf. **-nus, -anus, -ina**), **pet-**
being a form of an old root meaning *to fly,* as in **petere,** *seek, i.e.,*
fly after. Setting aside the suffixes we find 'pet' becoming *feth*
(*feath*).

pecus: *fee.* **Pec-us** (n.) was *a herd of cattle,* which in primitive
times constituted a basis of wealth; **pecus** (fem.), *a single head*
(cf. PECUNIARY, 202). For English, 'pek̂-' is *feh,* but the breath
sound was lost and *fe* was spelled *fee.*

pro: *for;* **pro,** *before, in place of, in behalf of,* with interchange of
ro we have *for,* also *fore.*

capere: *heave; to take* and *to take up; c* and *p* corresponding to *h*
and *v* (like *f*). It was the *-j-* of the Teutonic 'hafj-' (= **i** of **capio**)
which brought about the change of vowel for the English
word.

noscere: *know.* The root of **noscere** is **gno-, -sc-** making a pres.
stem (131). The *g* is retained in compounds, as **cognoscere,** but
as mentioned above (152), omitted in the simple verb on account
of the difficulty of pronunciation, exactly as we do not pronounce
the *k* of *know;* 'ĝno,' Lat. **gno,** Eng. *kno, w* being a vanish for *o.*

lassus: *late.* **Lassus,** *weary,* is made of **lad-** with the **-tus** suffix,
lad-tus becoming **lassus** (147); *d* shifts to *t,* and the *weary* man
is *late.*

nepos: *nephew;* the latter a modification of the Fr. 'neveu,' but
the Anglo-Saxon word was 'nefa.' The Latin meant *grandson,*
later also *nephew.*

dicere: *teach.* The older form of the Latin word was **deic-ere;**
the shift of *d* and *k̂* would give *t* and *(c)h,* and the Teutonic root
was 'tih' (Gothic 'teih-an'), but in Anglo-Saxon *c* appears for
the second consonant ('taecan'), later changed to our *ch.*

tumor: *thumb.* The root of **tumor, tumere, tumidus, tuber,** etc.
means *swell;* the *b* of *thumb* is a finishing sound for the final *m*

(AS 'thuma'); *t* changed to *th* and the **thumb** is but *a swollen finger*.

duo: *two;* *d* has become *t;* we spell it with double *u* (*w*) instead of *u*.

videre: *wit;* **vid-** is *wit;* *wit* is properly *knowledge*, and *seeing* is *knowing*.

jugum: *yoke.* Original *g* became *k* and the Gothic had 'juk,' which in Anglo-Saxon was written 'geoc' or 'gioc' (*ge* or *gi* with the *y*-sound); thus came Eng. *yoke.*

224. A root sometimes had different forms, and the kinship between Latin and English words may thus be disguised:

findere: *bite.* The inserted *n* for a Latin pres. stem is quite common; the perfect of this verb is **fidi,** its pf. pple. **fissus** for **fid-tus** (147). So we really have the root **fid,** *cut, split*, and the corresponding Eng. *bite* (AS 'bit-an').

frangere: *break.* The *n* again makes a pres. stem; **fractus** is for **frag-tus,** and the root is **frag** ('bhrag̑'), as also in **fragilis,** FRAGILE; the shift of *bh* and *g̑* gives 'brak,' the English either *break* or *brake.*

granum: *corn.* For *corn* as a single grain, cf. "Except a corn of wheat fall into the ground" (John 12 : 24); *g̑* here has become *c* and from different root-forms 'g̑er,' 'g̑or,' 'g̑r,' we have difference of vowel position in **gran-** and *corn.* A CORN on the foot is derived from Lat. **cornu** and thus cognate with *horn* (221).

pes, pedis: *foot.* The Indo-European had two forms of the stem, 'ped' and 'pod' (157); Latin extended **ped** to all cases, Greek 'pod' (cf. BI-PED and 'tri-pod'). Corresponding to 'pod' is the AS 'fōt,' spelled in Mid. Eng. as 'fot' or *foot.*

prehendere: *get.* The Latin verb has the inserted nasal, the root syllable being **-hed-** ('ghed'), *seize;* for English, *gh* and *d* became *g* and *t,* **hed** is *get.* The literal meaning of the Latin, *get hold of,* we have in the derivative adj. PREHENSILE (205), the figurative meaning in APPREHEND (198). Note also **praeda,** PREY, *booty,* probably **prae** + **hed-a,** *what is got beforehand.*

cella: *hall;* original 'k̂al' appearing in Latin as **cel,** and meaning, as in **celare,** *cover* or *conceal;* 'k̂al' became *hall, a covered* (or *covering?*) *place.*

collis: *hill;* *c* and *h* from *k;* and the vowel varied, *o* in **collis**, *u* in **cul-men**, *top*, (cf. CULMINATE, *reach a peak*), *e* in **cel-sus**, *lofty*, and Anglo-Saxon had *y*, 'hyll.'

genus: *kin;* *ĝ* changing to *k*, the root 'ĝon,' 'ĝen,' 'ĝn,' *beget*, suggesting *race* or *birth*, appeared in Gothic 'kuni,' AS 'cynn,' and our **kin**. Of the same origin the adjective **kind** denotes a quality characteristic of those of the same birth, while the noun **kind** means sort or class based on natural (inborn) qualities.

tenuis: *thin;* 'ten-' ('ton,' 'tn') meant *stretch*, and became Eng. **thin**, *i.e.*, **thin** because *stretched out*. **Tendere**, English derivative TEND (also ATTEND, INTEND, etc.) carries the same meaning of *stretch toward*, as also the Lat. **tener**, Eng. TENDER, since what is *stretched out* and **thin** is weak or delicate. From **tenuis** came **extenuare**, Eng. EXTENUATE, *make quite thin; extenuating* circumstances make the charge against one *thin*.

tonare: *thunder;* different vowels from different root forms; *t* becomes *th*, and since the noun (from which we use the verb) was 'thunor,' the *d* is plainly a development between *n* and *r* (154).

225. In a number of cognate words of Latin and English the law thus illustrated seems not to hold. The word *father* looks like an excellent example when compared with **pater**, *p* and *f*, *t* and *th*, but when we refer to our older English we find *faeder*, and likewise cognate with **mater** is *modor*, then *moder*. In fact *fader* and *moder* continued in use till after the time of Chaucer. An original *t* has changed to *d*, and not to *th*. The explanation of this was given by Karl Verner in 1875, that if the original Indo-European word was accented on any other than the syllable next preceding the changing consonant, the *p*, *t*, or *c*, within the word, became in Germanic the voiced stops *b*, *d*, *g*. The originals of **pater** and **mater**, as we know from Sanskrit, were accented on the last syllable; hence the change to *fader* (*faeder*) and *moder* (*modor*). What then of 'father' and 'mother' with *th?* The original of **frater** had its accent on the first syllable, and following Grimm's law exactly became **brother**. Clearly *fader* and *moder* after the fourteenth century adopted the *th* of *brother*, the influence spreading in the family. A very common accented final syllable was the adjective or participle suffix *-to-* appearing in Lat. **-tus** (*i.e.*, **-to-s**), and this *t* accordingly appears in English as *d*. This is the *-d* (*-ed*) of our passive participle. Note also the following:

crates: *hurdle.* The root which gave **crat-es,** *wickerwork*, meant *weave*, and had various forms, here 'krat,' Grk. 'kart,' and 'kurt' (κυρτία), *wickerwork;* so the shifts made 'hurd' when the accent followed, and the *-le* (earlier *-el*) is a diminutive suffix. The Engglish derivative is CRATE.

in-clutus: *loud.* In-clutus (Grk. 'klutos', κλυτός), meant *renowned* (*talked loudly about,* **cluere,** *hear, hear oneself spoken of*)*;* so 'klut' became AS 'hlud,' which later lost its aspiration and was altered to *loud.*

sat-is: *sad.* The root meant *satisfy*, and *-t* represents the *-to* suffix; *t* again becomes Eng. *d.* **Sad** thus meant *having had enough, surfeited, weary of life.* The heaviness is transferred from the spirit to material things (199), and we may have a '*sad* cake' or a '*sad* iron.'

hortus: *yard.* Hortus, *a garden*, meant *enclosed;* then *an enclosure;* ĝh became *g*, O. Sax. 'gard,' AS 'geord' or 'geard,' later to be spelled *yard.* The older 'gard,' borrowed by Mediæval Latin, came back through French into English as 'garden.'

226. Another reason for apparent violations of the general rule is that protection from change was afforded certain sounds by their union with other sounds. So, *sk* (*sc*), *st* did not change, and in *pt*, *kt* (*ct*), *t* remained unchanged:

piscis: *fish.* Our *f* corresponds to Lat. *p* and the Anglo-Saxon word was 'fisc,' altered afterward into *fish.*

hostis: *guest.* Hostis was *an enemy*, properly *a stranger;* *gh* became Eng. *g*, written *gu* to preserve the hard sound, the vowel varied (AS 'gast' and 'gaest' as well as 'gest'), and *t* was preserved by *s*. The enemy is commonly a foreigner, the *guest* is a stranger, and **hostis** is *guest* (cf. HOST, 202).

nox, noctis: *night.* The vowel was *a* in Gothic ('nahts'), becoming *ea, e,* and *i* in Anglo-Saxon; hence with *k* shifting and *t* preserved **noct-**('nokt') was '*niht*' in Old and Mid. Eng., later spelled *night.*

in-stigare: *stick;* **in-stig-are,** *to prick, spur on,* INSTIGATE; so *stick* was to *pierce, thrust in,* and as a noun a *stick* was for piercing or punching (cf. **stimulus,** 52). What is *thrust in* may *hold fast* and give rise to another meaning of *stick. St* remained, original *g* became *k* (*ck*).

stringere: *strike;* **stringere,** *bind,* also *graze, stroke, strike gently;* the *n* is inserted for the pres. stem, the root being **strig;** English keeps the *st,* while *g* shifted to *k.*

227. The alteration of certain sounds after a word had already come into Anglo-Saxon or later English has been referred to in connection with a word or two above. In a number of instances the modern form wears a disguise of this kind and only after being questioned acknowledges its relations; so the following:

flos, floris: *blossom, bloom;* **flo, blo;** to the latter in Anglo-Saxon were added two suffixes '-st' and '-ma,' making 'blostma,' which became *blossom,* while other Teutonic languages added only '-ma,' and 'blo-ma' gave rise to Eng. *bloom.* The same root is in Eng. *blow,* meaning *flourish* or *grow;* a full-*blown* rose is one *fully flowered.*

fugere: *bow.* Lat. *f* is our *b;* and for the AS 'bug-an' (infin.) Middle English wrote 'bugen,' 'bogen,' and 'bowen,' whence *bow.* The Indo-European root was 'bheugh' or 'bheuĝ,' the latter accounts for Lat. **fug-,** the former for Eng. 'bug-.' As to meaning cf. *bow, bend, give way, flee.*

gena: *chin.* **Gena,** *cheek,* should appear in English with *c* (*k*) for *g;* so it did, for the Anglo-Saxon word was *cin(n),* the spelling with *ch* occurring only from the thirteenth century.

homo: *groom.* The *r* of *groom* in the compound bride*groom* is evidently a mistake, possibly introduced from the word 'bride.' The Anglo-Saxon was 'bryd-guma,' *bride-man.* The **hom-** of **homo,** *man,* **hem-** of **nemo** for **ne-hemo,** *no-man,* **hum-** of **huma-**

nus, HUMAN, was *gum-* of *guma*. *Groom* meaning *servant* may be of the same origin, with *r* introduced from some other influence.

mors, mortis: *murder*. **Mort-,** *death*, our table tells us, should correspond to *morth*, which actually occurred in Old Saxon, while Anglo-Saxon added a suffix making 'morthor.' In Middle English this became 'morder' (and 'murther'); then *murder*.

dacrima: *tear*. **Dacrima** was an older form for **lacrima**, *tear*. To omit the suffix, **dacr-** corresponds to 'tahr,' and with loss of *h* AS 'taer' or *tear*.

tegere: *thatch*. **Tegere** was *to cover*, **tectum (teg-tum)** *a covering, shelter,* or *roof*. With variation of vowel '(s)teg' became 'thak,' which is found in Middle English, later altered to *thatch*.

torrere: *thirst*. Variation of the vowel is shown in the Lat. **torrere,** *be hot and dry*, and **terra,** *dry land* (157)*;* and these were for '**torsere**' and '**tersa.**' This root 'tors,' 'ters,' 'trs,' we keep in *thirst*, the final *t* being a remnant of an old Teutonic suffix.

domus: *timber*. The root occurring in **dom-us,** *house*, meant *build; d* became Eng. *t;* the *-er* was the English agent suffix, and *b* was a sound developed (epenthetic) between *m* and *r* (cf. 174)*;* **dom-us** then is *a building*, and *timber* is *a builder*.

digitus: *toe*. The *g* of **digitus**, *finger, toe*, was a modification of an older *k* or *c* ('decetos')*;* this 'dek̂' (also 'dak̂') was represented by Teutonic 'tah,' probably 'tahe,' which lost the *h* and contracted into AS 'tā,' changing later to *toe*. As meaning *a figure*, DIGIT relates to counting on the fingers. Cf. **dic-ere,** *say, point out*, and the "index finger."

228. Variation or development of vowel sounds may also sometimes help to obscure the origin of a word, as in the following:

flare: *blow*. *Bh* became Lat. *f*, Eng. *b*, **flā-** is *blo(w)*, AS blaw-an, Mid. Eng. 'blawen' or 'blowen.'

fagus: *book;* *ā* becoming AS *ō* (cf. **frater,** *brother*), bhāĝ (Lat. **fag**) became 'bōc,' the Anglo-Saxon word which later was written *book*. The use of a slab of beech-wood, or the beech bark, to write on is the explanation of the meaning. Cf. **liber,** LIBRARY, 71. 'Beech' itself is still another form of the same word.

purus: *fire*. It seems that from a root meaning cleanse the Latin got **pur-us**, PURE (Grk. 'pyr,' $\pi\hat{v}\rho$, *fire*); *p* shifted to *f;* then AS 'fyr' became *fire, a purifying agent.* Cf. **purgo, pur(i)go, pur** + **ago.**

anser: *goose.* From the Lat. **anser** had been lost an initial *h,* original *ĝh;* this should give us *gans,* but *n* was dropped and with *ā* becoming *ō* we have AS '*gōs*'; Mid. Eng. changed it to 'goos' and now we have added an *e.* With the suffix '-ra,' 'ganra' developed a *d*-sound (cf. 174), became AS 'gandra,' and our *gander.*

cor, cordis: *heart.* Lat. **cord-** (Grk. 'kard-,' $\kappa\alpha\rho\delta$-*ία*); the shift of $\hat{k}$ to *h,* and *d* to *t,* gave AS 'heorte,' and modern *heart.*

canere: *hen.* Our word in Anglo-Saxon was 'hen' or 'haen,' formed from 'hana,' *a cock,* from the same origin as **can-,** *sing,* *k* changing to *h.* The **hen,** or at any rate the 'hana,' is a *singer.* Cf. also the derived word CHANTICLEER (Fr.), *singing clearly.*

mulgere: *milk.* The vowel varies: Lat. **mulg-,** Grk. 'melg-' ($\mu\epsilon\lambda\gamma$-ω), 'meolc' in Anglo-Saxon, *ĝ* having become *c,* later *k.* With the Grk. *e,* AS *eo,* also Dutch and Danish 'melk,' compare the tendency on the part of some to pronounce the English word as 'melk.'

sudor: *sweat.* Lat. **sud-** represents 'swoid' (Sanskrit 'sved'); *d* became *t,* and 'swoid' *sweat.*

domare: *tame.* The **dom-** of **domare,** *tame,* is in Greek (and Sanskrit) 'dam' ($\delta\alpha\mu$-$\acute{\alpha}\zeta\omega$); *d* shifting to *t* gives Eng. *tame.* In DAUNT, UNDAUNTED, INDOMITABLE, we have borrowed from the Lat. **domitare,** *subdue,* on the same root.

tu: *thou.* *Thou* was Middle English, but AS *thu;* original *t* has become *th.*

dens, dentis: *tooth.* Lat. **dent-** (Grk. 'odont-' $\dot{o}\delta o\nu\tau$-) corresponds to Teutonic 'tanth' *d, t,* and *t, th;* then came the loss of *n* and the change of the lengthened vowel to *o,* making 'toth,' Middle English having both 'toth' and *tooth* (cf. **gans,** 'gos,' *goose*).

vehere: *wagon.* The 'veĝh' of **vehere,** *carry,* changing *ĝh* to *g* became 'wag' in the Dutch 'wagen,' from which our word was borrowed. Anglo-Saxon, however, had 'waegn' which became *wain.* Lat. **vehiculum,** *a carrier,* we have adopted as the more general term VEHICLE (91).

CONCLUSION

The story of Latin words in English has been told only in part. The number of examples in most of the lists given could be multiplied. The course of many a word's development might be studied in greater detail. Low Latin and Old French have much to say that could not be included in our account. The scientist must know a thousand terms purposely omitted from these pages, and the lawyer revels in Latin which has been mentioned here but briefly. Nor need we think that our borrowing from the Roman treasure house has ended; the years that come will bring occasions for new words and doubtless we shall supply our need over and over again from this same source. The derivatives which we have now examined should suffice to convince us that Latin is not dead, that all language lives and grows with the life of men and the growth of institutions, that words partake of the nature of their users, that they have character and personality. And in this conviction perhaps some reader may be inspired to a further and fuller study of subjects here suggested; and it is hoped that many will find a new and happy interest in the common words of our everyday life.

BIBLIOGRAPHY

BENNETT, CHARLES E., *The Latin Language*. New York: Allyn and Bacon, 1907.

BOURCIEZ, E., *Précis Historique de Phonétique Française*. Paris: Librairie C. Klincksieck, 1930.

BRACHET, A., *Grammaire Historique de la Langue Française*. Paris: J. Hertzel et Cⁱᵉ.

BRADLEY, HENRY, *The Making of English*. New York: The Macmillan Co., 1913.

BRUNOT, F., *Histoire de la Langue Française*, Tome I, Ch. I, II. Paris: A. Colin, 1917.

CONWAY, R. S., *The Making of Latin*. London: John Murray, 1923.

EARLE, JOHN, *Philology of the English Tongue*. Oxford: The Clarendon Press, 1871.

EMERSON, O. F., *History of the English Language*. New York: The Macmillan Co., 1895.

FREEMAN, E. A., *History of the Norman Conquest*. Oxford: The Clarendon Press, 1869–79.

GRANDGENT, C. H., *An Introduction to Vulgar Latin*. Boston: D. C. Heath and Co., 1907.

—— *From Latin to Italian*. Cambridge: Harvard University Press, 1927.

GREENOUGH, J. B., and KITTREDGE, G. L., *Words and Their Ways in English Speech*. Boston: Ginn and Co., 1906.

JESPERSEN, OTTO, *Growth and Structure of the English Language*. Leipzig: B. G. Teubner, 1905.

JOHNSON, C. F., *English Words*. New York: Harper and Brothers, 1891.

KENT, R. G., *Language and Philology*. Boston: Marshall Jones Co., 1923.

LEUMANN, M., und HOFMANN, J. B., *Stolz-Schmalz Lateinische Grammatik*. München: C. H. Beck'sche Verlagsbuchhandlung, 1928.

LINDSAY, W. M., *The Latin Language.* Oxford: The Clarendon Press, 1894.

LOUNSBURY, T. R., *History of the English Language.* New York: Henry Holt and Co., 1887.

MARSH, G. P., *Lectures on the English Language.* New York: Scribner's, 1860.

—— *Origin and History of the English Language.* New York: Scribner's, 1862.

McKNIGHT, G. H., *English Words and Their Background.* New York: D. Appleton and Co., 1923.

MEYER-LÜBKE, W., *Romanisches Etymologisches Wörterbuch.* Heidelberg: Carl Winter's Universitätsbuchhandlung, 1911.

MORRIS, RICHARD, *Historical Outlines of English Accidence.* (Revised by L. KELLNER, assisted by H. BRADLEY.) New York: The Macmillan Co., 1903.

MÜLLER, F., *Altitalisches Wörterbuch.* Vandenhoeck & Ruprecht, Göttingen, 1926.

MURRAY, SIR JAMES A. H., *A New English Dictionary.* Oxford: The Clarendon Press, 1888–1928.

PIDAL, R. MENÉNDEZ, *Manual de Gramática Histórica Española.* Madrid: Librería General de Victoriano Suárez, 1918.

ROEMER, JEAN, *The Origin of the English People and the English Language.* New York: D. Appleton and Co., 1888.

SCOTT, H. F., and CARR, W. L., *The Development of Language.* Chicago: Scott, Foresman and Co., 1921.

SKEAT, W. W., *An Etymological Dictionary of the English Language.* Oxford: The Clarendon Press, 1882.

—— *Principles of Etymology*, First Series and Second Series. Oxford: The Clarendon Press, 1891–1892.

—— *The Science of Etymology.* Oxford: The Clarendon Press, 1912.

STURTEVANT, E. H., *Linguistic Change.* Chicago: University of Chicago Press, 1917.

SWEET, HENRY, *New English Grammar*, Part I. The Clarendon Press, 1900; Oxford University Press, 1903.

The English-Latin Debt. Chicago: Syntactic Book Co., 1928.

TRENCH, R. C., *English Past and Present.* New York: E. P. Dutton, 1905.

—— *On the Study of Words*, (Supplée's ed.). Revised by A. L. MAY-HEW. New York: A. C. Armstrong and Co., 1907.

—— *Select Glossary*. New York: The Macmillan Co., 1879.

VANIČEK, ALOIS, *Etymologisches Wörterbuch der Lateinischen Sprache*. Leipzig: B. G. Teubner, 1881.

WALDE, ALOIS, *Lateinisches Etymologisches Wörterbuch*. Heidelberg: Carl Winter's Universitätsbuchhandlung, 1910.

WEEKLEY, ERNEST, *Etymological Dictionary of Modern English*. New York: E. P. Dutton, 1921.

—— *The Romance of Words*. New York: E. P. Dutton, 1912.

GENERAL INDEX

(References are to sections.)

a final, Fr. -*e* 161
Abbreviations 60
Ablaut 157
Abstract and concrete 7, 14, 198, 199
Abstract nouns, in -*y* (-*ia*) 74; *see* Nouns made from adjectives
Accent 149, 159; Verner's law 225
Accusative, survival of 158, 160
Action nouns 81–93; *see* Nouns made from verbs
Adjectives, derived, with Eng. nouns 40
  Lat. adopted 53; through Fr. 54
  Made from nouns 94–111
    -al (**-alis**) 98
    -an, -ane, -ain (**-anus**) 103
    -ar (**-aris**) 99
    -ary (**-arius**) 101
    -ate (**-atus**) 107
    -eous, etc. (**-eus**, etc.) 110
    -ern(al), -urn(al), (**-ernus, -urnus**) 108
    -ese, -ensic, (**-ensis**) 109
    -ic, -tic (**-icus, -ticus**) 97
    -il(e) (**-ilis**) 100
    -in(e) (**-inus**) 104, 105
    -(o)lent, -(u)lent (**-olentus, -ulentus**) 106
    -ous (**-osus**) 94–96
    -t, -te, -tous (**-tus**) 111
    -tory, -sory, -torious, sorious (**-torius, -sorius**) 102
  Made from verbs 112–127
    -acious (**-ax**) 119
    -ble (**-bilis**) 116–118
    -id (**-idus**) 112, 113

    -ile (**-ilis**) 114
    -nd (gerundive) 126, 127
    -nt (pres. pple.) 123
    -te, -ate, -ite (pf. pple.) 124, 125
    -t-ed 125
    -tile, -sile (**-tilis, -silis**) 115
    -tive, -sive (**-tivus, -sivus**) 120
    -ulous (**-ulus**) 121
    -uous (**-uus**) 122
Adverbs, Lat. adopted 55
  Prefixes 144, 145, 150, 151
-age (**-aticum**) 177
Agent nouns 80
Alphabet 14–16, 219
Angles 2, 3, 10
Anglo-Saxon 2, et passim; Anglo-Saxons 8
Art, Norman Fr. in 31
Assimilation 146–148, 150, 151, 175–177
Augustine 10, 16
Augustus Caesar 17
Ayenbite of Inwit 24

b becoming *f* (Fr.) 178
Bede 2
Borrowed Latin 59
Britain 1, 3, 9
Britons 1, 2
Burgundians 18

c and *ch* (Fr.) 36, 176 *a*
Caesar: Augustus 17; Claudius 1, 17; Julius 1, 17
Canterbury 10
Canute 20
Cases 160; case-forms adopted 56

Celts 1, 8, 9, 17, 220
Changes, form and meaning 195–202
Charles I 214 (Carolina)
Charles II 214 (Carolina)
Charles IX 214 (Carolina)
Charles the Simple 19
Chaucer, quoted 34
Cheke, Sir John 22
Christianity 10–16, 17
Church words 10, 11
Claudius Caesar 1, 17
Clovis 18
Cognates 220–227
Coined words 77, 144 (prae-) 203–206; see also Hybrids
College mottoes 63
Combination, phonetic 146–156
Compounds 139–143
   Dependent 140
   Descriptive 141
   Hybrid 212
   Possessive 142
   Prepositional 143
   Preposition and verb 144, 145
Concrete and abstract 7, 14, 198, 199
Conquest, Norman 14, 17–36
Consonants, added 154, 174
   Changed 175–179; see Assimilation
   Dropped 152, 153, 173
   Epenthetic 154, 174
   Excrescent 154

Danes 20, 21
Dee (Deva) 8
Degraded meaning 197
Dentals 221, 222
Dependent compounds 140
Descriptive compounds 141
di- becoming j- 176b
Dialects, Fr. 34, 35, 176a
Dignity of meaning 197
Diminutives 68, 69
Diocletian 10 N.

Disguised Latin forms 58
Dissimilation 155
Doublets 39 N.
   Eng.-Fr. 25, 26
   Eng.-Lat. 39
   Eng.-Literary Fr. 41
   French, Dialects 35
      Old-Modern 44
      Popular-Literary 43, 181
   Fr.-Lat. 42
   Legal and religious phrases 27
   see also Variant forms
Dover 1, 8

-e, mute 161, 163, 182, 183
Edward the Confessor 21
-ee from -atum 192
Elevated meaning 197
Emma 21
Epenthesis 154
es- for s- 180
Ethelbert 10
Ethelred 21
Etruscan 15
Euphony 155, 156
Excrescent consonants 154

Figurative meaning 196
Final syllables 161–163
Form, change of 195, 202
Formation of
   Lat. Adjectives 94–127
   Lat. Nouns 68–93
   Lat. Verbs 128–131
Forth 2
France 18
Franks 18, 19
French 19, 22
   Changes from Lat. 158–193
   Dialects 34, 35; see also Doublets
   Words adopted in Eng. 23–35, 194
Frequentative verbs 130
Futhork 15 N.
-fy, verbs in 187, 188

g and *j*, French 176*a*
Gaul, Gauls 1, 17, 18
Generalization of meaning 200
Geographical names 214, 215
Germans 1, 2, 3, 4, 18
Gerundive 126, 127, 191
Goths 18
Gradation of vowels 157
Greek words 10, 11, 33
Greeks 1, 220
Gregory 10
Grimm's Law 220–222

Harold 21
Hastings, Battle of 21
Hengist 2
Henry VII 38
Henry VIII 38
Horsa 2
Hrolf 19
Hybrids 11 (end), 207–212

i, consonantal 15 (p. 16) N., 170, 176*a*
  Before nasal 171
Inchoative verbs 131
Indo-European 1, 220
Infinitive, becoming Eng. noun or verb 185
Inflectional forms as Eng. words 56, 57
Intensive verbs 130
Irish missionaries 10 N., 16
Italian, changes from Lat. 47
  Derivatives 49; through Fr. 36, 48
Ivanhoe, quotation 25

j- and *g*-, Fr. 176*a*
  From *di*- 176*b*
Janus 52 (janitor), 216
Jespersen, quoted 14
John, King 22
Julius Caesar 1, 17
Juno Moneta 6
Jutes 2, 3, 18

l, vocalized 179
Labials 221, 222
Lachmann's Law 147 N. 2
Latin abbreviations 60
  Adjectives in Eng. 53, 54
  Adverbs in Eng. 55
  Inflectional forms in Eng. 56–58
  Mottoes 62, 63
  Nouns adopted 52, 54
  Prepositions in Eng. 55
  Proverbs, etc., 61
  Titles 64–66
  Word formation 67–157
  Words and phrases in Eng. 59–61
Law, Norman Fr. in 30
Legal and religious phrases 27
Lingua Romanica (Romana) 18
Literature, Lat. titles 64
Loss of consonants 152, 173
  Final syllables 162
  Vowels 159

Meaning, change of 195–202
Medical terms, Norman Fr. 33
Mental and physical 198, 199
Missionaries 10, 14, 16
Moneta 6
Months, names of 216
Mottoes, college 63; state 62
Music, Lat. titles 65
Mute -*e* 161, 163, 182, 183

Names
  Geographical 214, 215
  Months 216
  Personal 213
  Signs of Zodiac 217
  Trade 218
Norman Conquest 14, 17–36
Normandy 19, 21, 22, 34, 176*a*
Norman French 19, 22–36
Normans 19, 22
Norsemen 19, 21
Northmen, *see* Norsemen
Nouns, Lat. adopted 52, 58; through Fr. 54

Made from adjectives 72–79
  -acy (**-atia**) 77
  -ce, -cy (**-tia**) 76 (cf. 75)
  -ine (**-ina**) 105
  -mony (**-monia, -monium**) 79
  -nce, -ncy (**-ntia**) 75, 191
  -tude (**-tudo**) 78
  -ty (**-tas, -tat-**) 72, 73, 168
  -y (**-ia**) 74
Made from nouns 68–71
  Diminutives 68, 69
    -culus, -ulus 68
    -lus 69
  Office, -ate (**-atus**) 70
  Place, etc. (**-ius,** etc.) 71
Made from verbs 80–93
  Action, -ble, etc. (**-bulum,**
    etc.) 89, 91, 92
  -ce (**c-ium**) 71, 82, 83
  -c(h)re (**-crum**) 89, 92
  -cle (**-culum**) 89, 91
  -ge (g-**ium**) 71, 82, 83
  -ion 84
  -men 89
  -or 81
  -ter, -tre (**-trum**) 89, 93
  -tion, -sion 85, 86
  -ture, -sure (**-tura, -sura**) 87
  -t, -te, -se etc. (**-tus, -sus**) 88
  -y (**-ium**) 82, 83
  Agent 80
Numa 216
Numeral signs, Roman 219

Office, nouns denoting 70
ou from Lat. *u* 172

Paintings, Lat. titles 66
Palatals 221, 222
Palatalization 170, 176
Parisian Fr. 34, 35
Participles
  Perf. 124, 135
    -ed 125; -ee 192
    making Eng. verbs 132, 133
  Pres. 123, 190

Particular meaning 200, 201
Personal names 213
Petrarch 37
Phrases and sentences, Lat. 61
Phrases, legal and religious 27
Physical and mental 198, 199
Picardy 34, 35, 176*a*
Picts 2
-ply, verbs in 189
Portuguese, derivatives 51
Possessive compounds 142
Prefixes 144, 150; inseparable 145, 151
Prepositional compounds 143
Prepositions, Lat. adopted 55
  Prefixes 144, 150
Pronunciation, Lat. in Eng. 59 N. 1
Prothetic vowel 180 and N.
Proverbs, Lat. in Eng. 61

Quality nouns 72–79; *see* Nouns
  made from adjectives

Rask, R. K. 222 N.
Reformation 38
Religion, Norman Fr. in 32
Religious and legal phrases 27
Renaissance 37
Revival of Learning 37, 38
Rhotacism 156
Richard, Duke 21
Richborough 8
Rollo 19
Romance 18
Romans 1, 8, 220
Rome 1
Roots 67
Runes 15

s- becoming *es-* 180 and N.
s, ss from *dt, tt* 147
Saxons 2, 3
Scandinavians 19, 20
Scots 2
Scott 25
Seres 5

Sermo rusticus, militaris 17
Silent -e, see Mute -e
Songs, Lat. titles 65
Sound combination 146–156
Sound shift 222
Spanish, changes from Lat. 50
    Derivatives 50
Specialization of meaning 201
Spelling of
    Derived nouns and adjectives
        161–163, 193
    Verbs 182–184
State mottoes 62
State, Norman Fr. in 28
Suffixes 67–121, 193, 204, 210, 211
Syllables, Fr., closed 169
    Final 161–163
    Initial 165, 166
    Open 167, 168

t becoming ts, s 176
Tacitus 1
Teutons 220
Titles, Lat. 64–66
Trade names 218
Transfer of meaning 196–202
Triplets 46

University mottoes 63

-v becoming -f 178
Variant forms 45
Verbs, compound 144, 145
    Formation, Eng. 128–138, Lat.
        128–131
        Eng. from Lat. pf. pple. 128,
            130, 134, 136, 137

Lat. forms adopted 57, 58
    Forms in -fy 187, 188; -ish
        186; -ply 189
    From Lat. pres. 129, 135–137,
        182–189
Made from nouns and adjec-
    tives 128, 129
Made from verbs
    Frequentative (intensive) 130
    Inchoative 131
    -sc- 131, 186
Verner's Law 225
Vowel
    Alteration 228
    Gradation 157
    Loss of 159, 161, 162, 164
    Prothetic 180 and N.
    Weakening 149, 150, 151, 159,
        164
Vowels, Fr.
    In accented syllables, closed
        169; open 167, 168
    In final syllables 161–163
    In initial syllables 165, 166
    Influenced by y 170

War, Norman Fr. in 29
Weakening, see Vowels, weakening
    Final syllable 161–164
William of Normandy 21
Word formation 67–157
Writing 14–16

y, see i consonantal
Year, Roman 216

Zodiac, names of signs 217

INDEX OF WORDS

LOAN-WORDS, DERIVATIVES, AND COGNATES

(Numbers refer to pages. Latin words and phrases listed
alphabetically on pages 89–98 are not repeated in the index.)

abbreviate 42
abdomen 63
abduct 176
aberration 128
abhor 206
abject 161
able 152
ablution 128, 233
abnormal 175
abominate 217
aborigines 63
abortive 155
abound 199
abridge 42
abrupt 161
abscond 176
absence 122
absent 122, 158
absolute 168
absolve 168
absorbent 158
Absorbine 274
abstain 176
abstemious 138
abstract, abstracted 162
abundance 122
abundant 122, 158
abuse 176
accede 187, 206
accent 132
accept 174, 185
accession 128
accident 158, 187
accomplish 208

accord 217
accordion 217
accost 222
accumulate 163
accuracy 123
accusative 155
accuse 27, 155, 205
acerbity 40, 118
achieve 255
acid 151, 249
acquaint 240
acquire 187
acquit 241
acre 281
acrid 249
acrimony 124, 192
act (noun) 25, 114
act (verb) 128, 158, 167
action 114, 128
active 114, 156
activity 114
actor 63, 114
actual 114
acumen 63, 133
adapt 206
add 206
adduce 176
adequate 161
adieu 212
adjacent 158
adjust 218
administrator 63
administratrix 63
admirable 153

admire 30, 153
admissible 154
admit 206
admonish 192
adolescent 158, 166
adopt 156, 176
adoptive 156
adore 206
adorn 134, 206
advance 176
advantage 176
advent 132, 176
adventure 259
adversary 117
advise 218
affable 153
affect 128, 187
affection 128
affidavit 83
affinity 218
affirm 206
afflatus 63
afflict 167
age 203
agent 114, 158
aggravate 42, 187
aggregate 175
aggrieve 42
agile 114, 152
agility 114
agitate 114, 166
agitation 114, 128
agitator 63, 114
agree 255
agriculture 22, 171, 251

aid 25
aim 43
aisle 218
alacrity 119
alarm 50
alas 218
albino 60
album 64
albumen 64
alert 50
alias 81
alibi 81
alien 147
alienate 163
alimony 124
aliquot 78
allege 218
alligator 58
allot 256
allow 218
allude 187
alluvial 233, 249
alluvium 233
ally 253
Alma 263
altar 12
alter 205
altercation 128
altimeter 260
altitude 37, 124
alto 51
alumna 64
alumnus 64
Amabel 265
Amanda 263
amanuensis 64, 149
amateur 37, 212
amatory 37
ambidextrous 249
ambiguous 157, 181
ambition 136, 181
ambitious 136
amble 239
ambuscade 58
ambush 58
ameliorate 249

amenity 119
amiable 42, 50
amicable 37, 42, 50
ammunition 130
amount 245
amour 212
ample 124
amplify 208
amplitude 124
amputate 169
Amy 263
ancestor 218
anguish 218
angular 142
animal 64, 115
animalculum, -e 115
animate 64
animated 162
animus 64
annals 140
annex 187
annihilate 94, 175
annoy 218
annoyance 219
annual 42
annul 168
annular 142
ante-bellum 89, 177
antecedent 158, 177
antedate 177, 249
antediluvian 249
antenna 64
anterior 78
anteroom 256
antic 219
anticipate 171 N., 176
antiquary 117
antique 219
antiquity 119
Antony, -ia (Anthony) 263
antrum 64
anxiety 120
anxious 120
aperture 131
apex 64

apiary 117
apparatus 64, 132, 223
apparel 223
appellant 210
appellation 37
appellee 210
appellor 210
appendicitis 258
appendix 64, 258
appetite 132
applaud 154
applause 185
applicant 158
apply 158, 209, 257
apposite 187
appraise 219
appreciate 219
apprehend 216, 219, 283
apprentice 219
approach 202
apricot 239
April 272
apropos 212
apt 53
aptitude 53
aquarium 64, 117
Aquarius 273
aquatic 139
Aqua Velva 274
aqueduct 171
aquiline 147
arable 153
arbiter 64, 144
arbitrary 144
arbor 65
arc 195
arcade 51
arcana 65
arch 195 N.
ardor 126
arduous 138
area 65
arena 65
Argentina 267
argue 133

argument 133
arid 151
Aries 273
armada 58
armadillo 58
armament 133
armature 131
armor 26
arms 26
army 27
around 257
arrears 241
arrive 219
arrogance 122
arrogant 122, 158, 187
art 195, 258
article 115
articulate 115
artifice 117, cf. 127
artificial 140
artist 258
artless 258
asafœtida 260
ascendant (-ent) 210
asinine 147
aspect 132
asperity 119
aspirant 158
aspire 187
assail 27
assault 27, 204
assemble 25
assert 75
assess 157
assessor 65
assiduity 119
assiduous 157
assign 206
assist 187
associate 164
association 121
astral 140
astray 245
astute 150
atrocity 119
attain 188

attend 284
attendant 210
attitude 53
attorney 27
attribute 77
auction 128
auctioneer 143 N.
audacious 155
audit 132
auditor 117, 125
auditorium 65, 117
auditory 145
augur 65, 117, 231
augury 117
august 263
August 272
Augustine 263
Augustus, -a 263
aura 65
aural 39
auricle 115
aurora 65
auspices 117, 219, 231
Austin 263
Australia 267
author 125
authority 26
automobile 260
auxiliary 144
avarice 123
ave 83
avenge 199
aversion 128
avert 176
aviary 117
aviation 249
avidity 119
avocation 176
avoirdupois 212
axis 65

baccalaureate 220
bachelor 196, 219
bacillus 65
balance 197
bankrupt 220

base 66
basis 65
battle 27
bear 279, 280, 281
beast 140
beatitude 124
Beatrice 263
beau 194 N., 212
beauty 29
because 257
beech 287
beef 24, 197
belabor 257
believable 154
belladonna 53
belle 212
Belle 263
belles-lettres 212
bellicose 136
belligerent 171
benediction 45, 50, 173
benefactor 173
benefice 127, 255
beneficent 173
benefit 127
benevolent 173
benign 192
benignity 119
benison 45, 50
besiege 22, 257
bestial 140
betray 22
bib 220
bibulous 156
biennium 173, 250
bigamy 256
billion 253
biped 157, 174, 283
biscuit 220
bite 283
black 282
bloom 286
blossom 286
blow (blossom) 286
blow (of wind) 287
boa 66

boil 220, 236
bonanza 58
bondage 203
bonus 78
book 287
bore 281
botheration 131
bounty 197, 199
bow 286
box 13
break, brake 283
breakage 203, 259
brevity 119
brief 197, 204
brother 284
brute 258
brutish 258
buckle 220
budget 229
bugle 220
bulge 229
bull 220
bullet 51
bulletin 51
bus 82
bush 58
butter 6

cabbage 51
cadaver 66
cadence 45
caesura 66, 186
cage 202
caitiff 42
calamitous 136
calamity 136
calculate 115
calculus 66, 115
caldron 32
Caledonia 268
calendar 117
calends 117
callous 136
Calvary 117
Calvin 263
calyx 6

camera 66
camp 66
campaign 34
campus 66
canary, Canary, 220, 267
cancel 33
cancer 49, 66
Cancer 273
candelabrum 66
candid 151
candidate 220
candle 12, 66
candor 126
canine 147
canker 49
cant 42, 132
cap 13
capable 154 N.
capacious 155
cape 13
caper (capreoll) 53
capillary 142
capital 33, 39, 140
capitol 140
capitulate 221
caprice 54
Capricornus 273
capsule 115
captain 27, 34, 146 N.
captive 42, 156
captor 66
capture 131, 253
car 54, 217
carbon 221
carbuncle 221
card 33
cardinal 140, 221
career 68
caret 83
cargo 58
caricature 54
carnal 42, 140
carnival 51
carnivorous 172
Carolina 267

carriage 203, 217
carry 216
case 132, 156
cash 221
castle 116
casual 140
catch 33
cattle 33
caudal 39, 249
cauliflower 221
cause 191, 257
caution 129
cavalier 51
cavalry 34, 51
cave 202, 232
caveat 83
cease 165
Cecil, Cecilia 263
cede 207
celebrity 119
Celeste 263
celestial 41, 249, 263
cell 196, 274
Celloglass 274
Celotex 274
cement 133
censor 66
censure 131
census 66, 132
centennial 249, 250
centipede 174
centrifugal 250
centripetal 250
cereal 140
cerebellum 66, 116
cerebrum 66, 116
Ceres 140
certain 146 N.
certify 209
cessation 165
chafe 221
chafing-dish 212
chair 222
chaldron 32
chalice 6
chalk 66

challenge 202
chamber 58, 201
champagne 34
chance 45
chancel 33
chancellor 26
chant 42, 165
chanticleer 288
chap 6
chapel 221
chaplain 221
chapter 33, 221
charge 221
chariot 203
charm 198
charnel 42
chart 33
chase 33, 40
chattel 33
chauffeur 212
cheap 6
cheese 6
chef 48, 204, 213
Cherbourg 269
cherish 208
cherry 7, 221, 222
chest 6
Chester 8, 9, 136
chief 25, 48, 140, 213, 235
chieftain 27, 34
chin 286
Chinese 149
chisel 29
chivalry 34, 51
Christian 147
Ciceronian 147
Cincinnati 267
cinder 201
circle 217
circuit 132
circumnavigate 177
circumscribe 177
circumvent 174
circus 66, 217
cirrus 66

citadel 51
cite 205
citizen 222
city 200, 222
civic 139
civil 143
civility 119, 143
clamor 126
clang 66
clangor 66
Clara, Claire 263
Clarence 263
Claribel 263
Clarice 263
clarify 208
clarion 217
Clarissa 264
class 139
classic 139
classy 139
Claud, -e, -ia 264
clause 186
clear 215
clef 197
clemency 122
Clement 264
client 222
cloister 29, 136
close 136, 197, 258
closeness 258
clove 58
coadjutor 66
coalesce 166, 206
coast 222
cobble 222
cobbler 222, 223
code 67, 252
codex 66
codify 252
coefficient 250
coeval 177
cogent 114, 158
cogitate 114
cognate 187, 192
cognomen 67
cohort 223

coign 223
coil 188
coin 223
coinage 203
coincide 250
collapse 167
collar 142
colleague 117
collect 156, 188
collective 156
college 117
collide 206
colloquy 127
Colnchester 9
Colne 9
colonel 27, 51
colonnade 52
colony 9
color 29, 80
Colorado 269
colporteur 223
colter 6
columbine 147
combine 223
combustion 177
comfort 223
comfortable 155
comity 119
command 215
commence 24, 205
commerce 118
commingle 256
committee 211
common 261
commonwealth 261
companion 58, 258
companionship 258
compare 223
compatriot 256
compendium 67
competent 158
competitor 67
compile 223
complacent 158
complement 134
complete 134, 167

complex (noun) 224
complex (adj.) 78
complexion 224
compliment 134
comply 209, 257
component 158, 170
compose 169, 170
composite 170
composition 170
compound 170, 190
comprehend 206
comprehensible 154
comprehension 129
compunction 240
compute 42
comrade 58
conceal 29, 37
concede 207
conceit 45
conception 45
concern 206, 216
concert 52
concise 186
conclave 224
conclusion 129
concoct 167
concoction 129
concord 121
concourse 44
concrete 161
concur 44
concussion 187 N.
condense 206
condiment 134
condition 128
condone 168
conduce 169
conduct 169
confection 129
confederacy 123
confer 192, 205
confess 25
confessor 22
confidant 210
confident 158, 210
confiscate 229

conflagration 37
confusion 129
congenial 250
congregate 175
congress 132, 260
congruous 157
conjecture 131
conjugal 140
conjure 168
conscience 23
consecrate 178
consensus 67, 132
consequent 158
consider 161, 224
considerate 161
consistent 210
consolatory 145
consonant 160
conspicuous 157
constable 224
Constance 264
constancy 122
constant 122, 210, 264
constellation 131, 224
constitution 129
construct 169
construction 129
construe 169, 258
consul 67, 116, 142
consular 142
consulate 116
consult 26
consumer 125
contagion 128
contemplate 224
contemplation 224
content 186
contest 168
contiguous 157
continence 122, 210
continent 158, 186
contingent 159, 186
continuous 157
contraction 129
contradict 37, 177
contradictory 145

contralto 54
contrary 144
contrast 207
control 224
controversy 121, 177
controvert 177
contumacy 121
convene 177
convenient 210
convent 132
conversation 129
converse 165
convey 224
convict 169
convince 169
convoy 224
cook (noun) 6
cook (verb) 239
cope 13, 221
copious 136
copula 67
copy 225
Cordelia 264
cordial 31, 41
cork 58
corn (cognate) 283
corn (derived) 283
cornea 67
cornet 279
cornucopia 67
corolla 67, 116, 185, 225
corollary 225
corona 67, 116, 273
coronation 250
coroner 258
corporal (noun) 140
corporal (adj.) 36, 140, 191
corporeal 150
corps 48, 213
corpse 48
corpulent 37, 148
corpuscle 115, 191
correct 167
corridor 52

corroborate 164
corrupt 154, 188
corrupter 125
corruptible 154
costume 52
coulter 6
council 26
counsel 26, 67
counselor 67
count (title) 199, 225
count (verb) 42
counter 177, 199
countermand 177
counter-movement 177
counterpart 177
counter-roll 224
countersign 177
country 26, 225
county 85
couple 223
coupler 223
courage 41
court 26, 198
courteous 197
courtesy 49
courtier 258
covenant 210
coward 225
coy 42
crate 285
create 166, 167
creator 67
credible 153, 154
creditor 67
credulous 156
creed 12, 85
crescent 159, 166, 217
cretaceous 150
crevasse 226
crevice 226
crime 28
crisp 7
cross 68
crown 26, 67, 258
crucial 68
crucify 209

cruel 200
cruelty 197
cruise 225
crust 195
crux 68
cubit 225
cucumber 190
cull 188
culminate 284
culprit 225
culture 131, 253
cuneiform 250
cup 13, 52
cupola 52
curate 255
curator 68
curb 202 N.
cure 24, 40, 195
curious 138
current 159
curriculum 68, 135
cursory 145
curtail 225
curtsy 49
custody 121
custom 52
customary 52
cuticle 115
Cuticura 274

dainty 45
dame 226
danger 226
data 68
date 68, 192, 249
dative 156
daub 204, 226
daunt 288
dean 226
debauchee 211
debenture 85
debility 119
debit 177
debt 177, 201
debtor 125
decadent 187

decamp 57
decapitate 36
decay 200
December 80, 272
decemvir 68
decide 226
deciduous 157
decimate 163
declamatory 145
declivity 119
decorate 78
decoration 78
decorum 78
decrepit 226
defeat 42
defect 42, 43, 186
defence 228
defend 154
defendant 28
defender 125
defensible 154
defer 177
deficient 186
deficit 83
defile 256
definite 161
definition 129
deformed 177
defraud 206
defy 182, 209
deify 209
deign 199
dejected 162
delete 90
deliberate 226
delicate 148
delinquent 159
delirium 68
deliver 233
delude 206
deluge 233, 249
dementia 68
demolish 208
demonstrative 156
demonstrator 68
denizen 222, 226

dentate 148
dentifrice 172
dentist 258
depart 182, 196
depend 155
dependable 155
dependant 210
dependent 210
depict 29
deplore 178
deponent 170
depose 169, 170
deposit 45, 170
deposition 170
depot 45, 213
depreciate 219
deputy 169 N.
derange 256
derivation 227
derive 227
descend 178
descendant 210
descendent 210
desecrate 178
deserter 125
desideratum 78
design 29
desire 41, 78
desist 191
desolate 161
despair 22
desperado 58
desperate 161
desperation 129
despite 245
despondency 178
destine 161
destroy 154
destructible 154
desultory 145
detail 245
detect 178
deter 168
determine 76
detour 213
detriment 134

detritus 68
deuce 197
devastate 164
devious 138
devolve 206
devote 211
devotee 211
dexterity 227
diary 117
dictaphone 261
dictate 165
dictator 68
diction 129, 250
dictionary 250
dictum 68
differ 159, 185
different 159
difficult 119
difficulty 119
diffident 159
diffuse 188
digest 182
dight 14
digit 274, 287
dignity 45, 119
dilapidated 227
dilettante 54
diligence 122
diligent 30, 122
diminish 38, 56, 79
diminutive 37
dirge 86
disarrange 256
disaster 250
discern 168, 216
disciple 12, 157
discipline 148
discord 121
discreet 168
discrepancy 226
discuss 185
discussion 187 N.
disfigure 251
disgust 54
dish 7
dishonest 251

disinfect 250
disinherit 251
disloyal 251
dismal 227
dismiss 169, 251
disperse 182, 188
disport 244
dispute 168, 169
dissect 174
disseminate 182
dissent 206
dissertation 75
dissimilar 182
dissolution 129
dissonant 173
distemper 135
distil 206
distinction 129
distinguish 129, 208 N.
ditto 54
ditty 54
diurnal 149, 248
divers 168
diverse 168
divert 168, 192
Dives 68
divide 36, 129, 162
dividend 162
divine 147, 195
division 129
divisor 68
divorce 192
divorcee 211
divulge 182
docile 152
doctor 68
doctrine 148
document 134, 187
domestic 139
dominate 163, 226, 253
domination 129
Domingo 269
dominie 86
domino 58, 59, 226
donate 163, 192
Doncaster 9

double 195, 201
doubt 200
dozen 227
drilling 227
Drusilla 264
dual 140
dubious 138
ductile 152
duel 52
duet 54, 57
duke 23, 195, 258
dukedom 258
dungeon 226
duodecimal 171
duodecimo 82
Duofold 274
duplex 78, 273
duplicate 78
durable 153

eagle 147
eat 282
eatable 259
ebullition 220
Ecuador 269
edible 259
edifice 40, 171
edition 129
educate 68
education 129
educator 68
effect 155
effeminacy 123
effervesce 166
effervescent 166
efficacious 155
efficacy 121
efficiency 122
efficient 122, 178
effigy 86
efflorescent 166
effuse 188
effusive 188
ego 68
egotism 68
egotist 68

egregious 175
egress 133
ejaculate 227
elect 213
elegance 122
elegant 122
element 144
elementary 144
eliminate 227
élite 213
elocution 129
elope 256
eloquent 159
emaciated 38
emancipate 227
embellish 29
embody 257
emerge 169, 227
emergency 227
emeritus 78
Emily 264
eminent 159
emissary 117
emolument 134
employ 211
employee 211
enchant 42
encourage 40, 223
endure 196
enemy 27
enervate 137
engender 178
engine 227
engineer 143 N.
ennui 213
enormous 175
ensample 48
enter 93, 181
entertain 179
entire 78
entity 251
enumerate 153, 164
envious 137, 178
envy 137
epistolary 144
equal 118

equality 118
equate 163
equator 269
equestrian 249
equilibrium 69, 173
equine 147
equinox 174
equity 118
equivocate 239
era 228
eradicate 38
err 206
erratic 139
error 126
erudite 37
erudition 129
escape 228
especial 204
esprit 48
esquire 26
essence 241
establish 204
estate 45, 50, 204, 254
esteem 43
Estelle 266
estimate 43, 128
estimation 128
estimator 69
estray 245
estuary 117
eternal 118
eternity 118
étude 213
evanescent 159
event 133, 178
evict 169
evince 169
exaggerate 163
exalt 168
examination 189
examine 152
example 48, 209
exasperate 163
exceed 174, 207
exclamatory 145

exclude 29, 186
excoriate 163, 243
excruciating 228
exculpate 254
excursus 69
execution 129
exemplary 48
exemplify 48, 209
exempt 167
Exeter 9
exhume 255
exit, exeunt 83
ex-king 257
exonerate 38, 73, 164
exorbitant 175
exordium 69
expect 159, 166, 178
expectant 159
expectorate 175
expedite 169, 228
experiment 134
explanatory 145
explorer 125
exponent 170
expose 169, 170
exposition 170
expound 170, 190
expunge 240
exquisite 161
extant 159
extemporary 255
extenuate 284
exterior 80
exterminate 175
external 149
extirpate 164
extol 178
extort 167, 189
extra 81
extra-curricular 81
extraordinary 81, 178
extra-scientific 81
extravagance 54
extravagant 178
extravaganza 54
exult 187 N.

fable 135
fabric 46
façade 52
face 52, 181
facile 152, 186
facility 119
facsimile 86
fact 43, 186, 187
faction 45
factitious 60
factor 69, 117
factory 117
factotum 86
faculty 119
fairy 228
fallacious 155
fallacy 121
false 54, 258
falsehood 258
falsetto 54
fame 136, 195
familiar 142
familiarity 119
family 121, 142
famous 136
fanatic 139, 248
fanatical 248
fane 196
farce 228
farrago 69
fashion 45
fashionable 155
fastidious 136
fatal 140
fate 228
father 284
fathom 282
fault 204
faun 196
favor 126
fay 228
fealty 45, 46, 50
feast 48, 251
feat 43
feather 282
February 272

fee 282
Felix, Felicia 264
female 228
feminine 42, 147
fence 228
fennel 13
ferment 134
fertile 152
fervid 151
fervor 126
festal 251
festival 251
festive 156, 251
Festus 264
fête 48
fetich, fetish 60
fetid 260
fever 202
fiancé, -ée 213
fiat 83
fib 135
fiction 29, 129
fictitious 203
fidelity 45, 50
fierce 194 N.
figment 29
figure 29
filial 39
finale 54
fine 228, 229
finis 69
finish 165, 208
finite 161, 182 N.
fire 287, 288
firm 41
firmament 134
fiscal 229
fish 285
fish-monger 6
fissure 131
flagrant 282
flail 199
flexible 154, 274
Flexoglass 274
flirtation 131
Flora 264

floral 140
Florence 264
florid 151
Florida 270
florist 258
flotilla 59
flour 24
flourish 165, 208
flower 24, 140, 151, 165, 221, 270
fluctuate 163
fluent 159
fluid 151
flume 133
focus 69
folio 82
foment 134
font 12, 199
foot 283
for 282
forceps 69
fore 282
forefront 261
foreign 229
forensic 150
foreordain 261
forge 46
form 115, 177, 195
Formosa 267, 268
formula 69, 115
fortify 209
fortitude 124
fortuitous 150
fortunate 148
fortune 148, 150, 192
forum 69
Fossbridge 9
Fossbrooke 9
fossil 152
Fossway 9
found 251
fount 199
fracas 52
fraction 78
fracture 131
fragile 46, 152, 283

fragment 134
frail 46
fraternal 149
fraternity 197, 253
fratricide 253
fraud 163
fraudulent 148
Freeport 9
frequency 122
frequent 122
frigid 151
front 195, 229, 261
frontispiece 229
fruit 199
fruitage 203
frustrate 163
frustum 69
fugitive 156
fulcrum 69, 135
fume 237
fumigate 172
fundament 251
fundamental 251
fundamentalist 251
Fundy 270
funeral 150
funereal 150
fungus 69
furnace 69
furor 126
furtive 156
fury 55
fuse 191

gambol 52
gamut 229
gander 288
gaol 232
garden 285
garner 43
garrulous 157
gaud 127, 230, 258
gaudiness 230
gaudy 230, 258
gem 195
Gemini 273

general 54
generalissimo 54
generate 191
generator 69
generous 136, 141
genial 250
genius 69, 250
genteel 46
gentile 46, 143
gentle 46, 143
gentleman 46
genuine 148, 192
genus 70, 191
Georgia 268
germ 163
germane 146
germinate 163
get 283
gin (a drink) 230
gin (machine) 228
gist 230
glacial 142 N.
glacier 142 N.
gladiator 70, 125, 145
gladiatorial 145
gladiolus 70, 115
gland 230
glebe 9
globe 115
globule 115
glorify 208
Gloucester 9
goose 288
govern 26
governor 215
grace 122, 137, 202, 264
Grace 264
gracious 137, 202
grade 92, 140
gradual 140
graduate 148
grain 115, 117
grampus 238
Granada 270
granary 43, 117
grand 173

grandiloquent 173
granite 54
granule 115
grateful 259
gratify 209
gratis 81
gratuitous 151
grave 119
gravity 119
Greenwich 9
gregarious 143 N.
grenade 237
grief 41
groom 286, 287
guest 285
gullible 155, 259
gusto (gust) 54
guttural 39

habit 52, 133
habitat 84, 166
hall 283
haughtiness 230
haughty 230
hearse 230
heart 288
heave 282
heir 119, 261
heirloom 261
hen 288
herb 70, 117
herbarium 70, 117
Hercules 273
heredity 119
hesitate 166
hiatus 70
hibernate 163
Hilary 264
hill 284
hindrance 259
homicide 41, 172, 253
honest 101, 119
honesty 119
honor 80, 144
honorable 153
honorarium 70

honorary 144
Horace 264
horn 279, 280, 281
horrible 153
horrid 151
horror 70
Hortense 264
horticulture 251
hospice 118, cf. 127
hospital 46, 50, 118
host (hospes) 196, 231
host (hostis) 231
hostel 46, 48, 50
hostelry 46
hostile 143
hotel 46, 48, 50
hour 197, 264
human 146
humane 146
humble 70, 190, 201
humid 151
humility 119
humor 31, 126
humorist 258
humus 70
hurdle 285

ibex 70
identical 251
identity 251
igneous 37, 150
ignis fatuus 70
ignoble 189
ignominy 121
ignoramus 84
ignorance 22
ignorant 189
illegal 182 N., 251
illegible 38
illiterate 149
illuminate 168
illumine 168
illusion 188
illustrious 139
image 29
imbecile 65

imbed 257
imitate 29, 129
imitation 129
immaculate 182 N.
immanent 159
immediate 38
immediately 38
immense 182 N.
immerse 169
imminent 159
immolate 231
immune 141
immunity 119
impair 223
impecunious 251
impede 169, 228
impediment 134, 228
impel 187 N.
imperative 156, 186
impervious 138
impetus 70
import 206
impotent 189
impress 129, 188
impression 129
imprimatur 84
impromptu 86
improve 231
impudent 160
impulse 187 N.
impure 182
inability 182 N.
inactive 114
inaugurate 231
incandescent 166
incantation 42
incarnate 175
incense 167, 216
inch 7
incident 159
incipient 123
incision 178
incline 178
include 29
incognito 55
incongruous 157

incorrect 153
incorrigible 153
increase 134
increment 134
incubate 70
incubator 70
incubus 70
inculcate 231
incumbent 159
incur 168
indecorum 78
indelible 90
index 70
indicative 156
indigence 122
indigenous 138, 178
indigent 122, 178
indivisible 182 N.
indolence 231
indomitable 288
industrious 138
inept 182
inert 174
inertia 70, 121
inexorable 231
infamous 121
infamy 121
infant 232
infantry 232
infatuate 186
infect 250
infer 279
inferior 80
infernal 149
inferno 55
infinite 161, 173, 182 N.
influence 55
influenza 55
inform 216
infuriate 55
infuse 174
ingenious 137
ingenuous 232
ingrate 259
ingredient 159
inherent 159

inimical 38, 173
iniquity 118, 188
initial 141
injurious 137
injury 121
innocent 158
innocuous 157
innuendo 84
innumerable 153
inoculate 232
inquire 129, 191, 206
inquisition 129
inquisitive 191
inscribe 129
inscription 129
insect 232
insidious 137
insignia 70
insinuate 75
insistent 159
insolent 159
insoluble 182
insomnia 70
instant 253
instantaneous 253
instanter 81
instigate 286
instructor 38
instrument 134
insular 142
insulate 55
insult 232
insurgent 159
intaglio 55
integer 78
intelligent 188
intelligible 153
intend 284
intense 184 N. 1
intent 184 N. 1
inter 255
intercede 71
intercessor 71
interest 84
interfere 168, 205
interim 81

interior 78
intermittent 179
internal 149
internecine 192
interregnum 71
interrex 71
interrogate 192
interrupt 179
inter-stellar 255
interval 175
intimacy 123
intimate 123
intra-mural 179, 255
intra-state 179
intricate 161
intrigue 161
introduce 179
introspection 179
intuition 130
inundate 164
invention 130
inventor 125
invest 165
investigate 165
invidious 137, 178
invite 247
Iola 265
ire 36
irreligious 189
irrigate 188
isle 198, 232
isolate 55
italics 232
Italy 232
Itasca 268
item 81
iterate 164
itinerant 159

jail 232
jamb 203
janitor 71, 247
January 272
Janus 71, 272
jeopardy 232
jest 232

jocose 137
jocular 116, 142
Johnsonese 149
joke 137
journal 203
Jove 233
jovial 233, 234, 243
joy 127, 198, 230
judge (noun) 28
judge (verb) 206
judicial 141
judiciary 144
Julian, -ien 265
Juliet 265
Julius, -ia 198, 264, 265
July 272
juncture 131
June 272
junior 78
juniper 230
junk 60
Jupiter 233
jurisdiction 172
jurisprudence 172
juror 125
jury 28
just 28, 123, 150, 209, 218, 258, 265
justice 28, 123
justify 209
Justin 265
juvenile 42, 143

kennel 197, 233
kettle 6, 20
kiln 13
kin 284
kind 284
kindle 20
kitchen 6
know 282

labial 39, 142 N.
labor (noun) 42, 80, 138
labor (verb) 257

laboratory 251, 252
laborer 252
laborious 138
Labrador 270
lacerate 164
lacuna 71
lake 9, 71, 196
lament (noun) 135
lament (verb) 168
language 25
languid 151
languor 71
lapidary 118
lapse 133, 185
lares 71, 93
larva 71
lassitude 124
late 282
latent 159
lateral 141
Latin 147
latitude 124, 217
Latium 147
laud 206
laughable 155
launder 233
laundress 233
laundry 233
Laura, -etta 265
laureate 149
Laurence, Lawrence 265
lava 55
lave 55, 233
lavender 52
leal 46, 50
leaven 133
legacy 252
legal 46, 50, 141
legate 252
legation 130
legend 162, 233
legible 38
legion 128, 144
legionary 144
legislator 172

Leicester 9
leisure 207
lemur 71
lenient 165
lens 71
lentil 71
Leo 273
Leo, Leon, Leona 265
lesson 217
Letitia 265
letter 144, 149, 164, 198, 212, 213
levant 55
levee 233
level 116, 233
levity 119
levy 233
libel 116, 185, 233
liberal 141
liberate 164
liberation 130
liberator 71
Liberia 268
libertine 147
liberty 40, 120
Libra 273
librarian 118
library 118
lictor 71
lieutenant 27, 210
ligament 30
ligature 30
Lilly, -ian 265
limbo 82
limpid 152
Lincoln 9
line 135, 142 N.
lineal 142 N.
lineament 135
linear 142 N.
linen 13, 259
liniment 134
liquid 151
liquor 126
literary 144
literate 149

literati 71
literatim 82
literature 132
litterateur 213
littoral 141
livery 233
livid 151
lizard 58
locate 164
locomotion 252
locomotive 252
locus 71
long 124
longitude 124, 217
loquacious 155
loquacity 120
Lorenzo 265
Loretta 265
loud 285
Louisiana 268
loyal 46, 50
Lucian, -ien, -iana 265
lucid 151
Lucifer 71, 172
Lucius, -ia, -y, -inda 265
lucrative 156
lucre 213
Lucretia 265
ludicrous 138
Luke 265
lumbago 72
lunacy 123
lunar 39, 142
lunatic 123, 139
lurid 152
lustre 146
Lux 273
luxurious 137
luxury 137
lymph 139
lymphatic 139

Mabel 265
macadamization 259
madam, madame 55

Madeira 270
madonna 55
Magi 72
magistracy 116
magistrate 116
magnanimous 174
magnificence 122
magnificent 122
magnitude 124
maintain 234
maintenance 234
majesty 120
major 43, 78
malaria 55
male 200, 228
malediction 173
malefactor 173
malice 123
malleable 252
malnutrition 252
malpractice 257
mamma 72
mammal 72
manacle 115
Manchester 9
mandamus 84
maneuver 213
manicure 252
maniple 234
manipulate 234
manœuvre 46, 213
manor 207
mansion 130
manual 37, 39, 141
manufactory 252
manufacture 252
manure 46
manuscript 255
map 234
marble 190, 268
Marcellus 265
March 272
Marcus 265
marine 147
marital 140
Mark 265

marmalade 60
Marmora 268
marriage 203
Mars 265
martial 265
Martin 265
marvel 94
mass 12, 234
master 49, 80, 116, 200
mat 13
matador 59
material 270
maternal 149
matricide 253
matriculate 234
matrimony 124
Maurice 265
Max 266
maxim 234
Maximilian 266
maximum 78
May 272
mayor 43
meager 199
mean 146 N.
measure 182 N.
mediæval 252
median 146 N.
mediate 38
mediator 22
mediocre 192, 234
Mediterranean 268
medium 78
medley 48
mêlée 48, 213
member 41, 198, 248
membrane 248
membranous 249
memento 84
memoir 198
memorandum 79
memory 121
mendacity 120
mental 39
menu 197, 213
mercenary 144

mercurial 233, 234, 243
Mercury, mercury 234
mercy 196, 200
mere 196
merger 207
meridian 146, 190
merriment 260
mess 234
mica 72
mile 7, 10, 275
militant 160
military 142
militate 164
militia 72
milk 288
mill 6
millenium 250
million 253
Minerva 266
miniature 55, 56
minim 79
minimize 56
minimum 79
minish 38
minister 26, 49, 80, 216
ministry 118
minor 79
mint 7
minuend 162
minus 79
minute 235
minutiæ 72
miracle 30, 135, 235
Miranda 266
mirror 235
miscellaneous 150
mischief 235
misconstrue 257
miscreant 235
miser 79
miserable 25, 153
misery 121
mishap 257
misnomer 207
missal 12

missile 152
mission 130
mister 49
mix 150, 157
mob 235
mobile 153, 155, 260
mode 49
model 53
moderator 72
modern 149
modest 121
modesty 121
modicum 79
molar 142
molasses 60
mollify 41
moment 72, 134
momentum 72, 134
money 7
monger 6
monitor 72
monoplane 261
monster 136, 137
monstrous 137
Montana 268
Montenegro 270
Montevideo 270
monument 134, 187
mood 49
moral 141
morale 141
moratorium 72
morbid 152
morose 137
Morris 266
morsel 216
mortal 40, 141
mortar 6, 29
mosquito 59
mother 284
motion 130, 252
motor 73, 261
motorcycle 261
motorman 261
motto 56
moult 235

mount 9, 199
mountain 146
mountaineer 143 N.
mountainous 146
movable 155
move 130, 155, 206, 260
mulberry 190
mule 196
multiform 174
multigraph 261
multilateral 252
multiplex 79
multiplicand 162
multiply 162, 209
multitude 124, 216
mundane 42, 146
municipal 141
municipality 141
munificence 172
munition 130
mural 141
murder 287
murderous 139, 260
murmur 80
muscle, mussel 235
mutation 130
mutual 158

naïve 213
napkin 234
narrate 125
narrator 125
nasturtium 73
Natal 270
natatorium 118
nation 130
native 156
natural 141
nature 131, 141
nausea 73, 89
nautical 139
naval 141
nave 235
navigate 172
navy 27

nebula 73
necessary 144
necessity 120
nefarious 138
neglect 213
négligé 213
negligence 122
negligent 30, 122
negotiate 164
negro 59
nephew 282
nepotism 69
nerve 137
nervous 137
neuter 79
neutral 79
neutrality 79
neutralize 79
Nevada 271
nice 235
night 286
nihilism 94
nincompoop 94
noble 22, 153
nocturn, nocturne 149
nocturnal 149
nocuous 157
nol-pros 100
nominal 141
nominate 164
nominative 156
non- 81
Nona 266
non-combatant 81
non-conductor 81
nondescript 255
nonentity 251
nones 236
noon 12, 236
Nora 266
norm 141
normal 141
nostrum 82
notary 118
notice 123
notify 209

notion 130, 189, 192
notorious 145
nourish 43, 134, 197, 203, 208
nourishment 43
Nova Scotia 268
November 80, 272
noxious 138, 158, 192
nucleus 73
nuisance 158, 216
nullify 209
number 141, 164, 201
numeral 141
numero 82
nun 12
nurse 203, 252
nutriment 43, 134, 252
nutrition 252
nutritious 203, 252

obdurate 179
obedience 46
obedient 160
obeisance 46
obey 46, 160
objectionable 155
oblate 168
oblique 132
obliterate 164
oblivion 128
oblong 179
obnoxious 138
observe 206
obsolescent 160
obstacle 135
obstinacy 123
obstinate 123, 161
obtrude 179
obverse 179
obviate 179
obvious 138
occasion 188
occident 55, 188
occult 161
occupant 187 N.
occupation 130

occur 188
Octavia 266
octavo 82
October 80, 272
octogenarian 249
ocular 39, 142
oddity 260
odious 137
odium 73, 127
odor 80, 138
odorous 138
offer 14, 168, 188
office 127, 236
officer 27
officious 137
oil 262, 274
ointment 160
olive 266
Oliver, Olive, Olivia 266
omen 73
omit 188
omnibus 82
omnipotent 40
omniscient 252
omnivorous 172
onerous 40, 73, 137
onus 73
opera 56
operate 164
opinion 128
opportune 236
opposite 188
oppress 125
oppressor 125
optician 260
optimist 187
option 128
opulent 148
opus 73
oracle 135
oral 39
oration 41, 47, 50, 130
orator 63 N., 125
oratorio 56
oratory 56

orbit 175
ordain 261
order 141
ordinal 141
ordinary 144
organization 131
orient 55
orifice 127
orison 47, 50
ornament 134
Orthosonic 274
osseous 150
ossify 252
ostrich 261
outrage 236
oval 196
ovation. 236
overplus 261

pabulum 73, 135
Pacific 268
pacify 208
pact 196
pagan 146
pain 241
paint 29
pair 198, 223
palace 202, 236
palatial 202
Palatine 236
pale, paling 13
pale (adj.) 151
pall 12
palliate 36
pallid 151
pallor 73
palm 13
palpitate 236
pansy 226
pap 73
papa 73
par 79
parade 59
paramount 245
paramour 213
parasol 60

parboil 236
parcel 47
pardon 25
parent 160, 196
parliament 260
parricide 172, 253
parse 86, 189
parsimony 124
parson 49
parsonage 203
part 115, 189, 236
partake 261
partaker 94
participant 172
particle 47, 115
particular 142
partition 130
passive 156
pastor 73, 189, 237
patent 217
paternal 149
patience 122
Patience 266
patient 31, 122, 241
patriarch 12
patrician 249, 266
Patrick, Patricia, 266
patrimony 124
paucity 120
Paul, Pauline, Paulina 266
pauper 43
pause 170
pavilion 236, 237
pay 199, 211
payee 211
pea, peas 7, 222
peace 27
pear 7, 230
peccadillo 59
peculiar 237
pecuniary 237
pedal 39, 141
pedestal 261
pen 237
penal 28

penalty 28
penance 22, 47
pendant, -ent 210
pendulous 157
pendulum 79
penetrate 93
peninsula 73, 173
penitence 47
penitent 47
pennate 149
Pennsylvania 269
pension 130
people 24, 139, 197
Pepsodent 274
peradventure 255
perambulate 239
perceive 130
perception 130
perchance 257
perdition 179
peremptory 145
perennial 175
perfidious 137
perfidy 121, 179
perforate 281
perforce 255
perfume 237
perhaps 257
peril 200
perish 179, 208
perjure 179
permeate 179
permit 179
permutation 180
pernicious 137
peroration 130
perpendicular 135, 143
persecute 167
perseverance 122
persevering 122
persistence 210
person 49
personnel 213
perspicacious 155
perspicuous 158
perturb 168

pervert 180
pest 31
pester 237
pestilence 31
pestilent 148
petition 130
petrify 252
petroleum 262
petulance 123
petulant 123
piano 56
pianoforte 56
picture 29, 131
Piedmont 271
piety 47, 120
pigment 29, 134
pile (heap) 223
pile (pier) 13, 29
pilgrim 237
pillar 29
pillow 13
pin 13
pine (noun) 13, 196
pine (verb) 241
pinnate 149
pious 120
Pisces 273
pit 13
pitch 13
pity 47
placable 153
placebo 84
placid 151
plain 56, 261
plaintiff 28
plane 56, 261
plant 13
plaudit 86
plausible 154
plead 28
pleasure 207
plebs 73
plenipotentiary 252
plover 237
plum 7
plumb 29

plumber 217
plume 40, 195
plural 141
plus 79, 261
poignant 43
point 43, 160, 240
poison 47, 198, 202
pole 13
polish 161
polite 161
pollen 73
pomade 53
pomegranate 237
pommel 215
ponder 226
ponent 55
pontiff 116, 237
pontificate 116
poor 43
poppy 13
popular 143
porcelain 238
porch 56
Porchester 9
porcupine 238
pork 23, 24, 195, 238
porpoise 238
port 9
portal 198
portend 180
portent 180
portico 56
portion 175
portrait 29
portray 29
Portsmouth 9
Portugal 269
pose 170
posse 85
possess 180
possessor 73
post (office) 238
post (pillar) 238
postal 238
posterior 78, 79
posterity 120

posthumous 238
postpone 170, 180
postscript 180
posture 196
potent 160
potion 47
poultice 86
pound 7, 200
poverty 43
powder 201
power 26, 207
practitioner 31, 260
pray 25, 30
preach 30
preamble 238
preceptor 157
precious 22, 202
precipice 239
precipitate 239
precise 161
precocious 239
precursor 37, 73
predatory 145
predicament 239
predicate 30, 239
predict 37
predominate 252
pre-existence 180
prehensile 253, 283
prejudice 127
premature 239
premier 143 N.
premises 86
premium 74
prepare 186 N., 223
preposterous 239
prerogative 156
presage 155
prescribe 206
preside 180
press 131
pressure 131
prestige 190, 239
presuppose 180
preterite 180
preternatural 180

pretext 180
prevalent 160, 210
prevaricate 37, 239
prevent 240
previous 138
pre-war 180
prey 145, 283
price 198, 202, 219
primacy 123
prima donna 56
primary 143 N.
prime 189
primeval 248
primrose 246
prince 23, 259
prince-like 259
princely 259
princess 259
principal 141
principle 142
prior 79
Priscilla 266
prison 27
pristine 189
privilege 173
prize 198, 202
probable 153
probation 130
proceed 207
proconsul 175
procrastinate 163
proctor 125
procuracy 125
procurator 125
prodigal 180
prodigality 180
produce 180, 206
profane 240
professor 74
proficient 160
profile 56
profit 127
profiteer 143 N.
profound 24, 199
progress 133, 147, 185
promiscuous 157

prompt 189
proof 197
propaganda 85
propagate 85
propensity 253
proper 28, 120
property 28
proportion 175
proprietary 144
propriety 28, 120
prorate 96
prose 247
prosecute 43
prospect 133, 180
prospectus 74, 133, 180
prosperous 138
protect 37, 125, 213
protector 125
protégé 213
prove 130
Provence 271
proverb 180
provide 37, 43, 50
providence 123
provident 123
province 271
provision 37
proviso 82
provoke 206
prowess 231
proxy 125
prudence 123
Prudence 266
prudent 123
public 139
publish 208 N.
puerile 40, 143
pugilism 259
pugnacious 155, 248
pulchritude 124
pulpit 50, 217
pulsate 166
pulse 87
punch 240, 259
puncheon 240
punctuate 240

puncture 240
pungent 43, 160
punish 165, 208, 240
puny 255
pup 240
pupa 74, 240
pupil 240
puppet 240
puppy 240
purblind 262
purchase 40
pure 197, 262, 288
purgatory 30
purge 198, cf. 288
purity 197
pursue 43
purvey 43, 50
pus 74
pusillanimous 174
putrefy 74
putrid 74

quadrangle 174
quadrennium 250
quadrillion 253
quadruped 174
quaint 240
quality 120
quantity 120
quarantine 240
quarry 241
quart 56
quarter 56
quartet 56
quarto 82
quash 52
querulous 157
query 87
quiescent 160
quiet 42, 124, 241
quietude 124
quietus 85
quintessence 241
quit 241
quitclaim 241
quite 241

quorum 82
quota 56
quote 56
quotient 241

rabid 74, 151
rabies 74
radiate 164
radical 38
radio 43
radish 38
radium 43
radius 43, 74
rage 74
rally 253
ramify 209
rancor 126
ransom 47, 200
rapacious 155
rapid 151
rapidity 120
rapine 47
rapture 253
ratio 43, 50, 74
ration 47, 50, 130, 202
rational 142, 249
rationalist 249
rationalistic 249
rationalize 249
ravin, raven 47
ravine 47
ray 43
react 114
reagent 114
real (actual) 47
real (royal) 47
re-ally 253
realm 26, 41, 50
rear 241
reason 43, 47, 50, 142, 198, 202
rebel 242
rebellion 128, 242
rebus 83
recalcitrant 241
recapitulate 186

recede 207
receptacle 135
recess 133
recipe 85
recipient 187 N.
recognition 192
record 182
recourse 44
recover 187 N., 202
recreant 235
rectify 209
rector 74
recumbent 225
recuperate 187 N.
recur 44, 183
redeem 189
redeemer 22
redemption 47, 183, 189
redivivus 79
refer 169, 186
referee 211
referendum 79
refractory 143 N.
refuge 127, 211
refugee 211
refund 169
refuse 169
regal 47, 50
regalia 74
regent 160, 192
regicide 253
regimen 74, 133, 134
regiment 134
Regina 266
region 128
regular 143
regulate 44
rehearse 230
reign 26, 41, 50
reiterate 164
rejoinder 207
relate 169
religion 30, 137
religious 137
rely 257

remainder 207
remedy 127
remember 201
reminiscence 192
remit 169
remorse 23, 216
renaissance 213
render 207
renegade 59
renege, renig 59
renovate 164
rent 207
repair 223
repast 73
repel 169, 192
repellent 160
repent 22
repine 241
reply 209, 257
report 41
reprehend 241, 242
reprehensible 242
repress 162
reprimand 162, 210
reptile 152
repudiate 164
repugnant 160
repulse 169, 192
requiem 83
require 168
requisite 168
resemble 201
reside 40
residence 40
residue 74
residuum 74
resilient 166
resin 274
Resinol 274
resist 41
resistance 210
respect 43
respiration 130
respite 43
respond 206
response 185

rest 207
restaurant 213
restitution 130
restore 213
restrain 44
restrict 44
result 166
retail 245
retaliate 242
reticent 160
retort 242
retrograde 180
reveal 168
revel 242
revelry 242
revere 160, 162
reverend 162
reverent 160
reverse 179
revive 206
Rex 266
Rexall 274
ridiculous 137
righteous 139
rigid 151
rigor 126
Rio Grande 271
river 25, 196, 202
Riviera 271
rivulet 115
robust 150
Rochester 9
rodent 74, 160
rôle 224
roll 201, 224
Roman 146
romance 242
Rome 146
Rosa 266
Rosalie, -ind 266
rose 191
Rose 266
rosemary 242
rostrum 74, 136, 185
rotund 257
round 199, 245, 257

Roy 197
royal 41, 47, 50, 197
rubric 242
rudiment 135
Rufus 266
rule 44, 157
Rumania, Roumania,
    Romania 269
ruminant 242
ruminate 242
rumor 80
rural 191
rustic 139, 191

sacred 30, 75, 178
sacrifice 30
sacristan 146 N.
sad 285
safe 25, 30
sagacious 155
sage 202
Sagittarius 273
saint 30, 199
salad 53
salary 118
salient 160
saline 147
saliva 74
salubrious 38, 139
salutary 143
salutation 130
Salvador, San Salva-
    dor 271
sample 48
sanatorium 74
sanctimony 75, 124
sanction 75
sanctum 74
sane 120
sanguinary 40
sanguine 40, 150
Sanitas 273
sanity 120
sapient 214
Saragossa 271
sassafras 59

satiety 121
satire 242
satisfaction 172
Saturday 7
Saturn 7, 192
saturnine 233, 243
sauce 204
savage 203
savant 214
saviour 22, 30
saxifrage 59
scald 204 N.
scamp 56, 204 N.
scamper 56, 204 N.
scandal-monger 6
scintilla 38, 75
scintillate 38, 75, 164
scintillation 38, 75
Scorpio 273
scorpion 273
scour 204 N., 243
scourge 204 N., 243
scribe 184, 196
script 184
scripture 131
scrofula 75
scruple 116, 243
sculptor 75
scurrilous 139
seance 214
search 243
season 198
seasonable 155
secant 160
secede 183, 207
secession 130
second 144, 235
secondary 144
secret 243, 248
secretarial 248
secretary 243, 248
section 130
sector 75
secular 143
secure 44, 200, 243
security 120

sedate 157
sedentary 279
sediment 134
sedition 183
sedulous 138
segment 134
segregate 175
select 36
scmester 174
semicircle 173
seminary 118, 192
senate 116
senator 81, 145
senatorial 145
senile 81
senior 44, 79, 81
sense 133
sensual 142
sentiment 40
separate 44, 183, 223
September 80, 272
septuagint 87
sepulchre 135
sequence 192
serenade 53
serene 53
sergeant 27, 243
seriatim 82
series 75
sermon 30, 195, 217
serpent 152
serrate, -ed 149
serum 75
servant 27, 243
serve 127, 165, 243
service 30, cf. 127
servile 143
servitude 124
session 28, 185
set 279, 280, 281
settlement 134
sever 44
sexton 146 N.
shambles 243
shay 222
sherry 222

shirt 8
short 8, 204 N.
shrine 12
shrive 14
Siamese 149
sickle 14
siege 27, 257
sign 29
signify 209
Silas 266
silk 7
silvan 146
Silvester 266
similar 79
simile 79
similitude 124
simple 120
simplicity 120
simplify 209
simulacrum 75, 136
simultaneous 253
sincere 244
sincerity 244
sinecure 255
singular 143
sinister 80
sinuous 75
sinus 75
sir 44
sire 44
site 162, 170
situated 162
skirt 8, 20
sober 120
sobriety 120
society 121, 192, 262
sociology 262
sock 14
soil 14
sojourn 203
solar 38, 143
solder 244
soldier 27, 244
sole (noun) 14
sole (adj.) 57, 124
solemn 244

solicitous 124
solicitude 124
solid 152, 244, 252
solidify 252
soliloquy 127
solitaire 214
solitary 41
solitude 124
solo 57
solstice 22, 172, 202
soluble 153
solve 153
somersault 59
somniferous 139, 172
somnolent 148
sonant 160
soporiferous 253
soporific 253
soprano 57
sordid 151
sorority 253
sound 190, 199
souvenir 200
sovereign 26, 57, 146 N., 229
space 202
spacious 202
Spain 204 N.
sparse 185
specie 83
species 44, 75
specify 209
specimen 75, 133
spectacle 135
spectator 75
spectre 136
spectroscope 262
spectrum 75
speculate 244
speculative 244
speculator 76, 244
spend 14
spice 44
spine 197
spirit 48, 64, 216
spite 245

splendor 76
sponge 69
sponsor 63 N., 76
spontaneous 150
sport 244, 245
spouse 25
sprightly 48
sprite 48
spurious 138
squalid 151
squalor 76
Stabilator 274
stable (noun) 135
stable (adj.) 153, 274
stagnant 160
stamen 76
stamina 76
stanza 57
starvation 260
state 26, 45, 50, 253
statement 253, 254
station 130, 245
stationer 245
stationery 245
stature 131
status 50, 76, 254
Stella 266
stellar 38, 185
stick 286
stiletto 57
stimulate 164
stimulus 76
stipend 127
stop 14
story 204 N.
strait 44
strange 202
Stratford 8
Stratton 8
stratum 76
stray 245
Streatham 8
street 7, cf. 8, 245
strenuous 138
strict 44
strident 160

strike 286
stringent 44, 160
structure 131
student 160
studio 57
studious 137
study 57, 127, 204 N.
stupefy 209
stupendous 162
stupid 151
stupor 76
style 57, 87
stylus 57, 87
subdivide 180
subject 181
subjugate 176
sublunary 255
submarine 255
submit 168
suborn 181
subpoena 96
subscribe 181
subside 127
subsidiary 144
subsidy 127
substratum 76
subterfuge 181
subterranean 150
subtle 187, 246
subtrahend 162
suburb 176
suburban 146
subvert 181
subway 257
succor 188
succumb 206
sudden 201
suffer 188
suffrage 245
suggest 185, 188
suicide 254
suit 28, 214
suite 28, 214
summerset 60
summon 28
sumptuous 137

superannuate 254
supercilious 245
superficial 181
superfluous 181
superintend 181
superior 81
Superior 269
superlative 181
superman 257
supernal 149
superstition 130, 137
superstitious 137
superstructure 255
supervise 37
supervision 37
supine 147
supplant 245
supplicate 209
supply 209
support 188
supremacy 123
supreme 123
sure 44, 200
surge 206
surplus 261
surprise 27
surreptitious 188
surround 245
survey 225
susceptible 188
suspend 181
suspicion 128, 137
suspicious 137
sustenance 210
sweat 288
sylvan 146

table 195, 214
tableau 214
tabulation 131
tacit 161
taciturn 149
tact 133
tailor 245
talkative 260
tally 245

tame 288
tandem 81, 82
tangent 160, 186
Tanlac 274
tantamount 245
tarantula 57
tarpaulin 262
Tarvia 274
Taurus 273
tavern 202
teach 282
tear 287
tedium 76
tegument 135, 192
television 262
televox 262
temperament 135
temperate 161
temperature 132
tempest 41
temple 12, 224
temporary 144
tempt 190
tenacious 155
tenant 186, 210
tend 284
tender (adj.) 190, 201, 284
tender (verb or noun) 207
tenet 85
tenor 126
tentative 190
tenure 28
tepid 151
term 76, 201
terminus 76
terrace 53
terra cotta 57
terrestrial 37, 192, 249
terrible 154
terrier 246
terrific 37, 173
terrify 37, 208
terror 40, 126, 216

test 246
testament 25, 135
testify 209
testimony 124
textile 153
texture 132
thatch 287
thin 284
thirst 287
thou 288
three 281
thumb 282, 283
thunder 284
tile 14
timber 287
timid 40, 151
timorous 254
tincture 132
tinge 132
tiro 76
toe 287
toga 76, 192
toggery 76
togs 76
toilet 246
toils 246
tolerable 154
tonsorial 254
tonsure 132
Tony 263
tooth 288
torment 135
tornado 60
torpedo 76
torpid 151
torpor 76
torrent 160
torrid 151, 192
tower 27
tract 44
tractable 154
tradition 44, 130
traduce 181
trait 44
tramontane 146
trance 246

transfer 181
transgress 125, 174, 181
transgressor 125
transit 133, 246
transitory 145
translucent 181
transmute 206
transom 246
Transylvania 269
travesty 254
treason 44
tremble 157
tremendous 162
tremor 77
tremulous 157
triangle 174
tribe 77
tribunal 77
tribunate 116
tribune 77, 116
tribute 77
trident 174
triennium 250
trillion 253
Trinidad 271
trinity 31, 271
trio 57
trireme 174
triumph 236
triumvir 116
triumvirate 116
trivial 246
truculent 148
trustee 211
tuber 77
tuberculosis 259
tuberose 246
tuition 130
tumor 77, 126, 282
turbid 152
turbulent 148
turgid 151
turn 27, 60, 213
turpitude 124
turtle 190

tutor 125
two 283

ubiquity 254
ulterior 80
ultimatum 80
ultra-fashionable 97
ultramontane 146
ultra-violet 97
umbrella 57
umpire 247
unable 119, 182 N.
unanimous 174
uncle 115, 198
undaunted 288
understandable 154
undivided 182 N.
unguent 160
Unguentine 274
unicorn 174
uniform 174
unity 120
university 120
unjust 258
unmeasured 182 N.
unthinkable 155
urban 146
urbane 146
use (noun) 25, 133
use (verb) 133, 185
usher 247
usury 132
utensil 153
utility 120

vaccinate 254
vaccination 254
vaccine 254
vacuum 80
vagary 87
vain 199
valiant 210
valid 152
valor 40, 126
value 126
valve 215

vanish 208
vanquish 208
vapid 152
vapor 81, 152
vaporize 259
variegated 162
variety 121
various 121, 138
veal 24
vegetable 247, 249
vegetarian 249
vehicle 135, 288
veil 168
vein 199
velocipede 254
velocity 41
Velox 273
venerable 41, 154
venerate 154
venison 23, 24
ventilate 165, 187
ventricle 116
ventriloquist 173
venture 259
venturesome 259
Venus 273
Vera 266
veracious 38
veracity 38
Vera Cruz 271
verbatim 82
verbena 77
verbose 137
verdict 173
Verdun 271
verify 209
Vermont 271
vernacular 247
vernal 149
versatile 153
verse 12, 185, 247
version 131
vertebra 77, 136
vertex 77
Vertex 273
vertigo 77

vesper 77
vest 254
Vesta 273
vestige 165
vestment 135, 254
vesture 254
veteran 146
veterinary 144
veto 85
via 83
viaduct 254
viand 162, 210
vicar 118
vicarious 118
vice 138, 202
vicinity 120
vicious 138, 202
vicissitude 124
victor 77
Victor 266
Victoria 266
victorious 137
victory 121, 137, 266
Victrola 274
vie 247
vigil 121
vigilant 160
vigor 126
villa 77
villain 216
vim 83
Vincent 267
vinculum 77, 135
vinegar 201
Viola 267
violator 77
violent 148
violet, Violet 267
virago 77
virgin 31, 269
Virginia 267, 269
Virgo 273
virile 41, 143
virility 120
virtue 200
virtuoso 57

virulent 148
virus 77
viscera 77
viscous 138
vision 131, 185, 262
visit 166
vista 57
vitaphone 262
vituperation 173
vivacious 155
Vivian 267
vivid 152
vivisection 254
vocable 135
vocabulary 135
vocal 142
vocative 156

voice 142, 262
volatile 153
volcano 57
voluble 154
volume 224
voluntary 145
voluptuous 138
voracious 155
vortex 77
votive 156
vow 197
vowel 142
voyage 197
Vulcan 57
vulgar 143
vulnerable 39

wagon, wain 288
wall 9
Warwick 9
whimsical 260
Winchester 9
wine 6, 10
wit 283
withdrawal 260
wonderment 260
wondrous 139
Worcester 9
workable 155

yard 285
yoke 283